Plain English Rhetoric and Reader

THIRD EDITION

Gregory Cowan

Elisabeth McPherson

with Elizabeth Wooten Cowan
Texas A & M University

Random House **New York**

Third Edition
9876543
Copyright © 1970, 1977, 1982 by Random House, Inc.

Library of Congress Cataloging in Publication Data
Cowan, Gregory.
    Plain English rhetoric and reader.
    Includes index.
    1.   English language—Rhetoric.   2.   College readers.
I.   McPherson, Elisabeth, joint author.   II.   Title.
STUDENT'S EDITION ISBN 394-32655-5
TEACHER'S EDITION ISBN 394-32829-9
Manufactured in the United States of America.
Composed by American–Stratford Graphic Services, Brattleboro, Vermont.
Printed and bound by R. R. Donnelley and Sons, Harrisonburg, Va.

Text design by Kay Ward
Cover design by Lorraine Hohman
Cover photo by Jerome Kresch
Since this page cannot legibly accommodate all the copyright notices, pp. ii–v, constitute an extension
of the copyright page.

SHANA ALEXANDER, "An Equal Opportunity Occupation?" from *State-by-State Guide to Women's Legal Rights*, pp. 177–179, by Shana Alexander. Copyright © 1975 by Shana Alexander. Reprinted by permission of the author.

ALMADEN VINEYARDS, "What's the Right Wine for Candlelight and Saturday Night?" ad for Almaden, printed in *Sunset Magazine* (April 1980). Reprinted by permission of Dancer Fitzgerald Sample, Inc. Photo courtesy of Almaden Vineyards.

JONATHAN ALTER, "It's Your Funeral," from *The New Republic* (March 9, 1980), pp. 6–9. Copyright © 1980 *The New Republic,* Inc. Reprinted by permission of *The New Republic.*

BEN H. BAGDIKIAN, excerpt from *Guaranteed Incomes*, by Ben H. Bagdikian. Reprinted by permission of The Sterling Lord Agency, Inc. Copyright © 1968 by Ben H. Bagdikian.

SHARON BEGLEY and MARY HAGER, "The Plight of the Turtle," from *Newsweek* (January 14, 1980), p. 56. Copyright © 1980, by Newsweek, Inc. All Rights Reserved. Reprinted by Permission.

THOMAS G. BELL, "The Ospreys of Boca Grande," from *Sea Frontiers*, by Thomas G. Bell. Reprinted by permisson from International Oceanographic Foundation, Sea Frontiers © 1980, 3979 Rickenbacker Causeway, Virginia Key, Miami, Florida 33149 and the author.

HAL ZINA BENNETT, "When Is A Cold Not?" from *Cold Comfort*, by Hal Zina Bennett. Copyright © 1979 by Hal Zina Bennett, Used by permission of Clarkson N. Potter, Inc.

ELIZABETH BERCK, "Curb Program," letter to the editor, printed in *Sunday Oregonian* (April 27, 1980). Reprinted by permission of the author.

PETER L. BERGER, excerpt from *Invitation to Sociology: A Human Perspective*, by Peter L. Berger. Copyright © 1973 by Peter L. Berger. First published in 1973 by Overlook Press. Reprinted by permission of Doubleday & Company, Inc.

GWENDOLYN BROOKS BLAKELY, "Home," from *Report From Part One*. Copyright © 1970 by Gwendolyn Blakely. Reprinted by permission of Broadside Press.

NANCY BLAKEY-PATELLA, "If There Is a Draft I Believe Everyone Should be Included," letter to the editor, printed in *The Columbian* (February 12, 1980). Reprinted by permission of the author.

LYNN BLOOM, KAREN COBURN, AND JOAN PEARLMAN, "The Game," excerpt from "Be More Assertive," as edited in *New Woman* Magazine (May/June 1976), originally published as *The New Assertive Woman*, Delacorte Press, 1975.

LYNN Z. BLOOM, KAREN COBURN AND JOAN PEARLMAN, "Game II," excerpted from the book *The New Assertive Woman*, by Lynn Z. Bloom, Karen Coburn, and Joan Pearlman. Copyright © Lynn Z. Bloom, Karen Levin Coburn, and Joan Crystal Pearlman. Reprinted by permission of Delacorte Press.

ERMA BOMBECK, "Trash Is Winning," from *San Antonio Express* (January 9, 1980). From *At Wit's End* by Erma Bombeck © 1980 Field Enterprises, Inc. Courtesy of Field Newspaper Syndicate.

JULIAN BOND, "A Letter from Julian Bond at the Southern Poverty Law Center." Reprinted by permission of Southern Poverty Law Center, Montgomery, Alabama and Julian Bond.

THOMAS BOSWELL, excerpt from "Olympic 'Daredevil' Events Write History in Deaths, not Injuries," from *Sunday Oregonian* (February 17, 1980). Copyright © 1980 The Washington Post. Reprinted by permission of Los Angeles Times-Washington Post Service.

KAREN BROOKS AND GIDEON BOSKER, "There's a Thumb in My Soup," from *Willamette Week* (November 8–14, 1979). Reprinted by permission of the authors.

BROWN AND ROOT, INC., "Brown and Root may have designed and built the mill where this paper was made, . . ." ad for Brown and Root, Inc. Reprinted by permission of Brown and Root, Inc.

KATHERYN WATTERSON BURKHART, "Who Is In the Criminal Class?" adaptation of excerpt from *Women In Prison*, by Katheryn Watterson Burkhart. Copyright © 1973 by Katheryn Watterson Burkhart. Reprinted by permission of Doubleday & Company, Inc.

ii

TARBELL REAL ESTATE, "Are High Rates Discouraging You From Investing In A Home?" ad for Tarbell Real Estate, from *The Sunday Oregonian* (February 17, 1980). Reprinted by permission of Tarbell Real Estate.

TIME MAGAZINE, "Playing Rental Roulette," from *Time* (February 18, 1980). Reprinted by permission from TIME, the Weekly Newsmagazine; Copyright Time Inc., 1980.

MARY TRULLINGER and CAROL SANGER, "Energy Alternatives," from *Transportation USA* (Vol. 6, No. 1, 1979). Reprinted by permission of the publisher.

ANNE TYLER, "Three by Irving," from *The New Republic* (April 26, 1980). Reprinted by permission of The New Republic, © 1980 The New Republic, Inc.

UNION OF CONCERNED SCIENTISTS, "The Hazards of Nuclear Power," brochure distributed by Union of Concerned Scientists. Reprinted by permission of Union of Concerned Scientists.

UNITED FEATURE SYNDICATE, excerpt from *Slim Gourmet*. Copyright © 1980 by United Feature Syndicate, Inc. Reprinted by permission of United Feature Syndicate.

U.S. PIONEER ELECTRONICS CORPORATION, "Pioneer's National Truckload Sale," ad for U.S. Pioneer Electronics Corporation, printed in *Time* (April 14, 1980). Reprinted by permission of U.S. Pioneer Electronics Corporation.

ALICE WALKER, excerpt from "In Search of Our Mother's Gardens," from *Ms. Magazizne* (May 1974), pp. 97–101. Copyright © 1974 by Alice Walker. Reprinted by permission of Julian Bach Literary Agency, Inc.

STEVEN WEISS, "What You Expect Is What You Get," from *Psychology Today* (July 1973). Reprinted by permission of the author.

E. B. WHITE, excerpt from *Here Is New York*, by E. B. White. Copyright 1949 by E. B. White. Reprinted by permission of Harper & Row, Publishers, Inc.

WOMEN TODAY, "Remarriage of Women," from *Women Today* (March 7, 1980), p. 38. Reprinted from *Women Today*, copyright 1980, Lester A. Barrer, Today News Service.

WOODSTOVES & MORE, "Judge for Yourselves," ad for Woodstoves & More. Reprinted by permission of Woodstoves & More.

WORLD BOOK-CHILDCRAFT INTERNATIONAL, "Boll Weevil," from *The World Book Encyclopedia*. Copyright © 1981 World Book-Childcraft International, Inc. Reprinted by permission.

RONALD YATES, "Jojoba: One Important Bean," from *Air California* (August 1979). Reprinted by permission of the author.

Preface to the Third Edition

Experience has shown us that all students, of all ages and backgrounds, have things worth saying and that they can learn to say them clearly and effectively in writing. But good writing does take guidance and practice. Like its earlier editions, PLAIN ENGLISH RHETORIC AND READER, 3RD EDITION, advises students on every part of the writing process from finding a main idea, through planning the paper, to putting the plan into finished form. We tell students frankly that nobody, beginner or professional, writes just to be writing. All successful writers know why they write and whom they are writing for. Their purpose and their sense of audience guide them as they write. We remind students that if their only purpose is to turn in an assignment, and if the only audience they write for is the teacher, the likelihood of increasing their skill is not very great. Although the requirements in a writing class necessarily remain somewhat artificial, the more students can see a connection between the writing they are asked to do and "real writing" in the "real world," the more successful their efforts will be. The advice we give and the samples we provide are designed to show the relationship between what's practiced in a composition class and well in a job or other classes—in other words, as an educated person.

As the title suggests, PLAIN ENGLISH RHETORIC AND READER is similar to another text of ours, PLAIN ENGLISH PLEASE. In direct, nontechnical language both books provide inexperienced writers step-by-step guidance in giving directions, defining terms, comparing objects or ideas, classifying items or experiences, analyzing processes or causes, producing objective reports, finding the significance in their own experiences, persuading others, examining arguments through ordinary logic, writing reviews, and summarizing. Both texts have an appendix, which provides advice and examples on writing term papers and business letters. Both have a section on editing—how to make a paper look better by following the conventions of spelling, punctuation, and written usage once the paper has been completed to the writer's satisfaction. Both have a glossary of terms that will help students to use this book and to understand the terminology of their other English courses.

However, the detailed exercises following each chapter in PLAIN ENGLISH PLEASE are omitted here. Instead, PLAIN ENGLISH RHETORIC AND READER contains generous samples of the kinds of writing covered in the text. We believe that these readings help students in three ways: they illustrate what has been said in the chapters; they encourage students by showing them that writing very like what they are being asked to do has been published; and, perhaps most important, they help students with little experience in careful reading to see the relationship between reading well and writing well.

We know that many students, arriving in class terrified that college writing will demand some mysterious and esoteric quality far beyond their abilities, are paralyzed by a conviction that whatever they write will be "wrong." We have tried to relieve these anxieties by emphasizing how good writing comes from good ideas, carefully controlled and clearly communicated, and by insisting that "correctness" is a final, superficial step, a step they won't mind taking when they realize that no competent writer produces finished copy in the first draft.

We also know that many composition students have an unacknowledged, often justified, fear that they can't read well enough to cope with their college assignments. We have tried to help them develop greater reading comprehension by showing how to isolate main ideas, how to distinguish between esssential points and elaboration, how to recognize a writer's purposes and use that recognition in evaluating what they read. Because inexperienced readers do need analytical practice, most of the selections we have chosen come from current magazines and newspapers. The first few readings in each chapter are short, so that students will be intimidated neither by length nor by a too unfamiliar vocabulary, and the selections can be examined in fairly complete detail. The responses following each selection are directed almost equally toward better reading and better writing. By discovering how other writers have developed their ideas and met the needs of their audiences, students will better understand and appreciate whatever they read. Also by seeing how other writers have solved the same problems they themselves face, students will become more competent writers.

To provide teachers and students with a greater variety of choice, this edition contains almost twice as many readings as did the earlier editions, and so that the topics will be relevant to the interests of students and teachers, more than seventy-five per cent of the readings are new. Nevertheless, the responses emphasize (as previously) rhetorical principles rather than subject matter, and almost all the writing suggestions, expanded greatly in this edition, are directed toward writing purposes and how these can be achieved rather than toward reactions to the selection's topic. By paying attention to the process of writing and reading rather than to specific content, we have tried to avoid the schizophrenic effect of arguing about energy or the environment on Monday and returning to the problems of organization on Wednesday—discussions that usually seem to students quite unrelated. We hope, however, that students *will* see a relationship between the difficulties they face and those faced by professional writers, between what they must do to read with comprehension and to write with clarity.

If this book is an improvement over earlier editions, much of the credit goes to the students and teachers who have given us their suggestions. We continue to be grateful to Deborah Berman, David Dushkin, Richard Friedrich, Georgia-Mae Gallivan, Richard Hawkins, Rayna Kline, Glenn Leggett, Barbara Relyea, Judy Rosenberg, Jim Smith, Stanley Spicer, Susan Scarff Webster, and the members of the Clark College and Forest Park English Departments, all of whom helped with the first two editions. We'd also like to thank Richard Larson, George Haich, Kathleen O. Stearns, Lloyd N. Monnin, Gertrude P. Brainerd, and Mae Smith Williams for their thoughtful reviews, although they are certainly not responsible for any shortcomings that remain in the book. And without the patience, assistance, and encouragement of Richard Garretson and Christine Pellicano at Random House, this edition would not have been completed.

I should also add that the "we" in this preface accurately refers to both Gregory Cowan and me, since almost nothing in the chapters themselves has changed since his death in 1979. The book remains as much his as mine, although the new reading selections have been my responsibility. Elizabeth Wooten Cowan has been generous with her assistance throughout, but especially with the teacher's manual, which can be obtained by writing to Random House.

Elisabeth McPherson

Contents

Chapter 3   *Explaining: Definition*   53

READINGS: Definitions   71

Chapter 4   *Explaining: Comparison*   89

READINGS: Comparison   103

(*new to this edition)

Chapter 5   Explaining: Classification   123

READINGS: Classification   137

Chapter 6   Explaining: Analysis   163

READINGS: Analysis   173

(*new to this edition)

Chapter 7   *Telling What Happened: Objective Reports*   191

READINGS: Objective Reports   207

Chapter 8   *Telling What Happened: Personal Experience*   227

(*new to this edition)

Chapter 9   *Writing to Persuade*   263

Chapter 10   *Fair Persuasion*   301

(*new to this edition)

Chapter 11 *Summarizing and Reviewing* **341**

(*new to this edition)

(*new to this edition)

A Note to Students

Don't let anybody tell you you're not "good in English." If you were born in the United States, or any other English-speaking country, you've been pretty much an expert since you were five or six years old. Before you started school, you had so thoroughly absorbed the shape and pattern of ordinary sentences that you understood nearly everything said to you and could say a good deal for yourself besides. What you had learned, without self-consciousness or drills or any sense of strain, was the English spoken in your own neighbobrhood and your own home. It may have been a little different from the English spoken in other neighborhoods and other homes, but it was the same language. As you grew older and experienced more things, you learned more words and used longer sentences. You discovered that the same thing could be said in more than one way—that your language offered choices. What you could say on the playground, to the applause of your friends, did not always win praise when you tried it at home. You became expert, not just in the structure of your language—how it works—but in appropriateness—when to choose what part of it. What you mastered is a symbolic system so subtle and complex that linguists have not yet been able to describe it completely. But you, like any other normal child, simply absorbed it. Language became as much a part of you as running or breathing, and you used it, most of the time, with as little conscious thought.

In school, however, you had to learn a second system, the writing system: a method of "recording language" so people can communicate, or remember, across distance and time. This second system is much less complicated and much easier to describe than the talking system, but most people find it harder to learn. Mastering it becomes a deliberate act. Self-consciously and often with considerable strain, school children learn to read and write. But they keep right on talking. They ask questions about what they read, complain about their assignments, gossip with their friends, offer and take advice. We all talk, probably, fifty times as much as we read and a thousand times as much as we write. It's small wonder that most of us feel more comfortable talking, and do it better. We've had more practice.

But even in this electronic age, where television shows us the news and cassette tapes can preserve our conversations, talking is not enough. We still live in a literate society, in the sense that we receive most of our information and do most of our business through print and writing. We're bombarded with printed words: traffic directions and recipes, campaign promises and special sales, textbooks and treatises. Unless you can read with considerable skill, you will have trouble discriminating among this mass of material and pulling from it the information you actually need.

You won't have to write as much or as often as you have to read. But there is no job you can hold, and no place you can live, where you won't have to do some writing, unless you opt for a cave in the hills somewhere, and good caves are getting harder to find. When you do write, you'll need to write well.

Reading well will help you write well. Because the two skills are so intertwined, you can use the articles in this book in two ways—as samples that show the kind of writing you will be asked to do and as guides on how to do it. For instance, if you are asked to write an analysis, the job will be much easier if you can first see some successful analyses other people have written. To get a general idea of what you're being asked to do, one quick reading may be enough. But for the articles to help in the actual doing, you will need to read with more care. If you find an article lively and effective, discover what that writer did to arouse your interest. Then try the same methods in your own writing. If you find an article dull or confusing, analyze that article even more carefully, so you can keep from boring or confusing your own readers. What you read will show you how other writers express themselves, and your reading will suggest to you ways of organizing your own ideas, arranging your own sentences, and presenting your own ideas clearly and forcefully.

That is the kind of practice this book will give you. After you have accomplished the main job of writing, after you have put your ideas into a paper that pleases you, you may want to make it look better by some attention to the conventions of the writing system—spelling, punctuation, and so on—you may want to "edit" what you have written. If so, you can find some advice in the final appendix of this book.

But don't confuse the problems of editing with the problems of writing. For years you have been speaking English plainly, probably with some precision, variety, and sophistication. This book offers you practice in writing plainly—it gives help in putting your ideas on paper with precision, variety, and clarity. Your ideas and the words you find to express them are the nourishment in your writing; the editing you do later is merely the table manners that make the nourishment more palatable to others.

Chapter 1

Finding the Purpose

Why do people write? At first that sounds like a silly question. The answer seems obvious: people write because they have to or because they'll gain something or because, sometimes, they just want to. All those reasons will apply to you, too, for most of your life; and the writing you do will be made easier, and pleasanter, if you stop to examine why you are writing and what you want to accomplish.

While you are in college, you *will* have to write. You'll have to answer test questions, prepare a paper for history or medical technology, or complete a report for your physical therapy class. To earn your living you'll have to write, too, a lot or a little, depending on what your job is. Troubleshooters write reports, clerks write collection letters, lawyers write briefs, secretaries write minutes, engineers write specifications, department heads write proposals, politicians write speeches. All this writing has to be done. Getting through college or paying the rent depends on it.

Even at home some writing is necessary: a list of directions for the baby-sitter, a note to Uncle Arnold, a letter to the phone company saying just why you don't owe the $11.23 they've billed you for. From all this writing you have something to gain. Unless you remind the baby-sitter that Angie is allergic to eggs and needs her medicine at seven o'clock, you may come home to find her covered with rash. Unless you thank Uncle Arnold for the fifty-dollar check, he'll be less obliging the next time you need a loan in a hurry. And unless you can convince the phone company that the long distance call was made by somebody else, they'll soon be telling all your friends that your line is disconnected.

The writing you do because you want to is a little different. It may include love letters, diaries, journals, jottings, perhaps poetry or stories. We can call this kind "private writing," even though you may let other people read it or, if you like it well enough, try to get it published. Private writing is important: it helps us understand ourselves and our experiences; it lets us capture a moment we want to remember; it satisfies a deep human need and makes us more aware of our humanity. In private writing, we can make our own rules, play around with words, take off on tangents, skip or repeat, as the fancy takes us. The only readers we have to satisfy are ourselves.

But even though private writing is both important and enjoyable, we are not concerned with it in this book. Here, we are dealing with writing intended for other people to read. Somebody else, one person or a hundred, will read what you have written and do something or think something as a result of what they read. And it's in public writing that *purpose*—a reason for writing that goes beyond "have to" or "gain something"—becomes especially significant. In public writing, you must be able to answer such questions as Why am I writing this? What do I hope to accomplish? Who will my readers be? What do they need to be told? The answers to these questions will shape the way you write and influence the effect your writing has on the people who read it.

In some writing, those questions answer themselves so easily you don't think twice about it. You write the directions for the baby-sitter because you're concerned about Angie and hope she'll be well cared for; since the sitter is new, you realize you will need to give more details about Angie's habits than the regular sitter needed. You write to Uncle Arnold because both good manners and self-interest require it; knowing Uncle Arnold and what he likes to hear, you ask about his rheumatism, tell him your mother has a new job, and describe the last hockey game you saw, but you don't include the last concert—Uncle Arnold hates country-western. When you write to the phone company, you know why you're writing and what you want to accomplish—you want to get that charge taken off your bill —but you don't know exactly who will read the letter. You do know, however, that calling the company names and saying you'll never pay won't be enough. You keep your temper and provide details about who uses your phone, how you keep track of calls, and where you were on the day the call was made. In any of this kind of writing you may not stop to think much about your purpose, but you always know what it is; and that purpose controls what and how you write.

Confronted with college assignments, however, some people forget that public writing always has a definite purpose. The only reason they can think of for writing is that the teacher assigned a paper. They don't really expect anybody except their teacher to read what they've written, and they don't really believe the teacher will do anything different, or think anything different, because of what they've written. They don't see much relationship between college assignments and "real writing." Their purpose is just to satisfy the teacher, and their reason for writing is just that they have to.

People who think this way are right, in one sense. If they want the credit for the course, they do have no choice: they *have* to write the papers that are assigned. But if they never go beyond this simple-minded purpose—getting the credit and getting it over with—that's the *only* thing they will accomplish.

In this book we are assuming that you want to do more than just get it over. We hope you will see each assignment as a way of learning to control what you write. We urge you to share your writing with other students in the class—real people who may indeed be changed by something you have written. We want you to see public writing for what it is: a way of entering the minds of your readers, of affecting their consciousness, of expanding their horizons by letting them share your experiences, your insights, your knowledge and techniques, or your convictions. "Writing purpose" will mean more than "doing something to hand in on Friday."

Common Writing Purposes

Although we can name writing purposes in many different ways (such as thanking, advising, protesting, notifying, reassuring), most of them can be grouped under the five general purposes that are discussed in this book:

giving directions
explaining
telling what happened
persuading
summarizing

Knowing what your general purpose is will serve as a guide when you plan your paper; it will help you decide what to put in and what to leave out. And after you've written the first draft, it will help you to revise. You can pretend you're a reader, instead of the writer, and ask yourself what else you'd need to be told. In writing that history paper, have you assumed that everybody knows who Chief Joseph was? Would it help to give a little background about the Nez Percés before you tell what happened on that tragic thousand-mile flight through Idaho and Montana? On the other hand, if your purpose is to persuade readers that Joseph was a military genius, all that information about what the Nez Percés ate and what they wore will have to go, no matter how interesting it is. Throwing in everything you know, without relating it to your general purpose, results in muddled writing.

It's true that the writing purposes covered in this book seldom appear in their "pure" form. Much of what you read seems to have a mixture of many purposes: some explaining, some persuading, some telling what happened. But even though the purposes are mixed, when you read carefully you can usually find what the *main purpose* was and see how the other purposes were used to support it. In *explaining* why IQ tests are unfair to some students, a writer may *tell what happened* when city children were given questions about farming, *summarize* what leading psychologists have said about the tests, and even *persuade* some parents to protest the use of the tests in their district. The explanation (the main purpose) will succeed, however, only if the summarizing and persuading are skillfully done—if the writer has had some practice in performing those purposes separately.

Writers who can blend purposes effectively have probably already become pretty good at using each purpose by itself. A good blend is not a hodgepodge but a carefully prepared mixture. Composers cannot arrange music for a group until they can tell a flute from a trombone and understand just how much volume will increase the excitement without deafening the concert audience. Landscape architects cannot plan a formal garden until they have learned whether rhododendrons grow higher than azaleas, whether petunias clash with pinks, and whether lilies bloom in the spring or the fall. Gardeners who throw seeds at random are sure to reap chaos. Writing, like composing and gardening, is a skill that can be learned. Like learning any other skill, taking it one step at a time will bring the best results. By working on each purpose separately, you can learn to give directions, to explain, to tell what happened, to persuade, and to summarize. Then when you need to blend purposes, you'll have a much better chance of keeping the emphasis where you want it.

Consider the papers assigned in this book as exercises, much like the scales a pianist plays or the balls a golfer hits on a driving range. Of course, the scales are not the concerto the pianist will play later on and the practice swings aren't the trophy match, but without them music lovers may walk out on the concerto and the golfer may lose the match. The papers you write with a single purpose will make your later writing—and your thinking—surer and swifter. That's what practice is for.

Giving Directions

One common writing purpose is telling other people how to do something—giving directions. All of us give directions, and all of us follow them, every day. We consult recipes before we make a Bavarian chocolate cake; we follow the steps on assembling a tricycle; we read the labels on paint cans, the tissue sheets in dress patterns, and the owner's manuals for our automobiles. We say eagerly to our friends, "I'll show you"; but if the friends are far away, or if the project is complicated, we write it down. We leaves notes for the baby-sitter, and we post signs on how to operate the duplicating machine. Whenever we offer step-by-step advice on completing any kind of project, we're giving directions.

Explaining

Another common general purpose is to explain something. In one sense, of course, the experienced cook and the car manufacturer are *explaining* to their readers what steps to follow in baking the cake or adjusting the headlights. Their purpose, however, is to speak directly to readers who will actually do the job, rather than to readers who are mainly interested in the theory behind it. Although giving directions is often very reasonably considered a kind of explaining, directions have some important differences from other explanations. The writer giving directions is saying, "Do this, then do that." In other kinds of explanations, writers never talk to their readers as though the writers were giving commands. These examples show the difference:

> Take off your shoes before you come into the living room. [*directions*]

> Polite Japanese remove their shoes before they come into a house, just as automatically and naturally as Americans remove their coats and overshoes. [*explanation*]

> Don't run film backward through a projector with the sound on. [*directions*]

> The sound track on a film passes an exciter light, which converts the track to the sound you hear. If the film is run backward while the sound is on, the exciter light becomes overloaded and blows out. [*explanation*]

To avoid confusion, in this book we'll save the term *explanation* for the kind of writing that deals with meaning or relationships—writing that defines or compares or classifies or analyzes.

For instance, if you wrote a paper on IQ tests, you would be explaining when you gave a careful definition of what "standard deviation" means. You would also be explaining when you compared IQ tests and achievement tests, or when you classified the kind of tests given to children in your neighborhood school, or when you analyzed the effects the misuse of tests can have on schoolchildren who are labeled by them. Here are some other examples of explanation:

> A standard deduction is the dollar amount taxpayers are allowed to subtract from their income if they don't want to itemize what they have paid in medical bills, taxes, interest, etc. [*definition*]

> Although severe indigestion and heart attacks can cause similar symptoms, the first-aid treatment for the two conditions is very different. [*comparison*]

> Lizards, Gila monsters, and dinosaurs all belong to the reptile family. [*classification*]

> In order to understand the working of a welding torch, we must consider each of its separate parts. [*analysis*]

Many textbooks—in science or in English, for instance—are made up of explanation. Part of what we are doing here is explaining the difference between one writing purpose and another.

Telling What Happened

Some occasions call for reports instead of explanations. Reports are clear and complete accounts of what happened, not attempts to explain why the events occurred or arguments saying they shouldn't have occurred at all. The "minutes" that secretaries write are one example of a report; the minutes tell what happened in the meeting. Newspaper articles are another example. A front-page news story says, "Thirteen people were killed in weekend highway accidents" or "A severe earthquake left thousands homeless" or "The city council passed a zoning ordinance last night." But news writers do not, in their front-page accounts, warn you to drive carefully or urge you to send sandwiches and blankets to the homeless or tell you the council members are a pack of reactionary idiots. You may find these lectures and appeals and opinions on the editorial page or in syndicated columns, but the news story itself, if it is carefully written, will tell only what happened.

Reports are an objective record of events, with the writer's opinions carefully kept out. Sometimes, however, you will want to write about special events in your own life and make your readers understand why those events were important. You will still be telling what happened, but instead of just producing a record you will be trying to let your readers share the feeling and the mood of your experience. Here is the difference:

> On January 16, 1962, John and Mary Davis were granted a divorce. John Davis was given custody of the two children. [*report*]

> When my parents were divorced and I went to live with my father, I discovered that mothers do more than sew and scold. [*personal experience*]

Telling what happened, either as a report or as a personal experience, is often a useful part of other kinds of writing, and whatever your general purpose is, you will frequently find yourself using it. Reports, however, are so important in much college work, and in many jobs, that you must be able to recognize them and know what their requirements are.

Persuading

Probably the most common writing purpose is to try to get others to agree with you or do what you want them to do. Perhaps you wrote a letter to the newspaper, urging people to boycott a grocery store that was selling nonunion lettuce. Perhaps you wrote to an airline company, hoping to persuade them to pay for your lost suitcase, or hired a lawyer to persuade a judge that the company should be forced to pay. Perhaps your little sister, or your own child, wrote home from summer camp, pleading for a bit more spending money.

You not only do a lot of persuading yourself, you read and hear a lot from other people. Half the letters you get in the mail try to persuade you to subscribe to a magazine, vote for a candidate, take out an insurance policy, buy some product you never thought of needing, or send money to somebody's good cause.

In fact, we are overwhelmed by persuasion, some of it masquerading as something else. Senator Goodsell tries to convince the folks back home that voting for him means better schools and lower taxes. Ad writers try to convince us that Twinkle toothpaste will make our teeth a whiter white, that Manheim cigarettes will make us look like cowboys, that because Talaco Oil Company believes in the American way of life, whatever that is, we should buy their gasoline. If you go to church on Sunday, the sermon is designed to persuade you to mend your wicked ways or, if your ways are not wicked, to put some money in the plate. When you were little, your parents tried to convince you that good children pick up their toys, and perhaps you are trying to convince your own children that hitting each other is not acceptable behavior. Editorial writers persuade us that the new airport is (or isn't) a good thing; that building a new jail will (or won't) prevent crime; that Senator Goodsell should (or shouldn't) be elected to another term. *Persuading* is the main purpose of any writing that tries to get readers to change their behavior or their beliefs.

In its most straightforward form, persuasion uses such words as *should* or *ought to,* or tells us that we *must* do something or other to make ourselves (or the world) better and safer. Persuasive writing also uses words that praise—*good, safe, beautiful, economical, patriotic*—and words that blame—*bad, dangerous, ugly, expensive, treasonable.* Such words sometimes appear in other kinds of writing, of course, but whenever getting us to agree that something is "good" or "bad" seems to be the main purpose of the writing, we can be sure that somebody is trying to persuade us.

Summarizing

Although summarizing is a fairly common writing purpose, identifying it is not quite so straightforward. To summarize means to shorten and put into your own words what somebody else has written or said. When you summarize, you follow the writing purpose of whatever you are summarizing. If the original is a report, then your summary will be a report, too, but a little or a lot shorter.

If you read an article on IQ tests and condense into a single page what the original writer covered in fourteen, you are summarizing. If one of your readers further shortens what you said to three or four sentences, that reader is summarizing, too. Some digest magazines have made millions of dollars and gained millions of readers by cutting long articles in half. Students have earned very good grades by compressing into four or five pages of final examination what they think the important parts of the course have been.

Although summaries never have a purpose of their own, since they reflect the purpose of the original, they can be easily recognized because they announce themselves as summaries. They begin with, or end with, such phrases as "As yesterday's paper reported, . . ." or ". . . according to the United States Department of Agriculture." When you improve your explanations by giving a brief summary of what some expert has said, or strengthen your argument by summarizing the report of a survey, you always identify the expert or mention the name of the person who made the survey.

Choosing a Topic

In ordinary life, what you write *about* is usually chosen for you by the circumstances of your life or the requirements of the job you hold. In school, however, you're sometimes told to produce a paper with a certain general purpose, and the subject of that paper is left entirely up to you. Knowing that you're going to explain or persuade, naturally, isn't enough to start you writing. You have to explain *something,* or convince your readers to do *something,* and what that something will be can create a problem. Many beginning writers spend a lot of time worrying over what to write about. They see themselves as ordinary people who have had ordinary experiences and whose information is pretty limited. Caught in the conviction (almost always mistaken) that they aren't experts on anything, they hesitate to expose their ignorance. But we're all ordinary people; it's the way we see our experiences that makes them extraordinary, and the way we use those experiences that helps our readers to share them with us. When you write about something you care about, you can make your readers care, too, even if the topic is no more exciting than a ride on a bus or an afternoon at the zoo. If you're genuinely concerned about the telephone service in your office, you can get your readers involved in it, too, even if they argue that your views are wrong, that the telephone service is the best in town.

When you try to decide in this class—or in biology or business or embalming classes, for that matter—what the topic of your paper will be, keep two things in mind: first, the topic should be something you know about or something you're willing to spend the necessary time finding out about before you begin to write; and second, the topic should be something that seems interesting enough or important enough to be worth the time you will spend on it. If the subject seems dull or trivial to you, it's pretty certain your readers will be bored.

Narrowing Your Topic

Even though you have chosen a topic you find fascinating, you may think it safer to leave it as broad as possible. "After all," you say to yourself, "if I write about families, I'll be able to use everything I know—how to get along with relatives, what happened when my sister got divorced, what the laws of adoption are, why people say traditional families are disappearing, what a Chinese family is like (from that book I read last month), and even why I think parents should set a curfew for their kids. My general purpose will be to *explain* about families." If you fall into the trap of a very broad topic, however, you'll be saying way too little about way too much. Just as your readers are getting interested in one thing, you'll be off in another direction, and everybody will end up thoroughly frustrated.

Begin by choosing a broad topic, if you like, but go on to ask yourself what part of that topic you want to concentrate on. If families interest you, ask yourself what it is about families that interests you most at the moment. Is it the difficulty four people find in adjusting to one another's habits in a cramped apartment? That could lead to directions on how to share the bathroom, the dishwashing, and the television set. Is it your worry about the adjustments necessary when a divorce occurs? That could lead either to an account of what happened when your sister came home with her baby or to some research in the library, finding out what resources are available to help newly divorced women. Is it what present-day Chinese families are like? That might lead to a summary of the book you read, and it wouldn't give you much chance to explore your own ideas unless you've actually spent some time in China. Or are you troubled by fourteen-year-olds running about unsupervised at midnight? That could lead to a paper of persuasion in which you give sound reasons for your belief that parents should make, and enforce, rules for their children to follow.

It's possible, of course, that a topic has already been assigned; that does happen in some classes. "Write about education," the teacher says and disappears down the hall. The task in this situation is especially difficult, since the choice has not been yours and the assigned topic is enormous. Every newspaper you pick up says something about schools; "education" entries in the library catalog include more than fifty books; education in some form has always existed everywhere; and you've been being educated yourself for a sizable number of years. But just because the topic is so broad, it offers all kinds of possibilities. Your job is to focus on one little piece of it that you care about—one little piece that will interest other people because you've said something definite. Think about it for a day or two—on the bus, in the shower, just before you go to sleep. And when the idea comes, don't be afraid to talk about it—with your roommate or your wife or anybody who will listen. Talking will sharpen your ideas and make you more certain you've narrowed the topic to a size that can be dealt with in a short paper.

Writing a Main Idea Sentence

Before you begin to write, you should work out in your head (or on paper) a main idea sentence for your paper. A good main idea sentence will make clear what the purpose of the paper will be—giving directions, explaining, telling what happened, persuading, or summarizing—and it must state the idea or event on which the paper will be based. Here are some samples of what might be said about education.

1. High schools should require every student to take at least one course in speed reading.
2. Public school teachers should not be allowed to strike.
3. Standardized tests are unfair to many students.
4. British and American colleges operate on different systems.
5. People who oppose school bussing can be divided into three general groups.
6. The school bonds failed to pass because retired people were worried about taxes, employers were annoyed that some employees can't spell, and newspapers claimed that schools weren't teaching the "basics."
7. Six cases of school violence occurred in Woodside last year.
8. When I dropped out of school at fifteen, I found that having a high school diploma does make a difference.
9. To register for adult education classes by mail, you must follow four separate steps.

10. In a recent article in *Library Doings* called "Don't Censor Books," Arden Musgrave points out that students who aren't allowed to read what interests them often don't read at all.

Notice that these ten sentences have two things in common: First, they all narrow the general topic of education so that a definite statement can be made about it; and second, they suggest the purpose of the paper. The first three will be papers of persuasion. They all express the writer's opinion, and the papers will try to get readers to share that opinion. Equally good papers could be written by reversing the opinions:

1. High school courses in speed reading are a waste of time.
2. Public school teachers should be allowed to strike.
3. Standardized tests are the fairest way of measuring what students know.

The next three main idea sentences (numbers 4, 5, and 6) will lead to papers of explanation. Number 4 will compare British and American colleges, probably without saying which system the writer thinks is better. Number 5 will classify people who are against bussing and explain the characteristics of each group. Number 6 will analyze the reasons for the failure of the bonds.

Numbers 7 and 8 will tell what happened; number 7 will be an objective report, somewhat like a newspaper account, and number 8 will give details of a personal experience. Number 9 will give directions, and number 10 will summarize what another writer has said.

All these sentences show that the writers know what they intend to say. They are not just topics, but *main idea sentences.* Certainly the statement "I am going to write about education" is, in the grammatical sense, a complete sentence. But the sentence that contains the main idea must not contain such obvious evasions as "I am going to write about . . ." or "My paper will be about. . . ." To test whether you have stated your idea clearly, strike out all repetitions of the question you began with (What shall I write about?) and examine what remains. After you have crossed out "I am going to write about . . ." or "This paper will be about . . . ," do you still have a complete sentence? "A course in speed reading" is obviously not a complete sentence, but neither is "Requiring every student to take a course in speed reading." Each is only a piece of a main idea sentence and leads to such questions as Well, what about it? Are you for or against it? "When I dropped out of high school" will force people to ask you, What happened? Your main idea sentence must answer such questions before they are asked.

It's a good idea to check your main idea sentence to make sure your topic is not *too* narrow. "Sometimes teachers strike" is certainly a complete sentence, and so is "I don't know much about standardized tests," but neither of them will leave you anything to say after you have announced those facts. You have developed a good main idea sentence if the things you could use to support it or complete it suggest themselves easily. "Standardized tests are unfair to many students" will be followed by enough examples of unfair questions that readers will understand why you made the statement. "To register for adult education classes by mail, you must follow four separate steps" will be followed by more details about what the steps are and the order in which they should be accomplished. If you aren't sure where your main idea sentence will take you, discard it and find another that does provide you with a clear direction.

Developing Your Topic

Working out a clear main idea sentence and knowing in general what your paper will cover can get you off to a good start, but to write a good paper you'll need more than a start. You'll need to give lots of details, provide plenty of examples, and include solid support for what you say. Even though many other people have written about the same topic before, your paper will be worth reading if you add enough of your own experiences and your own reactions to make the paper genuinely yours.

At first that may seem hard to do, and it does take a bit of practice. You might begin by brainstorming a little. Jot down everything you can think of that's in any way connected with your narrowed topic, just as it comes into your head. List everything, no matter how unimportant it seems—colors, smells, sounds, times, names, memories, daydreams, contrasts, comparisons. When you begin to plan your paper, you can select the things that fit your purpose and main ideas and throw out the rest. Making such a random list is a kind of exploration—something like a woman who tries on all the clothes in all the most expensive departments in the store, even though she ends by buying one ten-dollar blouse, because that's what she really needs.

This kind of brainstorming, whether or not you actually write your ideas down, can be good insurance that your paper will be developed, that you'll do more than produce an outline in the form of a paper. You'll have something to say in each of your paragraphs and will be able to produce more than a sentence or two, written very big so it looks like more.

Different kinds of writing purposes require different kinds of development, of course, but there's no purpose, and no topic, that can't be made interesting by a writer who digs for the right material. There can be real pleasure in completing a piece of writing that says just what you want it to say. It may be a while before you regard writing as fun, but many people have learned to enjoy the process as well as the product of their writing. They like the intellectual workout of sorting their thoughts, putting mental pictures into words, and finding the best words to help their readers share those pictures. Such writers never find themselves in the position of the child who wrote to her father:

```
Dear Daddy,

I'm having a good time.  The nurse thinks it will be all right.

This letter is about money.

                    Love,

                    Rose Marie
```

Key Words

If you know exactly how these key words are used in the chapter, and if you can finish these statements in your own words, you can be fairly certain you have understood the most important points made in the chapter. If you have trouble, however, reread the section of the chapter where the discussion occurs until you are sure you do understand.

1. **Private writing** refers to . . .
2. **Public writing** is . . .
3. What questions should you ask yourself before you begin any kind of **public writing?**
4. Finding your **writing purpose** means . . .
5. Why is it important to know who your **readers** will be?
6. The five **writing purposes** covered in this book are . . .
7. Writing that **gives directions** tells the readers . . .
8. Writing that **explains** tells . . .
9. A **report** tells only . . .
10. **Personal experience** tries to . . .
11. In a paper of **persuasion,** you . . .
12. When you write a **summary,** you . . .
13. **Choosing a topic** involves . . .
14. **Narrowing the topic** means . . .
15. A good **main idea sentence** includes . . .
16. How can you **develop your topic?**

READINGS
Finding the Purpose

The following eleven pieces of writing all appeared in newspapers in the same area in the same week. Readers were expected to be members of the general public who subscribe to the newspapers.

Woodstoves and More

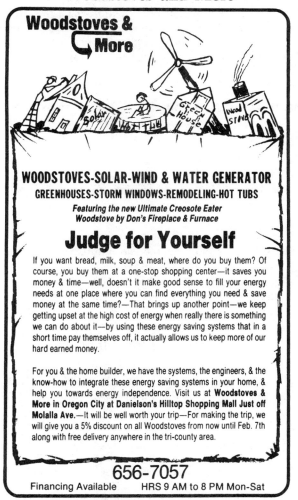

The Sunday Oregonian, January 25, 1981.

On Pruning Apple and Pear Trees

[1]   The production of fruit from your apple or pear tree will be directly affected by the pruning you do this month. Before cutting off everything in sight, take a look at where the tree bears its fruit. Apples and pears bear their fruit on limbs several years old. Peaches and apricots, on the other hand, bloom and bear fruit only on 1-year-old wood. Therefore, different pruning techniques are necessary.

[2]   Apple and pear trees need annual maintenance pruning to help thin out some of the long, crowding shoots and to top back some of the upper growth so the tree can be sprayed and harvested. Most of the pruning on these trees should be limited to thinning and cutting back to strong side shoots. Limbs in the center should be removed to allow better air circulation and sunlight penetration. Fruit is developed on the short, stubby spurs that grow on 2-year-old wood. If you cut off the spurs, you remove the crop. Also, you may have noticed in years past, the more you prune from an apple tree, the more water sprouts and long shoots you end up with by the end of summer, and the less fruit you get. If much needs to be cut out of a tree to bring it back within bounds, try to do it over several years.

Perch Family Member Makes Good Eating

[1]   What is a walleye?

[2]   Well, first it is not a walleye pike as so many writers and even biologists out here on the West Coast call it.

[3]   The walleye is a member of the perch family (*Stizostedion vitreum*), not the pike family.

[4]   Many people, especially those from the Midwest, call it the best eatin' fish in the world. Many prefer it to salmon, in fact.

[5]   In the Midwest, it is not only a game fish but also a food fish and is marketed commercially. . . .

[6]   It ranges in size from about 18 inches to 20 pounds or more and is all good eating. It doesn't fight much, although it is a wily one to get on a hook.

Fashion Trends for 1980

[1]   Two years ago, the look for spring was big, really big. Voluminous blouses and dresses that draped yards of extra fabric over the body came and then went with the first signs of fall.

Ray A. McNeilan, "On Pruning Apple and Pear Trees," *Northwest Magazine,* February 17, 1980, p. 14.

Don Holm, "Perch Family Member Makes Good Eating," *Northwest Magazine,* February 17, 1980.

Ellen Emry Heltzel, "Fashion Trends for 1980 Waver Between Extremes," *Sunday Oregonian,* February 17, 1980.

[2]   Last year, it was in to be in. Designers pulled in their seams for a close-to-the-body silhouette, and women went on diets to taper the tent look into an hourglass.

[3]   For spring 1980, women's wear is playing both ends against the middle.

[4]   Clothes are neither too tight nor too loose, but they hit other kinds of extremes. On the one hand, there are the frankly feminine dresses with lace collars and cummerbunds—lawn-party pretty. On the other hand, sculptural dressing has surfaced, with the chemise and the tube and accessories that have sharp, tailored angles.

[5]   The same dichotomy exists throughout women's fashions. Shoes have either very high heels (3 inches) or they are flatter than flat, and each type can be worn for both day and evening. Hairstyles have a similar duality, either softly curled or sharply geometric, blunt cut à la Cleopatra. (The Afro is a throwback to the '60s.)

Start Over as Chiropractors

[1]   KANSAS CITY, Mo. (AP)—John Clemens got the jolt of his life in June 1976. His job as a salesman was eliminated.

[2]   Clemens, 56, had been in sales for 30 years when his boss told him at a breakfast meeting that his sales territory was being phased out.

[3]   Clemens and his wife, Constance, were in their early 50s at the time. They had to consider their five children in high school and college when they sat down to decide what to do: find another sales job or begin a new career.

[4]   They decided to make a clean start. They sold their home in Wilmington, Del., and moved halfway across the country to Kansas City, where they both enrolled in a chiropractic college. . . .

Pass the Bread

Starch was less likely to raise blood-fat levels than sugar in an experiment performed by the U.S. Department of Agriculture. Ten men and nine women, aged 35 to 55, stayed on a 30 percent wheat-starch diet for six weeks, then transferred to another diet in which 30 percent of the calories came from sucrose (ordinary white table sugar). Triglyceride and cholesterol levels were significantly higher on the sugar diet, according to a report in the American Journal of Clinical Nutrition.

Robert Macy, "Start Over as Chiropractors," *Sunday Oregonian,* February 17, 1980.

Barbara Gibbons, "The Slim Gourmet: Nutrition Trends Glimpsed," *Sunday Oregonian,* February 17, 1980.

No Draft

[1]   To the Editor: No person should have their personal rights violated by a mandatory draft. The United States takes pride in the freedoms which this nation was founded on. One of these being freedom of choice. To be told one has to serve in a division of the armed forces, without choice, to me is the ultimate infringement of these rights.

[2]   There seem to be enough "war-loving" people out there ready for a battle to fill this so-called military crisis. I don't feel it necessary to draft anyone, female or male. Furthermore, I have yet to be convinced that we have been threatened as a nation or that war is the solution to all the problems of this nation and the world.

> K. M. Schriener
> 2600 Falk Rd.
> Vancouver

Olympic Daredevil

[1]   One man who expresses himself with courage is John Fee, 28, senior member of the U.S. luge team.

[2]   Fee has three passions, none of which he fully understands, and none of which seem to be linked with the others. He is an artist who has spent years making stained glass windows for churches. He is a fisherman who battles the 35-foot waves and gale force winds of the Bering Sea to fish for king crab off the Alaskan coast. And he is the U.S.' best hope for a top 10 luger here.

[3]   This combination of qualities—artist, explorer, sportsman—somehow seems to illuminate the confusing character of the daredevils in the Olympic to us.

Stepson Scores on First Duck Hunt

[1] My stepson Jody and I started out before daylight one freezing morning at the end of December. Jody was 16 then, just beginning his initiation into the rites and mystique of duck hunting.

[2]   We had to break ice to set out the decoys, but the day, when it broke, was clear, cold, still; the sun rose in winter splendor, creating the kind of day Lee, an old duck-hunting friend from way back, used to call a "sparrow day" because no ducks would fly.

Columbian, February 12, 1980.

Thomas Boswell, "Olympic 'Daredevil' Events Write History in Deaths, Not Injuries," *Sunday Oregonian,* February 17, 1980.

Jim Magmer, "Stepson Scores on First Duck Hunt," *Northwest Magazine,* February 17, 1980.

[3]   To make matters worse, tramping through the decoys to break the ice and keep the water open, I slipped and my hip boots filled with water.

[4]   I've been miserable before, but never quite that uncomfortable in a duck blind, even after I had poured the water in my boots back into the marsh. As nothing was flying, I told Jody I was going to walk back to the house and dry out.

[5]   I took my time, had an extra cup of coffee and read the paper before starting back. When I arrived at the blind, Jody was jubilant with a limit of ducks.

[6]   "Right after you left, they started coming and never stopped until you got back just now," Jody said. "What a great shoot. If you'd stayed, you'd have gotten your limit, too."

[7]   Jody's only a year older—very young as duck hunters go—but already he has his "great shoot" story to tell.

High Interest Rates

Sunday Oregonian, February 17, 1980.

Draft Everybody

[1]   To the Editor: If there is a draft I believe everyone should be included. I don't think there should be exemptions for students, mothers, married people, etc. Also, everyone between the ages of 18 and 50 should be included in the draft.

[2]   There are plenty of jobs to be done in the military that aren't in actual combat. Although, I don't think a person should be exempted from combat just because she happens to be female.

[3]   If there is a draft, if there is a war, what makes your daughter more precious than my son?

Nancy Blakey-Patella
3100 Columbia St.
Vancouver

Responses

1. What is the purpose of each of the pieces of writing you have just read: giving directions, explaining, telling what happened, persuading, or summarizing? What is there in each piece that helped you decide?

2. From a week's issues of a newspaper (or newspapers) in your own area, find pieces that illustrate each of these five writing purposes. Select one of them, and write a short paragraph in which you say what the purpose, the topic, and the main idea sentence of the piece are. If it seems to you that the piece does not have a main idea sentence, say in your own words what you think that sentence must have been.

Columbian, February 12, 1980.

Chapter 2

Giving Directions

Giving directions often sounds easier than it is. You understand clearly enough how to do whatever you're writing about—how to bake bread, read a subway map, or do a magic trick—and it ought to be simple enough to tell other people to follow your example. If the other people could watch you do it—see you pounding the dough, pointing to the colored lines on the map, or spreading out the cards—it might indeed be fairly simple. The difficulty comes when you try to find words for actions that may seem almost automatic. To write good directions, you must solve two problems: first, you must examine your own actions carefully so that you won't leave out anything important; and second, you must find words exact enough so that your readers can see in their minds what you're doing, almost as well as if they were watching you.

Choosing a Topic

In many of the directions you write, at home or on the job, the topic chooses itself. You write out for Angie's baby-sitter just where her pajamas are, just what time you want her put to bed, and just what light to leave on so she'll go to sleep without fretting. Or you leave directions for the new office assistant, giving step-by-step instructions on what to do when the duplicating machine starts flinging the papers all over the floor. In writing your English assignment, the situation is only a little different: you get to choose the topic for your directions, but you are still sharing with other people in the class something you know how to do.

You probably won't have a specific topic assigned; after all, not everybody in the class is an expert on the same things. But everybody is an expert on something, and your first job is to select one of the many things you can do well. Don't worry too much about being obvious or boring. Nothing is obvious to readers who need the advice you can give, and nothing is boring to people trying to do something new or to do an old thing in a new way.

You will, however, want to choose a topic complicated enough to give you some real practice in direction writing and simple enough that you can do a thorough job. How to lubricate a bicycle chain or how to change flashlight batteries may be important things to know, but the process is probably too short for you to get much practice in giving directions. On the other hand, how to program a computer or how to change jobs in midcareer are both much too complicated. It takes most people an entire year to learn computer programming, and planning and executing a career change is likely to occupy several months. If you try either of these things, your advice will be so superficial that only people who already know how to program computers or switch jobs will understand you, and in that case your directions will indeed be obvious and boring. Instead of something that requires only one tool and one action—an oil can and a squirt of oil on the bicycle chain—or something that requires a long list of equipment and more than a hundred steps, choose something that can be done in five or ten operations, with only four or five pieces of equipment. How to act during a job interview is probably something you could explain thoroughly enough that your readers, by following your directions, could keep the interviewer's attention fixed firmly on their accomplishments and attractive qualities; how to stop the bleeding until the doctor comes might be a step-by-step explanation that could save somebody's life.

In choosing your topic, however, try to choose your audience, too—that is, try to figure out *who you are writing the directions for.* People who work in a personnel department are likely to know what to do and say during interviews; your directions will be interesting and useful to people who haven't had a job interview for several years or perhaps have never had one. Nurses know how to deal with bad cuts; your directions should be written for frightened parents who have never before coped with a wound that a Band-Aid wouldn't fix.

If you decide to give directions on changing a tire, assume that you're writing for a wealthy person who has always depended on garages. If you decide to give directions on changing a diaper, assume you're writing for a new grandfather who has always foolishly assumed that changing diapers was woman's work. The field is wide open: how to cut a younger brother's hair is a good topic, and so is how to keep a five-year-old still during a haircut. Lots of people don't know how to make candles at home or how to sharpen scissors or how to put in a zipper. Because *you* know, you can do a successful job of telling your readers how to do it.

Main Ideas for Papers Giving Directions

After you have picked your topic, but before you begin to write, work out a main idea sentence. You'll already know what your purpose is—giving directions—and what your directions are going to cover—how to make an extension cord, for instance—but put the main idea sentence down on paper anyway. Writing it out will help clarify your own thoughts and will help to remind you that you're writing for people who don't know what equipment they'll need or whether it's really possible for them to learn whatever it is you're trying to teach them. A main idea sentence for a paper giving directions must include two things:

1. what the directions will cover
2. the most important thing the reader needs to have or do in order to follow the directions successfully

For instance, you might say:

You can't bake good bread unless you have the proper utensils.

(This main idea sentence tells what the job is—baking bread—and what is needed —the proper utensils.)

Almost anyone who knows the basic symbols can read a subway map.

(This main idea sentence tells what the job is—reading a subway map—and what is needed—understanding of the basic symbols.)

You can't keep babies from catching colds, but you can certainly keep a baby with a cold more comfortable by following a few simple rules.

(Here your readers are told what the directions will cover—keeping a baby with a cold comfortable—and are encouraged by the information that it isn't really hard to do.)

Planning the Paper

Working out the main idea sentence is the first step; planning the paper is the second. Beneath your main idea sentence, list all the steps needed to do the job. Check to see that you have not omitted any necessary step. Because you are dealing with a subject you are very familiar with, it's easy to leave out something that seems obvious to you. Your readers are not familiar with the subject, and nothing will be obvious to them. If you are giving directions for baking bread, for instance, don't jump from "dissolve the yeast in hot water" to "knead the dough." Your readers are not likely to know that if the water is too hot it will kill the yeast. What seems obvious and maybe even common knowledge to you may, for them, be crucial information; lacking that information may cause them to fail miserably in the whole project.

For the topic "how to repair a broken window," your main idea sentence might be:

To repair a broken window successfully the only tools you need are a tape measure, a chisel, and a tack hammer.

A list of the steps in the paper might be:

1. Measure the size of the glass.
2. Remove molding or putty.
3. Remove the old glass.
4. Clean the edges of the frame.
5. Fit glass in frame.
6. Install glazier's points.
7. Replace molding or putty.

Have any necessary steps been left out? Apparently one step is missing. Measuring the size of the glass won't provide a new piece cut to size. The list must be expanded, either telling readers how to cut the glass—a procedure difficult enough that it might be the subject of an entire set of directions by itself—or telling them to buy a pane of glass already cut to the exact size.

Are the steps in the right order? Near enough, probably; but since the size of the glass must be exact if it is to fit properly, it might be better to begin with step 2, "Remove molding or putty," go on to step 3, "Remove the old glass," step 4, "Clean the edges of the frame," and only then give step 1, "Measure the size of the glass." If you list all the steps you can think of and then go back over the list, asking yourself, "Is that exactly what I do?" you can probably avoid leaving out anything important or getting things in the wrong order. If your list is complete and orderly, writing your paper will be much less difficult. The groundwork will be done.

Writing the Introduction

Like any other paper you write, a paper of directions will sound better if it has an introduction. How long should an introduction be? Like a lot of other questions about writing, this one has no absolute answer. The length of an introduction is in proportion to the length of what you are writing. For very short papers, a short paragraph is enough; a ten-page essay may have as much as a page of introduction; and a book may have a whole chapter.

The purpose of an introduction is to tell your readers what the writing is going to be about and to give them a chance to decide whether or not to continue reading. The introduction becomes a contract between writer and reader. You must not go beyond what your introduction agrees to do, nor should you do less than it promises. If the main idea sentence in your first paragraph promises to tell the reader how to bake bread, then your paper must be limited to mixing the ingredients, kneading the dough, and leaving the bread in the oven for the right time at the right temperature. You must not get sidetracked into a tirade about whether or not men belong in the kitchen, no matter how strongly you feel on that subject.

A good introduction, however, ought to contain more than just a main idea sentence. It may give reasons for doing the job, it may offer encouragement, it may list the necessary equipment, it may justify the need for the first step, or it may simply arouse the readers' interest. The first paragraph certainly should include all the information your readers will need before deciding to start the job.

These samples show three ways of introducing a paper giving directions. In each one, the main idea sentence is italicized.

1. If you really love the taste, texture, and smell of delicious bread and can't stand that bland, doughy white junk the supermarket sells, you may want to try your hand at baking your own. *You can't bake good bread without the proper utensils.* However, since all you need is a mixing bowl, a spoon, a flat surface (countertop or cutting board will do), and a baking pan, you probably have everything already on hand.

2. You've daydreamed it hundreds of times: there is a pause during the party when the conversation slacks off and everything is kind of quiet. You step forward to the attractive woman you've wanted to meet all evening. You take a deck of cards out of your pocket and with one deft motion of hand and wrist, spread them into a perfect fan. "Take a card, any card," you say. Everyone at the party may think it's magic, and they may envy you your skill. But it's not magic. *The real secret to doing card tricks successfully is plenty of practice, plenty of patience in trying the basic moves over and over again, and a natural flair for the dramatic.*

3. *You can't keep babies from catching colds, but you can certainly keep a baby with a cold more comfortable by following a few simple rules.* New parents especially are thrown into a panic when their baby gets sick; but frightened, panicky parents often make babies feel worse instead of better. The thing to do is relax and just follow these rules.

Notice that there is no single best place for the main idea sentence. It can come at the beginning, in the middle, or at the end of your introduction. In these samples, the first introduction gives reasons for doing the job and lists the necessary equipment. The second introduction encourages readers by telling them they can do something it probably never occurred to them to try. The third introduction is also encouraging, but it mainly emphasizes how important it is for readers to follow the rules that will be given.

Developing Your Plan

Writing the main part of a paper of directions should be fairly easy. All you need do is follow your plan. But just as the main idea sentence is not enough for the first paragraph, simply repeating the list of steps is not enough for the main part of the paper. The student who made the list on page 28 won't have a very useful paper if all it says is:

> First, remove the old glass. Then clean the edges of the frame. Measure the size of the glass and buy exactly the right size at the hardware store. Fit the glass into the frame. Install the glazier's points and replace the molding. Now the job is finished.

These are the proper steps all right, now arranged in the proper order, but readers who have never repaired a broken window may not know how to get the old glass out without cutting themselves, and they certainly won't know how to get the new glass in without breaking it. The writer's job is to explain exactly how each step must be done.

Instead of just repeating the list, the writer must get a mental picture of what happens when the broken glass is being taken out, and then use that picture to explain in detail what to do if the glass is cracked, what to do if it is shattered. The writer will probably have to explain what holds the old glass in—putty or molding or metal—and how to remove the glazier's points. Making the directions useful to somebody who has never repaired a broken window will mean writing at least one full paragraph for each step in the plan. If you look at the sample paper on pages 35–39, you can notice the differences between the writer's first attempt, where not enough details were given, and the second attempt, where the writer did considerably more than just copy the plan.

Writing the Conclusion

Just as every paper needs an introduction, every paper ought to have a conclusion. The last paragraph of a paper of directions need not be very long, but it should give readers the feeling that they have come to the end, not that you got tired of writing and just stopped. One sentence is usually enough to make a short paper of directions sound complete:

1. Now that you know how to bake your own bread, you can have that delicious, warm-from-the-oven treat any time you want to—and a wonderful aroma all through the house besides.

2. By practicing these techniques, you'll soon be ready to do your magic tricks in public, and in no time at all you'll be saying smoothly, "Pick a card, any card."

3. The baby will not only be more comfortable, it will probably get well a lot quicker than if you had fretted yourself sick about an ordinary cold.

Single sentence conclusions such as these are all you need for papers of simple directions. Longer, more complicated papers will probably need longer conclusions.

But whether the conclusion to a thousand-word paper of explanation uses three paragraphs to summarize the main divisions of the paper, or whether a book defending a point of view includes a whole chapter intended to clinch the argument, all good conclusions have one thing in common: they make the writing sound finished.

Checking for Clarity

Even though you have written the conclusion, your work is not quite finished. You still need to do the careful detective work that makes the difference between good writing and almost good enough. Read through what you have written. Is everything you have said perfectly clear? Clarity is important in most writing, but it is essential in giving directions. Just one confused sentence, where your readers aren't sure what you mean, can get them so mixed up that the whole job will be a failure.

Short sentences are more likely to make for clarity than long, involved ones.

> Although I'm not absolutely sure how you do it, you start with the clay you want to mix up, and then you add the water to it. Some say add it all at once and others say dribble it in—and by the way, there are lots of different kinds of clay, too, so be sure that you have the right kind for your use—and then work it up good, maybe by pounding it, or squeezing it, and sometimes people use a kind of shovel, and sometimes even tromp it with their feet, and pretty soon you'll have it ready so you can make you a pot or something and then fire it in the kiln, if you've used that kind of clay.

"Add one-fourth of a cup of water to five pounds of clay and mix with your hands until it's smooth" is not only clearer, it is more likely to inspire confidence.

Avoiding Apologies

Extra, unnecessary information may make your readers wonder whether you really know what you're talking about, but a long stream of apologies will make them pretty sure you don't. Whenever you are tempted to say "Although I am not sure, but I think . . . ," stop and ask yourself whether you are really not sure. If you do know, leave the apology out; there's no need to be overmodest. If you don't know, find out. After all, you are writing about something you understand fairly thoroughly and you want your readers to feel confident that you do understand it. Naturally you want to be accurate and honest, but the best way to achieve honesty—and accuracy, too—is to write in a straightforward way on topics you already know something about.

Other phrases you will probably want to cut out are "it seems to me," "in my opinion," or any of their variations. Your readers can figure out that if it didn't seem that way to you, you wouldn't be saying it. And the phrase "in my opinion" is usually just a way of taking up space, very like the habit some people have of saying "you know" every other sentence when they talk. Sometimes, of course, you may want to make it clear that your opinion is different from the opinion of most other people. If that difference seems important enough to emphasize, you will probably do better to come right out and say so: "Many people think that . . . ; I think, on the other hand, that. . . ." But that situation is not likely to come up in papers giving directions. When you are telling your readers how to do something, you're the expert.

Using Transitions

Another way to write clearly is to take your readers with you as you move from one step to the next. These attempts to help readers see the relationships between the parts of your writing are called *transitions*. Sometimes the transition from step to step occurs almost automatically. It is natural to say "First, make sure you have all the supplies you need" and "Second, find a place where you can work without being disturbed." Other words and phrases that help to suggest order are:

You begin by . . .

Next . . .

Then . . .

After you have . . .

The last step is to . . .

Finally . . .

These transitional words and phrases show how things are related in time. Using them sensibly makes for smoother, easier reading, but overusing any one of them can become tiresome: *"Then* you do this *and then* you add this *and then* you do that *and then.* . . ."

Other transitions show how things are related in space (*in front of, behind, next to, underneath,* etc.). Still others show how things contrast in our minds (*however, nevertheless, but, in spite of, although,* etc.). We might call all three kinds of connectors—those that show time, those that show space, and those that show contrast—*link transitions.* Link transitions are either single words or groups of words that we think of as belonging together: *but* and *in spite of* are good examples.

Sometimes, however, you will want to show the logical relationship between one set of ideas and another, and no ready-made link transition seems adequate for the job. Then the best way to show this logical relationship is to pick up an important word or phrase at the end of one paragraph and repeat it at the beginning of the next paragraph. For example, in this chapter we ended one paragraph by saying ". . . all good *conclusions* have one thing in common: they make the writing sound finished," and we began the next paragraph with "Even though you have written the *conclusion*. . . ." We might call this kind of connecting device, which repeats an important word, an *echo transition.*

Echo transitions make for smooth-sounding writing if they are used smoothly. But just as a single link transition can become tiresome if it is overused, so echo transitions can annoy your readers if they are used awkwardly. Ending one paragraph with "Now I have told you how to scrape the *wires*" and beginning the next paragraph with "Now I am going to tell you how to connect the *wires*" sounds a bit flatfooted. Your readers may not like to be told that they have already been told.

Both link and echo transitions are good ways of helping your readers, and they will help most if they sound easy and natural. Lead your readers by the hand; don't pull them by the nose.

Keeping the Same Attitude Toward Your Readers: Pronouns

Good writers not only help their readers get from paragraph to paragraph, they help them within paragraphs, too. One way of doing this is by always speaking to your readers in the same way. If you begin by speaking directly to them, keep on speaking directly throughout the rest of your paper. "Before one can change their tire, you must stop our car" is almost frightening. Is "our" car trying to run over "their" tire, and are "you" chasing behind trying to grab the bumper before "one" is smashed to a bloody pulp? Such confusions usually come from writers who have been told that saying "I" and "you" is wrong. No advice could be more mistaken. Especially in papers of directions, it's a good idea to address your readers as though you were speaking to them face to face. If you mean "Stop the car before you change the tire," then say so. When you are talking about yourself, it is natural to say "I found . . . ," "we tried . . . ," and so on. Feeling natural will make your writing sound natural.

Some handbooks that give advice on college writing will still tell you, however, that you should use more impersonal expressions such as *people, others, students, anybody,* and so on. And it is true that avoiding *I, me,* and *you* will make your writing sound more formal. But struggling for formality sometimes makes for very stilted writing: *one should, one tends,* or even *in the judgment of this writer.* It's better to be informal than to sound stilted or affected. Such sentences as "One should not stay in the bathtub for more than an hour at a time" lead flippant readers to say, "Okay, but can two do it?" And such circumlocutions as "this writer" establish a sense of distance between you and your readers that is surely inappropriate in a paper giving directions.

The best rule is to decide on whatever makes you feel comfortable and then stick to it. Feeling comfortable will probably help you to write more clearly.

Finding a Title

After you have written your paper and revised it as carefully as you can, the last step is to give it a title. Sometimes the simplest titles are the best. In a paper of directions, a phrase that shows clearly what the directions will cover is probably better than an attempt to be clever. "Baking Your Own Bread" is a more effective title than "To Bake or Not to Bake." "How to Do Card Tricks" is more effective than "Sheer Magic."

If you can think of a title that is both clever and clear, fine; but in general it is better not to parody a quotation so familiar that it has already been overworked ("To Bake or Not to Bake" is an obvious parody of "To be or not to be"), and it is always a good idea to avoid clichés—phrases that have been worn out by overuse (such as "Sheer Magic"). These titles are bad because they are corny. But they are also misleading, and that is a more serious fault. The titles don't tell readers what the paper will be about. Because paint manufacturers don't want to mislead their customers, paint cans are usually labeled "Directions for Mixing," not "Invitation to a Fun Mixer" or "The Enamel Can that Can Cancan." And you seldom see the directions for assembling a chair with the title "Fun and Games with a Screwy Screwdriver."

In other words, worry more about whether your title is direct and appropriate than about whether it is dull. If you make the title informative, your readers will be grateful rather than bored.

And although there is no absolute rule about how long a title should be, very short titles may seem to promise too much and very long titles may tell your readers more than they want to know at that point. "Baking" sounds like an encyclopedia entry rather than a paper on how to make bread; and "Magic" might refer to an explanation, a report, or even an advertisement for a Caribbean cruise.

Perhaps the best reason for not making your title too long is that you will have to repeat yourself too much. If you use your entire main idea sentence, or even part of it, for your title—"Almost Anyone Can Read a Subway Map"—you have only two choices: either you will have to repeat the sentence in the introduction or you will be tempted to say, in the first sentence, "If you need to read one. . . ." (You can avoid this particular temptation by writing the paper first and finding the title last.)

When you have decided on a title that pleases you, center it at the top of the first page. It's conventional practice to capitalize the important words but not to use quotation marks or underline the title. For example, if you have written a paper telling readers how to bake bread, your title should look like this:

Baking Your Own Bread

A Check List for Revisions

If you are like most people, whatever you write will seem perfectly clear to you at the time you're writing it. If it didn't seem clear, you wouldn't write it that way. A useful trick is to put the paper away for a day or two and then reread it as though somebody else had written it. You may find confusions you missed. Reading your paper aloud to yourself also helps; sometimes the ear can hear what the eye misses. And it's even better to read it to somebody else, especially if you have friends who will tell you honestly what they think instead of just saying "Good, good" to make you feel better. If you do find places that seem confusing either to you or to your friends, don't be afraid to change them.

Before you present your directions to the class, make one final check. If you can answer yes to these questions, you probably have a good paper:

1. Have you done everything your first paragraph promised and no more?
2. Have you told your readers about all the equipment they will need?
3. Have you included all the necessary steps in logical order?
4. Have you developed each step by giving exact details?
5. Have you avoided sounding apologetic?
6. Have you used enough transitions to take your readers comfortably from point to point?
7. Have you talked to your readers in the same way all through the paper—stayed with "you" if you began with "you"?
8. Does your conclusion make your paper sound finished?
9. Is your title clear and appropriate?

Examining a Sample Paper of Directions

Here is the first version of a paper on how to replace a broken window, based on the plan shown on page 22:

How to Replace a Broken Window

Introduction is good: tells what the job is; why you should do it; how easy it is; what equipment is needed.

[1] Everybody that owns a house, or even rents an apartment, is likely to get a window broken some time or other. Some kid will throw a rock, or a ball will go in the wrong direction, or a heavy wind will just blow the glass out. You can call the landlord, if you're renting, and wait a month for the repairman to come. If you own your own

house, you can pay somebody twenty-five dollars or more to come fix it for you. But a way that is both quicker and cheaper is to fix it yourself. Replacing a broken window is an easy home-repair job that requires only a tape measure, a chisel, a tack hammer, and a reasonable amount of care.

Problems begin here: What if the glass is just cracked, rather than broken into pieces that will lift out? What if the window is put in with molding or metal rather than putty? What do you use the hammer for— breaking the glass or pounding the chisel? And what are glazier's points? Many people have never seen them.

[2]   The first step is to remove the old glass. Be careful not to cut yourself. You can chip out the old putty with a chisel and you may have to use a hammer. Then take out the glazier's points.

What does "thorough cleaning" mean? The step on cleaning needs more details, in a paragraph of its own. And do even amateurs need to be told that if the glass is too big, it won't go in?

[3]   After you have cleaned the edges of the window frame thoroughly, measure the size of the glass carefully and write down the measurement, because the right size is very important. If it's too big, it won't go in and if it's too little it will fall through the hole.

Are there any tricks to making the glass fit? And here are those glazier's points again, still not explained. Is this the same putty that was chipped out? Do you use putty no matter how the original glass was put in?

[4]   Next, fit the glass into the frame and install the glazier's points. Then roll the putty into little strips and press it in.

A problem with order here —this warning should come much earlier in the paper. Perhaps the main idea sentence should be changed to read: "If your window is reasonably small and set in a wooden frame, . . ."

[5]   This system won't work if the windows are framed in metal, and it isn't practical for glass much bigger than thirty-six inches in any direction. If you have a broken picture window, you'd better call the repairman after all.

This sentence does try to make the paper sound finished—but can one person actually do the job alone? Maybe. And would the ending be more effective if it referred back to the good introduction?

[6] Now you can be proud of a window you fixed all by yourself.

Here is the second version of the same paper. Now the writer can honestly answer yes to all the questions in the check list on page 29.

Replacing a Broken Window

Introduction stays the same, except for the changed main idea sentence, which eliminates the need for paragraph 5 in the first version.

[1] Everybody that owns a house, or even rents an apartment, is likely to get a window broken some time or other. Some kid will throw a rock, or a ball will go in the wrong direction, or a heavy wind will just blow the glass out. You can call the landlord, if you're renting, and wait a month for the repairman to come. If you own your own house, you can pay somebody twenty-five dollars or more to come fix it for you. But a way that is both quicker and cheaper is to fix it yourself. If your window is reasonably small and set in a wooden frame, replacing it is an easy home-repair job that requires only a tape measure, a chisel, a tack hammer, and a little bit of care.

Writer has given more details on dealing with both cracked and jagged glass, and advice on handling both molding and putty. Writer has also considered problems that might occur.

[2] The first step is to remove the old glass. If the window is broken into jagged pieces, probably they will just lift out, but be careful not to cut your hands on the sharp edges. If the window is just cracked and won't come out easily, you will need to remove whatever holds it in place. Some windows are put in with wooden molding and some are put in with putty. If yours has molding, loosen the molding gently with the back side of the hammer. If the window has had several coats of paint, you may have to pry a little with your chisel before you can use the hammer. Once the molding is loose, you should be able to lift it off. Save it carefully, because you will want to put it back on after the new glass is in. If your window was put in with putty, you will need to chip the putty out with a chisel. This is harder to do be-

cause old putty hardens. Try it with just the chisel first, and if that doesn't work, hit the end of the chisel with your hammer.

Step 1 has been given two paragraphs, and glazier's points have been explained.

[3] When you have gotten the molding or the putty out, you will see that the glass is held in place with glazier's points. These are little triangular pieces of metal pushed into the wood of the window frame just far enough to hold the glass securely. But don't worry about them. After you have gotten the molding or the putty off, you can lift the pieces of old glass out and the glazier's points will probably come with them.

"Thoroughly cleaned" has also been explained.

[4] The next step is to clean the edges of the window frame. Run over the edges lightly with your chisel to make sure the old paint is out of the way and the edges are perfectly smooth. This is also a good time to make sure that the glazier's points all came out with the glass.

The importance of exact measurements is made clearer, and the unnecessary "too big/too little" sentence has been left out. Readers are reminded that they will need new glazier's points and new putty. (Although it's usually a good idea to list needed supplies earlier in the directions, the delay is all right here since the glass can't be bought until the window is carefully measured, and one trip to the hardware store can cover all the purchases.)

[5] Now you are ready to measure the size of glass you need. Getting exactly the right measurement is very important, because even a quarter of an inch too much or too little will keep the glass from fitting. Double-check your measurements, and write them down so that when you get to the hardware store to buy the glass you won't have to depend on your memory. When you are buying the glass, pick up a box of glazier's points—you won't be able to reuse the old ones. (Sometimes these little metal gadgets are called *push points.* That's all right. They all do the same thing.) And if the window was put in with putty, buy some of that, too.

Writer has given suggestions on what to do if the glass doesn't seem to fit; mentioned the value of a helper; and told how to put the new points in.

[6] When you get home with your supplies, try fitting the glass into the window frame. If it doesn't fit exactly, don't be discouraged. Most old windows are not perfectly square, and the glass may fit better the other way up or the other way around. After you have found the way it fits best, you are ready to use the glazier's points. Here is where an assistant will be a good thing. You *can* hold the

glass in place with one hand and push the points in with the other, but it is a lot easier if someone else holds the glass in place while you cope with the points. Although push points are meant just to be pushed into the wood, I've found that tapping them in with a hammer is a good deal easier and a lot more secure.

New information tells readers what to watch out for in replacing molding. The conclusion is better, too. Instead of a single sentence in a paragraph all alone, the writer has added a new idea (washing the finished window) and made the ending livelier and more personal by mentioning Mary and her baseball.

[7]   Once the glass is securely held in place, you can put the molding back on or replace the putty. If you're replacing molding, be sure to hammer the nails in very gently so you don't break the new glass. If you're using putty, roll it into little strips with your hands and press it neatly in place all around the glass. Now the job is almost done. When you have washed the finger smudges off the new glass, you can say proudly, "Sure, Mary threw a baseball through the window, but I fixed it without any trouble."

Key Words

Here are some of the important terms used in this chapter. See whether you can answer these questions about them.

1. The **main idea sentence** of a paper giving directions should include two things. What are they?
2. What should the **plan** for a paper of directions include? What two questions should you ask yourself about your plan?
3. What does the **introduction** for a paper of directions do that the main idea sentence does not do?
4. What is meant by **developing your plan into a paper**?
5. What does a good **conclusion** do? How long should it be in a paper of directions?
6. How can you make sure that what you have said will be **clear** to your readers?
7. Why should you **avoid apologies**?
8. What are the two kinds of **transition**? How does **using transitions** help your readers?
9. How do **pronouns** show what attitude you are taking toward your readers? What is the best attitude to take in a paper of directions?
10. What makes a good **title**?
11. When is the best time to **check for revisions**?

READINGS
Giving Directions

Rubbings

archaeologists: scientists who study the way prehistoric people lived
bas-relief: a shallow carving in which the figures stand out only slightly from
    the background, like faces on coins
deteriorating: wearing out or crumbling away
commemorative: put up in memory of a person or an event
incised: cut down from the surface, like cut glass or cut crystal
recipient: person who receives something

"Remember when" opening is catchy, and also explains the process. Introduction gives a reason for attempting the project and encourages the reader. It also lists the materials needed to do the job.

Second paragraph gives another reason

[1] Remember when, as a child, you covered a penny with paper and rubbed a pencil back and forth across the surface to reproduce the likeness of Abraham Lincoln? Attractive rubbings to decorate the home may be made in much the same way and are not much more difficult to do. The inexpensive materials are easily available; all you will need is some paper, a marker, a whisk broom, a soft nail brush, and masking tape.

[2] The technique of taking rubbings has long been used by archaeologists, scholars, and artists to record bas-reliefs in danger of deteriorating. Such reproductions make wonderful gifts, for they can be tailor-made to suit the interests of the persons to whom they are given. For a history lover, a rubbing of a historical marker would make a perfect gift. For a friend who is moving away, you might make a rubbing of some familiar landmark to serve as a reminder.

Gifts You Can Make (Menlo Park, Calif.: Lane Publishing, Sunset Books, 1965), pp. 12–13.

Where to look for suitable subjects

[3] There are many places where you will find suitable subjects. Part of the fun is finding them in unexpected spots. The ideal relief is not too deep or sculptural, with the raised surface flat and smooth. Good examples can usually be found among historical markers, cornerstones, manhole covers, gravestones, low reliefs on buildings and commemorative plaques, to suggest a few. It doesn't harm the original to make a rubbing, but stay on your paper. And if the object to be rubbed is on private property, be sure to get the owner's permission.

Kinds of paper for the job

[4] Once you have located your subject, you can easily assemble your materials. Smooth-textured, lightweight papers produce the cleanest prints. The paper should be strong, yet thin enough to make good contact with the object being rubbed. White poster paper was used by the writer to reproduce a Mexican stone carving. You may also use newsprint (which eventually turns yellow), rice paper, lightweight bond, tissue paper, and shelf paper, all with good results.

Markers, suitable and unsuitable

[5] Markers with a wax base are best. Shoe finishing wax may be bought in a one-pound block from shoe repair shops and broken into manageable pieces. You may also use Conte crayon, litho crayon, ordinary wax crayon, and medium grade lumberman's marking pencil (available at building supply dealers). Charcoal and graphite are too soft and pile up on the surface of the paper. Use the side of the crayon to get a flat, smooth marking surface. Conte crayon should be sprayed with artist's fixative when you are finished; the other markers will not smear as easily.

Preparing the rubbing

[6] To make the rubbing, first brush the carved or incised stone free of dirt with your whisk broom. Cut the desired length of paper and tape it in place over the stone to prevent shifting.

Making the rubbing

[7] Using the soft nail brush, go over the surface of the paper, easing it into the depressions of the stone in order to locate the design outlines. When this is done, you are ready to begin rubbing with your marker. Go over the entire surface of the stone. Be careful to stay within the desired boundary lines and to keep the tone even.

Conclusion restates a reason for doing the job

[8] This project combines fun with the satisfaction of making a gift that is out of the ordinary and thoughtfully chosen to suit the taste of the recipient.

Responses

1. What are the two reasons for making rubbings? Why does the writer give a separate paragraph to each reason? Why does the list of materials appear where it does?
2. Where does the introduction end? In what paragraph does the writer stop encouraging readers to try the project and begin giving information useful to people who have decided to do it?
3. Skillful writers sometimes encourage the reader beyond the introduction. In this article the writer weaves the encouragement into the whole article. Find those words, phrases, or sentences that provide encouragement to the reader.
4. What is the main point of each paragraph from 2 through 7? Would it be fair to say that paragraphs 2 through 7 each develop a point already mentioned in the first paragraph? If you think that this statement is a fair one, find the particular word or phrase in paragraph 1 that hints at each of these points.
5. The list of necessary materials given in the first paragraph includes five things. Why does the writer go into considerable detail about two of them and not discuss the other three at all?
6. The conclusion to this article is a single sentence. Does it seem satisfactory to you? Why or why not? If you think it is unsatisfactory, what would you add?
7. Think of some very simple thing you know how to make. Then make a plan for a paper. Include in your plan at least one reason readers might want to make whatever it is, a list of materials that will be needed, and the steps that need to be followed.

Fixing Leaky Faucets

corroded: eaten away; uneven or pitted
access: ability to reach or get at

[1]   The exact point where a leak appears on a faucet is the best clue to finding the cause. A spout drip is caused by a worn faucet washer or a corroded valve seat. A leak at the stem suggests a loose cap nut or worn cone bonnet packing. Water oozing below the cap nut indicates a worn bib washer. Water coming from the base of the faucet body seeps through a worn washer there.

Basic Home Repairs (Menlo Park, Calif.: Lane Publishing, Sunset Books, 1974), p. 6

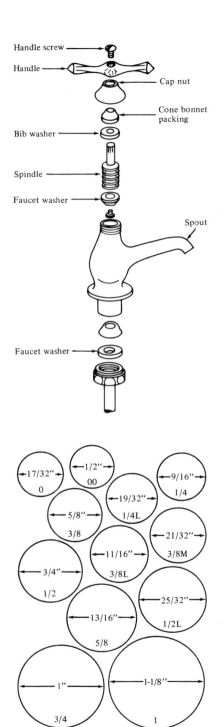

Handle screw

Handle

Cap nut

Cone bonnet packing

Bib washer

Spindle

Faucet washer

Spout

Faucet washer

17/32"
0

1/2"
00

9/16"
1/4

19/32"
1/4L

5/8"
3/8

21/32"
3/8M

11/16"
3/8L

3/4"
1/2

25/32"
1/2L

13/16"
5/8

1"
3/4

1-1/8"
1

ACTUAL SIZE DIAMETERS

[2]   To dismantle a faucet: (1) Shut off water at valve below sink, then open tap to drain the faucet. (2) Remove handle screw and handle. (3) Unscrew cap nut, covering jaws of wrench with adhesive or friction tape to avoid marring the chrome finish. (4) Unscrew stem with finger pressure and lift it out.

[3]   These steps give access to all points except the washer at the base of the faucet body. It is reached by loosening the slip nut that connects the faucet body to the pipe. Raise the faucet body away from the pipe rather than trying to bend the pipe if the fit is too close to remove the washer.

[4]   The chart shows washers at exact size, with their trade designations as well as actual measurements. It can be used to match sizes of washers too worn to be read for size. The code size embossed on the washer should be turned toward the seat when the washer is installed. Before buying replacements, check also to see whether you want a flat washer or a conical one. Make sure it's like the old one.

[5]   In replacing a faucet washer, check the seat to be sure it is not pitted or otherwise rough. If the seat is rough an inexpensive "reseater kit" can be purchased to grind it smooth again.

[6]   On reassembling the faucet, tighten the cap nut just enough so it does not leak. Screwing the nut down hard can cause rapid wear on the stem.

Responses

1. What is the main idea sentence of this short article? If you think the article contains a main idea sentence, be ready to say what it is; if you think the sentence does not appear, work out in your own words what it should be.
2. Decide whether the writer of this article could have answered yes to the nine questions given on page 29. If the answer to some questions is no, explain what the problem is.
3. If you have ever fixed a faucet yourself, is this the procedure you followed? Has anything been left out or any unnecessary information added? If you've never fixed a faucet, do you think you could follow these directions? Why or why not?
4. This article was written for people who have never done any home repairs and are probably unfamiliar with plumbing terms. How does the diagram help them? How much longer would the article need to be if the pictures were not included?
5. Write a paragraph or two giving directions for some easy household repair. Include a simple sketch to make it easier for readers to follow your directions.

Learning to Keep Your Cool During Tests

peripheral: around the edges
optimum: best or most favorable
interspersing: scattering here and there
intuitive: understanding something without thinking about it

[1]   Have you ever felt so panicky during an examination that you couldn't even put down the answers you *knew?* If so, you were suffering from what is known as test anxiety.

[2]   According to psychologist Ralph Trimble, test anxiety is a very real problem for many people. When you're worried over your performance on an exam, your heart beats faster, your pulse speeds up, hormones are secreted. These reactions trigger others: you may sweat more than normal or suffer from a stomach ache or headache. Your field of vision narrows and becomes tunnellike, leaving you with very little peripheral sight. Before you know it you're having difficulty focusing.

[3]   "What I hear students say over and over again," says Dr. Trimble, who is

Margot Jerrard, "Learning to Keep Your Cool During Tests," *Family Weekly,* February 10, 1980.

involved with the Psychological and Counseling Center at the University of Illinois, "is, 'My mind went blank.' "

[4]   For a number of years, Dr. Trimble helped many students learn how to function better during exams and to bring up their grades. Some of these students were interested in sharing what they learned and, with Trimble's help, began holding workshops on overcoming test anxiety. For many students, just being in a workshop with other sufferers was a relief. They realized they weren't freaks, that they were not the only ones who had done poorly on tests because of tension. The workshops were so successful that they are still given.

[5]   In the workshops, students are taught that anxiety is normal. You just have to prevent it from getting the best of you. The first step is to learn to relax. If before or during an examination you start to panic, stretch as hard as you can, tensing the muscles in your arms and legs; then suddenly relax all of them. This will help relieve tension.

[6]   But keep in mind that you don't want to be *too* relaxed. Being completely relaxed is no better than being too tense. "If you are so calm you don't *care* how you do on an examination, you won't do well," Trimble says. "There is an optimum level of concern when you perform at your best. Some stress helps. There are people who can't take even slight stress. They have to learn that in a challenging situation, being keyed up is good and will help them to do better. But if they label it anxiety and say, 'It's going to hit me again,' that will push them over the edge."

[7]   As a student you must also realize that if you leave too much studying until a day or two before the examination, you can't do the impossible and learn it all. Instead, concentrate on what you *can* do and try to think what questions are likely to be asked and what you can do in the time left for studying.

[8]   When you sit down to study, set a moderate pace and vary it by interspersing reading, writing notes and going over any papers you have already written for the course, as well as the textbooks and notes you took in class. Review what you know. Take breaks, and go to sleep in plenty of time to get a good night's rest before the exam. You should also eat a moderate breakfast or lunch, avoiding drinks with caffeine and steering clear of fellow students who get tense. **Panic is contagious.**

[9]   Get to the exam room a few minutes early so you will have a chance to familiarize yourself with the surroundings and get out your supplies. When the examination is handed out, read the directions twice and underline the significant instructions, making sure you understand them. Ask the teacher or proctor to explain if you don't. First answer the easiest questions, then go back to the more difficult. If you are stumped on a multiple-choice question, first eliminate the impossible answers, then make as good an intuitive guess as possible and go on to the next.

[10]   On essay questions, instead of plunging right in, take a few minutes to organize your thoughts, make a brief outline and then start off with a summary sentence. Keep working steadily, and even when time starts to run out, don't speed up.

[11]   After the examination is over, don't torture yourself by thinking over all the mistakes you made, and don't start studying immediately for another exam. Instead, give yourself an hour or two of free time.

[12]   Among the students who are working now as volunteer leaders in the workshops are a number who started out panicky and unable to function on exams. They learned how to deal with test anxiety and are now teaching others. It's almost as easy as ABC.

Responses

1. Who are the readers of this article expected to be? How can you tell? What does Jerrard say to encourage them?
2. Where does the introduction end and the actual directions begin? Are the directions given in the order in which readers should follow them? If you think they aren't, make a plan showing the steps in chronological order.
3. Make a plan that shows the steps you follow in studying for and taking an exam. How is what you do like what Jerrard recommends? How is it different?

Home Garden in a Flowerpot

versatile: usable in several ways
receptacle: container

[1] Soybeans, now cultivated extensively in this country, are becoming almost as familiar to [Americans] as they are to the Chinese, who have made them an important part of their diet for 5,000 years. In addition to having wide use as an ingredient for industrial products and as both fodder and fertilizer on farms, soybeans are common on many dining tables in a variety of dishes.

[2]   One way of using this versatile bean as a food, however, probably isn't so well known. Sprouting converts the dried bean into a fresh vegetable that not only rivals tomatoes in vitamin C, but contains healthy amounts of protein, calcium, iron, thiamine, niacin, and riboflavin, which are found in beefsteak.

[3]   Any wide-mouthed receptacle can be used for sprouting beans at home, provided it has a hole in the bottom for water to drain through. [Most people] will probably find an ordinary clay flowerpot best suited for the raising of a small crop of sprouts for a tryout in some of the appealing new dishes.

[4]   Dry soybeans for successful sprouting need possess no higher quality than a mere ability to grow, and they are pretty sure to do so if they are less than a year old. The more expensive, higher-grade beans are not necessary. Field beans generally used as fodder are good enough if they are free from other seeds, and a half

Complete Home Workshop Cyclopedia (New York: Grosset and Dunlap, 1945), pp. 283–284.

pound of them will return an abundant family supply of sprouts in from three to five days.

[5]   Aside from the pot and the beans and water, the process calls for nothing except a little chlorinated lime. Dilute solutions of the lime are used to prevent mold.

[6]   Rules for sprouting are simple. Inspect and wash a half pound of beans and soak them overnight in 1½ pints of water to which has been added a pinch of the chlorinated lime. After soaking, the beans should be strained and poured into a sprouting pot large enough to hold them, as they swell to twice their original size. A piece of wire screening over the hole in the bottom of the pot will keep any beans from falling through and scattering when the pot is moved about.

[7]   Now cover the beans with a wet cloth and also place on top of the pot a piece of wet cardboard or a plate to keep light out. Sprinkle the beans with plain water three or four times a day, taking care after each sprinkling to joggle the pot so that all excess water will drain out the hole. A last sprinkling each night should be made with a solution formed by dissolving ⅓ teaspoon chlorinated lime in 1 gal. water as a guard against the formation of mold.

[8]   Sprouts are fully grown when they are about 1½″ long. They grow faster in warm weather than in cool, but they seldom take more than five days to mature. In very hot weather, mold may develop despite the chlorine treatment, but ice cubes placed on top of the wet cloth will help to avert it.

Responses

1. How does the introduction to this article work? by giving reasons for doing the job? offering encouragement? justifying the need for the first step? encouraging readers? Where does the introduction end?
2. Is the list of equipment given in paragraph 5 complete? If not, what has been left out and why do you think the writer omitted it?
3. Does this article have a satisfactory conclusion? If you think it does, what is the conclusion and why does it make the article sound ended? If you think it doesn't, write a conclusion that seems more satisfactory.

Replacing Broken Plugs the Easy Way

[1]   Let's suppose your check of the wiring turns up a smashed plug hidden behind the living room sofa. It's the plug for a lamp that doesn't carry too much current, and the wire from the lamp to the plug is in good shape. Only the plug needs to be replaced, and a light-duty one will work.

Arthur Symons, *The Fix-it Book* (New York: Gramercy Publishing, 1967), pp. 114–116.

[2]   Your local hardware store has the answer to this one, and you can fix it in less than three minutes. It is a patented plug (called a "pin-on plug cap") with a removable core, and it looks like this:

[3]   Trim your wire off even; do *not* strip any insulation. Remove the core of the plug from the outer case. Run the wire through the outer case of the plug. Be sure the "wings" on the inner core are in the "out" position. Run the two strands of the wire into the holes in the core as far as they will go. Squeeze the "wings" together. Slip the core back into the outer case. The job is done, and the "wings" are the prongs that go into the wall socket.

[4]   Perhaps the hardware store doesn't have the type of plug that is so very easy to attach, or perhaps you want something a bit stronger to resist the shock when the sofa is jammed against the wall again. Or perhaps there is one of the older types of plugs in your junk box. You had better know how to replace this kind also.

[5]   Cut the end of the cord clean, as close to the plug as you can. Push the end of the cord through the hole in the plug from the rear, like this:

Strip off several inches of the braid that holds the two wires together, being very careful to avoid damaging the rubber insulation beneath the braid. If the cord has two rubber-covered wires pressed together, separate them carefully for a couple of inches.

[6]   Now tie an electrician's knot. Then pull the plug against the cord so the knot fits tightly in the space provided for it. This little trick, rarely done by most home fix-it experts, will protect the wire and the plug from those people who insist on pulling out plugs by the wires instead of by the plug itself.

[7]   Next, cut off the ends of the wires at a length that will permit them to make a full turn under the screws in the plug. Then, very carefully, strip off the insulation from the ends, being sure you don't injure the wire strands. Twist the strands into a solid rope. Scrape them with a knife until the copper is bright. Bend the brightened ends under the screw heads in a clockwise direction, so that when you tighten the screw the friction between screw and wire will tighten the wire around the threaded portion of the screw. If you were to wind the wires counterclockwise, tightening the screw would have the effect of loosening the coil.

[8]   Check to be sure that your two wires are not touching at any place where there is no insulation. Replace the fiber cap if there is one; if not, perhaps a piece of friction tape will make a satisfactory cover.

[9]   Try the lamp, or appliance. No fuses blown? You did it!

Responses

1. See whether you can answer these questions about this article:
   a. What is "too much current" (paragraph 1)?
   b. What tools are needed to replace the plug? Where are you told about them?
   c. What is "an electrician's knot"? How do you know?
   d. Why does the writer say "or appliance" in the last line of the article?
   e. What makes the article sound finished?
   If you cannot answer the questions, what changes does the writer need to make?
2. Could you follow these directions? Why or why not?
3. What is the effect of such comments as "hidden behind the living room sofa" and "when the sofa is jammed against the wall again"? What other such comments can you find? (See paragraphs 4 and 6.)

First Aid for Household Emergencies

[1]   Accidents do happen, but would you know what to do if you found yourself in a situation where you or someone else needed immediate help? Here's a quiz to test your knowledge of some first-aid basics.

1. Preoccupied with worries about work, you cut your finger with a knife. You treat the wound by
   _____a. Cleansing it, stopping the bleeding and allowing it to "air heal"
   _____b. Cleansing it, applying medication and covering it with an adhesive bandage
   _____c. Immersing it in cold water
2. Your friend is baking her favorite quiche when she burns her finger on the oven. You advise her to
   _____a. Submerge the burned finger in cold water
   _____b. Spread a protective layer of butter on the burn
   _____c. Wait until a blister forms; then "pop" it

Family Weekly, February 17, 1980.

3. You enter the kitchen to discover that your child has taken a drink from a bottle of cleanser beneath the sink. You should

_____a. Force the child to vomit

_____b. Phone your regional Poison Control Center

_____c. Rush him to the hospital

4. As you carry a load of parcels home, your lower back begins to ache. You decide to

_____a. Jog a mile to smooth out the kinks in your muscles

_____b. Ignore the pain and continue with your plans

_____c. Apply wet heat to the sore muscles and get some rest

ANSWERS

[2]   1. You're right if you chose the "b" response. The four simple steps to remember when treating a minor wound are *cleanse, treat, cover* and *tape.* Gently wash in and around the wound and rinse it thoroughly. Blot the wound dry, then apply medication and a fresh, dry, nonstick sterile pad. Don't forget to replace the dressing as often as necessary to keep the wound clean and dry. If infection or other complications occur, seek medical attention.

2. Like most people, you probably believe "b" is the best burn remedy. But this is an old wives' tale. The best method for soothing minor burns is applying cold water—response "a." Cover the burn with a nonstick bandage, and resist any impulse you might have to break a blister.

3. The National Safety Council reports that accidental poisoning is a major cause of death and illness for children under 5. If you chose response "b," you're aware of the right procedure for this type of accident. Find the container of poison so you'll know what the substance is, and then call your regional Poison Control Center for prompt assistance. They may advise you to administer either syrup of ipecac or activated charcoal to induce vomiting, so it is a good idea to keep both substances on hand. However, don't act unless you have been directed to do so.

4. A back strain means it's time to pamper yourself, and "c" is the way doctors recommend you do it. And again, you'll want to have medical attention if the problem persists. A good general, preventive measure might be to invest in a firm-support mattress.

[3]   Other general, preventive first-aid measures you might consider are enrolling in Red Cross community first-aid courses and keeping a first-aid manual or wall chart on hand that gives basic first-aid information. Maintaining a household inventory of such first-aid supplies as adhesive bandages, gauze, sterile absorbent cotton and aspirin or an aspirin substitute is also advisable.

Responses

1. Which of the following would be the best main idea sentence for this article?
   a. Everybody should know something about first aid.
   b. Most people don't know what to do in an amergency.
   c. Only four kinds of accidents are likely to occur at home.
   d. People who get the right answers to the questions don't need to read any further.
   If none of the above seems suitable, write one that you think is better.
2. The method of presenting these directions is unusual. What is the effect of beginning with a quiz? Why are the answers to the quiz longer than the choices given in the questions?
3. From the information given in the answer section, could you cope with a cut finger, a burned finger, a poisoned child, or an aching back? What medication would you use on the cut? How would you apply wet heat?
4. After you have decided on something you know how to do—cleaning a room, washing a car, fitting a pair of shoes—write three multiple-choice questions about it, followed by the "right" answers, as has been done in this article.

A Free Supply of Fuel: Newspaper Logs

maxim: a generally recognized truth
ultimate: final
caveat: a warning
ambidextrous: ability to use both hands equally well

[1]   In these days of low energy supply and high energy prices, it is well to remember the old maxim, "true conservation is the maximum utilization of one's resources." This brings to mind one of America's truly plentiful natural resources. Nuclear, coal, natural gas, solar, wind or ocean waves? No. A resource as close as your garage, attic or old storage area—old newspapers, magazines and mail order catalogs!

[2]   From time to time, I've read about various complex machines or technologies by which newspapers are converted to useful fuels. The means discussed range from complex compacting in industrial plants to elaborate paper logs put together with string, soaked in water overnight and dried until ready for ultimate use. This

Vernon Cook, "A Free Supply of Fuel: Newspaper Logs," *Northwest Magazine,* February 17, 1980, p. 20.

is like purchasing an expensive machine to roll your own cigarettes when brown papers, Bull Durham and spit will produce a better product; or renting complex computers and hiring expensive computer operators to reapportion the Legislature when a pencil, a piece of paper and a fourth-grade education will produce just as good a result.

[3]   The true source of knowledge of how best to utilize this great natural resource, the newspaper and magazine, has been passed down by oral tradition from one generation of newspaper carriers to the next. This is the old reliable technique of "rolling a paper" which makes both newspapers and magazines excellent sources of fuel for fireplace, stove and outdoor barbecue. It may soon be a lost art, since most contemporary newspaper carriers are using either rubber bands, a newspaper box or plastic bags. Here's how it's done.

[4]   It still is common knowledge that crinkled single sheets of newspaper are almost as good as kerosene and diesel oil to use to start a fire (never use gasoline unless you are bent on suicide or a quick trip to Kingdom Come. Gas fumes are as explosive in a wood stove as in a carburetor). To start a fire in a wood stove or fireplace with paper, I'd recommend about six full sheets (24 pages of a standard newspaper) at the bottom of the fireplace or grate. Crisscross with three or four "rolled" newspapers of from 12 to 20 pages. Top off with a rolled 36 or 48-page newspaper log or a 12-page newspaper with a magazine folded inside. This fire will start and keep burning as well as any fire you might start and stoke with conventional wood. Why? Because you are merely returning the paper to its original form —a stick of wood, with a little ink mixed in.

The "newspaper carrier roll" is made as follows:

[5]   Take any newspaper, local, national, daily or weekly. It makes no difference although some, like the Wall Street Journal, are packed more tightly. They will roll easily and burn well. The front page of this newspaper has six columns. How you should roll a paper depends primarily on the number of pages contained. The "lap over" (first fold) distance may be changed, and the width of each standard fold may be different. Generally, the thicker the newspaper the wider the first fold should be. To try the basic technique, take a 36-page newspaper and lay it down, looking at the top and center of the newspaper as it is displayed on a news stand. Fold from right to left, from the open edges of the pages to the page folds. Begin with a fold of one column, about 2½ inches (crease for beginners). Fold and crease and fold and crease until you reach the end, a total of four folds to the page fold edge. This creates five sections. Then back off two folds, exposing two sections.

[6]   Now the "art." Turn the last folded edge (section 5) backwards, over section 4. Take the outer (leading) edge of section 2, lay it on the outer edge of section 5, and roll the inner edge of section 2 into the inner edge of section 5. You now have a loose log. As a final touch, grasp the open edge of the circular newspaper "column" with the palm of your hand and twist clockwise as tightly as you can. You now have a tight newspaper log suitable for all purposes. Caveat: I'm right-handed. A non-ambidextrous left-hander (like my daughter, Patricia), probably would reverse these directions.

[7]   Now to the refinements. While it is possible to roll a tabloid (like a magazine

section) even though it has no "folded edge," I prefer to insert tabs and advertising inserts into a conventional newspaper of 12 pages or more. Magazines in their original form are almost impossible to use for burning in a home. They can, however, be fairly efficiently burned on a fireplace by placing them tentlike over the other fuel, split in the middle. I've found, though, that they make excellent centers for rolled newspapers. Simply open them up in half, center up, and insert in a 12 or 16- page standard newspaper. Fold in the usual way. Use these "magazine logs" after you have the fire started, as the leaves are tighter and the log doesn't burn as easily as standard newspaper logs made of looser newsprint.

[8]   With a properly prepared and maintained fire, folded newspaper will burn as cleanly as wood and leave no more ashes. In our old fashioned Crown Sterling kitchen range, manufactured in 1910 by the Portland Stove Works, I last stoked the fire with rolled newspaper at 10 p.m. It was still warm, with glowing coals, at 5 a.m. the next day.

[9]   After the outer edge is burnt off, you can't distinguish between burning newspaper logs and burning wood logs of the same size. The heat is identical. Any wood fire, during the first hour, is like the old husband was described by the old wife. She said, "Every time I look the other way he goes out." Newspaper logs are no different. They burn at a rate very close to dry cottonwood or split dry fir. Logs with magazine centers burn at a rate nearer to that of oak or alder.

[10]   We use newspaper logs in combination with conventional wood in all applications: campfire, outside barbecue, fireplace and woodburning stove. We don't own a modern airtight stove, but I'm sure newspaper logs would work there just as well as anywhere else. With campfires, barbecues and other uses, newspaper logs have the advantage of being easy to start. They are also easy to store in their original flat form.

[11]   *A word of caution.* While no significant amount of lead or chromium is used in printing black and white pages or newsprint, lead and chromium sometimes are used in the printing of colored pages. It has been demonstrated by numerous tests that some colored printing inks have caused significant increases in the level of lead in the blood of "pica" children (those who eat such things as paper, rather than the usual food). Tests have also been conducted which show that colored pages mixed with food materials and fed to sheep cause residual lead deposits in their bones. Where colored newsprint was mixed with soil there was an observable increase in the lead content of the vegetation grown in such soil.

[12]   A literature search at the Environmental Protection Agency's Research Triangle Park in North Carolina about Dec. 12, 1979, revealed only one article relating to the possible dangers of burning colored newsprint. This was a case study reported in the March 3, 1976, issue of *Pediatrics,* which found an elevated blood lead count in a 6-month-old breast-fed infant who spent most of the time in front of a fireplace which regularly burned newsprint and magazines, as well as wood.

[13]   Since the use of inks containing lead is a matter of choice with the publisher, in view of the increasing use of wood stoves and fireplaces it would seem that lead-free inks should be required for all publications. Continued use increases an already existing risk, pica children eating colored pages. The body does have a consider-

able capacity for handling the ingestion of lead, whether by mouth or nose. The real question is whether or not the amount one might breathe would cause one to exceed that permissible level. There are presently no authoritative answers to this question. A conservative approach would be to discard all colored pages and burn only the black and white printed material. This is not too hard to do if one has a mind to do it.

[14]   Rather than fill up our garbage cans and community garbage dumps with our old newspapers and magazines, we should be like the squirrel is with the nuts he gathers. Store up our old newspapers during the mild months for use during the cold winter months. Then enjoy the beautiful flames and the wonderful heat of delightful old newspapers, magazines and racing forms. It's the cheapest fuel we can use—no cost and just a little elbow grease.

Responses

1. What do the directions in paragraph 4 cover? In paragraphs 5, 6, and 7? Which set of directions is more important? Why?
2. Cook gives a good deal of space to the advantages of paper as fuel. What are these advantages and where do you find them in the article?
3. How seriously are you expected to take the "word of caution" discussed in paragraphs 11, 12, and 13? How can you tell?
4. The tone of this article is cheerful and light-hearted. How does Cook make his directions entertaining as well as informative? Consider "truly plentiful natural resources" in paragraph 1, for instance; what is the usual meaning of "natural resource"? What other similar examples can you find?

Landmark Prison Reforms Won

comprehensive: including many things
revamp: change
habitation: place where people live
rampant: running wild
blatant: obvious, glaring
virtually: mostly
composition: makeup

[1]   In the most comprehensive order ever directed to a state correctional system, a federal judge here has set detailed guidelines for prison reform which, when implemented, will totally revamp Alabama's prisons. . . .

Poverty Law Report (Montgomery, Ala.: Southern Poverty Law Center, March 1976).

[2]   In a Jan. 13 order, U.S. District Court Judge Frank M. Johnson said Alabama prisons were "wholly unfit for human habitation," and that their vast overcrowding, rampant violence and filthy conditions were blatant violations of constitutional rights.

[3]   To correct the gross abuse, Johnson issued a tough ruling covering all aspects of prison operation—from a weekly change of bed linen and "three wholesome meals" a day to almost halving the current 4,400 inmate population and nearly doubling the 383 guards at the state's four major prisons.

[4]   Every inmate must be given "a meaningful job," a chance to take basic educational programs, and an annual classification check to determine whether he or she should be transferred to a more appropriate facility, such as a mental hospital, the judge said. . . .

[5]   Virtually no aspect of prison life escaped Johnson when his long-expected prison order was released. Although he applied his order to 11 basic areas, Johnson left no room for guessing as to what the specific relief should be in each area. He spelled out in simple language exactly what the state must do to upgrade the prisons to meet constitutional standards.

[6]   Among those standards were:

> Each prisoner must have at least 60 square feet of living space, and the prison must give him or her a complete supply of personal items at no cost to the inmate.
>
> A system of internal security must be established to assure the safety of inmates from physical violence. To accomplish this, the number of guards at the four major prisons must be increased from 383 to 692. The guards should reflect the cultural composition of the inmate population.
>
> Each prison must have a recreational program supervised by a college-trained person.
>
> No more than one prisoner can be placed in an isolation, or punishment, cell, and that inmate must have at least 60 square feet of living space. [Currently, none of the prisons' isolation cells meet this standard.] Each isolation cell must have a working toilet and a sink with hot and cold running water. A prisoner cannot be held in punishment longer than 21 days.
>
> The prison system must develop and implement a comprehensive classification program which takes into consideration an inmate's offense, prior record, vocational and educational needs, and physical and mental health care requirements.
>
> Only minimum custody prisoners may be housed in dormitories, currently used to house the vast majority of inmates with no regard to a prisoner's tendency to violence.
>
> All prisons must be adequately heated, lighted and ventilated, and windows and doors must be screened.
>
> Each prison must have one working toilet per 15 inmates, one shower per 20 inmates and one lavatory per 10 inmates.
>
> The prison system must provide postage and paper for up to five letters a week for each inmate. . . .

[7]   Although several other states have been hit with prison orders, Judge Johnson's is believed to be the first which outlines in such great detail the specific conditions that must be met to correct the constitutional violations. Attorneys for the inmates think the Alabama order will be used as a model in other prison suits.

Responses

1. This article is actually a news report—an account of what happened—but the report does contain a set of directions. Where do the directions begin and what do they cover? Write a main idea sentence to fit the directions that are given.
2. Because this is a newspaper article and news reports follow a slightly different system than other kinds of writing, each of the first four paragraphs contains only one sentence. If this report were intended as a magazine article, how would you combine these first four paragraphs? How many paragraphs would you use?
3. The directions themselves are written in the form of statements rather than commands. Pick any two of them and rewrite them in a "do this, then do that" form. Which form do you like better for this article? Why?
4. What readers might actually follow these directions? Are the directions complete enough that those readers would know exactly what to do? If you think they are not complete enough, what other information would the readers need?
5. What is the difference between "guidelines" and "directions"? between "guidelines" and "standards"? between "standards" and "rules"?
6. Imagine that you have been made the inspector of a school cafeteria or the manager of a busline or whatever supervisory job interests you. Write a short set of guidelines that could help to improve conditions in your imaginary situation.

More Suggestions for Writing

How to:

hitch a ride
answer a police officer
look for an apartment
explain why you're late
use a sled
use a pool cue
buy a wedding present
refuse an invitation politely

clean the inside of an automobile
wax a linoleum floor
do a week's grocery shopping in one trip

How to make:

candles
a sling shot
a whistle from a willow branch
a bonfire without matches
a fire in a fireplace
a swing
a bird feeder
a coffee table, perhaps out of a wooden box
a one-piece apron

Chapter 3

Explaining: Definition

When people ask, "What do you mean?" sometimes they are playing for time, sometimes they are expressing doubt about what has been said. Usually, however, they are asking for a genuine explanation. Perhaps they want to know what some unfamiliar term means, or perhaps they don't understand the precise sense in which you are using a word that can mean several things. Often, what they're asking for is a definition.

Defining words is not as simple as it sounds. We get nowhere with the childish demand "Just tell me what the word *really* means," because words, in themselves, don't "really mean" anything. Words are just symbols—puffs of air that stand for meanings—and it is people who put the meaning into those puffs of air. A moment's thought will make that clear. For instance, English-speaking people have agreed that the sound "milk" will represent a nourishing white fluid, but French speakers represent that same fluid by the sound "lait," Spanish speakers by the sound "leche," and speakers of Chinese or Swahili by still different sounds. Whatever the sound, the milk stays the same—the "meaning" exists in the minds of the speakers and listeners. We know, too, that meanings shift and change with time. What does the sound "outrageous" mean to you? A few years ago, most people would immediately have said, "something grossly offensive, disgraceful, shameful." Now, some of us at least might use it to express unqualified approval and appreciation, as in: "I'm dating an outrageous lady."

Furthermore, most of us learn the words we know through our experiences with them, and all of us have different experiences. Just as a baby learns what the sound "dog" represents by associating the word with the dogs in the neighborhood, so as we grow older we absorb meanings from the conversations we hear or the books we read. If we all lived in the same neighborhoods or read the same books, we might all agree on the same "meanings." Since we don't, we have to do the best we can.

Remembering that the purpose of language—or words—is to get "meaning" out of one mind and into other minds will help. We can never accomplish that aim perfectly, but we can come a good deal closer if we watch out for two things. First, although words don't have any "real meaning" in themselves, we can't communicate satisfactorily unless the people we're talking to, or writing for, put about the same meaning into the words they hear or read as we put into the words we speak or write. They must share our agreement as to what the words refer to. Saying *lait* to people who don't know French won't communicate, and neither will saying *paratoluidine* to people who haven't studied chemistry. Second, we must take the time to explain carefully what *we* mean by some words whose agreed-on meanings may be fuzzy. Suppose someone tells you that Arnold Watkins, the new city supervisor, is "very patriotic." All of us can agree that "patriotism" means love of one's country—we can find dictionaries that will tell us that. But we still don't understand much about what the new supervisor thinks, or how he behaves. Does he paste a bumper sticker on his car saying "America—love it or leave it"? Does he wear a small flag in his lapel? Does he support a large military budget, because he wants his country to be the strongest in the world? Or does he oppose that budget, because love of country makes him believe in peace? Until we get a more precise definition, we can't tell whether Arnold Watkins's behavior fits our notion of "patriotic."

Kinds of Definition

The simplest kind of definition is a *synonym* definition—giving another word that means the same, or almost the same, as the one you are defining:

> *Obese* means "fat."
>
> *Lepidoptera* means "butterflies and moths."
>
> *Sodden* means "thoroughly soaked."
>
> *Vacuity* means "emptiness."
>
> *Eccentric* means "peculiar."
>
> To *vacillate* is to oscillate.

Such definitions are completely satisfactory if they begin with words most people don't know and move to words they do know. They are not much good if they move from one little-known word to another. To be told that *vacillate* means "oscillate" will not help unless you know what oscillate means. And you won't be helped much by being told that "vacillate means having the qualities or characteristics of vacillation." That kind of definition just goes in circles and leaves you no wiser than before.

> *Good synonym definitions always move from difficult words to simpler words, and they avoid going in circles.*

Because often we can't find single words or short phrases to explain difficult words, a more usual (and usually more satisfactory) kind of definition comes in three parts: (1) the word that's being defined, (2) the big group or class it belongs to, and (3) the way to tell it from other things in the big group. For convenience, we'll call this kind a *class* definition. Here are some examples:

1. An **augur** (word being defined) is
   2. a person (big group)
      3. who claims to foretell the future (how an augur is different from other persons).

1. **Euphemisms** (word being defined) are
      3. mild or indirect (how they're different from other expressions)
   2. expressions (big group)
      3. used in place of harsher, more direct expressions (more ways they're different).

1. **Typhus** (word being defined) is
   2. an infectious disease (big group)
      3. caused by microorganisms carried by fleas, lice, or mites (how it's different from other infectious diseases).

1. **Bionics** (word being defined) is
   2. the application of biological principles (big group)
      3. to the study and design of engineering and electronic systems (how it's different from other applications of biological principles).

1. To **stipulate** (word being defined) means
   2. to specify (big group)
      3. certain things as part of an agreement (more exact details of what's being specified).

These class definitions are probably satisfactory. If somebody tells you that "sanitary engineer" is a *euphemism* for "garbage collector," you understand what you're being told. Or if somebody protests against using *bionics* in surgical operations to replace human bodily parts with artificial ones, you can decide whether or not you agree with the protest.

In writing class definitions, it's important to make sure that the third part of the definition, the part that distinguishes your term from other members of the big group, actually does give enough differences. A good definition will fit only the word you are defining and nothing else. Look, for instance, at these two unsatisfactory class definitions:

1. A **pencil** (word being defined) is
      3. a long, narrow (how it's different from other instruments)
   2. instrument (big group)
      3. used for writing (more ways it's different).

1. An **elephant** (word being defined) is
   3. a large, wild (how it's different from other animals)
  2. animal (big group)
   3. with four legs (more ways it's different).

The problem is not that these two statements aren't accurate—they're both accurate enough as far as they go. The problem in both definitions is that they don't go far enough. The definition of *pencil* would do just as well for several other instruments used for writing: a fountain pen, a ball-point pen, a felt-tip pen. However, if we change it to say:

1. A **pencil** (word being defined) is
   3. a long, narrow (how it's different from other instruments)
  2. instrument (big group)
   3. used for writing (more ways it's different)
   3. made of graphite and wood (still more ways it's different).

it can then apply to nothing except a lead pencil.

One good way to test the completeness of a class definition is to try turning it around to see whether the result makes sense:

A large wild animal with four legs is an elephant.

Of course it doesn't. The definition could apply equally well to a lion, a zebra, a hippopotamus, or a giraffe. Our job, then, is to add more ways of distinguishing elephants from other large, wild, four-legged animals. When we have found three more differences, we can reverse the definition and be sure that it does refer only to elephants:

Any large, wild animal with four legs, large flapping ears, tusks made of ivory, and a nose and upper lip stretched out into a trunk that reaches the ground *is an elephant.*

Good class definitions
 put the word being defined into a big group
  and tell how it differs from other members
  of the big group;
 avoid going in circles;
 can be reversed and still make sense

But there are situations where even good class definitions don't work very well. Then we need *stipulative* definitions. Suppose somebody calls you a "fanatic." A dictionary can give you a three-part definition:

1. A **fanatic** is
 2. a person
  3. with uncritical enthusiasm or zeal.

We know that fanatics are people—you probably knew that much anyway, if you were called one—and you know that "zeal" means intensity, but you don't know just when enthusiasm becomes "uncritical" or how that enthusiasm is shown.

We've already seen that *patriotic* is a word that can give trouble. A dictionary can tell us that

   1. **patriotic** is
      2. characteristic
         3. of a patriot.

No good at all. It goes in a circle. If we try to get rid of the circle, we may come up with:

   1. **patriotic** is
      2. characteristic
         3. of people who love their country.

Better, but we're still left with those same questions. How can we tell whether people love their country? Does love mean supporting it without question? Or does love mean caring so much that questions are asked, often?

We run into problems like this whenever we try to explain words that describe human behavior or words that make judgments about the way people behave. And the problems come up not just with fairly unfamiliar words, such as *fanatic,* but with ordinary words that everybody more or less understands: *cowardice, brutality, prejudice, devotion.* The trouble lies in "more or less understands," and the trouble arises because words like these are *abstractions*—we have *abstracted,* or pulled out, what we think is alike in a lot of different situations and given a name to that likeness. We see a collie run the other way when a German shepherd barks at it. We see a prize fighter fall back to the corner of the ring when his opponent aims a blow at his head. We see a soldier run away from the battle rather than toward it. We see a legislator who believes in abortion vote against it because she thinks that a vote for it might make her lose the next election. We think there is something alike in all these behaviors, so we call the likeness "cowardice" and the people who behave like that "cowards."

There's nothing wrong with abstractions; it would be hard to get along without them. The trouble comes when we treat them as though they were things rather than just ideas, when we forget that people's experiences have been different and that therefore their definitions may be different, too. Some people would say that the collie is not a coward; it's just been trained not to fight. The prize fighter is not a coward either; he's just been made so dizzy by earlier blows that he can't control his actions. The soldier is not a coward; he knows he's out of ammunition. And the state senator, although she believes in abortion herself, also believes it's her job to represent the wishes of the people who elected her, and the mail has been running five to one against the proposed law. To define *cowardice* clearly, neither a synonym nor a class definition will be enough.

We can use synonym or class definitions for words that refer to things we can see or hear or touch or count—coffee, computers, collies, barking, abortions, votes. But to define words like *cowardice* or *patriotism, fanatic* or *enthusiasm,* we have to do more than that. We have to show what is happening when we say that people are being cowardly or patriotic, fanatic or enthusiastic. We have to limit the kind of behavior we will include in our definition; we have to *stipulate* what our meaning will be. In other words, we make an agreement with our readers.

Stipulative definitions are usually much longer than synonym or class definitions. Showing what happens in one situation probably won't be enough; we'll have to use three or four different situations, and sometimes we may have to describe the situations in some detail. We may even have to describe situations where the word we're defining doesn't fit—that's part of the way we limit our definition. But stipulative definitions limit meaning in another way, too: they may limit the definition to the person who is using it or the occasion on which it is being used. You sometimes hear people say, "For purposes of this discussion, let's agree that *freedom* means . . ." or "When I say *loyalty* I mean . . ." and then go on from there. They remember that most words cannot be defined absolutely, for all time and for all occasions, so that everybody will agree; they remember that most words, and especially abstractions, have no "real meaning." Instead, these people try to answer the question What do you mean? by offering stipulative definitions that explain what *they* mean in *that* discussion or *that* paper, and they do it in words that are as specific as possible.

General and Specific Words

If you aren't used to thinking about whether words are general or specific, you may need some practice before you understand what people mean when they say to you, "That's too general—be more specific."

We can explain *general* words by saying that the more things a word refers to, the more *general* it is. The fewer things a word refers to, the more *specific* it is. Thus *general* and *specific* are relative terms. The word *pig* is more specific than *animal,* less specific than *Cheshire pig. Cheshire pig,* in turn, is less specific than *Wilbur, the pig in* <u>Charlotte's Web</u>. In the same way, *human being* is more general than *woman; woman* is more general than *coach; coach* is more general than *gymnastics coach at Limestone College;* and *gymnastics coach at Limestone College* is more general than *Harriet Wong, the new gymnastics coach at Limestone College.*

In fact, *Harriet Wong* is about as specific as you can get. It works like this:

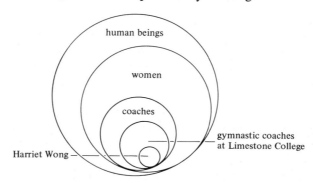

The diagram makes it easier to see that almost no words can, by themselves, be considered either *general* or *specific.* Whether or not a word is considered specific depends on what you're comparing it to.

General and specific words are not bad or good in themselves; words are bad or good depending on whether they fit the writer's needs and whether they make the meaning clear. A newspaper story with the headline "Teachers Get Raise" is likely to mislead its readers if the cost-of-living increase applied only to Limestone College and not to the other colleges in the state nor to the elementary and secondary teachers in the region. Here "teachers" is too general a word. On the other hand, "gymnastics coaches" is too specific if everybody on the staff at Limestone College got the increase.

Inexperienced writers sometimes deliberately choose rather general words, probably because general words seem safer. If you're not pinned down to anything very definite, then there's less chance of anybody proving you "wrong." But there's also less chance that what you say will be worth reading. Nobody wants to be *too specific,* but you won't make many mistakes if you follow this rule:

> *Always choose the most specific word that will fit the subject you are discussing.*

Generalizations and Examples

The more general the words you use in making a statement, the more inclusive the statement will be. If the statement refers to a group of people or things, or covers more than one situation, we call it a *generalization.* The statement "Americans like sports" is a generalization; it includes all the people, young and old, who live in this country, and it includes all the active recreation you can think of, from watching professional football to roller skating and skin diving. The statement "Water skiing is a dangerous sport" is a generalization, too. Although it's true that the term *water skiing* is much more specific than the general term *sports,* the statement includes all the times that anybody goes water skiing; it includes an unlimited number of situations.

Just as there is nothing wrong with general words if they fit the situation and make the meaning clear, so there is nothing wrong with generalizations when they do the same thing. Actually, we'd have a hard time doing without them. If we had to say "In 1975 there was a hurricane in September," "In 1974 there was a hurricane in September," "In 1973 there was a hurricane in September," "In 1972 there was . . . ," and so on, back as far as we can remember, we'd waste a lot of time and our readers would probably go to sleep. It's much easier to say, "September is a bad month for hurricanes."

Sometimes, of course, people will question our generalizations. If you say to a friend, "Many people believe that there is a solution for world hunger," your friend may respond with, "Who believes that?" When you answer, "Robert S.

McNamara, president of the World Bank; John Gilligan, administrator of USAID (United States Agency for International Development); and the International Labor Organization," your friend may still want to know what you mean by "a solution for world hunger." If you reply by quoting the National Academy of Sciences' *World Food and Nutrition Study* (1977), "It should be possible to overcome the worst aspects of widespread hunger and malnutrition within one generation . . . ," your friend may persist and ask, "What do you mean by 'worst aspects'? and how will they be 'overcome'?" Your friend is forcing you to make a more specific statement.

A generalization includes many things and many occasions; a specific statement concerns one particular thing that happened at one particular time. If the general statement and the specific statement are related, we say that the *specific statement is an example of the generalization.*

> **Generalization:** Many people believe that there is a solution for world hunger.
> **Example:** Robert S. McNamara, John Gilligan, and the International Labor Organization believe that there is a solution for world hunger.
>
> **Generalization:** The teachers at this college grade unfairly.
> **Example:** Professor Oglethorpe gave me a *D* on last week's test, even though I got all but one of the questions right.
>
> **Generalization:** Railroad service is very unreliable.
> **Example:** The train from Kansas City to Chicago was four hours late last Sunday.
>
> **Generalization:** First aid, promptly given, can save lives.
> **Example:** When a six-year-old nearly drowned in Blue Lake last summer, the life guard gave him mouth-to-mouth resuscitation until the doctor came; the doctor said she saved the child's life.

There are two or three things to notice about these examples. In the first one, no attempt has been made to give an example of the solution; only the subject (many people) has been dealt with, and even there you might not consider that two men and one organization really represent "many people." Neither do the second and third examples prove the generalizations: one train being four hours late does not prove that all railroad service is unreliable, any more than one *D* on one test, whether or not it was deserved, proves that all teachers grade unfairly. What these two examples do accomplish is to show what one person sometimes means by "unfairly" and what another sometimes means by "unreliable."

Notice, too, that the fourth generalization doesn't say, "First aid, promptly given, saves lives"; it just says that it *can.* We are more likely to accept this generalization, not because the example is more specific, but because the generalization is more limited. What is true for words goes for statements too:

Never make a more general statement than the occasion demands or the circumstances justify.

Main Idea Sentences
for Stipulative Definitions

When you write a stipulative definition, you will want it to apply to more than one situation, so the main idea sentence will be a generalization. The generalization will begin with the term you are defining, and that term will probably be an abstraction, because words that represent things we can see or hear or touch don't need long definitions. If you need to define what a *child* is, to distinguish children from infants or adolescents, you can do it very quickly: "For purposes of this discussion," you can say, "a *child* is a human being more than two years old and less than thirteen." If what you want to define is *gifted child,* however, you are dealing with an abstraction, and the problem is not nearly so simple; *gifted child* will probably take three or four paragraphs of definition.

Probably the safest way to begin is to make your main idea sentence a three-part definition. You might say, "Gifted children are children who have more outstanding physical or mental qualities than their parents have." That's a generalization and a class definition, but it's not very satisfactory. For one thing, it's pretty close to being a circle: *gifted* means almost the same as "having outstanding qualities." But another problem is that the statement is too general in one way, and probably too specific in another. It's too general because we don't know what "outstanding physical or mental qualities" refers to. Does it mean being able to walk a month earlier than other children in the neighborhood? learning Greek at age three? knowing how to tie their shoelaces without instruction? being able to work long division in their heads at age four? making pitcher on the Little League team? Some of these questions could be answered later on by showing specific examples of "gifted" children, but for a short paper it would probably be better to deal with physical gifts or intellectual gifts rather than try to cover everything that "gifted" might mean. On the other hand, "parents" may be too specific. Do children have to have parents to be gifted, or might gifted children be living with grandparents or in foster homes or orphanages? And is it true that anyone who can do something a parent can't do is "gifted"? Whatever you decide to say about gifted children should be as specific as you can make it without leaving out any situations you want to include. "Children are mentally gifted when they are able to solve math problems, learn languages, compose music, or carry on other intellectual activities that would be impossible for their classmates and extremely difficult for most adults" might be a more satisfactory main idea sentence. Here, "parents" has been broadened to include classmates and most other adults, and "gifted" has been limited to intellectual ability.

The main idea sentence is especially important in stipulative definitions, and you may have to experiment a little before you find the one that says exactly what you mean. If you are defining *prejudice,* you may already have one situation in mind that will influence your generalization. Perhaps you have had some bitter experiences with attempts to integrate neighborhood schools, so you say, *"Prejudice* means white parents who resent Black children coming to their schools." Then you realize that you don't want to limit prejudiced behavior that much, so you try again, first asking yourself *why* the white parents were out there picketing: *"Prejudice* means looking down on other people."

That main idea sentence is better because it includes more situations, but maybe it includes too many. Does it really fit the example you already had in mind? Now you ask yourself more questions. Why did the white parents picket the school and some of them actually throw rocks at the new students who had been bussed in? Was it just that they looked down on the new students? Why did they look down on them? Was it because the new students were Black? Would the parents have looked down on white children? If you decide it was because the new children were Black, you need to add something to your generalization. You have already put *prejudice* into a big group (people looking down on other people). Now you need to make clear that the "looking down" that comes from prejudice is not like other kinds of "looking down." Your new main idea sentence might read: *"Prejudice* means looking down on people because they are different."

Planning a Stipulative Definition

Now that you have found a main idea sentence that looks workable, you need to back it up with more than one example. Is prejudice always limited to a single group? Or can you think of some instance where Black people have shown they were prejudiced against whites? And is prejudice always a result of racial differences? Can it result from religious differences, too? What about Hitler and the Jews? Or, more recently, the Jews and the Arabs? Maybe you know a Catholic family who refused to accept a Jewish son-in-law—or a Protestant one, for that matter.

And does prejudice always show itself in bomb dropping or rock throwing, in refusing to let other people attend school or come to Sunday dinner? Is it possible that people who think of themselves as unprejudiced still do things that you believe show prejudice? Perhaps you have a long-haired friend, a qualified data processor with two years' experience, who habitually dresses in sandals, dirty jeans, and a faded T-shirt. When he applied for a job at Numbers, Inc., he was told there were no vacancies, but an hour later another applicant, with neatly trimmed hair and a five-dollar tie—and only six months' experience—got the job your friend had applied for. That personnel director was so prejudiced in favor of conventional appearance . . . but wait a minute. Can people be prejudiced toward people as well as against them? Remember, your examples and your main idea must fit together, with no overlapping.

Now you have three choices: you can change your main idea again; you can throw out the last example; or you can use your introduction to explain that there really are two kinds of prejudice, for and against, but that in this paper you are planning to deal only with the "against" part of it. It's your definition, and it's up to you to decide what goes in it. One of the gains from writing a long definition is that as you write the paper, you will straighten out and sharpen your own thinking. You will be a good deal more certain, the next time you call somebody "prejudiced," just exactly what you do and do not mean.

To make sure your readers, too, understand what you do not mean, you may want to include an example of behavior that is sometimes called prejudice but that you think isn't. What about that same personnel man at Numbers, Inc., who advertised for a secretary last year? Two whites and three Blacks applied, and one of the whites got the job—the only one of all the applicants who knew shorthand. In that example, was the personnel man prejudiced?

Once you're satisfied with both your generalization and your examples, all you need do before you begin to write is to put your examples in order. In arranging your examples, you may want to show what the term means before you show what it doesn't mean, but that's not a hard-and-fast rule. The main thing is to put examples that seem to fit together next to each other. That way you'll avoid jumping around from place to place, and you'll make things easier for your readers. The examples used in defining *prejudice,* for instance, might go something like this:

Religious prejudice: Hitler and the Jews
Jews and Arabs
Catholic father-in-law, Jewish son-in-law

Racial prejudice: white parents throwing rocks at Black kids

Cultural prejudice: refusal to hire freaky-looking friend

What prejudice is not: hiring on qualifications, not race

Or, if it makes more sense to you, reverse the order. The point is not that one arrangement is always better than another, but rather that there needs to be a deliberate arrangement.

At the end of your stipulative definition, you should pull all your ideas together by reminding your readers what your general definition is. One way is to repeat the generalization you began with. A better way is to say the same thing in slightly different words: "Prejudice, then, is looking down on people who are not like you, whether the difference is religious, racial, or cultural."

But remember that the purpose of your definition is to make clear what you mean, not to defend your own ideas or to attack other people's ideas. If your definition is only part of a longer paper—an argument against prejudice, perhaps—your argument will be more convincing if you have kept your definition impartial. Words such as *should* or *should not, ought* or *ought not, good* or *bad, better* or *worse,* express your opinion and can be part of your argument, but they do not belong in the definition or in the examples that illustrate it. Because you have written a clear main idea sentence, you are more likely to stick to defining. You will be less tempted to say "Prejudice is what's wrong with this country" and think it is part of your definition.

Paragraphing

As you begin to write, use the plan for your definition to help you decide where to paragraph. Probably, you will need a paragraph for the generalization and the comments you make about it, and probably you will need a paragraph for each of your examples. Don't worry about making all your paragraphs the same length. Some of your examples will naturally take less space than others, or perhaps one of them will be so long it will take more than one paragraph to make your meaning completely clear. The best rule to follow is to begin a new paragraph whenever there is a shift in what you're talking about, just as you would move from room to room when you shift what you're doing at home. When you finish your example of religious prejudice and move to racial prejudice, start a new paragraph, just as you move from the kitchen to the living room when you shift from cooking dinner to watching TV. If you use several examples in your definition, you may need more paragraphs than your house has rooms, but the idea is the same. The plan you have already made has kept your paragraphs in convenient order; now the transitions discussed in the last chapter will serve as the "doors," getting your readers from place to place without stumbling.

Following this rule—giving a paragraph to each part of your plan—will keep you from writing a tiresome series of single-sentence paragraphs. By the time you have given enough details to make your example clear, your paragraph will have expanded and your readers will have room enough to understand your meaning. A group of one-sentence paragraphs is like an apartment containing nothing but closets: the writer is cramped and the readers are frustrated.

It's true, of course, that there is no "right length" for a paragraph, no way of counting words or sentences that will tell you when it's long enough. A glance at any magazine will show you paragraphs varying from one to six sentences long, and sometimes more. But five-sentence paragraphs occur more often than one-sentence paragraphs, which are used only now and then for special emphasis. Readers are accustomed to how paragraphs should look on a page, and if your pages don't look that way, readers tend to become uneasy. Appearance—how your paper looks—is one reason for making your paragraphs longer than a single sentence; but successful communication—saying enough to help readers share your ideas—is a more important reason. Writers who want to have an effect on their readers, writers who want to put their own ideas into their readers' minds, must not stop with throwing out a series of general statements.

One-sentence paragraphs often seem all right to inexperienced writers because they are perfectly certain of what those single sentences mean to them. In their minds, that one sentence completely expresses all of the experience and images and ideas they're thinking about. But for the reader, who lacks that experience and those pictures and ideas, the single, general sentence is almost worthless. Not completely worthless, because it may suggest a hazy idea of what the writer was thinking; mostly, however, the overlap between the reader's ideas and the writer's ideas is very small indeed.

If you are defining prejudice, for instance, it won't be enough to say, "An example of cultural prejudice occurs when a business won't hire people because of the way they look," and then begin a new paragraph with your next example. All you've done is produce another generalization only a little more specific than your main idea sentence. And it won't help much to add one more sentence that still fails to create a picture: "That happened last year to a man I know." The picture is probably clear in your own mind—you can see those ragged blue jeans and long blond hair, and you can remember how Numbers, Inc., ignored experience and skill in favor of a short haircut and a neat striped shirt—but your readers have no such memory to guide them. Their mental picture may show fat women or frail, pretty girls being turned away. Readers may think all the applicants were equally skilled and that the "business," which you left very vague, was right in considering appearance. Should a reducing studio hire an overweight receptionist? Should a furniture-moving company hire a ninety-pound sixteen-year-old to move a piano? Unless you give enough details so that readers can see the same situation you see, your example won't help much; and good-natured readers willing to say, "Yes, that's so, businesses shouldn't judge by looks," may not be sure what they're agreeing with.

Agreement is no guarantee of understanding. If you take a sentence such as "Success is difficult to measure" and ask a random sample of ten people whether they agree with it, probably all of them will say yes. But what are they agreeing with? If you ask what they mean by "success," what they mean by "difficult," and what they mean by "measure," you're likely to get thirty different answers. Even though they think they agree with the statement—and maybe they actually do—all of them are looking into their own minds and memories for the experiences that back up their agreement, and all those experiences will be different. The writer who made the statement about success will have had almost nothing to do with what happens in the readers' minds, except to provide a starting point for their own thoughts.

When readers have to imagine (or guess) what you are thinking about, very little communication is taking place. For real communication to happen, paragraphs must be "developed." "Developing a paragraph" means putting into words the experiences, ideas, and pictures that were in your mind when you made the general statement. When you give examples of what you see when you use such words as "success" and "difficult" and "measure," you start to share with your readers what is actually in your mind. Communication may not be complete, but it will certainly be closer. You will have done more than provide a series of inkblots that readers must interpret for themselves.

Pronouns—Making Clear What They Stand For

When you have finished the first draft of your definition, put it away to cool; and when it is thoroughly cold—in a day or two—go over it to make sure that everything you have written makes sense, and that nothing you have said will confuse your readers.

One thing that may confuse readers, or at least slow them down, is not being sure what a pronoun stands for. If you have said, "The personnel director told Jesse Maracheck that he got promoted that day," your readers can't tell who got promoted, Jesse or the personnel director. Maybe your readers could figure that one out if they worried over it a little but some sentences are even more confusing: "When the newspapers left the presses, the strikers burned them." What was burned, the newspapers or the presses?

Sometimes readers are confused because pronouns don't seem to stand for anything: "Max Lincoln had a degree in physical education, but the park superintendent was so prejudiced he never got to be one." First, who is "he," Max or the superintendent? And what didn't whoever it was get to be? A person can hardly be "an education," although people can be recreation directors or soccer coaches. Such sentences are bad not because they are "wrong" but because they are confusing. Reread your definition carefully, making sure that your readers won't be slowed down trying to figure out what your pronouns stand for.

Finally, make one more check. Before you decide your definition is finished, ask yourself these questions:

Does your first paragraph contain your main idea?

Does the rest of your definition fit the generalization you began with?

Are all your paragraphs developed enough for readers to share your ideas?

Does the last paragraph relate clearly to the first generalization without repeating it exactly?

If the answer to any of those questions is no, rewrite that part of the definition until you are fairly sure that nobody who reads the finished definition will have to ask, "What do you mean?"

Examining a Stipulative Definition

Here is the plan for a definition paper:

Definition of **fanatic.**

Main idea sentence: Being a fanatic means being so hung up on one thing that you can't think sensibly about it.

Examples (*including one thing that it isn't, but that might be confused with it*):

1. My uncle loves streetcars.
2. My aunt hates dirty ashtrays.
3. Mr. Abernathy goes to church every Sunday.
4. Mr. Baumgartner thinks everybody should have the same religion he has— he's not a fanatic but a bigot.

Conclusion (*a variation of the main idea*): A fanatic has uncritical zeal or enthusiasm for something, such as religion or politics.

Here is the first version of the paper written from this plan:

Fanaticism

Introduction is not very lively. The class definition is all right:

> fanatic **(term)**
>> **being so hung up on one thing (big group)**
> **that you can't think**
>> **sensibly about it (how it differs)**

but the synonym definition isn't needed; anybody who knows *zealot* **will know** *fanatic.* **And the judgment (Nobody likes . . .) is out of place here.**

Being a fanatic means being so hung up on one thing that you can't think sensibly about it. A fanatic is a zealot. Nobody likes being around a fanatic.

Example is not developed. How does he show love? What does "talks about them all the time" mean? And what is "a long way"? A mile? A hundred miles? It would be better to *show* **us that it's boring than just to say so.**

My uncle is a fanatic about streetcars. He loves them so much he talks about them all the time and goes a long way to ride on them. I think that's boring.

If this example were better developed, we could share the writer's nervousness instead of just being told about it in a general way.

My aunt is a fanatic because she can't stand to have anything in ashtrays. It makes me nervous to have her emptying them all the time.

The monotonous start of all these paragraphs is boring—"My uncle . . . My aunt . . . Mr. Abernathy . . ." Transitions are needed. How can going to church harm either Mr. Abernathy or other people?

Mr. Abernathy is so fanatic about going to church that he does harm to himself and other people. He won't miss a single service.

What pictures does "hasn't any use for" create in your mind? What do you see *happening* when Mr. Baumgartner "wasn't nice"? Why wouldn't he let the man in the house? Is that the difference between fanatics and bigots —not letting people in the house?

Mr. Baumgartner goes to church, and he hasn't any use for people who don't go too. He wasn't nice to his daughter's boyfriend and wouldn't let him in the house. He's a bigot.

The single-sentence conclusion is a restatement of the main idea, but it sounds as though it came straight out of the dictionary; politics hasn't been mentioned in the paper at all.

A fanatic has uncritical zeal or enthusiasm for something, such as religion or politics.

Do you understand what the writer means by fanaticism—that is, could you say to yourself, "According to this definition, *this* kind of behavior would be fanatic, but *that* kind wouldn't"? Would the writer consider that putting on a freshly laundered shirt every morning is being fanatic about cleanliness? What about changing shirts three times a day? Is the person who buys a new mystery story every week a fanatic? Or the person who never misses the late, late show on television? Is the person who travels 500 miles to carry placards for (or against) the Equal Rights Amendment a fanatic? the Catholic mother who refuses to let her son marry a Protestant? In other words, has the writer made clear what "uncritical enthusiasm" is?

Unless they were being very obliging, most people would agree that the writer has not shown any very clear examples of uncritical enthusiasm. We are given only a fuzzy notion of what happened, what things looked like, sounded like, felt like. The writer, in other words, has left the readers to do all the work.

In the second version of the definition paper based on the plan outlined earlier, we are given some clear pictures. Here the writer is coming much closer to real communication. We don't have to agree with the definition, but we can tell what the writer means. The transitions help to take us smoothly from one example to the next, and the sentences have been combined so that the effect is not so choppy. In this second version, the new material has been underlined so that you can see the changes easily, and the omitted material has been crossed out.

Fanaticism

[1]   Being a fanatic means being so hung up on one thing or one idea that you can't think sensibly about it. [A fanatic is a zealot.] Whatever form your fanaticism takes, the thing you're hung up on gets bigger and bigger, until it

pushes other things or ideas right out of the picture. Your "thing," whatever it is, makes you ignore other things that may be more important, and you get so enthusiastic that you stop being reasonable. [Nobody likes being around a fanatic.]

[2] For instance, I have an uncle who is a fanatic about streetcars. He loves them so much he drags them into every conversation. If I say something about coming home on the bus, he says, "Now if that had been a streetcar, you wouldn't have had that trouble. Let me tell you about. . . ." and then he goes into some long-winded account of where the streetcars used to run and how much cheaper they were to operate. He has a scrapbook full of old pictures, and it isn't enough for him to look at them by himself, he makes everybody who visits the house look, too, even though we've already seen those pictures a thousand times. If you tell my uncle about some town that still has a streetcar, he'll make my aunt go two thousand miles on their next vacation, just so he can ride the streetcar before that city, like all the rest of them, decides that busses would be better. My uncle is sensible enough about most things, but about streetcars [he's a terrible bore] he loses all sense of proportion.

[3] My aunt is a fanatic, too, but her fixation is ashtrays. She can't stand to have anything in them. Although she doesn't smoke herself, she never tries to get anybody else to stop. Smoking is all right; it's just dirty ashtrays she objects to. As soon as my uncle puts his cigar out, there she is, jumping up to put the butt in the garbage and wipe the ashtray out with a Kleenex. Sometimes when I'm smoking a cigarette, she empties the ashtray two or three times before I'm through and makes me so nervous I wish my slacks had cuffs so I could put the ashes there and leave that little glass dish entirely alone.

[4] Streetcars and ashtrays are fairly harmless things to be fanatic about, but other kinds of fanaticism can really be dangerous. [But] I know another man who is so fanatic about going to church that he does harm both to himself and to other people. Mr. Abernathy won't miss a single service, no matter how sick he is or what other more important things people try to get him to do. Once when he had the flu, and a fever of 104 degrees, the doctor told him to stay in bed. Instead, he got up and went to church because it was Sunday. Nobody knows how many other people caught the flu from him, but we do know he got pneumonia and was in the hospital for two weeks. He refused to be sensible about it. He forgot that he might be exposing the rest of the congregation to his germs; the harm he did was unintentional. He doesn't try to make other people go to church with him or complain about people who don't go. He just goes himself, to every single service.

[5] On the other hand, Mr. Baumgartner goes to church just as often as Mr. Abernathy, but he insists that everybody else go, too, and he doesn't have any use for people who don't go. He doesn't even put up with people who go to a

different church. If it isn't his church, it doesn't count. The first thing he asked when his daughter brought home a new boyfriend was, "How often do you go to church?" And then, "What church do you go to?" When Mr. Baumgartner found out that the boyfriend went to a different church, one Mr. Baumgartner thought was wrong, he wouldn't let the young man in the house and ordered his daughter not to be seen with the young man again. Mr. Abernathy is just a fanatic, but Mr. Baumgartner is a bigot.

[6]   A fanatic, then, is a person who [has uncritical enthusiasm or zeal for something, such as religion or politics] is uncritically enthusiastic about something and carries that enthusiasm further than ordinary people would. The enthusiasm can be for a small thing, like emptying ashtrays or keeping a desk straightened up, or it can be about important things, such as religion. It is not the same as bigotry. Bigots are intolerant of what other people do; fanatics confine their wild enthusiasms to their own behavior.

Key Words

Here are some of the important terms used in this chapter. See whether you can answer these questions about them:

1. Why can't we say what the **real meaning** of a word is?
2. What is a **synonym definition?**
3. What are the three parts of a **class definition?**
4. How do **stipulative definitions** work?
5. What is an **abstraction?**
6. What is meant by the statement **"General and specific are relative terms"?**
7. How should you decide whether to use a **general** or a **specific word** in your own writing?
8. What is a **generalization?**
9. What is a **specific statement?**
10. How do **examples** relate to **generalizations?**
11. Why will the main idea sentence of a **stipulative definition** be a **generalization?** What three parts should the generalization have?
12. What should the **plan** for a stipulative definition include?
13. How can the plan help in deciding where to **paragraph?**
14. Why should you avoid **one-sentence paragraphs?**
15. How can **pronouns** sometimes confuse readers?

READINGS
Definition

Instinct

species: classification by kind or family
migratory: moving from one part of the world to another

First definition (somewhat incomplete): Instincts are built-in patterns.

[1]   For the daily routine of living and meeting the need for food and shelter, nature has provided animal life with built-in patterns known as instincts.

Example: Birds' nests:
a. Orioles
b. Robins

[2]   All birds of a given species build a similar nest. The orioles swing their cradle from the weeping-willow branch. Robins plaster their sturdy nest bowl in the shaded crotch of a maple, elm or oak tree.

Example: Long-distance flying:

a. Geese

[3]   Migratory birds have a built-in sense of direction which guides them to their destination on their annual migrations of thousands of miles from north to south in response to climatic changes. The geese form their V in the sky and start south in fall, led by the call of the lead gander. They do not argue about the reasonableness of it, or debate whether to set their compass to right or left. Day and night they fly on, through bright moonlight or stormy sky, reaching their destination close to schedule. It is traditional that the swallows of Capistrano, California, will arrive on March 19. They vary little from schedule year after year as they return to build their nests in the old Spanish mission.

b. Swallows

Example: Spawning of salmon

[4]   On the West Coast the salmon return after four years at sea to the stream where they were hatched. There they lay their eggs and die, completing nature's life cycle for them.

Paul H. Landis, *Sociology* (Lexington, Mass.: Ginn and Company, 1972).

Example: Social life of insects:

a. Bees
b. Ants

Three-part definition:
1. Instinct =
2. Behavior pattern +
3. Provided by nature and functioning when environmental forces are brought to bear on the creature

[5] Nature provides some insects with the built-in equipment for a very complicated social life. Instinct accounts for the complex community organization of bees and the complicated homes and habits of ants. Among such social insects one sees cooperation, specialization of work, and even division of labor. These patterns work perfectly, or nearly so, yet they are not learned.

[6] Instinct is never learned by an animal. It is by definition a behavior pattern provided by nature, which functions when environmental forces are brought to bear on the creature.

Responses

1. Although Landis begins with a simplified general statement, he does not give us his complete definition until after he has produced several examples. Does this order make his definition harder or easier to understand? Why?

2. Just before the complete general statement definition, we are given a brief negative definition. Does this statement of what instinct is *not* belong in the definition? Defend your answer. Does this negative definition help you see why the term is not precisely used in the comment, "Some instinct told me to stay away from Andy's martinis"?

3. Using the definition given in Landis' last paragraph, decide which of the following kinds of behavior could be called instinctive. Why do you think so?

   a. A newborn baby crying from hunger
   b. A two-year-old's fear of a hot stove
   c. A man swearing when he hits his thumb with a hammer
   d. A cat suckling her kittens
   e. A boy swallowing his gum when the teacher comes in
   f. A girl dodging when a car swerves toward her
   g. A child liking ice cream
   h. A child disliking spinach

4. This six-paragraph selection, taken from a college textbook, is a fair example of the kind of definition you will need to understand, remember, reproduce, and apply in many of your college classes, especially in the social sciences. Using a different term from another class you are taking

or have taken, write a short paragraph in which you define the term by giving a class definition backed up by at least two specific examples.

Lagniappe

facility: ease, skill
equivalent: like, equal to
gratis: free
countenance: face
edifice: structure, large building
gill: about half a cup

[1]   We picked up one excellent word—a word worth traveling to New Orleans to get; a nice, limber, expressive, handy word—"lagniappe." They pronounce it "lanny-yap." It is Spanish—so they said. We discovered it at the head of a column of odds and ends in the *Picayune* the first day; heard twenty people use it the second; inquired what it meant the third; adopted it and got facility in swinging it the fourth. It has a restricted meaning, but I think the people spread it out a little when they choose. It is the equivalent of the thirteenth roll in a "baker's dozen." It is something thrown in, gratis, for good measure. The custom originated in the Spanish quarter of the city. When a child or a servant buys something in a shop—or even the mayor or the governor, for aught I know—he finishes the operation by saying: "Give me something for lagniappe."

[2]   The shopman always responds; gives the child a bit of licorice root, gives the servant a cheap cigar or a spool of thread, gives the governor—I don't know what he gives the governor; support, likely.

[3]   When you are invited to drink—and this does occur now and then in New Orleans—and you say, "What, again?—no, I've had enough," the other party says, "But just this one time more—this is for lagniappe." When the beau perceives that he is stacking his compliments a trifle too high, and sees by the young lady's countenance that the edifice would have been better with the top compliment left off, he puts his "I beg your pardon, no harm intended," into the briefer form of "Oh, that's for lagniappe." If the waiter in the restaurant stumbles and spills a gill of coffee down the back of your neck, he says, "For lagniappe, sir," and gets you another cup without extra charge.

Responses

1. Where does Mark Twain give a class definition of "lagniappe"? What is it? What are the four examples he gives of the word in use?

Mark Twain, *Life on the Mississippi.*

2. Can you think of three more occasions where the word would fit? Make up three such situations, and see whether the other students in your class think "lagniappe" would be appropriate.
3. Although Twain works from the unfamiliar (lagniappe) to the familiar (the kind of situation we might all find ourselves in), he does use uncommon words. He could have said *ease, free, face,* and *structure,* for instance, instead of *facility, gratis, countenance,* and *edifice.* Why do you think he doesn't use the easier words?
4. The last situation Twain mentions is a little different from the other three. What do *thrown* and *free* mean this time that they didn't mean before? Why do you suppose Twain saved this situation for the last?
5. This article, written about a hundred years ago, defines a word you aren't likely to run into either in your reading or in your conversation, but it is a good illustration of two important things: first, how we learn unfamiliar words by hearing them, asking about them, and then using them ourselves; and second, how an unfamiliar word can be explained in writing so that readers almost feel as if they had heard it used. As an experiment, make up a word (to be sure nobody has ever heard it before), and write a paragraph showing readers at least three situations in which your invented word would be appropriately used.

Discrimination in Rental Housing

impose: require, insist on
statute: a state or federal law

[1]   What is illegal discrimination? It is unlawful for a landlord to refuse to rent to a person or impose different rental terms because of a person's sex, marital status, race, creed, color, or national origin, or because the person is handicapped. It is important to understand that a landlord's actions may be unfair and unreasonable and still not be unlawful discrimination. In order to be unlawful, the discrimination must be based on your being a member of one of the groups or classes of people protected by an antidiscrimination statute or ordinance. It is not illegal for a landlord to refuse to rent to you because he does not like the shoes you are wearing. His decision might be arbitrary and unreasonable, but there is no law which prohibits discrimination based on shoe styles.
[2]   Landlords are free to treat individuals differently. You cannot prove illegal discrimination simply by showing that a landlord did something to you that he did

Barbara A. Isenhour, James E. Fearn, Jr., and Steve Frederickson, *Tenants' Rights: A Guide for Washington State* (Seattle: University of Washington Press, 1977).

not do to other people. In order to prove illegal discrimination you must show that the landlord treated you differently *because* you are a member of a group which is protected by antidiscrimination laws. For example, a single woman living in an apartment building in which all the tenants are single women is the only tenant to receive an eviction notice. Although her different treatment may be unfair, it is not sex or marital status discrimination.

[3]   What to do about discrimination: If you have been denied rental housing because of discrimination, you may be able to force the landlord to rent to you and, in addition, get money damages and attorney's fees. Unlawful discrimination is also a defense to an eviction. If you think you have been the victim of housing discrimination, you can do any of the following:

1. Start a lawsuit immediately.
2. File a complaint with the Fair Housing Section of the Department of Housing and Urban Development.
3. File a complaint with the Washington State Human Rights Commission.
4. File a complaint with your city human rights department if there is one.

No matter what you decide to do, it is important to act quickly. In most cases a discrimination complaint must be filed shortly after the discrimination takes place. If you do not file in time, you will lose your right to file your claim. There is no cost for filing a housing discrimination claim with a government agency, and you do not need a lawyer. Once you contact the agency, its staff can provide you with helpful information on how to pursue your claim.

Responses

1. Finish the statement, "Illegal discrimination in rental housing means . . . ." Then check your dictionary to find the more general definition of "discrimination." What are some of the differences between the two definitions?
2. The authors give two examples of what illegal discrimination is not, but no specific examples of what it is. Would the article be easier to understand if such examples were added? Why or why not?
3. Legal definitions must be as clear and specific as possible so that individuals, commissions, and judges can understand and apply what the law means. The first two paragraphs of this article give the definition; the next two paragraphs explain how ordinary people can apply the definition to their own situations. Make up an example that you think illustrates a case of illegal discrimination, and see whether your classmates agree that you would have a justifiable complaint.
4. Find, in your college library, another legal definition—reckless driving, for instance, or manslaughter—and write a paragraph giving the definition and at least one example of a situation in which the term would not legally apply.

The Ospreys of Boca Grande

adept: expert
predatory: living by preying on weaker creatures
plummets: dives

[1]   With the beginning of the warm spring months, many fishes return to the waters of Boca Grande Pass, the entrance of Charlotte Harbor on Florida's west coast near Fort Myers. At about the same time, an airborne fish-eater, a year-round resident that cruises the skies, begins to nest. This magnificent predatory bird is the osprey, or fish hawk (*Pandion haliaetus*).

[2]   A close relative of the hawks, the osprey is found world-wide along seacoasts, lakes, and rivers. It has crooked wings that are long and narrow, with an average spread of 54 to 72 inches. This arrangement is ideally suited for soaring over water, where there are fewer uplifting currents of warm air than there are over land. The keen eyesight of the osprey, which enables it to spot prey from a distance of 30 to 100 feet, is the result of two adaptations: the strong muscles in the osprey's eyes enable them to focus sharply on a range of distances, and each eye contains several specialized areas for acute central vision (as opposed to only one of these areas in the eyes of most animals, including man). The osprey also has a small spikelike appendage, called a spicule, on the bottom of each foot, as well as an unhawklike outer toe that moves backwards and forwards, allowing the bird to grasp slippery fish.

[3]   Although it will eat an occasional small bird, water snake, toad, or lizard, the staple of the osprey's diet is fish. When hunting, the bird alternates between flapping and gliding, until it sights its prey. If the fish is a top-feeder such as the striped mullet (*Mugil cephalus*), the osprey swoops down and strikes parallel to the water's surface, lifting the fish out of the water with its strong talons. If the prey is a deeper-swimming species, however, such as the sea catfish (*Arius felis*), the osprey folds its wings, plummets beneath the surface of the water, grabs the fish with its claws, and then lifts off into the air. In the Boca Grande area, the sea catfish constitutes the most common food item of the osprey.

[4]   Once the osprey takes to flight with its prey, it appears that the bird always turns the head of the fish forward, regardless of which method was used to capture the fish. This may be done to reduce wind resistance during the return flight to the nest.

[5]   The nests, or aeries, of ospreys are composed of sticks, branches, and driftwood, and they may exceed 3 feet in diameter. They are commonly lined with seaweed, leaves, moss, or other soft materials. In Boca Grande, the locations of these nests have changed considerably over the last ten years. Huge structures, once built by the ospreys but now occupied by crows and sparrows, can be seen in the tops of solitary trees along the shorelines of LaCosta, Sanibel, Captiva, and Useppa

Thomas G. Bell, *Sea Frontiers,* January–February, 1980.

islands. These nesting sites were abandoned by the ospreys in favor of rather unlikely locations, such as water towers, channel markers, air vents, radio towers, and even wagon wheels placed in the tops of trees for them. These newer nesting sites seem to afford the ospreys more protection from predators, except man.

[6]   Usually two, but as many as five, brown or reddish-brown, blotched eggs are laid in the nest. During the 35- to 40-day incubation period, the female osprey is almost always found with the eggs. Once the osprey chicks hatch, they are fed by both parents until they reach six weeks of age, at which time they begin making short, mostly unsuccessful hunting excursions on their own. At this stage, the young ospreys are about the same size as the parents; only their clumsiness around the nest and their higher-pitched cries distinguish the young from the parent birds.

[7]   The osprey is an adept hunter, a devoted parent, and a handsome bird. For those who are boating or fishing or just bird-watching in the Boca Grande area, the osprey is an admirable sight to behold.

Responses

1. The *Random House Dictionary* (college edition) defines an osprey as "a large hawk, *Pandion haliaetus,* that feeds on fish. Also called *fish hawk.*" Where does Bell include this definition? What details does he add that might be considered part of his class definition?
2. In defining an actual thing, rather than an abstraction, how can examples be given? Would you like this article better if it included a photograph of an osprey? Why or why not?
3. The magazine in which this article was originally published did show five pictures; try to decide what the photographs probably showed. What does Bell do in words to compensate for the absence of pictures?

What Is Custody?

sufferance: acceptance of a situation because there's no other choice
distraught: very upset
prescribed: laid down as a rule
literal: meaning exactly what it says

[1]   Who will take Jimmy to the pediatrician? Should he go to Sunday school? What about a speech teacher for his lisp? Who will pay for summer camp? Where will he go for his birthday? Should he take music lessons? Is his friend Alec a bad influence? How much television should he watch?

Suzanne Ramos, *The Complete Book of Child Custody* (New York: Putnam, 1979), pp. 47–51.

[2]   Normally, these responsibilities and decisions are part of the daily lives of two parents. However, where there is no longer a two-parent home, they are assigned to one or the other parent and become part of what is meant by having custody. Essentially, custody means being the primary caretaker and authority in a child's life. It involves having him physically around for the majority of the time, as well as providing him with food and clothing, deciding what type of education he will have, and seeing to it that he has appropriate opportunities to make and meet friends.

[3]   On a more emotional level, it involves caring—caring enough to give a child standards; to provide structure; to demand reasonable and consistent discipline; to make him feel loved and wanted and not there by sufferance; to allow him to express his aggression and help him learn to control it; and to involve oneself in his life. Caring, too, may mean putting a child's interests above one's own needs, including, in some instances, accepting a custody arrangement one did not wish for or living up to a visitation agreement only because it is best for a *child's* emotional well-being.

[4]   Mary and Bert had been married ten years when they decided to separate. Six-year-old Alexandra was their only child. Mary worked as a fabric designer in an office six blocks from their apartment in downtown Atlanta, while Bert's job as a producer for a local television station included irregular working hours and frequent out-of-town business trips. Bert had always been very much involved with his daughter and after the separation was distraught at the thought of seeing her only once or twice a week. He disapproved of his wife's marijuana smoking and her occasional "oddball" parties with her artist friends. He decided to talk to his lawyer about suing for custody.

[5]   "Does she give the stuff to your daughter to smoke or even smoke it in front of her?" his lawyer asked Bert.

[6]   "Well no," Bert answered.

[7]   "Does she neglect or abuse the child?"

[8]   "No, certainly not."

[9]   "You see," the lawyer explained, "the thing is, Bert, Mary works from nine to five, she has a good housekeeper there when Alex gets home from school and the truth is she's a damn good mother who's at home on most nights and when she's out the child is well taken care of." . . . "And look at you, Bert," he went on. "Some nights you work until ten. You're out of town every other week. The child wouldn't see you enough. I don't think you have much of a case."

[10]   After thinking it over, Bert agreed to Mary having custody providing he could spend most weekends with his daughter.

[11]   There are various custody arrangements: "exclusive," "joint," "sole," "divided," "one-parent," "split," and "shared" are some of the terms used to describe those arrangements. When any custody provision is discussed, the terms should be clearly defined because such labels as joint or split custody are often used interchangeably or are misunderstood.

[12]   One parent (sole or exclusive) custody is the most commonly used arrangement, and it means most importantly that either the mother, which is the usual case, or the father cares for the child on a daily basis and assumes responsibility for most of the child's needs. The noncustodial parent usually sees the child according to

a prescribed yet generally somewhat flexible schedule negotiated as part of the custody settlement.

[13]   Kurt and Maria separated, with Maria taking sole custody of nine-year-old Kim and eleven-year-old Nils. On alternate weekends Kurt picked up the children Friday afternoons and returned them Sunday evening. He kept them for a month in the summer until they were old enough to work, at which point they stayed at their mother's house during the week.

[14]   In joint custody, sometimes called co- or shared custody, two parents share responsibility and authority over a child. It is a plan chosen by a small but growing number of parents and can work in several different ways. For example, in a joint-custody plan, children can move back and forth between parents' homes or parents can move in and out of the main house. The children's time can also be handled in various ways. Some parents alternate half weeks, while others exchange the children every week, month, or half year. Still other parents are less literal about their living patterns, and they agree, for example, that it would be best for the children's school schedule for them to live with one parent on weekdays and with the other parent on weekends.

[15]   The Robertsons ran their joint-custody arrangement in a typical manner. Billy and Matt lived in their mother's house and in their father's apartment on alternating weeks, making the change on Sunday evening.

[16]   Split (divided) custody means separated children. One or more children live with one parent and the other(s) with the other parent. This is not a commonly used arrangement and is generally found where there are special circumstances such as in the case of Nadine and Tom, where Tom, who worked for an oil company, was frequently transferred to different South American countries for stays of six months to a year at a time in each place. His fourteen-year-old son, Anthony, felt he would rather go with his father than not see him for such long stretches of time. Anthony visited his mother, who stayed in Texas with his nine-year-old sister, Christine, whenever his dad returned to the States. Each type of custody has advantages and drawbacks for children as well as parents.

Responses

1. Actually, this article contains not just one but four class definitions. What are they, and where are they found? Ramos gives only one example for each definition. Is one enough? Why or why not?
2. How many paragraphs does Ramos use to give the first example of custody? Does this number make the example seem out of balance with the others given? Why or why not? Discuss with your teacher and the other students why paragraphs 5, 6, 7, and 8 are so extremely short.
3. Are you at all bothered by the writer's assumption in paragraphs 2 and 3 that all children are boys (the child/him, etc.)? Does it make any difference that the first paragraph talks about "Jimmy" and the fourth about "Alexandra"?
4. The movie *Kramer vs. Kramer,* based on a best-selling book, is the story

of a custody fight. If you have read the book or seen the movie, write a paragraph explaining the type of custody the Kramers had, using their situation as your example. You may, of course, add your own comments if you like.

The Southern Lady

antebellum: before the Civil War
exhortation: strong advice
sensibility: capacity to respond to aesthetic and emotional stimuli
piety: dutiful religious attitude
paragon: a model of excellence
injunction: rule or command

[1]   If talking could make it so, antebellum southern women of the upper class would have been the most perfect examples of womankind yet seen on earth. If praise could satisfy all of woman's needs, they would also have been the happiest. Literary journals, sermons, novels, commencement addresses—wherever men spoke there was praise of Woman, and exhortation to further perfection.

[2]   This marvelous creation was described as a submissive wife whose reason for being was to love, honor, obey, and occasionally amuse her husband, to bring up his children and manage his household. Physically weak, and "formed for the less laborious occupations," she depended upon male protection. To secure this protection she was endowed with the capacity to "create a magic spell" over any man in her vicinity. She was timid and modest, beautiful and graceful, "the most fascinating being in creation . . . the delight and charm of every circle she moves in."

[3]   Part of her charm lay in her innocence. The less a woman knew of life, Ellen Glasgow once remarked bitterly, the better she was supposed to be able to deal with it. Her mind was not logical, but in the absence of reasoning capacity, her sensibility and intuition were highly developed. It was, indeed, to her advantage that "the play of instincts and of the feelings is not cramped by the controlling influence of logic and reason." She was capable of acute perceptions about human relationships, and was a creature of tact, discernment, sympathy, and compassion. It was her nature to be self-denying, and she was given to suffering in silence, a characteristic said to endear her to men. Less endearing, perhaps, but no less natural, was her piety and her tendency to "restrain man's natural vice and immorality." She was thought to be "most deeply interested in the success of every scheme which curbs the passions and enforces a true morality." She was a natural teacher, and a wise counselor to her husband and children*. . . .

[4]   Oddly enough this paragon of virtue was thought to need the direction and control of some man. A person identified only as "president of the oldest college in

Anne Ferar Scott, *The Southern Lady* (Chicago: University of Chicago Press, 1970), pp. 4–7.

Virginia" published a letter to his newly married daughter in an early issue of the *Southern Literary Messenger*. The wife's conduct alone, he asserted, determined the happiness or misery of a marriage. She must resolve at the outset never to oppose her husband, never to show displeasure, no matter what he might do. A man had a right to expect his wife to place perfect confidence in his judgment and to believe that he always knew best. "A difference with your husband ought to be considered the greatest calamity," wrote the father, adding that a woman who permitted differences to occur could expect to lose her husband's love and all hope of happiness. He concluded with the usual injunctions that she should be amiable, sweet, prudent, and devoted, that she should regulate her servants with a kind but firm hand, cultivate her mind by reading history and not corrupt it with novels, and manage her domestic concerns with neatness, order, economy, and judgment.*

[5]   A novelist echoed the opinions of the college president. "In the heart of woman, uncorrupted by a false philosophy which would unfit her for her proper sphere, the proudest feeling is that of admiration for her husband . . . . this is as God meant it should be. To this state the natural feelings of a woman's heart will tend, let quacks in education do what they will."*

[6]   From earliest childhood girls were trained to the ideals of perfection and submission. A magazine for children published in Charleston, recording the death of a seven-year-old, spoke of her as "peculiarly amiable and engaging; her behaviour marked with a delicate sense of propriety, happily mingled with an artless innocence." She was praised for being kind and considerate to her servants. The fiction in the same magazine was filled with pious, obedient little girls.* Boarding schools for young ladies, to which more and more girls were sent as the century wore on, emphasized correct female behavior more than intellectual development. In at least one school the girls wrote their English compositions on such subjects as modesty, benevolence, and the evils of reading novels.*

[7]   By the time they arrived at their teens, most girls had absorbed the injunctions of the myth. One young woman wrote in her diary that she longed to die because she had not found a husband, adding, "I know I would make a faithful, obedient wife, loving with all my heart, yielding entire trust in my husband."*

Responses

1. Scott doesn't give a class definition of a Southern lady in a single sentence. Instead, she spreads her definition through all seven paragraphs. See if you can add adjectives to complete the sentence, "A Southern lady before the Civil War was . . . ." Then compare your definition with those written by other students.

2. The quotation marks scattered throughout the article indicate that this writer is quoting from earlier writers. In footnotes, marked by asterisks, she explained who those writers were and gave the dates of the magazines and books. Does the fact that most of the statements quoted were written before the Civil War, and none of them later than 1897, help to explain their rather formal language and the somewhat unusual words used?

3. There are no specific examples of actual women in the article. What kind of examples are used? Why are they appropriate to what Scott is trying to do?
4. What impression of Scott's attitude toward this "Southern lady" do you get from such phrases as "if talking could make it so" and "wherever men spoke" in paragraph 1? Find other examples of comments that show her attitude. Does she believe such women actually existed? Back up what you say by reference to the article.
5. The asterisks in this article represent footnotes in which Scott carefully gave the exact sources for all the material she quotes. Most of the material was a hundred years old and is no longer available in an ordinary library. If the information had been given here, under what circumstances might you want to look it up? What could you find out from looking at the children's magazine mentioned in paragraph 6, for instance?
6. Write a paragraph or two in which you define some idealized picture of a human being—the liberated woman, the chauvinistic man, the modern child, for instance.

Child Abuse and Neglect

explicit: openly stated
prone: likely to
incapacity: inability to understand or do something

[1]   Would you help a friend in trouble? Sure you would. Loyalty in a tough situation is what friendship is all about. For most people this is an informal understanding, though some make it explicit by forming gangs or clubs. On a personal basis, if you have a buddy who is getting beaten up regularly, you come to his aid. If your girl friend is sexually molested, finding the guy who did it gets top priority. If your younger or smaller pal seems to have a fresh black eye, bruise, or welt every time you see him, you find out who is whipping him and even the score.
[2]   But would your answer change if the people responsible for your friend's distress are his or her parents? It probably would. Most of us are trained to accept the authority of parents in family matters. We know that many of the rules that govern public life simply don't apply in the home. A mother or father can order their child to work around the house without pay, something that would be laughable if attempted by an employer. Confining a youngster to his or her room would be an offense called "false imprisonment" for anyone but a parent or legal guardian. Laying hands on a stranger is against the law, but the legality of striking a son or

Leland Englehardt, *You Have a Right: a Guide for Minors* (New York: Lothrop, Lee & Shepard, 1979), pp. 96–102.

daughter is unquestioned. Double standards like these make us reluctant to counsel resistance to parental discipline, however severe.

[3]   In most situations, of course, parents try to be firm but kind in correcting their children. Many people regard an occasional spanking or slap as the proper punishment for disobedience. Without doubt, this is a parent's right. But if carried too far, punishment can easily become cruelty. Worse, some adults who suffer from alcoholism, mental illness, or an extremely violent temper may *want* to hurt their kids. When this happens they have exceeded their legal authority. The name of their crime is child abuse, and many social scientists see it as a modern plague.

[4]   Child abuse is much more widespread than you might suspect. Between 1967 and 1975 the number of cases reported in the United States rose over 2,800 percent. In 1978 it was estimated that between one million and a million and a half American children were physically abused or neglected. In one state alone over forty-two thousand cases were reported in a single year, and undoubtedly there were many more that were never reported.

[5]   Experts agree that the problem does not respect economic status. Abused children are as likely to come from comfortable middle-class homes as from tenement buildings. Saddest of all, it is also known that the victims of child abuse are prone to continue the cycle by brutalizing their own children years later.

[6]   Scary as these statistics are, they do not begin to tell of the suffering and death caused by child abuse. For the human side of the issue, we must look at case histories.

> In California, a mother blinded her five-year-old daughter by smashing an empty glass in her face. The reason: "Jeannie had a sore throat and wouldn't stop whining."
>
> In New York, a twelve-year-old girl was raped by her father. When his daughter was found to be pregnant the man refused to give permission for an abortion.
>
> In Michigan, an alcoholic mother tried to drown her four-year-old son while bathing him.
>
> In Massachusetts, a two-year-old boy was beaten to death by his mother's lover because he wouldn't swallow a doughnut.

[7]   Child abuse doesn't exist alone. It has a companion known as child neglect. Child neglect results from one simple fact: it is far easier to make a baby than it is to raise a baby. "Giving birth doesn't carry a dose of instant wisdom," says one social worker. "Every parent has to be taught how to care for a child. In school we spend years learning civics, history, and math, but we don't even mention the responsibilities of parenthood—probably the most important role in anyone's life."

[8]   From this incapacity, child neglect is born. In one case a poor woman fed her children almost nothing but ice cream because, she said, "Ice cream is frozen milk and milk is good for babies." The result was malnutrition. In another instance a mother, abandoned by her husband, sank into a deep mental depression and left all the household duties to her five-year-old son. In a short time the house was filthy, infested with cockroaches and empty of food. These people had no desire to harm their children. The source of their problems was ignorance of nutrition,

health, and sanitary conditions. Nonetheless, it was necessary to call in social agencies to assist in working things out.

[9]   You and your friends are entitled to proper care while you're dependent on parents or guardians. You also have a right to freedom from abusive treatment. These rules seem simple enough. But, like most other legal rights, they have little meaning without some method of enforcement. This is where child abuse laws have always run into trouble, because every form of "family regulation" has major drawbacks.

[10]   The U.S. Constitution guarantees everyone the right of privacy in his or her own home. This means that it would be illegal for police or other government agents to patrol our houses the same way they watch over public streets. Cops must have good reason to suspect that something is wrong before they enter private property. Therefore they can't just "check up" on the way kids are being treated.

[11]   Every state requires doctors, dentists, nurses, interns and other hospital personnel to report suspected cases of child abuse. Many states extend this requirement to include public and private school teachers, guidance and family counselors, social workers and policemen. Filing a report of possible abuse or neglect usually sets off an investigation by state welfare workers. If the case turns out to be serious—involving a crime like assault, murder, or rape—legal action may come later.

[12]   This sounds like an efficient system. The problem is that it does nothing to prevent child abuse in the first place. A report is made only after the injury is bad enough to put the victim in the hospital or to be noticed by others.

[13]   You may be wondering why abused children don't report the situation themselves. On its face, this seems the easiest and more direct method of enforcement. But experience has shown that kids who are brutalized by their parents rarely go to outsiders for help. The reasons are complex. "They are confused by conflicting emotions," says a psychologist who has worked with many abuse victims. "On one hand there is basic, natural love for their parents. On the other side is a terrific fear of what will happen if dad or mom finds out they went for help. I've seen young people come in with awful bruises or broken bones and say, 'I don't want to get my parents in trouble.' "

[14]   Where does this place the task of child abuse prevention? Mostly on the shoulders of young people like yourself. There are several reasons for this. It's logical that the first ones to notice signs of abuse or neglect in a child would be the friends he or she hangs out with every day. If your buddy shows up one morning with an ugly gash on his forehead, you're more apt to notice it than a teacher who looks at hundreds of kids every day or a cop who sees thousands. Because he *is* your buddy you're more likely to ask about the injury than would an official who doesn't know him from Adam. In addition, young people confide in each other. Your friend would probably tell you things he'd never reveal to an adult. If quizzed about that gash by a teacher or doctor, your pal might say, "It was just an accident—I tripped." But to his friends he will admit, "My old man got mad and threw me against a door last night." . . .

[15]   Let's suppose that you have good reason to suspect that your friend is being abused at home. Although things show no sign of getting better, he refuses to seek outside help. Do you have the right to go "over his head" and report the matter

anyway? You do indeed. In fact, anyone with knowledge of this sort of situation has a *duty* to try to get aid. This duty isn't written in law books the way a doctor's or teacher's may be; it should be inscribed on your conscience and motivated by an honest concern for your friend's health and safety. When a young person is being injured or molested it doesn't matter whether the attacker is a parent or a street-corner tough. He or she needs help. Fast.

[16]   There is no breach of faith in telling someone about your friend's problem. It isn't "ratting" or "squealing," because child abuse isn't a private matter. If your pal contracted a sickness and no one would care for him you wouldn't hesitate to call in a doctor. You'd notify the police if he were being beaten by hoodlums you couldn't handle on your own. Like sickness and crime, brutality to children is a social problem that should be handled by experts.

Responses

1. The class definition of child abuse is given somewhat indirectly in paragraph 3; what is it?
2. In paragraph 4, Englehardt says children are "abused or neglected": does he intend the two words as synonyms? If they are not synonyms, where is the distinction made clear? What is it?
3. What group of readers was this article intended for? What is said in the article to support your decision? Do the kind of language used and the examples given fit with what you have decided? How?
4. This article is an example of mixed purposes. What is the other writing purpose for which the definition is being used?
5. If you have known about, either in your own experience or through newspaper articles, any cases in which children were abused or neglected, write a short paragraph describing the situation and saying whether the parent involved should have been charged with abuse or with neglect.

Redlining

revitalize: bring back to life
entity: something that has a real existence of its own; self-contained
exodus: mass departure
fiscal: having to do with money

[1]   Who would have thought that a revolution was brewing in places like East Flatbush, Logan Square, Crown Heights or South Shore? Yet it is in these com-

John A. Collins, "New Hope for Old Neighborhoods: Redlining vs. Urban Reinvestment," in Evelyn Geller (ed.), *Saving American Cities* (New York: H. W. Wilson, 1979), pp. 98–103.

munities and hundreds like them across the US that working-class ethnics, white and Black, are getting angry and getting organized.

[2]   This time around, the neighborhoods are not organizing to keep Blacks out, or to cut welfare benefits, or to put muggers away for life; they are organizing to get power to take on the giants that control many aspects of their common and individual lives—big utilities, insurance companies, bureaucrats and banks.

[3]   These people are true conservatives. They want to preserve and revitalize the thousands of stable, well-built, energy-efficient, older neighborhoods of America. They have decided that the cities and older towns are *worth saving,* and they have concluded that the main threat to neighborhood stability and revitalization is coming from the banks, and especially "neighborhood" banks. Their battle cry: Redlining!

[4]   The current concern with world hunger has made us all aware that protein deficiency leads to malnutrition, lowered resistance, loss of energy, disease, and even death. Not so obvious is the fact that neighborhoods are entities that exhibit similar symptoms when systematically deprived of essential nutrients. An urban neighborhood starved for credit shows such early symptoms as stagnation, lowered property values and a shabby, run-down look. Later comes a reduced ability to combat crime, a middle-class exodus, open sores on the commercial strip and finally the advanced stages of deterioration, abandonment and arson.

[5]   Community groups have discovered increasingly that, with neighborhoods as well as with human beings, an ounce of prevention is worth a pound of cure. A steady flow of life-giving credit prevents a neighborhood from reaching that point of illness where more radical, expensive and often less effective measures become necessary.

[6]   Redlining is the arbitrary denial of credit to an entire geographic area by financial institutions. In the classic form of redlining, a bank draws a red line around an area on a map and says, "No more loans in this area." Before the issue became controversial, bankers would often flatly declare: "We don't give loans in this neighborhood." For instance, when Blacks began to move into a neighborhood, mortgage and home-improvement money "moved out," apparently on the racist assumption that an integrated neighborhood would soon become a Black neighborhood, and a Black neighborhood would soon be a slum. The practice has not been limited to racially changing neighborhoods. Community groups in recent years have charged banks with redlining entire sections of major American cities.

[7]   Redlining has many faces. As public criticism against the practice has mounted, outright refusal of loans has been replaced by higher interest rates, shortened terms, high down payments, low appraisals, application fees and red tape. The social injury resulting from redlining has "macro" and "micro" dimensions. Credit is refused without regard to the soundness of the property or the credit-worthiness of the prospective borrower. One middle-class family seeking a mortgage on a brownstone building in Brooklyn's Park Slope section went to 63 banks and was turned down by all 63. When a family owns a home in a redlined neighborhood and prospective buyers cannot get mortgages, the value of their property declines. If no one in the neighborhood can get a home-improvement loan, it won't be long before buildings start to deteriorate. The practice of redlining thus becomes its own self-fulfilling prophecy. . . .

[8]   When first confronted with charges of redlining, the banks' answer was simple: "We don't redline." When asked to disclose mortgage-loan data which would verify or disprove the charges, the banks said that the information was classified. The response of community groups and national networks like Gale Cincotta's National People's Action was to fight for and get the first piece of banking legislation not written by the banking industry in 40 years—the Home Mortgage Disclosure Act of 1975. Under this law, a community group or local church can learn the number and total dollar amount of mortgages a bank has given in any census tract.

[9]   Armed with the tools of disclosure legislation, community groups have produced some amazing evidence. In St. Louis, ACORN, an association of neighborhood groups, has concluded that 90 percent of the city is being redlined and that city lending institutions have invested only 5.5 percent of their total home mortgage money in the city. The New York State Banking Commission reports that the ten largest Brooklyn savings banks draw 85 percent of their deposits from Brooklyn but reinvest only 15 percent there.

[10]   Confronted with clear evidence of redlining, the banks play their ace—they contend that they are simply following sound banking practices to safeguard their depositors' money. A growing body of evidence suggests that the bankers' decisions involve more subjective/social bias than prudent economic judgment. (Blacks and women have long been victims of such bias.) In Philadelphia, where banks and community groups worked out a plan for the granting of loans in previously redlined lower-income area, 2,500 mortgages totaling over $25 million have been made in the first two years of the plan. There have been no foreclosures, and the low delinquency rate is no higher than that of most suburban communities. In fact, mortgage and home-improvement loans have always been one of the most secure places to invest money. Redlining is not based on sound fiscal policy.

[11]   Indeed, the banks *have* made some very bad investments, but not on home mortgages in urban neighborhoods. What outrages many people is not only the effects of redlining, but what the banks do with their depositors' money—money they refuse to invest in the depositors' neighborhoods. . . .

[12]   When middle-class urban residents, already upset by what is happening in their neighborhoods, learn that *their* banks take *their* money but refuse to reinvest it in *their* neighborhods, they become angry. Redlining serves to unite neighborhood groups across lines of class and race as perhaps no other current social issue does, and offers the potential for a new broad-based politico-economic movement. As one ACORN organizer in St. Louis told me, "We seek issues which do not divide people along lines of race or class and on which we can *win,* even if it's getting a traffic light at a busy intersection. Victories build momentum."

Responses

1. Is "true conservative" used in the same sense that Cook used it on page 45? If you think there are differences, what are they? Based on what both Cook and Collins say, write a class definition beginning, "A true conservative is a person who . . . ."

2. What comparison is made in paragraphs 4 and 5? How does it help you to understand the effects of redlining? How is the comparison related to what is said in paragraphs 3 and 6?
3. This article, like the one on child abuse, seems to have mixed purposes. The definition is needed so that readers can understand the problem. Collins never says openly that he is against redlining, but it would be hard to read the article and suppose that he favors it. What phrases, sentences, or sections show his attitude?
4. How does redlining differ from illegal discrimination as it was defined in the article on the rights of renters?
5. If redlining has occurred in your city, or a city you are familiar with, write two or three paragraphs in which you explain what happened and what is being done about it. [Consult the files in the college library if you need help.]

More Suggestions for Writing

Synonym definitions for:

    con carne
    delineate
    numismatist
    à la carte
    ditto

Class definitions for:

    to fast
    a patsy
    a cameo
    to bifurcate
    a hotcake
    garbage

Stipulative definitions for:

    racism
    independence
    dishonesty
    success
    justice
    trust
    prude
    innocence
    uptight

Chapter 4

Explaining: Comparison

The kind of explanation that points out similarities or differences between two things is called *comparison*. You are comparing whenever you explain something new by contrasting it with something familiar. If your readers have hot Cream of Wheat every morning but have never tasted grits, a comparison between Cream of Wheat and grits will help them understand the new food. If someone knows nothing about hockey but quite a bit about basketball, a comparison between the two games will help explain the rules for moving the puck from one end of the arena to the other.

Sometimes we make comparisons to learn something new, and sometimes to come to a better understanding of things already familiar to us. If you like both science fiction and detective stories, figuring out how those two kinds of novels are alike, and how they are different, can increase both your understanding and your pleasure. If you listen to the radio, comparing the lyrics played on a country-western station with the songs played on a top-forties station may give you some interesting new insights.

Perhaps you're more intrigued with differences. Take the twins you've known since childhood, Augustus and Pete. They shared the same parents and milked the same cows; they hated the same high-school teachers and liked the same girls. Yet Augustus now pays taxes on $90,000 a year and barely has time between board meetings and international flights to snatch a twenty-dollar lunch at the Union Club. And here is Pete, making and firing his own pottery on the Oregon coast, and barely earning enough money to make ends meet, but with plenty of time to hunt in the woods, fish in the mountain streams around his cabin, and watch the sun rise and set. Each man claims he likes his life. If you contrast, point by point, exactly what each man considers important, who knows what you may discover. Your chances of making a discovery are much greater, though, if you look for the actual differences before you generalize about what they are. Don't begin with the belief that you already know: examine each part with new eyes. And don't begin with a prejudice for one or the other. If you aim for understanding rather than judgment, at least at first, you'll almost always discover something useful.

Of course, comparisons can also be used as a basis for evaluation. In that case, the point is to arrive at a judgment as to which of the things being compared would be better for whatever your purpose is. Some jobs require you to compare one piece of equipment with another, and some decisions in your own life require you to choose between two alternatives. Should the farm cooperative buy a Ford tractor or a John Deere? Which will give the ice-cream parlor better service: repairing the old walk-in box or buying a new but smaller Freezecold unit? Does the Humpty Dumpty Nursery School have any advantages over the Tiny Tot Day-Care Center, and are those advantages worth the extra money? Should you buy or rent a house?

Comparisons can help even if you're not faced with an immediate decision. Sometimes a "what if" question can make contrasts clear. A man working a lathe turns to the man next to him and says, "What if I went to college and got a degree in architecture?" An English teacher looks at a classroom full of nursing students and asks, "What if I went to med school?" A retired woman asks her niece, "What if I wrote a book review and sent it to the local newspaper?" As you can see, a "what if" leads pretty directly to "What will happen if I do?" and "What will happen if I don't?" Making contrasts like that can change the direction of people's lives; writing about the contrasts can remind readers that they also have choices.

What to Compare

Comparison writing usually arises out of some problem or question that already exists, and writers seldom have to say to themselves, "Let's see now, what can I compare to what?" The topic comes ready-made if you're asked, on a health exam, to "compare and contrast" two methods of physical therapy, or if you're asked for a report evaluating a new system of repairing cement leaks—obviously you're expected to compare the new method with the one now in use. The topic is half there when you're trying to help readers imagine an experience they've never known: you start with the experience and then need only find some other experience that's roughly similar. Suppose you want to explain how you felt when you had temporary amnesia; you might make a quick comparison by saying, "It was like being lost in a strange city, without any money, without any baggage, and without any notion of where to get help, except it was worse than that. I not only didn't know where I was, I didn't know *who* I was."

The situation in a writing class is a bit more artificial. Here, you are developing your skill in comparison writing, and finding a topic will be up to you. When you look for subjects to compare, don't just grab two items out of the air and start making a list. Instead, ask yourself what point the comparison would make. What new knowledge or clearer view would you and your readers have when the comparison was finished?

You'll find out something worth knowing if you begin with two things that seem at first thought to be very much alike: RN's and LPN's, perhaps, or the $100.00 gown in the tenth-floor salon and the bargain-basement copy for $8.95. Then you can go on to find out what the real differences are.

Equally good comparison can be made, of course, by starting at the opposite end. Instead of beginning with two things that seem alike, you can begin with a pair that most people think entirely different and then go on to show that there's not much difference after all. For example, guppies are so small they get lost behind the seaweed, and sharks so big that a bathtub won't hold them, but they do have some things in common. Writing poems and baking cakes seem entirely different occupations, but good papers can be written showing their similarities. Whether you compare guppies and sharks, cheap dresses and expensive gowns, or poetry and pastry is less important than what you do with the comparison; the main problem is to choose a pair of things that will lead to better knowledge, better judgment, or better understanding for whoever reads your paper.

If you're trying to find a topic for a comparison paper, make sure that you are giving yourself enough room. In comparing two things that seem much alike, it is easy to make what you are emphasizing too narrow, to leave yourself nothing to say. A student comparing the Statue of Liberty with the Eiffel Tower, for instance, might say, "You can get a good view from the top of both the Eiffel Tower and the Statue of Liberty, but from the first one you see Paris and from the other you see New York." That statement is perfectly accurate, but it will bring most writers to a dead stop. Everything has been said, and there's nowhere to go from there.

Making your topic too broad is just as dangerous. If you think that saying "from one you see Paris, from the other you see New York" wouldn't leave you at a dead stop but would inspire you to list everything you could see from the top of either monument, certainly the topic is too broad. The list could go on and on forever.

To make a successful comparison, you must find some middle ground between nothing to say and everything. Now is the time to ask yourself, "Why do I want to make this comparison? What do I want to find out?" and, if you're planning a paper, "What do I want my readers to understand after they've read my paper?"

Whatever topic you choose, you increase your chances of producing a discovery for yourself or a clarification for someone else if you *look* at whatever you're examining and see beyond obvious similarities. Discover similarities that you hadn't suspected before, and note differences that are actually important. You can, if you want to, point out that both Babe Ruth and Hank Aaron are professional baseball players, both batters, both with incredible records. Okay, so what? Go on and ask yourself, "What happened when Babe Ruth hit his world-record home run? What happened when Hank Aaron hit his?" Right away it's obvious that the public reaction to those two events, while enormous, was different in each case. When you see those differences, you experience a discovery; when you write them for someone else to read, you share your understanding.

Main Idea Sentences for Comparisons

When you have found a topic that seems worth your time and are pretty sure what point you want to make, you already know whether you want to emphasize similarities or differences. Now is the time to write a main idea sentence, to help tie down that clear vision before it shifts to something else—to "fix" it, as a photographer fixes film to keep it from developing itself right out of sight.

A good main idea sentence for a paper of comparison has two parts. The first part states what things are being compared; the second part makes clear whether you are primarily interested in likenesses or in differences. The two parts are usually joined by such words and phrases as *although, even though, in spite of, notwithstanding,* or *but.* Using these words and phrases will help you avoid such a useless main idea sentence as "Clocks and wristwatches are both alike and different." A better version would be *"In spite of* the obvious difference in size, Big Ben in London and the Mickey Mouse watch my son wears contain very similar parts that work in a very similar way."

Here are some main idea sentences that emphasize differences. Notice that the first part of each sentence tells what two things will be compared and suggests that the likenesses don't matter much; the second part says definitely that the differences do matter.

(1) Many people think that judo and karate are alike because they both originated in Japan, *but* (2) as anyone who has seen a karate expert split an oak beam with a bare hand can tell you, the art of karate is quite different from the art of judo.

(1) *Even though* grocery stores in the ghetto and in the suburbs are run by the same company and go by the same name, (2) there are important differences in the choices available, the quality of the food, and the prices that are charged.

(1) *Although* either renting or owning a house can cause problems, (2) homeowners have several advantages that renters don't have.

(1) *Even though* a suitable site for a hot-dog stand is available both in Magnolia Groves and downtown, (2) several differences must be considered before a decision is made.

In the following main idea sentences, the order is reversed, and it is easy to tell that the writer will be concentrating on similarities:

(1) *Except for* the difference in setting, (2) a game of baccarat at a Monte Carlo casino and a crap game under the Chicago el are practically identical.

(1) The political philosophies of Jefferson and Lincoln differ on many points, *but* (2) on the fundamental issues of human freedom and the importance of the individual, they agree.

(1) *In spite of* the obvious difference in size, (2) Big Ben in London and the Mickey Mouse watch my son wears contain very similar parts that work in a very similar way.

(1) *Although* most advertisers would have you believe there are big differences between their gasoline and all the other brands you can buy, (2) the ingredients that go into all gasolines are much the same.

Planning the Order

Nearly all good papers begin with what the writers think is least important (though perhaps catchy) and work up to what they consider most important. That arrangement will probably seem natural to you as you plan your paper of comparison. The main idea sentence, in fact, serves as a miniature outline. The writer comparing a ghetto grocery store and a suburban grocery store will probably use the first paragraph to show in what ways the stores seem alike—the same name in big letters over the door, the same company collecting the profits. Next, the writer will probably tell everything that happens to shoppers in the ghetto grocery, from the time they go through the door of the store until they have paid the clerk for what they bought, and then do the same for shoppers in the suburban store. In the suburban account, the differences can be emphasized by such phrases as "In contrast with the scratched wooden door . . . ," "Instead of being treated . . . ," "Unlike the dirty floors and broken packages . . . ," "The vegetables, instead of being bruised and wilted. . . ." The plan will look like this:

> *Main idea sentence:* Even though grocery stores in the ghetto and in the suburbs are run by the same company and go by the same name, there are important differences in the choices available, the quality of the food, and the prices that are charged.

> *Similarities:*   same name
> same company

> *Differences:*   ghetto store
> few choices
> stale, unattractive food
> high prices
>
> suburban store
> several choices in each section
> fresh, appetizing food
> lower prices, more specials

Such a plan will work well for this material because the shopping trip gives a natural unity to each part, while the contrasting phrases help focus on the differences between the first store and the second, linking the two parts together.

The trouble is that not all topics fit so well into an "all about the first thing, then all about the second" arrangement. Unless you are very skillful, you risk at least three dangers: your comparison may be incomplete, your connecting phrases may be mechanical and dull, and your paper may wind up sounding like two separate essays. Once the less important part has been covered, it may be better to deal with the more important one point by point, comparing as you go.

The writer comparing casino gambling with street gambling, for instance, will probably show the apparent differences early in the paper—the elegant surroundings, dress, and manners in the casino; the squalor and noise under the el. By the end of that contrast, there should be a whopping difference established. After all, a jeweled duchess looking bored as she shoves another $5,000 toward the dealer certainly *seems* much different from the sweating, cigar-chewing man in ragged clothes who puts his last crumpled single on the next roll of the dice. If, at that point, the writer says the differences really aren't important, the readers' curiosity is bound to respond.

After the differences are taken care of, the writer can spend the rest of the paper, probably several paragraphs, explaining how the two events are alike. Both cards and dice are symbols, important only in games. Both the duchess and the man are playing by rules that are clearly understood and as binding as law. Though both people *seem* to be playing a game, they are in fact wagering their money in a situation they do not control. Mathematically, the odds are always against the player, and psychologically, both people are "playing" in order to prove their worth by showing that they are indeed "lucky." When the game is over, despite the duchess's apparent boredom and the man's obvious intensity, both will feel excited or depressed, as though they had proved something about themselves. The plan looks like this:

> *Main idea sentence:* Except for the difference in setting, a game of baccarat at a Monte Carlo casino and a crap game under the Chicago el are practically identical.

> *Differences:*   luxurious surroundings; windy, cold, dirty ugly
> satin and diamonds; threadbare overcoat, stump of cigar
> huge sums bet; fifty cents or a dollar wagered

> *Similarities:*   both use symbolic equipment
> both play by unchanging rules
> both play against odds
> both believe in their luck
> both end up excited or depressed

Neither of these methods of organizing a comparison is necessarily better than the other; the plan that will work best is the one that best fits whatever you are comparing. In comparing judo and karate, it would probably be a mistake to tell everything about judo, then everything about karate. That method would not only be less interesting for this subject, it would provide a danger of leaving something out. The writer might discuss the aims of judo but forget to mention the aims of karate; or go into great detail about the special hand training in karate but over-look whatever special training is needed for judo. If the comparison is to be complete, the two sections must balance point by point.

Even the second kind of plan, discussing the likenesses first and then comparing the differences one by one, may seem unsuitable here. Since the writer wants to show that things which seem alike are actually different, interweaving the similarities and differences all through the paper will make for a smoother paper. Each paper will begin with likenesses and then go on to differences. The plan will look like this:

> *Main idea sentence:* Many people think that judo and karate are alike because they both originated in Japan, but as anyone who has seen a karate expert split an oak beam with a bare hand can tell you, the art of karate is quite different from the art of judo.
>
> I. Both—Expert must learn and practice certain moves.
>   A. Judo expert learns to throw opponent.
>   B. Karate expert learns to disable opponent.
>
> II. Both—Physical discipline is required.
>   A. Judo expert disciplines all muscles and works for quick reactions.
>   B. Karate expert disciplines certain parts of the body until they are extremely tough.
>
> III. Both—Expert takes advantage of opponent's weight and movements.
>   A. Judo expert takes advantage of balance and gravity.
>   B. Karate expert tries to break arms or legs.
>
> IV. Both—Main use is for defense.
>   A. Victim of judo expert is merely thwarted.
>   B. Victim of karate expert is often dead.

In making your own plan, don't worry about producing a formal outline. The roman numerals and capital letters have been used here to show how the parts of this more sophisticated plan fit together, to make it easier for you to see how the paper will be balanced. If you are asked to make a sentence outline for a paper, you will need to construct a plan that follows this pattern. Meantime, however, you might want to try both methods and decide which works better for you. Some writers are more comfortable when everything is written down in sentence form and carefully labeled; others are more at ease with a sketchier plan.

Writing a Comparison Paper

When you have worked out a clear plan by whatever method you choose, most of the work is done. But you need to remember that the plan is no more than the bare bones. You won't have a satisfactory paper if all you do is put that skeleton into paragraph form, adding a few connectors here and there. The next step is developing each point you've decided to include. Begin by looking—actually seeing—the reality of what you're explaining. Let readers see the differences as clearly as you see them. Give some examples. Put in some specific details.

The writer of the judo-karate paper could just say that a judo expert works on moves that will land an opponent flat on the ground whereas a karate expert develops the hands until they become lethal weapons, and then go on to the next point. It will be a better paper, though, if the writer lets us see *how* the expertise is developed—that the karate expert begins to toughen the side of the hand by hitting a board or table hundreds of times a day, gradually increasing the force of the blows until the hand has developed a horny pad tougher than the soles of most people's feet, building up hardness and strength until boards, bottles, and bricks can be broken with a single stroke. The first sentence tells, in a general, colorless way, what the karate expert does; the second has been developed with specific details. By the time the writer has explained what the karate expert's hands can do to something as flimsy as the human body, there will be plenty to say, and it will be said interestingly and forcefully.

As you finish your paper, remember that usually you want just to compare, not to praise or condemn. A single sentence summarizing the main points will do very well: "The ghetto shopper finds the choices more limited, the quality poorer, and the food more expensive." Another way is to echo the main idea: "Even though they'll never meet, and wouldn't speak to each other if they did, the dignified duchess and the skid-row crap player have a lot in common." Or the conclusion may simply pick up the most important point and assume that the readers will remember the rest: "Judo is for sport; karate is for real."

Even though the point of your comparison has been to arrive at a judgment, to decide which of two possibilities would work out better, most of the conclusion should still emphasize what the differences would be. If your employer has asked you to investigate the advantages of opening a hot-dog stand in the suburbs as compared to opening one at a busy downtown intersection, you probably won't want to finish by saying, "Anybody would be crazy to start any kind of new restaurant in Magnolia Groves; there's too much competition." Instead, it would be better to say: "The people in Magnolia Groves have more money to spend, but there are seven other quick-lunch places in which they can spend it."

Examining a Sample Comparison Paper

One student who wanted to compare the advantages of buying a house with the advantages of renting began by making a list of everything that came into her mind, just as she thought of it:

expensive to buy
do you get more?
high interest rates

might get bored and want to move
landlords supposed to repair, often don't
leaky faucets
leaky roof
Uncle Jeff's house
threat to withhold rent
sense of permanence
moving every year—all those boxes
down payment
interest and taxes deductible
house we rented in Lunaville
beautiful old cherry tree
climbing and hiding
who plays in our tree house now?
father out of work that year
basements
can't make alterations
build up equity?
prices go up, make money
prices go down, payments don't, rent may
danger of foreclosure
insurance for dying
insurance on house
pride of ownership
no pets allowed
apartments into condominiums
closing costs
Aunt Jessie crying

Probably this list doesn't make much sense to you, but it isn't intended to. As a reader, you were never expected to see it. What the list did was give the writer a collection of memories and ideas from which her plan could be made. She began by pulling out the most important points and then arranged them in what seemed a sensible order. Her plan looked like this:

Main idea sentence: Although either renting or owning a house can cause problems, homeowners have several advantages that renters don't have.

Similarities: available houses about the same size
                  monthly payments about the same
                  utilities extra in both

Differences: short-term financial considerations
                    renting — only month's rent and damage deposit
                    buying — down payment
                              high interest rate
                              closing costs
                              taxes
                              insurance
                              cost of repairs

long-term financial considerations
    renting — nothing to show but receipts
    buying — equity built up
                    possibility of profit
responsibilities
    renting — landlord makes repairs but often slow
                    tenant can't make changes without permission
                    pets often not allowed
    buying — pay for your own repairs but can decide
                      when to do them
                    make whatever changes you want
                    keep pets if you want
permanence
    renting — might be asked to move any time
    buying — can stay as long as you choose

Intended audience: young people who need a bigger place to live

Here's the first draft of the paper:

Buying a House

[1]   Many young people have to decide whether they should rent a house or buy one. Although either renting or owning a house can cause problems, homeowners have several advantages that renters don't have.

[2]   Money is the first thing they consider. Then they discover that either renting or buying will cost more than they have been paying for a little apartment. When they ask people they know who have houses what they pay, they find out that it costs about the same to rent or buy and that there isn't much difference in the houses. They are both pretty old, both their roofs leaked last winter, and it cost a lot to heat both places.

[3]   When they start looking at some houses for sale, they find out that if they rent, all they need is a month's rent and a damage deposit. If they buy, they'll have to find money for a down payment, and pay some closing costs that they didn't know about, and then interest on the mortgage might be pretty high.

[4]   Maybe they can borrow enough money for the down payment from somebody. But if they buy a house, they'll have to pay a lot of taxes and insurance, and pay a good deal of money to have the roof fixed if it leaks. If they rent, the landlord has to pay for those things. It seems like renting would be better.

[5]   Then they think about later on. If they buy, they are building up equity, and if they want to sell the house, they'll be able to get their down payment

back and some of the money they've paid every month. Maybe prices will go up and they'll even make some money. If they rent, all they'll have at the end of ten years is a bundle of receipts.

[6]   If they rent, they'll never be sure they won't have to move if the landlord decides to sell the house. When I was a little girl, we rented a lovely house in Lunaville, with a big yard. It had a nice big tree where we used to climb and hide. We even had a tree house. Then all of a sudden, when my father got laid off, the landlord made us move. We lived in three other places before my parents finally bought their own place. It seemed like we were always putting stuff in boxes and taking it out again. One place we rented the furnace blew up and the landlord didn't fix it for two months, until we threatened not to pay the rent. We had to wear sweaters. Another time my mother wanted to change the kitchen around and the owner wouldn't let her.

[7]   My uncle always rented houses and never stayed any place very long. I remember my Aunt Jessie crying every time they had to move. She said she never felt she belonged anywhere. They never lived any place where they were allowed to keep a dog, and Aunt Jessie always wanted one.

[8]   When my family finally did buy a house, we were all a lot happier. We felt permanent. My mother sewed curtains and painted all the rooms. When we wanted to tear out a wall we could do it without asking anybody. We didn't have to worry about putting dishes into crates any more because that house was ours.

When the writer finished her first draft on Monday, she was fairly pleased. She had used almost everything on her brainstorming list, and she had followed her plan—or thought she had. When she read the paper on Wednesday, however, it didn't sound as good. She realized that the first five paragraphs didn't say anything very definite; they were filled with such phrases as "costs more," "costs about the same," "costs a lot," "pretty high," "pay a lot," "a good deal of money." Those five paragraphs were not much more than a restatement of the plan. The only place she had given any real examples or details was in the last three paragraphs, where she told about her own childhood experiences. Even that didn't sound quite right. Paragraph 7, about her uncle and aunt, seemed out of place; and although the final paragraph did say how much happier her own family had been, it wasn't a satisfactory conclusion. The paper seemed to be divided into two parts, one about "they" and one about "we." Some of the sentences were all right, but some of them sounded childish.

Before beginning to revise the paper, she did three things. First, she looked at her list again and noticed that she had omitted one fairly important item—that taxes and interest payments can be deducted from income tax. She also reminded herself that the list was just to get her started; she didn't have to use everything it contained. She decided to add the point about tax deduction and cut the part about Aunt Jessie. Next, she telephoned a savings bank to find out what was actually involved in buying a house: how much down payment was required, and what the current interest rates were. That gave her some accurate information. Finally, she showed her paper to two friends. They suggested that even though her memories were interesting, what she said in the paper ought to apply to more than just her own family. One friend pointed out that the title was misleading: it didn't mention renting at all.

She was better satisfied with her revised paper—and rightly so. The details in the first part are more specific, those in the last part less personal. Using the informal "you" all through has taken care of the break between the parts, and the sentences sound smoother. Rewriting the conclusion has made the paper sound finished.

Renting or Buying—An Important Decision

[1]   Living in a two-room apartment can be fun when you're very young, but if you're like most people, you'll wake up some morning and discover that the place is so crowded you can't get from the door to the bed without falling over something, and the only place to store your winter boots is either on top of the refrigerator or in the oven. You know you have to have a house. The question is, should you rent or buy? When you start to investigate, you find that although either renting or owning a house can cause problems, home-owners have several advantages that renters don't have.

[2]   Cost is the first thing to consider. If you want a house with two bed-rooms, either renting or buying will be more expensive than that two-room apartment. Monthly payments will be about the same. One available five-room house rents for $215 a month; mortgage payments on a very similar house would come to about $210. In either house, you will have to pay extra for gas, electricity, and garbage collection.

[3]   If you decide to buy, it will be more expensive in the beginning. You will have to find or borrow at least 10 percent of the selling price for a down payment, pay somewhere between $100 and $300 for closing costs, and at the current rate of 11.5 percent, expect that more than half of your monthly payments will go toward interest. You will have to take out homeowner's insurance and pay the taxes. Besides that, if a faucet leaks, you'll have to hire a plumber or fix it yourself. If the roof leaks, there won't be any landlord to pay the repair bill.

[4]   You may begin to think that owning a house will cost too much; renting sounds a lot cheaper. But if you think about five years from now, it looks a little different. Every year you have deducted the taxes and interest from your income tax, and that has cut Uncle Sam's bill almost in half. The higher the interest you pay, the lower your income tax is. Even though the interest rates are high, you've also been paying something on the principal. Add that to the

down payment you made, and you've built up some equity. If real estate prices keep going up, you could even make a profit. All a renter has at the end of five years is a worthless bundle of rent receipts.

[5]   It's true that if the furnace breaks down in a rented house, the landlord is supposed to fix it. But it isn't the landlord who has to shiver around in three sweaters for two months. It's you. And the only defense you have is refusing to pay the rent. The landlord is supposed to do the painting, too, and some landlords do; but they can be pretty nasty if you ask for alterations. When you own a house, you can paint whenever you want, whatever color you want; and if you decide to knock out a kitchen wall, there's nobody to say you can't do it. If you want to keep a dog, or even three dogs, you don't have to get permission.

[6]   Homeowners have a sense of permanence that renters never have. If you own your house, no landlord can tell you to move just when you're nicely settled in. You won't have to repack your dishes every year or so, and your children won't be upset at leaving a favorite climbing tree. You can plant your own fruit trees and know you will be there when they start to produce. You can take pride in the improvements you make, because it really belongs to you.

[7]   Wherever you live there will be problems. If letting somebody else worry about the repairs and the taxes makes you more comfortable, then renting is the solution. But if building up some equity, being able to change things when you want to, and getting a sense of permanence is what you like, then buying a house has some advantages.

Key Words _____

Here are some of the important terms used in this chapter. See whether you can answer these questions about them.

1. What are the **uses of comparison** in everyday life? Give an example of each use from your own experience.
2. What makes a suitable **topic for comparison?**
3. What happens if the topic is **too narrow? Too broad?**
4. What are the **two parts** of a **main idea sentence** for a paper of **comparison?**
5. How does the two-part main idea sentence help to show readers whether the paper will emphasize **similarities or differences?**
6. How is the **order** of the paper affected by an emphasis on **similarities?** By an emphasis on **difference?**

7. What do you have to watch out for in a **plan** that calls for "all about the first thing, then all about the other"?
8. When should you use a **formal outline?**
9. In **developing** a paper of comparison, what must you do besides following the plan?
10. What are three acceptable ways of **concluding** a paper of comparison?

READINGS
Comparison

Nursing in England and the USA

sutures: surgical stitches to hold a wound together
theoretically: according to the theory; usually means what actually happens
is different

The writer introduces the subject, gives her qualifications, and refers to differences

[1]   I left my native Ireland after I had completed a high school education. I studied to become a nurse and midwife in England, and I eventually came to the United States of America. Because I have worked five years in hospitals in England and the U.S.A., my friends frequently ask about differences, as I see them, in the practice of nursing on both sides of the Atlantic.

Licensing laws (difference 1):
a. In Great Britain

[2]   Until I realized how different the licensing laws of Great Britain are from those in the United States, I was surprised at the number of restrictions placed on a nurse's actions in this country. A nurse licensed in Britain may practice anywhere in the British Isles and in some countries abroad; in the United States, the nurse must apply in every state in which she hopes to work.

b. In the U.S.

Responsibilities (difference 2):
a. In Great Britain

[3]   In Britain, a nurse is a deeply respected, devoted woman, entrusted with a vast amount of responsibility. The patients place unquestioned confidence in her judgment and advice. The doctor relies on her report of her observations, and he seldom interferes in what is considered a nursing duty.

[4]   The nurse decides when the patient is allowed out of bed or what type of bath he may have. I do not recall ever seeing an order on a physician's chart such

American Journal of Nursing, April 1968.

as "OOB in 24 hours" or "may take a shower." The nurse judges when a wound is healed and when sutures may be removed. She is always consulted about the patient's requirements and his progress. And because of the structure of most hospitals in England, the nurse is in view of the patient constantly. Whenever he needs attention, the nurse is there in the ward, and she may observe him, too, unobtrusively.

[5]   Furthermore, the nurse is a member of the health team who sees the patient most frequently. To the patient she is the most familiar person in the strange hospital world.

b. In the U.S.

[6]   In the United States, the patient is likely to be under the care of the same doctor both in and out of the hospital, so the doctor is the person the patient knows best and the one in whom he confides most easily. But though the patient's treatment and care are discussed with the nursing staff, a nurse is not allowed much freedom to advise a patient. Also, I have seen doctors visit patients without a word of communication to the nurse. Personally I think it difficult to be ignored when a patient's care is concerned and I think it prevents full utilization of the nurse's knowledge and skills.

Socialized medicine (difference 3):
a. Nursing is easier under socialized medicine in Great Britain because:
   1. All drugs and supplies are kept on the ward.
   2. A nurse tends a patient who is free from worry about costs.

[7]   I myself found nursing practice easier, in a way, under the so-called "socialized medicine" of Great Britain than the more individual type of medical care found in the United States. It involved much less writing and left me at the patient's bedside, where I am happiest. There was no need to write several charges and requests for the needs of the patient. Stocks of drugs and other medicines were kept on each ward, so that when medication was ordered, it was at hand. All charges were met by "National Health"—including all supplies and equipment used on the ward. The nurse tends a person who is free from much anxiety and hence more easily cared for while he is an inpatient.

Orientation (difference 4):
In the U.S., hospitals have helpful orientation programs.

[8]   On the other hand, I found that my introduction to an American hospital was a happy experience. As a new nurse, I was guided by an orientation program given by another nurse and quickly found my place on the patient care team. I had never experienced such an orientation in England.

Reference books and information (difference 5):

[9]   Policy, drug reference, and procedure books at the nurses' station provide a ready reference where a nurse may check facts when she is in doubt, and she

U.S. practice keeps a nurse better informed than in Great Britain.

can instruct a new nurse on the staff without confusion. The active U.S. nurse, while working, can keep informed about new trends, discoveries, and inventions in a rapidly changing word of medicine.

Personal Life (difference 6):

a. In the U.S., a nurse has more time for outside activities.

[10] Here in the United States the nurse is regarded as an individual person and her personal life outside the hospital is given consideration. She develops interests in arts, sports or a creative hobby; she is encouraged to further her education. Time and means are available to her to expand her horizons and to enrich her personality. Many nurses combine marriage and a career very ably in this country, but not in England or Ireland. All this tends to involve her more with people other than the sick. She is an interesting, informed, and happy person, and at the bedside she can show understanding and perception.

b. In Great Britain, a nurse lives a more isolated life and has a more demanding schedule.

[11] In Britain, like most nurses, I lived in a nurses' home on the hospital grounds and was thus isolated in a special hospital community. Theoretically I worked eight hours each day that I was on duty. But these hours were so arranged that one went to work twice in one day. One might work four hours in the morning, have a few hours free, and then go back to the ward for the evening. This schedule demands most of one's waking hours, and so mingling in the larger community outside the hospital was quite limited. The nurse was expected to find full satisfaction in her vocation, and thoughts of increases in salary were considered unworthy. Now, such attitudes are beginning to change and the winds of unrest are blowing through nursing in England, ruffling many a well placed cap.

Conclusion: In Great Britain, nurses are now beginning to want changes in their profession.

Responses

1. The nurse who wrote this comparison is clearly evaluating—measuring—the advantages of nursing in England against the advantages of nursing in America. Does she reach a clear-cut decision as to which is better? If you think she does, back up what you say by reference to the essay.
2. On the basis of what you are told in this essay, decide whether an American or a British nurse would be more likely to be able to do these things:
   a. decide that a patient with a sprained ankle would be better off walking
   b. offer an aspirin to a patient with a headache
   c. attend a night school class in sculpture
   d. deliver a baby

    e. move from the north of the country to the far south without taking another examination

    f. suggest to a patient that it's time to go home

    g. notice a restless patient about to fall out of bed

    h. get a baby-sitter for her four-year-old so she can take a job in a hospital

    i. recommend expensive medicine for a patient without worrying about whether the patient can afford it

    j. discover where things are kept in an unfamiliar ward without wasting time looking for them

    k. offer advice to a doctor about a patient

3. Would this comparison have been more effective if the writer had told all about Great Britain, then all about the United States? Why or why not?

4. Did you notice any sexist language in this article? If so, where does it occur and why does it seem sexist?

5. Write a paragraph or two comparing two different jobs you have held. It will be easier if you use two jobs of the same type—two restaurants you have worked in, two families you baby-sat for, etc.—but even if the jobs are quite different, you can still make an interesting comparison.

Temperature: Mud Pies and Climate

unpalatable: bad-tasting
perceptibly: noticeably
infinitesimal: very tiny
sultry: hot and humid
incursions: sudden entrances
unhindered: without any obstruction
fluctuates: changes back and forth

[1]   No one has ever earned a fortune selling homemade mud pies. They're unpalatable, indigestible, and hard to cook. If you put one under the broiler on a gas stove, the upper crust may burn to a crisp. But the filling will remain raw and muddy because heat is not easily transmitted through the pie.

[2]   You'll be more successful if you set a dishpan of water under the broiler in place of the pie. Water cooks readily. As the surface warms under the gas flame, heat gradually circulates through the pan. Water at the bottom grows about as hot as water on top. Yet there is a drawback here, too. Although water can be cooked, it cannot be sold for pie.

[3]   Broiling either mud pies or water seems impractical. But the experiment has important implications for the weather. Suppose the mud pies were the continent

Robert Moore Fisher, *How About the Weather?* (New York: Harper & Row, 1958), pp. 34–35.

of the United States, the dishpan of water the ocean around it, and the gas flame the sun. When the sun rises, what happens?

[4]   The surface of the earth, like the upper crust of the mud pie, warms rapidly. All the heat it receives from the sun is absorbed within the first foot or so of top-soil. But the dishpan of water—the ocean—warms little. The sun's rays are distributed through a large volume of water. All this water must be heated before the temperature at the top changes perceptibly. By midafternoon, the surface temperature of the land may have risen 10 degrees. That of the ocean may be less than 1 degree higher.

[5]   After sunset, the process is reversed. The earth cools quickly. Much of its heat stays close to the surface and escapes. The ocean, on the other hand, keeps at about the same temperature. The heat it gives off during the night represents an infinitesimal part of what it has stored up in its depths. Over a twenty-four-hour period, the surface temperature range may equal 20 degrees for land but only 1 degree for water.

[6]   Because the mud-pie earth cannot be cooked to any great depth—and because the dishpan ocean can—a blizzard in San Francisco occurs as rarely as a winter without snow in St. Louis. Westerly winds travel over San Francisco from the Pacific Ocean, which evens out the season by being relatively cool in summer and warm in winter. Average monthly air temperatures in San Francisco vary over a narrow 12-degree range—from about 50 degrees in January to 62 degrees in September. At no time on record has the mercury risen above 101 degrees or dipped under 27 degrees.

[7]   The mild climate of the west coast, however, extends only a few miles inland. For our western mountain ranges, which run almost north-south, keep the tempering influence of the Pacific Ocean close to shore. At the same time, they leave the rest of the continent open to invasions of frigid air from the north and sultry air from the south. These incursions of comparatively cold and hot air seldom reach the mountain-protected west coast. But they sweep unhindered over St. Louis.

[8]   The people of Missouri thus live surrounded by a continent of land over which the air temperature fluctuates widely. St. Louisans first shiver and then perspire as average monthly temperatures vary over a 48-degree range—from about 33 degrees in January to 81 degrees in July. Although St. Louis lies at nearly the same latitude as San Francisco, the mercury in St. Louis goes to much greater extremes.

Responses

1. Which of the three uses of comparison mentioned on pages 89 and 90 applies best to this article? Be ready to explain your answer.
2. There are three comparisons in this essay, one beginning in paragraph 2, one in paragraph 3, and one in paragraph 6. What is being compared in each paragraph? How do the comparisons relate to one another? Which is most important to the main point of the paper? Why do you think so?

3. How does Fisher use his first paragraph to arouse the reader's curiosity? Does the fact that mud pies are not good to eat have anything to do with his main point? Does the fact that they are hard to digest and hard to cook matter? Why does he make all three of these comments in the same sentence?
4. In paragraph 6, how does Fisher remind us of the comparison he made in paragraphs 3 and 4? What does this reminder do for the reader?

When Is a Cold Not?

self-practitioners: people who do for themselves what is normally done by a professional
mucosal tissue: membranes in the nose, throat, etc.

[1]   Although most of us have no difficulty recognizing the symptoms of an upper respiratory illness when we have one, even the medical profession may have trouble saying with absolute assurance that what you have is a cold or the flu. It is true that laboratory tests of cultures taken from your throat can give positive identification of the kind of virus you have, but doctors rarely do this in everyday practice. What's more important is that the throat culture is out of the question for the self-practitioner. How then do you determine whether you have a cold or the flu? Although not even the best doctors are 100 percent right 100 percent of the time, even with laboratory tests, there are some good criteria by which you, the self-practitioner, can make an educated guess.

[2]   Researchers tell us that cold viruses and flu viruses are completely different organisms. Although they're all viruses, the similarities end there. From what we know about the differences between cold and flu viruses, it seems that most flu viruses have a greater ability to overcome the first hurdles of our defense mechanisms than do most cold viruses. Thus the antibodies and other virus-destroying substances in our mucosal tissue, which are extremely effective against cold viruses, may be less efficient against the flu.

[3]   Most physicians say that the presence of chills, fever, headache, generalized muscle aches, and sometimes a feeling of tiredness or even exhaustion are present with the flu to a greater extent than with a cold. On the other hand, sore throat, hoarseness, cough, nasal congestion, and discharge are present with both. It is also said that flu comes on suddenly. You feel great one moment and terrible the next. A cold creeps up on you more gradually.

Hal Zena Bennett, *Cold Comfort* (New York: Clarkson N. Potter, 1979), pp. 39–41.

[4]   Most flu infections occur on an epidemic or pendemic scale—that is, infecting a large community or the whole continent or even the whole world, at one time. In a sense, flu viruses are much more ambitious than common cold viruses.

[5]   As a simple guideline for deciding whether you have a cold or the flu, you would be safe in assuming that you have flu if you answer yes to the following:

> Did you have a *dry* cough?
> Did you feel great yesterday and lousy today?
> Does your head ache?
> Do you have chills and fever?
> Do you have a sore throat?
> Do you ache all over?
> Did you recently hear that the flu was going around?

[6]   So what difference does it make, in terms of self-treatment, to know that you have the flu or just a cold? For most people, the greatest benefit of this knowledge will be to reduce anxiety about what it is they have. At first glance this may seem like a small thing. But emotional stress, in this case worrying about what disease you have, can actually inhibit the healing processes.

[7]   Moreover, knowing what you have will give you some idea of how long it will take your body to heal. In general, you can usually calculate that a cold will last from two to four days and the flu from four to ten. Many people, when they have colds or flu, get impatient with the length of time it takes to recover. Their impatience may take different forms: returning to regular work routines too soon, getting angry with themselves for becoming sick, or getting worried that the cold or flu, because it is taking so long, is really something more serious. All these factors impose additional stress, and they divert energy from your body's healing processes. But knowing the normal terms for the cold or flu allows you to have a more realistic perspective about the infection and your body's needs for healing it.

Responses

1. Which comes closest to being the main idea sentence of this article—the first sentence of paragraph 1, the last sentence of paragraph 1, or the first sentence of paragraph 2? Be ready to defend your answer.
2. What use does Bennett expect readers will find in this comparison? Where does he say why the comparison is being made?
3. Is the information complete enough for you to tell the difference between flu and a cold? If it isn't, what else would you need to know?
4. Make a plan for this short article, similar to one of the plans shown on pages 93, 94 or 95. What do you discover about the order Collins followed?

Love, Like—How Different!

asperity: sharpness of tone
chided: scolded gently
scribes: those who in ancient times copied manuscripts and official documents
coessential: sharing the same nature
perverted: twisted, used unfairly

[1]   I took part in a college seminar recently at which one of the participants was a nun. She was attacking some public figure with a great deal of asperity.

[2]   "Sister," the chairman gently chided her, "I thought you're supposed to love your enemies." The nun smiled thinly. "I love him, all right," she returned. "But I just don't like him one bit!"

[3]   Her answer was neither flip nor hypocritical. She knew that the verb "to love" is not an intensive of the verb "to like." Most people think it is, and that is why they often confuse the two.

[4]   We cannot help what we like, but we can help what we love. Liking is a matter of taste and inclination, background and temperament. The food we like, the music we like, the kinds of people we like, are not subject to commandment or moral law.

[5]   But we are commanded to love our neighbors and our enemies—who are so often the same people. How could the Bible be so psychologically stupid as to command us to love if love were merely a matter of personal preference, like choosing vanilla ice cream over chocolate?

[6]   Anybody can learn to love what he already likes; there is no trick in that. But the love spoken of by the scribes and prophets is love of what we do not especially like, or even actively dislike. This is the only kind that has any particular merit.

[7]   Like is a feeling, and love is an act of the will. The nun may have intensely disliked the public figure she attacked, but nevertheless at some deeper stratum of her being she had trained herself to love him—which means to regard him as a human being coessential with herself, as worthy of the same treatment, as sharing the same mark of creation.

[8]   And only this kind of love can save the world from chaos and self-destruction. Without this absolute commandment—which is also a commandment of self-preservation of the human race—we embrace what we like and destroy what we do not like, and there is no end to killing.

[9]   Modern man looks with suspicion on "moral laws" and absolute commandments of any kind, because in the past they have so often been perverted for evil ends. We must learn, however, to look upon them as psychological laws, which are true for the character and destiny of man. For if a moral law does not express a deep psychological truth, it is useless and ultimately false.

Sydney J. Harris, Field Newspaper Syndicate.

[10] "Love thine enemy" is not a piece of "spiritual" sentiment; it is a rule as imperative for our human survival as our need for air and water.

Responses

1. The main idea sentence of this article doesn't appear until almost the end. What is it? At what point in the article did you realize that the purpose was persuasion? How did you know?
2. In the first two paragraphs, Harris shows a situation in which the word "love" is being used; in the third paragraph he tells us that the nun understands what the word means. Why does he wait until paragraph 7 to give us her definition (and his)?
3. What does Harris mean by saying that "to love" is not an intensive of the verb "to like"?
4. How does Harris deal with the similarities between the two words? Why does he put all the emphasis on the differences?
5. Is the distinction Harris makes between "love" and "like" the same one you would make? If it isn't, write a short paragraph explaining what your distinction would be; give some examples of situations in which each word would fit. If you agree with Harris, write a short paragraph in which you give examples of the word "love" being used incorrectly according to Harris' definition.

Parliamentary System Differs from Congress

dissent: disagreement, voting no
ceremonial: used for show purposes, without real power
coalition: two or more groups working together

[1] The parliamentary system used in Canada differs significantly from the American congressional system in the way the government operates and is chosen.

[2] To put it simply, the party that gains a majority of seats in Parliament holds all the cards. The leader of the party, chosen at a party leadership convention between elections, becomes the prime minister, who selects his cabinet from among members of his party who have been elected to Parliament. The cabinet introduces all legislation into Parliament. While "private members' bills" are sometimes introduced, they are rarely debated, and even more rarely passed.

Sunday Oregonian, February 17, 1980.

[3]   Armed with its majority, the party that forms the government can pass any legislation it introduces, restrained only by rules requiring debate with opposition parties, and by dissent from within its own membership if the cabinet or prime minister appears to be going off the deep end.

[4]   In theory, the parliamentary system gives enormous power to the majority party, but in practice, this power is restrained by the power of public opinion as expressed informally outside of Parliament, formally on the floor of Parliament by opposition members and in the ballot box by the voters. Any leader or party that abuses power will quickly find the party itself falling apart in dissent, and at the next election voters can throw the government out of office.

[5]   What happens when none of the parties gains a majority, which can happen when more than two parties vie for power? Canada has four federal parties, none of which gained a majority in the last election. The result is a minority government, the life of which is usually quite short. In such cases, the party with the largest number of members usually forms the government, selecting the prime minister and Cabinet. The process is watched over by the governor-general, a primarily cere-monial official who, as the queen's representative, serves as head of state.

[6]   A minority government maintains power by walking a parliamentary tight-rope. As long as it can get enough support from any of the other parties to muster a majority for any given vote in Parliament, it will remain in power. In some coun-tries, leaders of other small parties are sometimes given a cabinet post to assure the loyalty of their party to the government, but "coalition government" has not been used in Canada at the federal level.

[7]   When a government loses a vote in Parliament, either because it has been deserted by its own members or it has lost the support of other minority parties on which it depends, the leader of the party usually goes to the governor-general and announces that he cannot govern. The governor-general then dissolves Parliament and calls an election, although in some circumstances he may ask the leader of one of the other parties to try to form a government.

[8]   Unlike the United States, elections in Canada do not occur at regular inter-vals. The only requirement is that they be held at least every five years. Most elec-tions are called either because the governing party thinks the time is ripe to go to the voters for a renewed mandate or because it has "lost the confidence" of Parlia-ment by being defeated on a major bill. Voters in Canada do not vote directly for the prime minister. Instead, they vote to elect a local member of Parliament.

Responses

1. The main idea sentence of this article is the first paragraph. Does it make clear whether the emphasis will be on similarities or on differences? Does it make clear what parts of the two governments will be compared? How does this main idea sentence serve as a contract with the reader? Is the contract kept? Why or why not?

2. This article first appeared in a general-circulation newspaper. Who were

the readers expected to be—how informed or educated were they expected to be? What information were they expected to have? What kind of vocabulary were they expected to have? How can you tell?

3. Many political commentators have written articles deploring the stalemate that occurs when Congress and the President take opposing sides on legislation or belong to different political parties. Is this writer complaining that under the American system government often operates very slowly? Can you tell whether he thinks the Canadian system works better than the congressional system? If you think you can tell, what evidence can you find in the article to support your belief?

4. Write an article similar to this but intended for Canadian newspaper readers, beginning with the sentence: "The congressional system used in the United States differs significantly from the Canadian parliamentary system in the way the government operates and is chosen."

Appalachia Then and Now

sinister: evil, threatening
passel: a large amount
holler: valley in the hills

[1]   I felt a sinister change had come over that part of Appalachia that was mine. The river seemed the most changed, and all for the worse. I remember it as clear and clean and deep, and sparkling in the sun. I suddenly recalled a particular summer afternoon when my father took me fishing for the first time. We seated ourselves comfortably on the giant roots of an ancient sycamore growing beside the river, and I was instructed by my father that I must not talk aloud else the fish would be scared away. He first baited my hook and put the rod in my hand. Then he baited his own, and dropped it into a deep pothole. There we sat companionably, with the sun going down at our backs and casting long shadows across the water, my father speaking to me now and then in a low, quiet voice, I answering in whispers. He caught the fish, a "passel" of them, we would have said, strung them on a twig, and put them back into the water until we were ready to go home. I did not recall that I caught any fish. But I remembered the thrill that went through me every time I had a nibble. It was as if I had received a message from some kindly inhabitant of a deep, dark, underwater world. Perhaps catching a fish might have been more exciting. I, however, was quiveringly satisfied with nibbles.

[2]   Now there were no fish in the river. There were no deep potholes where fish could live. I had not been mistaken as I rode along in the bus, thinking that the

Rebecca Caudill, *My Appalachia: A Reminiscence* (New York: Holt, Rinehart and Winston, 1966).

rivers were shallower than I remembered them. The Poor Fork now was not only low; it was apparently the local refuse dump. Tin cans, pop bottles, and discarded automobiles lined the banks, while the river itself was full of debris which apparently it was too sluggish to move along. Across the river, on the mountainside, both above and below the road, clung unbelievably unsightly shacks. Dirty-faced, ragged children played on coal piles in dirty dooryards. Open privies drained into the river. Here was poverty of the most shameful sort.

[3]   "Nobody ever lived like that!" I heard myself saying in despair. "Nobody was rich. But certainly nobody was poor. Not like that."

[4]   "Oh," said my cousin, "there are plenty of rich people about. They own the mines or manage them. Those people you see up there are miners. They've come in here from every holler in Appalachia and every country in the world, I reckon."

[5]   Late that afternoon I took a bus for home, refreshed by the renewal with my childhood, chilled by the ugliness and devastation I had witnessed in a part of the world that had been intimately mine, and with my mind filled with a torment created by one question: Who is my brother's keeper?

Responses

1. Which of the three uses of comparison mentioned on pages 89 and 90 applies to this article? That is, what does Caudill expect to gain, or expect her readers to gain, from this comparison?

2. Which type of comparison plan (see pages 93, 94, 95) is followed in this article? Why is that kind of plan the most appropriate to the comparison being made here?

3. What words and details in paragraph 1 help to create a picture of peace and comfort? What details in paragraph 2 show the contrast between then and now?

4. Why does Caudill use regional words such as "passel" and "holler"? How do these words relate to her use of "mine" in the first sentence?

5. What do you learn from the brief conversation quoted in paragraphs 3 and 4? Would this information be more effective if Caudill had simply given the reason for the change? Is Caudill blaming anybody for the change? What does the question with which the article ends have to do with the short conversation?

6. Write a paragraph or two comparing the way some place you knew as a child looked then and looks now. The change can be for the worse or for the better, but make sure that the details you give show what your attitude toward the change is.

Antiperspirants: How Effective? How Safe?

prevalent: common
impede: make more difficult

[1]   If humans didn't sweat, heat stroke would be as prevalent as the common cold. Sweating is a normal physiological mechanism, one of the prime regulators of normal body temperature. Millions of eccrine glands, distributed over most of the body's surface, deposit perspiration on the skin in response to warm weather or the body heat caused by exercise. As this moisture evaporates, it cools the blood in the capillaries of the skin. Eccrine sweat is virtually odorless; it is more than 99 percent water, less than 1 percent salt and other chemicals.

[2]   As advertisers are fond of reminding people, however, there's also something called "nervous perspiration." Eccrine glands in the armpits, soles, and palms respond to emotional stimuli—anxiety, fear, pain, sexual excitement—as well as to heat. Further, a second type of sweat gland, the apocrine gland, responds *only* to emotional stimuli.

[3]   Apocrine glands differ from eccrine glands in several ways. Apocrine glands don't start to function until adolescence. Rather than being widely and plentifully distributed over the body, apocrine glands are limited to only three areas: the armpits, the genital area, and the area around the nipples. Apocrine sweat, un-like eccrine sweat, is rich in organic material. When metabolized by bacteria normally present on the skin, that organic material decomposes, producing the odor associated with perspiration.

[4]   Odor appears to be the main biological function of the apocrine glands. Many animals, including man's close relatives among the primates, communicate through scent. Some scientists now believe that the odor of apocrine secretions may play a role in human sexual communication. If so, conditions in the human armpit could scarcely be more ideal: The apocrine sweat provides food for the bacteria resident on the skin; the eccrine glands provide a plentiful supply of moisture, which permits bacterial growth; the armpit limits evaporation and offers a warm environment favorable to the growth of bacteria; and the hairs act as wicks for transmitting the odor.

[5]   If the biological function of the apocrine glands is uncertain, their economic role is much better understood. The apocrine glands help support a $750-million-a-year industry devoted to products that *Tickle, Ban,* and *Right Guard* people's armpits *Hour After Hour* so they'll stay *Arrid, Secret,* and *Soft and Dri.*

[6]   Such products fall into two classes—antiperspirants and deodorants—which are not identical. The U.S. Food and Drug Administration classifies antiperspirants as drugs because their active ingredients reduce sweating, and thus affect a function of the body. Deodorants are considered cosmetics. But that's a fine distinction, since deodorants contain not only perfume, to mask the body odor,

Consumer Reports, November 1979, pp. 648–649.

but also antimicrobial chemicals, to inhibit the odor-causing bacteria. There are also products that bill themselves as "antiperspirant deodorants"—they are merely antiperspirants that, like other antiperspirants, also help to reduce odor.

[7]   Today's market offers several types of antiperspirants in a baffling variety of shapes, sizes, aromas, and textures. All of them, however, contain aluminum salts, usually aluminum chlorhydrate, as the active ingredient. Thus, they are more similar than their advertising would make them seem. As Derwyn Phillips, president of the Gillette Co.'s personal care division, remarked: "The wetness-stopping properties in *Dry Idea* aren't any better than competing products. But the consumer thinks it keeps her drier."

[8]   This is not to say that all antiperspirants are equally effective. As part of its review of all over-the-counter drugs, the FDA in 1974 appointed a panel of experts to review the safety and effectiveness of antiperspirants. In its final report, issued in October of last year, the panel found that product type—aerosol, cream, roll-on, lotion, liquid, or stick—can affect the product's ability to reduce perspiration.

[9]   Manufacturers of antiperspirants evaluate how effectively their products reduce moisture by testing them on men and women. One armpit is treated with an antiperspirant, the other with the same formulation minus the active ingredient. An absorbent pad is then placed in each armpit for a specific time. The weights of the pads are later compared. If the pad from the antiperspirant-treated armpit comes out 20 percent lighter than the pad from the other armpit, the product is assumed to have reduced perspiration by 20 percent.

[10]   The FDA panel examined test results submitted by 15 companies for 60 products. Products that use aluminum chlorhydrate as the active ingredient—*Ultra Ban* lotion, *Right Guard Powder Dry* aerosol, *Tickle* roll-on, *Sure Super Dry* aerosol, and *Arrid XX Extra Strength* roll-on, among many others—reduced perspiration by 20 to 46 percent under test conditions.

[11]   The FDA found that test subjects could not tell which armpit had been treated with antiperspirant when perspiration was reduced by less than 20 percent. For that reason, the panel recommends that only antiperspirants proven by tesing to be at least 20 percent effective should be allowed on the market.

[12]   Aerosols were singled out by the panel as the least effective product type, reducing perspiration by only 20 to 33 percent. The panel suggested that certain inactive chemicals used in aerosol containers, such as chemicals added to prevent clogging of the spray nozzle, can impede the effectiveness of the active ingredient.

[13]   The consumer, of course, pays extra for those inactive chemicals, the propellant (about 80 percent by weight of the product), a sturdy can, valve, diptube, and elaborate packaging.

[14]   Lotions were the most effective product type in reducing perspiration. Behind the lotions were the creams, the sticks, and the liquids. Roll-ons were the most variable.

[15]   The modest reduction in perspiration attributed to many antiperspirants would not by itself be sufficient to reduce odor, the panel said. The panel concluded that antiperspirants reduce odor mainly because their metallic salts kill odor-producing bacteria on the skin, not because they reduce perspiration.

[16]   Though aluminum chlorohydrate is the active ingredient most commonly used, a different ingredient works better. The FDA panel found that *Certan-dri,* which contains aluminum *chloride,* was significantly more effective than other over-the-counter products in inhibiting perspiration. But aluminum chloride is more likely to irritate the skin and discolor and corrode fabrics. The panel suggested that products containing aluminum chloride carry this label: "Warning—some users of this product will experience skin irritation."

[17]   Does putting more of the active ingredient in an antiperspirant make that product more effective? Products such as *Arrid XX Extra Strength* roll-on would have you believe the answer is yes. Not so, the panel concluded. A product's formulation—how the active ingredient is combined with the other materials—is apparently the key factor, rather than the amount of active ingredient used. If the FDA accepts the panel's conclusion on this point, extra-strength claims could not appear on antiperspirant labels.

[18]   There is one way that anyone can make an antiperspirant somewhat more effective: Apply it daily, well before its action is needed, perhaps as early as the night before. The panel found that antiperspirants are not effective immediately after being applied to the skin. Some become effective after a few hours, while others require more time and repeated applications to reach their maximum effectiveness.

[19]   Over-the-counter antiperspirants generally offer little help to people with abnormally heavy sweating—a condition known as hyperhidrosis. *Drysol* has been promoted as a treatment for hyperhidrosis of the armpits, palms, or soles. This product, which is available only by prescription, contains a form of aluminum chloride in alcohol. Like other products with aluminum chloride, it can irritate the skin and damage clothing.

[20]   Regular users of aerosol antiperspirants inhale the spray every day over many years. When the panel began studying antiperspirants in 1974, the possible danger from inhaling metallic salts was one of its prime concerns. The panel concluded the following year that inhaling metallic salts of zirconium over a long period may pose a serious threat to consumers, and it urged the FDA to ban those salts from use in aerosol antiperspirants. The recommendation was based on evidence that zirconium compounds can produce granulomas (inflammatory lesions) in the skin of humans and in the lungs of experimental animals. The FDA later adopted the recommendation.

[21]   Now, in its final report, the panel has also questioned the safety of aerosol antiperspirants containing aluminum salts. That would include all aerosol antiperspirants now on the market. The panel asks that manufacturers be required to conduct long-term inhalation tests to examine the hazards of their products' ingredients. The report suggested that pressurized aerosols pose a greater inhalation risk than either finger pumps or squeeze bottles.

[22]   The panel cited animal studies indicating that it may take years for inhaled aluminum chlorohydrate particles to be cleared from the lungs. In two other studies cited, aluminum chlorohydrate in aerosol form caused lung changes in animals. Both studies used heavy doses of aluminum chlorohydrate in a very small particle

size, a size that increased the likelihood the chemical would reach the lungs. The inhalation studies suggested by the panel would more closely approximate exposure in normal human use.

[23]   The panel was much less concerned about nonaerosol antiperspirants. When applied directly to the skin, their metallic salts have virtually no chance of being absorbed or inhaled into the body. Local skin irritation can occur, but such reactions are neither serious nor frequent. *Consumer Report's* medical consultants suggest that if a rash or evidence of irritation appears, you should discontinue use of an antiperspirant immediately. If improvement doesn't occur within a few days, you should consult a physician.

[24]   According to the FDA panel, neither antiperspirants nor deodorants are as important as daily bathing in controlling body odor. If you believe you need something more than cleanliness to be socially acceptable, you might be satisfied with just a deodorant.

[25]   If your main concern is wetness, you probably want an antiperspirant. Most brands reduce perspiration by between 20 and 40 percent under test conditions. That may be enough to keep you from soaking through a shirt or blouse. The antibacterial action of antiperspirants also helps to reduce odor.

Responses

1. How is the information in the introduction helpful to an understanding of the rest of this article? Where does the introductory material end? How can you tell?

2. What is being compared in paragraph 3? Why does the writer make this comparison?

3. Find the transitions used between paragraphs 1 and 2, paragraphs 2 and 3, paragraphs 3 and 4, and paragraphs 4 and 5. How does the transition between paragraphs 4 and 5 call attention to the purpose of the article?

4. What is being compared in paragraphs 7 and 8? in paragraphs 9, 10, and 11? in paragraphs 12, 13, and 14? in paragraph 16? in paragraphs 21, 22, and 23? How are these three different comparisons related?

5. In paragraph 5, the trade names of several products are used as though they were ordinary verbs—there's also one used as an adverb. (You can tell that these are trade names, even if you don't recognize some of them, because they are set in italic print.) What does this sentence tell you about how trade names are chosen?

6. Why does the writer mention the U.S. Food and Drug Administration nine different times? What effect does mentioning the FDA have on your attitude toward these comparisons?

7. Many of the words used in this article are technical. How many of the unfamiliar terms did the writer explain? Which ones were not explained? As you read, did you have to look up some of these technical terms? Do

you see any way that this information could be given in more ordinary language? How and where?

8. Which of the comparisons in this article lead to better understanding of things with which most readers are not familiar? Which comparisons lead to a judgment? In many technical comparisons, judgments lead to recommendations—the intention behind the comparisons in the first place. What recommendations are made in this article? Where do they appear?

9. Imagine that you are the owner or inventor of a new gadget or product not much different from other products already being sold. Write a paragraph in which you identify the kind of product and suggest several names under which it might be marketed.

An Equal-Opportunity Occupation?

mayhem: the act of crippling or damaging another person
invoked: used
mandatory: required
coerced: compelled by force or threats

[1]   Crime is in one sense an equal-opportunity occupation; no one is barred from participation on grounds of race, religion, age, or sex. A woman is as capable as a man of committing murder, manslaughter, mayhem, burglary, larceny, robbery, arson, and so on. It is true that more men commit crimes than women do, and that only about one inmate out of twenty in correctional institutions is female. It is also true that women are more likely to commit embezzlement, forgery, and fraud, rather than more aggressive crimes such as auto theft, burglary, robbery, and assault. Only one out of every six murders is the work of a woman.

[2]   But the rate at which women are being arrested for violent crimes is increasing much faster than it is for men. From 1960 to 1972, arrests for serious crimes rose 81 percent for men and 256 percent for women. Violent crimes committed by boys increased by 203 percent; the rate for girls was an astronomical 388 percent.

[3]   Some observers see a relationship between these statistics and the broader implications of the women's liberation movement, but Dr. Eleanor Emmens Maccoby, Professor of Psychology at Stanford University, the outstanding expert on male-female sex differences, states in her new book, *The Psychology of Sex Differences:*

> Males are more aggressive than females. A sex difference in aggression has been observed in all cultures in which aggressive behavior has been observed. Boys are more aggressive physically and verbally. They engage in mock-fighting and

Shana Alexander, *State-by-State Guide to Women's Legal Rights* (Los Angeles: Wollstonecraft, 1975), pp. 177–179.

aggressive fantasies as well as direct forms of aggression more frequently than girls. The sex difference manifests itself as soon as social play begins, at age two or two and a half. From an early age, the primary victims of male aggression are other males, not females.

Although both sexes become less aggressive with age, boys and men remain more aggressive through the college years. Little information is available for older adults.

[4]   Certain crimes, by their very nature, are difficult for a woman to take an active part in—rape, for example. Yet even here a woman may be charged as a principal in the first degree if she aids a man in his scheme to rape another woman, or if she is voluntarily present while another person is being raped. The penalties for a woman found guilty of this charge can be as severe as they are for the rapist himself.

[5]   The only crime for which more women than men are consistently arrested is prostitution. Some estimates place the female-to-male arrest ratio at forty to one. While prostitution may be engaged in by men with men or by women with women, the crime is almost invariably defined in terms of a male-female relationship. For example, prostitution is variously described in law as: "The practice of a female in offering her body to an indiscriminate intercourse with men for money or its equivalent," "indiscriminate sexual intercourse with males for compensation," and "common lewdness of a woman for gain."

[6]   A prostitute's customers may sometimes be prosecuted for secondary crimes —criminal fornication, lewdness, solicitation, trespassing, or association with a prostitute. But even where such laws exist, courts usually protect the prostitute's patron. Studies indicate that these secondary laws are invoked less to punish the man than to force him to cooperate with the authorities by testifying against the prostitute. Arrest and conviction of men for these crimes is rare, and a much milder sentence is commonly imposed than for prostitution.

[7]   Recent efforts in New York to prosecute the customers of prostitutes proved futile because of the difficulties in gathering evidence, thereby making it impossible to build solid cases against the men. The police in Washington, D.C., began a campaign against the predominantly suburban clientele of urban prostitutes during the summer of 1970, but the resulting clamor by men was so overwhelming that the program was dropped within a month. Though everyone recognizes that without customer demand prostitution would not exist, it seems clear that the prostitution laws—and the discriminatory way in which they are enforced—will not be changed until they are successfully challenged on constitutional grounds.

[8]   But if crime is an equal-opportunity occupation, punishment sometimes is not. More often judges give harsher penalties to men than they do to women who commit the same crime. Yet there are some instances of longer prison sentences being given to women than to men guilty of the same crime. Recent federal court decisions in Connecticut, New Jersey, and Pennsylvania have reversed unequal sentences because they violate the constitutional guarantee of equal protection under the law. When an unequal sentence is imposed, however, it is often due less to a specific law mandating a different penalty for men and women than to the

discretion of the judge who is handing out the sentence. The variations in sentencing may well be within the limits set by law.

[9]   In well over half the states, a wife cannot be found guilty of certain minor crimes if she performs them in her husband's presence or with his knowledge. Here the law assumes that he coerced her and that she is not to be held responsible for her inability to resist his influence. This distinction is a vestige of the old common-law concept of husband and wife as one person, that one person being the husband. Such laws are a prime target for reform. They smack of the same paternalism which underlies "protective" labor laws.

[10]   Utah is the one state that still recognizes another kind of discrimination in the operation of criminal law, which is called the "unwritten law defense." This statute permits a man to kill "in the heat of passion" to prevent "rape or defilement" of a wife, daughter, sister, or mother. It has been interpreted by court decisions to be a valid defense for a husband who kills a man he finds committing adultery with his wife. This defense may not be used, however, by a wife who kills the "other woman" under identical circumstances. Texas and New Mexico have recently repealed similar statutes. This law is now being challenged in California courts in the Inez Garcia rape case.

[11]   In the field of criminal law, discrimination in America is less likely to be sexual than it is racial and economic. Nonetheless, a basic familiarity with our criminal procedures is essential to understanding how our society works.

Responses

1. How does the comment that crime is an equal-opportunity occupation prepare readers for the comparison made in this article? How does the beginning of paragraph 8 relate to the introduction and to the comparison?
2. In this comparison, three general areas are considered: number of criminal arrests, kinds of crimes for which arrests are made, and amount of punishment given. In which paragraphs do you find these areas compared?
3. Alexander obviously believes that men and women should receive equal treatment for equal offenses. Find the sentences which show her belief. Is the main purpose of the article explaining by comparison or persuading? Find the sections of the article that support your decision.
4. Who are the readers of this article expected to be? If you can't tell from the article itself, what does the name of the book from which the article was taken tell you?
5. Write a short paper explaining how "the Southern lady" [page 80] would probably react to paragraphs 8, 9, and 10 of this article; or write a paper explaining how you react to it. Make your paper a comparison between Alexander's attitude and the Southern lady's—or yours.

More Suggestions for Writing

A comparison between:

two books you've read
two movies you've seen
two courses you've taken
mothers and grandmothers
food stamps and cash
two places you've lived
paying cash and using credit cards
traveling by bus and traveling by plane
coffee and tea
two fast-food restaurants
the effects of alcohol and the effects of marijuana
anthropology and sociology
two teachers you've had
two children you know
used cars and new cars
rock and jazz
astrology and astronomy
oil heat and gas heat (or electric)
last year's prices and this year's

Chapter 5

Explaining: Classification

Sometimes you need to explain one term; that's *definition*. Sometimes you need to explain two somewhat similar terms or things; that's *comparison*. And sometimes you need to explain the connection between a number of things that are somehow related to each other; that's *classification*. Classification is a way of grouping things, of sorting out relationships. You are using a classification system whenever you attempt to explain things by sorting them into groups and then sorting each group into smaller groups.

Classifying our experiences is a way of understanding them, of putting into order what has happened to us or what we have learned. Farmers classify crops, ranchers classify cattle, librarians classify books, doctors classify diseases, and lawyers classify crimes. Classification, in fact, is a method commonly used in specialized fields whenever people need to make the work easier and the subject more understandable. But classification is not reserved for specialists. It is a method of explanation anybody can use, and it can be applied to almost anything. In fact, it's impossible to be human and not classify things.

We classify because we want to, because we have a reason. We decide to organize our information for some purpose—to help us clear up what we think. And we can use our classification to explain our view of things to other people—our readers.

What to Classify

Almost any group of things or ideas or people that interests you can be usefully classified. Cars or clothes, jobs or jewelry, furniture, foods, or fads—it doesn't really matter. The method (not the topic) is the important consideration.

Almost any subject can be classified in a number of ways, and the method you choose depends on what your aim is.

For example, students can be classified according to income, size, grade-point average, activities, or even their reasons for coming to college; and that list doesn't begin to cover all the possibilities. Students can be classified as contributors or consumers, as audience or participants, as resources or specimens, and in many, many more ways. The system you choose depends on what you know about students and what you think your readers need to know. If you are writing for a dean who is wondering whether or not to raise the tuition, you can classify students by income and show how many will be unable to come back next term if costs are raised. If you are working for the Scholastic Honors Society, you might classify students by their grades to find out who should be invited to join the society. You can classify students by activities if you're interested in how students spend their time or which activities draw the most students or which students are most involved.

Whatever system you choose, choose it because it will provide the information you need or make something clearer and easier to understand. That's the *why* of classification. The *what,* the subject, will always yield to a wide variety of approaches, but so long as you relate your topic to your purpose and make the classification with care, whatever method of sorting you use will make a point, and you may provide your readers with a fresh way of looking at some part of their lives.

Classifying and Stereotyping

Sometimes we classify physical things—recipes, cars, books; sometimes we classify people; sometimes we classify our experiences. Classifying our experiences is a way of understanding them, of grouping events according to their similarities. Occasionally you hear a very small child call all little animals "kitties." The child has taken a first step in classifying—it's clear that puppies and kittens and squirrels belong in a different group than trees or people. As the child grows older and sees more animals, however, it becomes apparent that although puppies and kittens and squirrels all belong to a big group of small furry creatures, there are enough differences that people call these animals by different names—that is, people put them into different groups. Indeed, if we didn't learn at an early age to classify, it is hard to imagine that our lives would have much order.

In fact, language itself is a giant classification system. If you hadn't learned, even before you started school, which words fit which positions in English sentences, you wouldn't be able to talk at all. It would never occur to you, for instance, to say "A bit dog man the," because you learned very early to classify "dog" and "man" as nouns, and "bit" as a verb, even though you were totally unfamiliar with those technical names for the groups. Language helps us classify in other ways, too. We see things in the physical world as separate objects because we have words to separate those things. In English we can say "That's an orange shirt, those slacks are red" because our language classifies the two colors into different groups. In other languages, where colors may be classified differently, people may regard an orange shirt and red slacks as being the same color, only slightly different in shade, much as we see light blue and dark blue as belonging together in the general group of "blue."

So we classify to bring order to the things we experience, to separate bits out of the whirling chaos surrounding us, to label those bits and to group similar bits. It is a very convenient shortcut for dealing with the outside world. For example, we only have to learn once about telling time. Thereafter, we recognize "clocks" whether they are wristwatches, alarm clocks, digital radio clocks, grandfather clocks, cuckoo clocks, or whatever. And by recognizing each new, unexperienced timekeeper as a "clock," we don't have to begin from scratch but can fit the new thing into the framework of information we already possess. We learn to tell time once, and that once is enough for the rest of our lives, whether we're focusing fuzzily at a bedside alarm or squinting through the fog at the courthouse clock.

Classification is a shortcut to orderly thinking. If we had to figure everything out each time we encountered it, we wouldn't have much time or energy for anything else. It's when we start classifying other human beings that we may run into trouble—we may slide over into stereotyping. *Stereotyping* means putting one label on a person or a group of people and disregarding everything else: "Quincy Monroe is a radical" or "All Irishmen are drunkards." Stereotyping is a special kind of classifying—a faulty kind—and though it, too, works as a shortcut and a timesaver, it is nearly always used to "prove" something unpleasant about other people. There's a difference between calling an animal "kitty" or "puppy" and labeling a person a "fat cat" or a "hippie." People who stereotype generalize about the whole human being from partial evidence. They start with one part of a person —name, hair style, skin color, age, neighborhood, job, or whatever—and forget all about the rest of the person. They call the person "a typical whatever" and don't look any further.

Let's take an example: Richard Arnold is thirty years old, a Black veteran majoring in political science. He lives two and a half miles from the campus with his wife and two-month-old son. He works from 4:00 to 9:00 P.M. as a police officer, and he voted Democratic in the last election.

This very short description shows at least ten different ways of looking at one man, at least ten different classification systems into which he would fit. Whether you classify Mr. Arnold as a husband or a veteran or a working student depends entirely on whether you are interested in finding out about the marital status, the draft status, or the employment status of college students. If you are classifying students according to income, for instance, neither Mr. Arnold's age nor his political beliefs have anything to do with it. Whatever classification system you use will leave out some of the "real Mr. Arnold"; it has to, because the system is set up from a single point of view, for one purpose, and for one time.

When you stereotype, on the other hand, you get hold of one detail and think you have the whole Mr. Arnold. Instead of remembering that there are other systems by which he could be classified, you assume that he can be placed permanently in a single group. When you stereotype, you decide that he's "one of us" or "one of them"—whatever "us" or "them" means at the time. Students who are only eighteen might regard him as "typically middle-aged," and thereby dismiss his character, opinions, accomplishments, and potentials as not worth bothering about. If his superiors are over fifty, though, they may regard Richard Arnold as "a mere kid" and disregard his abilities and suggestions for that reason. Racial bigots, white or Black, will think they know all they need to know simply by noticing his skin color.

Honest classification is a way of thinking about reality; stereotyping is a short circuit that actually prevents thinking. If when you classify people you remember to do so for a particular purpose at that particular time, you will avoid stereotyping. You will say, for example, *"For now, because I'm interested in jobs,* I'll group Richard Arnold with other policemen"; you will not say, "Oh, Richard Arnold. Don't ask him—he's a cop."

Stereotyping is logically flawed, because it leaps to unjustified conclusions from just a tiny bit of evidence. But because it is nearly always harmful to people, it is also immoral.

Sorting Up and Sorting Down

Once you realize that classifying is not the same as stereotyping, that it can enlarge rather than limit your understanding, you can go on to examine the ways classification can work for you. Classification systems can begin with individual things and put them into larger and larger groups. That's what happens when a child picks up a small brown object from the ground and asks, "What's that?" "It's a pecan." "What's a pecan?" "It's a kind of nut." "What are nuts?" "They're the kind of fruit some trees produce," and so on. We can call this "sorting up." Or classification systems can begin with a big group and divide it into smaller and smaller groups, like a woman unpacking her suitcase. She starts with a big batch of clothes and sorts them into piles that could be labeled "underwear," "scarves," "suits," and "shoes." She may then sort the underwear into smaller groups, panties, slips, bras, etc. We can call this process "sorting down."

For example, you might begin with "cats" and explain that they are members of a larger group, "felines," which includes jaguars, lions, and lynxes; mention what characteristics that group shares; and move up once more to put felines into a larger group, "mammals." What you are doing here is much like what you did when you were working with general and specific words. When you sort up, you begin with a specific term and move up to increasingly general terms.

When you sort down, you get more and more specific. You might divide the group, "cats," into smaller groups—pedigreed and common—and then sort down further by dividing pedigreed cats into smaller groups—by country of origin (Siamese, Persian, etc.), by hair length (short, medium, long), by coloring (light to dark, or perhaps solid to patterned), or by size, health, disposition, cost, rarity, or any other way that interests you. When you sort your recipe collection to fit the categories in a new recipe file, you are sorting down: beginning with one big higgledy-piggledy pile and ending with a lot of smaller piles.

Whether you are sorting up or sorting down, stick with one system. To jump back and forth will surely confuse both you and your readers. Either approach will lead to enlightenment; sorting up will more likely put your topic into larger perspective, whereas sorting down will narrow the perspective so you can look at one thing more carefully.

Main Idea Sentences for Classification

All of us classify automatically most of the time, but when we undertake a more formal classification, a main idea sentence will help. When you are writing a classification paper or, more likely, a classification paragraph—something you may often need to do for other college classes—the main idea sentence will show the direction you have chosen. It can't, however, serve as a miniature outline as easily as main idea sentences for definition or comparison papers usually do. In classification, your main idea sentence shows where you will begin but not where you will end. A good main idea sentence will let readers know what is being classified (the topic); what method of explanation you are using (classification); and the point of view you are taking (what the first division is based on).

Here are some main idea sentences for classification papers or paragraphs:

Three kinds of people consult fortunetellers: those who believe, those who are not sure, and those who are just spoofing.
Topic: people who consult fortunetellers
Point of view: degree of belief

In early April, many American taxpayers spend time sorting last year's expenses into those that can be deducted and those that can't, as a preliminary to listing deductible expenses under the six categories the Internal Revenue Service allows.
Topic: personal expenses
Point of view: deductibility

Prehistoric people had tools made of horn, tooth, and bone, each kind used for a specific purpose.
Topic: prehistoric tools
Point of view: material from which made

Commercial advertisements can be classified according to the way they appeal to potential customers.
Topic: advertisements
Point of view: type of appeal

Depending on the amount of training they have had, nurses fall into three general groups—registered nurses, practical nurses, and aides—all with quite different responsibilities.

Topic: nurses
Point of view: amount of training

The Adventures of Huckleberry Finn is sometimes classified as a picaresque novel, even though it has some characteristics of other kinds of fiction.
Topic: Mark Twain's *Huckleberry Finn*
Point of view: kinds of fiction

All these main idea sentences show the direction the classification will take. Because they illustrate a clear point of view they are likely to lead to classifications that help both you and your readers understand the subject better.

It's just as important in classification as in other papers to know who your readers will be and what their needs are. The main idea sentence can guide you here, too. In the first example, the main idea sentence might lead to a single paragraph in a more general essay on fortunetelling; it will appeal to readers who know little about the people who claim to predict the future. The classification of personal expenses will be read by people preparing their income taxes, perhaps for the first time. A classification of prehistoric tools will demonstrate—to a teacher or to anyone eager to learn more about prehistoric peoples—that the writer understands the subject. The classification of advertisements will distinguish between the kinds of appeal and may be intended either for a class in mass communications or for ordinary readers interested in the way clever advertisers try to sell their products. The classification of nurses is probably written for people investigating a career in the health sciences. The last sentence will place the single book *Huckleberry Finn* into at least one larger group. It might answer a test question in a course on the American novel, or it might be a paragraph in a longer paper on the works of Mark Twain.

Planning a Classification Paper—Making a Chart

Just as a main idea sentence will show the direction your classification is going to take, an actual chart of your classification will help to keep it straight in your head as you write. Sometimes such a chart is quite simple:

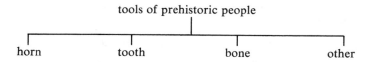

The category "other" has been added, even though it doesn't appear in the main idea sentence, as a kind of insurance against leaving anything out. Although you mean to concentrate on tools made of horn, tooth, and bone, it seems probable that early people did use rocks or stones for some purposes.

A chart placing nurses into groups according to the training they have had will be almost as simple, although you might want to add one more step to the chart:

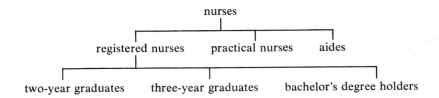

If you are quite sure there are no other kinds of training for nurses, you will not need an "other" category at either step. But you will need to make sure your categories are real divisions and that they don't overlap. If you were making a chart of people who go to fortunetellers, for instance, you could not make a chart that looks like this without getting yourself seriously muddled:

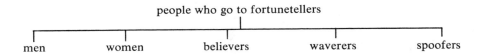

The problem, of course, is that all of the last three categories—believers, waverers, and spoofers—assuming they are human beings, have to be either men or women. If you want to classify Mary Jones, who has gone along for a joke, where do you put her? Under "women" or under "spoofers"? A better chart, one that avoids overlapping, would look like this:

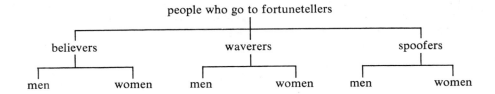

These charts are based on main idea sentences already written; they are suitable for writers who already know the point of view they mean to take. But let's consider for a minute a situation in which you don't yet know the point of view you are going to take, although you do know that your general topic is going to be advertising and you are already sure you are more interested in commercial advertisements than in want ads placed by private citizens. Some of the ways commercial advertisements might be divided are:

Local and national
Illustrated and nonillustrated
Selling goods and selling candidates
Newspaper, radio, and television
Straight and humorous

Obviously, if a system begins with "selling goods and selling candidates," the subdivisions will include different things than would be found in a system beginning with "straight and humorous." The first division you make establishes the system that the rest of the classification will follow. Suppose you decide that your first division will be "straight and humorous." Before you go any further, you will need to work out some satisfactory definitions of these terms. A straight advertisement, you may decide, is one that is completely serious both about the product it advertises and about the consumer it appeals to. A humorous advertisement, on the other hand, tries to sell its product by making you laugh, by irritating you with its nonsense, or by taking some other nonserious approach. Your attempt to define "straight" and "humorous" has led you automatically to the next step in your classification. So far the chart looks like this:

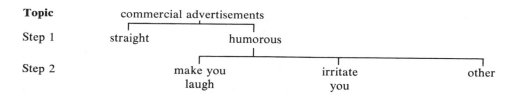

Topic   commercial advertisements

Step 1   straight   humorous

Step 2   make you   irritate   other
          laugh   you

A glance at this chart shows a couple of things. First, you are more concerned with humorous advertisements than with straight ones, since you have already subdivided that group. The next steps, if there are more, will probably further subdivide the "humorous" categories. When you write the paper, an example or two of what is meant by "straight" advertisements should dispose of that part of the topic —for instance, the sensibly dressed, middle-aged lady who tells you with great sincerity that you will look five pounds thinner if you buy her girdle, or the intellectual-looking young man who offers statistical evidence showing that his particular pill cures more headaches than any other variety does.

Second, the chart shows that you don't have to subdivide—you can, for example, leave "straight" just as it is—but if you do subdivide, you must make the categories inclusive. Every time you take another step, the new subdivisions must include everything that was in the original group. Step 2 in the advertisement chart would have been incomplete if it had mentioned only ads that amuse you and those that irritate you, since some ads clearly take a light approach without aiming for either a belly laugh or a groan. If you are doubtful about the number of items, or if you are not sure you have included all members of the previous group, you can create that catchall category, "other," designed to pick up whatever is left over.

Your next task is to decide which category in step 2 interests you most and then to subdivide that category. Suppose that your main interest is in advertisements that really make you laugh. If you ask yourself what you are laughing at, you should be able to isolate the types of ads that appeal through laughter. For example, ads provoke laughter by (1) poking fun at the product; (2) poking fun at the prospective buyer; or (3) poking fun at both of them. When you have supplied examples for these three subdivisions and have described them to your readers, you will have straightened out your own ideas about the various advertisement types and also made clear to your readers the distinctions between each type.

Again, you may get rid of the category that interests you least—ads that irritate you—by giving a quick example. The singing jingles that repeat over and over again the same simple-minded words may seem to you more annoying than funny, even though they are accompanied by cartoon characters doing absurd things. Once you have disposed of that category, you can give examples of advertisements that make you laugh. For ads that make fun of the product, you can include those that tell you how cheap, homely, and serviceable Hush Puppy shoes are, or those that show you a car rental agency delighted at being "No. 2." The ads that show ordinary-looking people hopelessly embarrassed by bad breath or wet armpits are poking fun at the consumer. And the ad showing smokers in ridiculous predicaments because the cigarette they are smoking is too long invites you to laugh both at the product and at the consumer.

Here is how the finished chart will look:

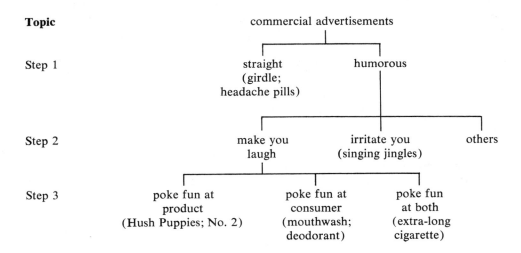

Writing a Classification Paper

When you use a chart as the basis for your writing, you must do more than just turn the chart into sentence form. A good paper requires an introduction that includes your main idea and serves as the usual contract with your reader; a thorough discussion of your main categories; a clear explanation of your examples; and a conclusion that nails down the point of your paper.

Here is an introduction that might do for a paper based on the classification chart for commercial advertisements that has just been worked out:

> On TV, four minutes out of every fifteen are devoted to ads. Radios broadcast ads after every record and on both ends of every station break. On everything except the front page, newspapers run more ads than news. Nevertheless, it is possible to make order out of this confusing assortment by grouping ads by type, noticing how they are related, and seeing that while all ads try to sell something, they go about it by different methods. In fact, all ads can be classified according to the way they appeal to potential consumers. Some of them make a straightforward announcement; others try to sell a product by making you laugh.

This introduction does three important things: it gives a reason for the classification (bringing a kind of order to the confusing array of advertisements); it includes the main idea sentence (". . . all ads can be classified according to the way they appeal to potential consumers."); and it mentions what the first subdivision will include (straight and humorous ads).

Each of the subdivisions important enough to be given an example should probably have a paragraph of its own, and the order of the paragraphs will be determined by the steps of the chart. First, perhaps, would come a paragraph disposing of straight ads; then a paragraph distinguishing among humorous ads and disposing of those that annoy you. The three categories in step 3 undoubtedly deserve a paragraph apiece.

Here is a conclusion that might work for a paper developed according to this plan:

> Straight ads concentrate on the merits of the product, whereas humorous ones, whether they work by irritating you or amusing you, try to get you to remember a brand name. It would seem that quite a bit more imagination goes into humorous ads than goes into straight ones. But whether the ads are straight or humorous, their purpose is the same, to get you to buy the product. When they succeed, and you buy something because it's an advertised brand, it's interesting to understand how the ad has made its appeal.

Classification for Readers

If you have followed your chart carefully and written your paper clearly, your readers should be able to reproduce the chart from which you were working. Good readers often make such charts as they study, either in their minds or actually on paper. Just as classification charts can help you sort out your own thoughts before you write, so "reconstructed" charts can help you sort out the ideas behind other people's writing. For example, a chart of writing purposes as they have been presented in this book would look like this:

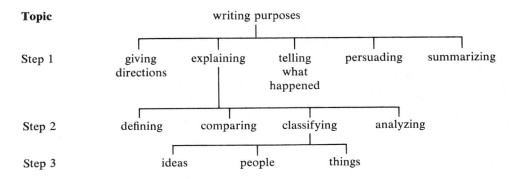

Because at this moment we are especially interested in classification, we did not subdivide all the categories contained in step 1 or all those in step 2. Notice, however, that we did not jump from step 1 to step 3; it would be misleading to go directly from "explaining" to "kinds of people or ideas." Instead, we showed that classifying is one method of explanation and that kinds of people or kinds of ideas are things that can be classified. Although such a chart may be primarily useful in straightening out what you have learned so far in this course, it could also serve as a writing plan if you were answering a test question.

Examining Two Sample Classification Papers

The first paper was written for an examination question in a class on the nature of language. The question was: "Identify and discuss three different meanings of the word 'grammar.'" The student quickly recognized that this question required a paragraph of classification and made a brief chart:

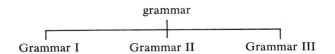

Here is the paragraph that was turned in:

Nelson Francis says that what people understand by "grammar" can be divided into what he calls Grammar I, Grammar II, and Grammar III. Grammar I is the real grammar, Grammar II is talking about it, and Grammar III is correcting it.

When the answer received only half credit, the student was indignant and demanded to know why. The teacher—an unusually generous type who believed that the purpose of tests is to teach—gave some advice and allowed the student to rewrite the paragraph. Here is the student's second, and much improved, attempt:

> Nelson Francis says that what people understand by "grammar" can be divided into what he calls Grammar I, Grammar II, and Grammar III. Grammar I means the way a language actually operates. That knowledge was built into us when we learned to talk, and that knowledge lets us understand sentences we've never heard before. It's the thing that tells us the difference, in English, between "John ate the pig," and "The pig ate John," even though the words in both sentences are the same. Grammar II means analyzing how Grammar I works. It's what we do when we learn about subjects and predicates, or about what a verb is. Grammar III really means conventional usage. That's the kind people mean when they say, "If you're an English teacher, I'll have to watch my grammar." It's also the kind parents mean when they tell their kids not to say "ain't."

Notice that the main idea sentence, which was clear and accurate in the first attempt, has been kept; everything else has been expanded upon. The three meanings of "grammar" have been made understandable to readers not familiar with Francis's divisions, and more important, the writer has provided examples. In other words, the paragraph has been *developed*. Most people, when they ask for a paragraph, expect more than a main idea sentence and one other simple statement.

The second paper, which was written as an essay assignment, was probably intended as much for other members of the class as for the teacher:

Classifying Me

[1]   When you turn sixty-five, you learn about classification systems. Four years ago, I found myself in a room surrounded by friends from work, drinking coffee and eating a cake that said, "Congratulations Fred." The occasion was my forced retirement. I had suddenly become a "senior citizen," and I sure wish I'd had this class before I went to that party. It would have helped me to make the shift from "seniority"—which meant I had spent plenty of time learning a job and becoming valuable—to "senior citizen"—which meant "on the street, ya bum!"

[2]   Now, of course, I know that I was *me* back then, no matter what the words said. But back then it was quite a blow. I guess you could classify my whole time as a worker, if you wanted to. I began as a "beginner," then moved up to "assistant," then became "senior." At each step, the categories felt just fine, and I knew I was progressing. But when I was forced to retire just because I had had one birthday too many, I didn't like my classification at all.

[3]   What to do? Get reclassified, don'tcha know! So I reclassified myself, first by going back to school, as a "student," which means young and full of beans and learning about stuff—and I like that category. And I'm also self-

employed. That nasty cake I got at the retirement party—yuk! I knew I could bake better, and now I do. I sell cakes and pies to three restaurants—when I feel like it, which is most days. My desserts are so good that the restaurants are glad to get them when they can. And the customers understand that sometimes they can eat my cooking and sometimes they can't. And so they come back to the restaurant to find out, and it's exciting for them and good business for the restaurants. If I've got a test to study for, I don't bake. But I'm careful to bake *most* of the time so I keep classified as a good baker *and* a reliable businessman.

[4]   Pepperidge Farm I'm not, but who knows where I'll be ten years from now? After all, as a "student" I'm also a "man with a future."

[5]   I guess I'm bragging a little bit, but I'm really proud of myself. I think I've got something to say: don't get classified unless it's on your own terms! And don't settle for less than you can be. That's it for now.

If you look for a main idea sentence in the first paragraph, you will not find it. Nevertheless, the student who wrote this paper did have a clear main idea sentence in his head, and if you look back at the first paragraph, you can make a fairly good guess at what it was. By the time you have read the whole theme, you should be able to work it out yourself: *People can be classified into two main divisions: those who work and those who are retired.*

Although the writer has not stated his main idea, he has used his introduction to gain interest. Starting with the retirement gives the theme a certain dramatic flair, certainly much livelier than simply telling what the system is. But despite the personalized beginning, this introduction does serve as a contract. The introduction makes it clear enough that the paper will deal with the categories of "worker" and "senior citizen." If the rest of the paper did not classify, readers would feel cheated. But it does, and the readers don't.

The dramatic beginning implies another promise, too. Readers expect to be told a story, and they are told one. In other words, the writer has blended telling what happened with explaining, but he never lets his eagerness to tell a story interfere with his main purpose—classifying his life. And although he maintains the same tone throughout, he cheerfully emphasizes what he has learned: that instead of being victims, we can all reclassify ourselves. When the writer says at the end of the second paragraph "I didn't like my classification at all," he's really saying "I resented being stereotyped as a retired person." There's another reference to stereotyping in the last paragraph: "don't get classified unless it's on your own terms!" Emphasizing this point is what makes the paper sound finished. The last sentence—"That's it for now"—is not a clumsy way of telling readers the paper is finished; it's a way of telling them again that the writer's life is *not* finished.

Pretty obviously, the student who wrote this paper had a good time doing it. But he also accomplished his main purpose. The classifications he makes for various stages of his life are sensible enough, and as he wrote the paper, the examples followed the order of the subdivisions. The theme is lively and informal, and it succeeds in following the assignment clearly and well. It is easy to make a classification chart showing the system that was followed. Notice that the writer took only one step at a time, and that each subdivision includes all the members of the group it subdivides:

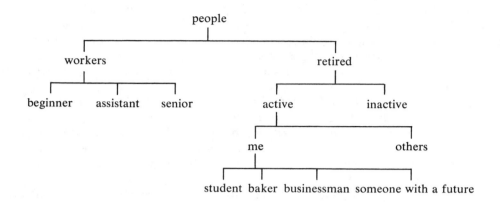

Key Words

Here are some of the important terms used in this chapter. See whether you can answer these questions about them.

1. How does **classification** differ from definition or comparison?
2. Once you have decided on a topic, how should you decide which **classification system** to use?
3. What is the difference between **classifying** and **stereotyping?**
4. What is the difference between **sorting up** and **sorting down?** What are the advantages of each?
5. What should the **main idea sentence** for a **classification** paper contain?
6. If the **main idea sentence** cannot serve as a model outline, what does it show about what the rest of the paper will do?
7. Explain why the category **"other"** is used in **classification charts.**
8. What is meant by **overlapping categories?** Why should they be avoided?
9. How can **readers** use **classification charts?**

READINGS

Classification

Whales

latitude: geographical distance north or south from the equator
untenanted: not lived in
quarry: prey; thing being hunted
writhing: twisting violently and painfully

Main idea sentence

Eventually the whales, as though to divide the sea's food resources among them, became separated into three groups: the plankton-eaters, the fish-eaters, and the squid-eaters. The plankton-eating whales can

Information about first group

exist only where there are dense masses of small shrimp or copepods to supply their enormous food requirements. This limits them, except for scattered areas, to arctic and antarctic waters and the high temperate lati-

Information about second group

tudes. Fish-eating whales may find food over a somewhat wider range of ocean, but they are restricted to places where there are enormous populations of schooling fish. The blue water of the tropics and of the open ocean basins offers little to either of these groups. But

Information about third group

that immense, square-headed, formidably toothed whale known as the cachalot or sperm whale discovered long ago what men have known for only a short time—that hundreds of fathoms below the almost untenanted surface waters of these regions there is an abundant animal life. The sperm whale has taken these deep waters for his hunting grounds; his quarry is the deep-water population of squids, including the giant squid Architeuthis, which lives at depths of 1500 feet or more. The

Rachel L. Carson, *The Sea Around Us* (New York: Oxford University Press, 1961), pp. 44–45.

head of the sperm whale is often marked with long stripes, which consist of a great number of circular scars made by the suckers of the squid. From this evidence we can imagine the battles that go on, in the darkness of the deep water, between these two huge creatures—the sperm whale with its 70-ton bulk, the squid with a body as long as 30 feet, and writhing, grasping arms extending the total length of the animal to perhaps 50 feet.

Responses

1. How is the classification developed? That is, what additional information are you given about plankton eaters? about fish eaters? about squid eaters?
2. Can you write a synonym definition of plankton from what Carson says in the first part of this paragraph? What would it be? Compare your definition with the definition given in your dictionary. Which is easier to understand?
3. What does the "But" with which the sixth sentence begins tell you about Carson's main interest in this classification? Does the amount of space Carson gives to each group tell you which is the most important to her? How?
4. From the information Carson gives, can you make a chart classifying whales according to appearance? according to the battles they engage in? according to the part of the ocean they live in? Choose one of these different points of view and make a one-step classification system.

When Do You Need Tires?

carcass: framework or body

[1]   Since 1968, all tires have come equipped with tire wear indicators. When your tread becomes dangerously low, you'll see a series of bars that are worn smooth across the tread. In many states, it's illegal to drive on tires with less than $\frac{1}{16}$ inch of tread. You can measure this easily yourself. Take a penny and put it in the tread. The distance between the edge of the penny and Lincoln's head is $\frac{1}{16}$ inch. If the top of his head shows, you need to replace the tire. The tire industry

Richard George, *The New Consumer Survival Kit* (Boston: Little, Brown, 1978).

estimates that 90 percent of all tire problems occur after the tread is worn down to less than $\frac{1}{16}$ inch.

[2]   The *beads* of a tire are the edges of the hole, the part of the tire that attaches to the wheel rim. The tread is the part that touches the road, and the carcass of the tire is everything else. The *centerline* is an imaginary line around the tire in the middle of the tread.

[3]   There are three basic tire types: In *bias-ply,* the body plies running from bead to bead intersect the centerline at about a 35-degree angle. *Bias-belted* is the same as bias-ply, with the addition of a reinforcing belt, usually made of steel or fiberglass, under the tread. In *radials,* the body plies intersect the centerline at a 90-degree angle. Radials also usually have a belt under the tread, like the belted bias.

[4]   The body plies themselves can be made of either rayon, polyester, or nylon. They all perform well. Nylon, however, has a tendency to develop flat spots in cold weather. When you first drive the car on a cold morning, the tires will "thump" for the first mile or so until they warm up, a minor inconvenience.

[5]   Choosing tires is largely a matter of personal driving habits and budget. The least expensive are good, old-fashioned bias-ply. However, the tread life of bias-plies is usually less than the other two types and they are not as strong. Bias-belted tires offer more strength and tread life, at a higher price, to be sure.

[6]   Radials cost the most, but they also last the longest. A good set of radials, properly maintained, can last 40,000 to 60,000 miles. And although they may cost more to buy, when the extra mileage is considered, they end up being a sound investment. If you intend to keep your car for another 40,000 miles, radials will be your best investment in the long run. Radials have been shown to have better rupture resistance, cornering ability, and tread wear than the other two types.

[7]   *Never* mix tire types on the same axle. The handling problems that result pose a substantial danger. For the most part, radials should not be mixed with other tire types on the same vehicle, although in some cases it may be all right to have radials on the rear wheels, and another type on the front. Consult your car's owner's manual.

Responses

1.   The method of explanation used in this article is classification, but the writer is using the classification for another purpose. What is it? How can you tell?
2.   For what group of readers was this article written—tire salespersons, garage mechanics, experienced drivers, new car owners, or some other group? Why does the writer begin paragraph 2 with four quick definitions?
3.   From which of these points of view is the classification made: cost? type of construction? material from which the tires are made? length of service? On the basis of the information given in the article, from which other points of view could the tires be classified?
4.   Pick some other product on the market—shoes, record-players, soaps,

soups, writing implements, milk, whatever—and suggest two different points of view from which the product could be classified. Then choose one point of view and write a short paragraph of classification. As you write, make your categories clear enough that other students could make a classification chart from what you have written.

Bank Accounts: Which Kind Will Serve You Best?

[1]   As banks become more and more competitive, it gets more and more difficult to understand how to deposit your money. In the simple old days you had two choices: a checking account or a savings account. Today when you open a new account with a bank, saying "savings" or "checking" is just the beginning.

[2]   There is still the regular old-fashioned checking account, where the customer usually pays a regular fee, either by the month or by the check, for the privilege of writing checks to pay the bills. However, there are a wide variety of "automatic" checking accounts, too. You can get an account that automatically pays some of your bills: utilities, telephone, insurance, certain credit cards. You can get one that automatically transfers money from your checking account to your savings account. You can even get one that automatically dips money out of your savings account in case you've written an overdraft.

[3]   In savings accounts the mystery deepens. Of course there is the regular savings account, very much like the one you had as a child. You expect to put in smallish amounts from time to time and to accumulate a reasonable amount of interest. These regular accounts are just a way of saving money, like the Model T was just a way of getting around—plain, simple, and serviceable.

[4]   Now, however, there are also special purpose accounts. Want to save up for Christmas? Open a special Christmas account. Planning to go to Disneyland next summer? Then by all means open a special vacation account. These are similar to the old-fashioned "regular" account, with small amounts regularly deposited (or automatically taken out of your checking account), except they are earmarked for a specific purpose, and they are savings intended to be spent when December or August rolls around.

[5]   Finally, there are the limited-access, long-term savings accounts. To attract big investors, the bank offers especially high interest for deposits that will stay in the bank for a definite period of time and that cannot be taken out until that time is up—as short a time as thirty days, or as long a time as five or ten years. The interest is greater the longer the depositor agrees to leave the money with the bank. These savings accounts are called "certificates of deposit," and you have to put in a fairly large amount of money each time—usually starting at $500. Recently most banks have started selling money market certificates, which require an even larger

Based on advertising brochures from several banks.

deposit—$10,000—but the money has to stay on deposit only six months and the interest rate is very high, sometimes more than double what a "regular" savings account earns.

[6] Banking is more complicated than it used to be, but if you are willing to uncloud the mysteries, you are sure to find a winning combination that exactly fits your own needs and plans. Once you are familiar with the various kinds of bank accounts, both checking and savings, you can make a wise decision.

Responses

1. Here is the classification chart on which this paper is based:

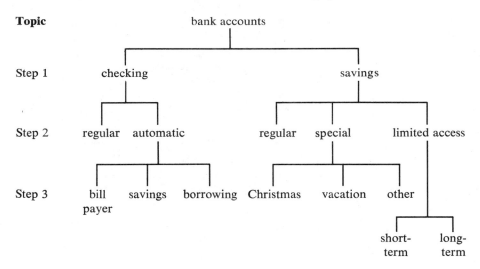

Using the chart as a guide, look back through the article to see where each item is mentioned. For which items does the writer provide additional information? Which items are just listed? Would an ordinary reader need additional information about the listed items? What kind of information would be needed?

2. Part of this article works by comparison. What two things are being compared? For what is the comparison being used? Support what you say by referring to the article.

3. Who are the readers of this article expected to be? How can you tell?

4. What kind of new bank account is not mentioned in this article? Where would you place it in the classification chart? Why? Write a short paragraph explaining how this kind of account works.

Who Is in the Criminal Class?

manipulate: use for personal gain
infractions: the breaking of rules
discretionary: left to one's own judgment
ironic: pertaining to the contrast between what is and what is expected or
    ought to be

[1]   Fresh thinking about our prison system is needed, and it is needed badly. We need to break with the past. For one thing, we can stop placing blame for the immense problems of our society on a "criminal class." Who is in that class, anyway?

[2]   I know there is a large group of people who are imprisoned unjustly and punished unfairly. They are held in jail long periods of time awaiting trial. Or they are people who are being punished for punishing themselves.

[3]   There is a second group of people—the vast majority—who do not get punished because of an ability to manipulate the system or avoid detection. The discretion of the law protects the majority of middle-class people. They break laws—fornication, adultery, traffic, liquor, drug laws, business infractions, tax evasions—crimes other people are serving time for. Studies have told us that the average urban resident commits eighteen felonies a year, each punishable theoretically by a year or more imprisonment.

[4]   There is a third group of people—some of them fall into the first category—to whom prison is an essentially normal part of culture. These are people unprotected by the discretionary power of the law. They serve as "examples" for the rest of us. Many of this group give lip service to such concepts as rehabilitation and getting out of the system—but essentially lack the tools or the motivation to do so. Some of this group resist all attempts to make them do what they say they want to do. They do not want to give up drugs or the minor moneymaking systems of survival that involve hustling and stealing and living fast and dangerously. They do not want to give up the life. They demonstrate this by not giving it up—no matter how much punishment they suffer as a result.

[5]   It is an ironic cycle: society has an exaggerated fear of crime because of the minority of truly violent experiences, and they lock a minority of lawbreakers away to help them feel safer. . . . The cycle must be broken if any of us are ever to go forward.

Responses

   1.   Does the introduction give a reason for this classification? What is it?

Adapted from Katheryn Watterson Burkhart, *Women in Prison* (Garden City, N.Y.: Doubleday, 1973).

2. Do any of the categories in this classification overlap? If you think they do, which ones are they and where is the overlapping? Does the overlapping help or hinder the argument? How?

3. Notice that the author includes the element of guilt in her first two classifications. The first classification deals with persons who are punished even though they are not guilty; the second deals with persons who are not punished even though they are guilty. Yet in her third group she does not emphasize guilt. She refers to this group as those "to whom prison is an essentially normal part of culture." What is she attempting to do in this third group?

4. Paragraph 5 tells you what the main purpose of the paper is. What is it? How does that main purpose relate to the classification?

5. The essay does not tell us what kinds of "crimes" have been committed by "people who are being punished for punishing themselves." In a short paragraph, give some examples of the things people do that involve "punishing themselves." You may want to classify the kinds of "crimes" that fit under this category.

Cheese

phenomenon: an observable fact or occurrence
facilitated: helped; made easier
pasteurization: heating milk to a high temperature to destroy some micro-organisms and prevent the milk from fermenting
accelerate: speed up
unadulterated: with nothing extra or foreign added
emulsifier: something that suspends one liquid in another
enhanced: made better or more attractive

[1]   Cheese is a man-made food phenomenon stemming from a highly developed art form centuries old. Cheese-making is basically a process of separating the milk solids (the curd) from the liquid portion (the whey), facilitated by the action of the enzyme rennin and/or lactic acid bacteria. The characteristic flavor and body are produced by varying the milk source (cow, goat, sheep), by the addition of salt and other added seasonings, by using different molds and bacteria for ripening the cheese, and by changing the time, temperature, and ripening climate. The result is hundreds of different tastes, textures, and varieties of cheese.

[2]   The bacteria added to milk during cheese production are lactic acid bacteria; these are the same bacteria that bring about the normal souring of milk. Because

Adapted from Nikki and David Goldbeck, *The Supermarket Handbook* (New York: New American Library, Signet, 1976), pp. 26–29.

the required pasteurization has destroyed this bacteria there is no choice but to put this "starter" back. The rennin used to accelerate the liquid-solid separation is a natural enzyme obtained from the stomach of young calves. Because these constituents of cheese—the milk, the rennin, and the bacteria—are real, as opposed to manufactured, ingredients, cheese is included in the classification of whole or natural foods. Not all cheese, however, is unadulterated.

[3]   The composition of cheese is regulated by a government standard of identity which specifies the ingredients that may be used, the maximum moisture content and minimum fat content, and sets requirements for pasteurizing or holding the milk to remove the chance of harmful bacterial growth. Many chemical additives are also permitted in this government standard, with some exempt from labeling; we will delve into them shortly.

[4]   Since there are so many possibilities when it comes to cheese buying, we'd best first evaluate the different cheese-making processes to eliminate those not fit for a whole foods kitchen. The labels of all cheeses, with the exception of natural cheese, will indicate by which process they were made.

[5]   "Natural" refers to a cheese made directly from the milk solids (and sometimes the whey) by separating the curds and whey, heating, stirring, and pressing the solids until the desired cheese characteristic is obtained. The milk itself may come from a cow, a goat, or a sheep, and is usually whole milk, although certain cheeses include skim milk, cream, and whey. Salt is added to almost every cheese. In this country, unfortunately, certain unnatural steps may enter the process, like the addition of calcium salts and acidifying agents along with the bacteria, rennet, or clotting enzymes, the use of artificial coloring agents, and the use of potassium or sodium sorbate as preservative. Where preservatives are used, the law requires a statement on the label, but as to other chemical intervention, it is most often in the form of hidden (unlabeled) ingredients. . . .

[6]   Those cheeses that are not "natural" are known as "process" cheeses and must be so labeled. During the "processing" they are heated to halt ripening and keep the flavor and texture constant. An assortment of emulsifiers and stabilizers are added to guarantee their consistency. Their supposed advantage over natural cheese is that they melt and spread easily and smoothly and are thus considered more convenient. The flavor, however, never approaches the richness of natural cheese, the controlled texture is dull, and a large part of the price goes toward the purchase of chemicals.

[7]   Processed cheese is always described with the adjectives "pasteurized process" on the label (although you might have to read the fine print to locate it). It is made by grinding and blending one or more natural cheeses, which are then heated and mixed with water and emulsifier, which may be any combination of thirteen different chemicals not appearing on the label, and some optional acids, artificial coloring, and flavoring ingredients in an effort to create a smooth, homogeneous, "plastic" mass. Some of the more popular forms of pasteurized processed cheese are American cheese (from Cheddar or colby), pasteurized process Swiss, sweet munchee, and brick. Unlike natural cheese, which continues to develop flavor with age, the flavor of a pasteurized process cheese is controlled. These cheeses

are often enhanced with bits of fruit, vegetables, or meat. Most varieties are packed with preservatives but listing is mandatory on the label.

[8]   Blended cheese is made by combining one or more natural cheeses and differs from the pasteurized process cheese in that cream cheese or Neufchatel cheese may be included. Blended cheeses usually contain added bits of fruits, vegetables, or meat. Added coloring must be stated on the label, but many other chemicals used in these spreadable cheeses do not have to be given. Do not despair. Your own cheese blends cost less and have a much more lively taste.

[9]   Process cheese food is almost the same as pasteurized process cheese except that it contains less cheese, with a dairy product (milk, nonfat dry milk, cream, or whey) plus water used as a replacement. The resulting cheese has a lower fat content and more moisture. It is mild in flavor, melts easily, and is chock full of chemicals. The only advantage of the process cheese food over the process cheese is that all the optional ingredients (color, salt, acidifying agents, flavoring, preservatives) must appear on the label; don't waste your time reading it.

[10]   Pasteurized process cheese spread is just another version of the pasteurized process cheese, only this time the moisture content is even higher in order to produce a food that is spreadable at 70°F (as specified in the government standard). This necessitates yet another chemical, a stabilizer, to prevent the separation of the ingredients. This item is usually packaged in pairs or loaves and often has added pimientos, fruits, vegetables, or meat. *Velveeta* and *Cheese Whiz* are among those commonly known. All ingredients are listed on the label and there are always a number of undesirable ones.

[11]   The only difference between cold-pack (club or comminuted) cheeses and the pasteurized process cheeses is the absence of heat in the processing; the chemicals remain the same, and sweetening agents like sugar or corn syrup may be added. Leave them on the shelf along with the pasteurized process variations. You can identify them by the term "cold-pack, club, or comminuted" on the label. In the case of cold-pack American, the word "American" may appear alone on the label, but the undesirable processing is still there. There is no such thing as natural American cheese, so don't be deceived by the lack of descriptive adjectives here.

[12]   Smoke from hardwood sawdust is used to impart a "smoked flavor" to many cheeses. Compounds known as hydrocarbons enter the picture here, and since hydrocarbons have been inconclusively investigated in connection with cancer, we suggest selecting unsmoked varieties. The label will always indicate when a cheese has been "smoked."

[13]   Choosing process cheese: don't!

Responses

1. In paragraph 1, you are given one quick classification of cheese, according to milk source. Why don't the writers give more information about this classification? Where is this classification referred to again? What other

point of view is suggested for classifying cheese according to what it is made from?

2. Paragraph 2 gives another brief one-step classification. What is it? How many things are included in this division? What are they?

3. Who are the readers of this article expected to be? Where are you first given a hint as to who the readers are?

4. What definitions do the writers of this article give? Do you think ordinary readers would need these definitions? Why or why not? Are any very technical terms—terms that are likely to be unfamiliar to ordinary readers—not defined? What are they?

5. Although the writers spend most of the article in classifying cheese, the classification is being used for another writing purpose. What is it? How does the conclusion relate to that other purpose? Find other sentences in the article that are connected to the other purpose.

6. The writers' main interest is in classifying cheeses according to how they are made. Make a two-step chart showing this classification, with two divisions in the first step. Which part of the first step is subdivided? How many kinds of cheese are included in the subdivision? How did the paragraph divisions help you to decide?

7. Make a classification chart showing some other supermarket product; breakfast cereals or packaged milk are two possibilities, but there are lots of others. Then write a paragraph or two of explanation based on your chart.

Natural Disasters

solace: comfort
puny: small and weak
aesthetically: artistically or beautifully
unmitigated: without any qualification; absolute
incapacitator: something that makes something else unable to function

[1]   The weather satellite 22,300 miles out in space reveals a beautiful but deceptive picture of earth. The view we see is of a placid world floating peacefully in the blackness of space, patterns of white clouds winding like ornaments across the planet's disk. But we know how misleading that serene scene can be. Within those clouds, within the rest of the atmosphere so invisible, and beneath the surface of what we think of as a solid planet, lurk awesome energies that need only the proper conditions to unleash their havoc.

Kendrick Frazier, *The Violent Face of Nature* (New York: William Morrow, 1979), pp. 13–18.

[2]   The wait need not be long. At any given moment, 1,800 thunderstorms are in progress over the earth's surface. Lightning is striking the earth 100 times each second. If the season is late summer, one or more of the some 50 hurricanes or typhoons that swirl into existence each year is likely to be moving toward a populated coastline. If the time is late afternoon, the odds are good that a tornado is raking across the American heartland; 600 to 1,000 times a year they do so, and in the prime months they can strike with a frequency of four or more a day. Somewhere at any given moment people's homes or crops are under flood waters. Half a billion people live on floodplains, and the crops grown on floodplains supply food for a third of the world's population.

[3]   There's no solace beneath the reach of the turbulent atmosphere either. More than 2,000 earth tremors strong enough to be recorded course through the planet every day. Twice a day somewhere in the world earthquakes strike with enough force to damage homes and buildings. From 15 to 20 times a year a quake strikes with enough energy to cause widespread death and destruction. And all the while there are 516 active volcanoes waiting to spring loose their violence. An eruption begins somewhere every 15 days.

[4]   There is no way to switch off the energy that continually feeds such violence. Storms derive their energy from the life-giving flow of heat from the sun. Earthquakes and volcanoes get their energy from the heat of radioactive decay of the material within the earth itself. This slow but unending release of heat from the interior to the earth's surface amounts to 10 times all the energy used by man. Even then, it is equivalent to only one five-thousandth the energy that the sun delivers to our planet.

[5]   Clearly we're talking about forces of nature that dwarf the puny efforts of humankind. A single thunderstorm three miles in diameter may hold half a million tons of water and contain energy equal to 10 atomic bombs the size that devastated Hiroshima and Nagasaki. Larger ones carry the potential energy of several one-megaton hydrogen bombs. Such comparisons are unsatisfactory both technically and aesthetically, but a single great earthquake of the size that occurs about four times each year releases the energy of a 10-megaton hydrogen bomb, or nearly twice the daily U.S. consumption of electrical energy. A large volcanic eruption produces almost exactly the same amount. . . .

[6]   In one important sense there is no such thing as a natural disaster. A disaster is a social phenomenon. Across our planet for about four and a half billions of years, the forces of nature have shaped, molded, and changed the earth. Oceans have come and gone, continents have assembled and split apart, mountains have grown and eroded. Awesome changes indeed. But what we call a disaster requires the presence of humans, caught up as victims in the violence of nature. A huge volcanic eruption on an uninhabited ocean island may not be a disaster at all. But even a small earthquake beneath a densely populated urban area can be an unmitigated tragedy. A hurricane that sweeps over a coastal fishing village where the storm-wizened residents have taken all possible precautions may cause some destruction. But if the same hurricane strikes a fast-growing Sun Belt coastal city where the residents are unfamiliar with such storms and ignore the warnings to evacuate, the death toll as well as the property damage could be catastrophic. A

once-a-generation flood of a major river could have little ill effect if humans have respected that potential. But when people build their homes and communities on a floodplain, the flood that undoubtedly will come is a disaster. Since populations nearly everywhere are on the rise and people are occupying vulnerable areas to a greater extent, the potential for most kinds of disasters is on a steady increase.

[7]   The decade of the 1970s has been plagued by extraordinary natural disasters. The second most devastating earthquake in recorded world history struck in 1976 in China, killing an estimated 700,000 persons. The greatest tornado outbreak in recorded history occurred in 1974 when 148 separate tornadoes in a two-day period ripped across the eastern third of the United States, killing 315 persons, injuring 6,142, and causing $600 million in property damage in 10 states. The Bangladesh storm of 1970 that left 300,000 dead may have been the deadliest tropical cyclone (hurricane) in history. The United States' worst disaster in amount of damage ($4 billion) was the widespread flooding from the rains of Hurricane Agnes in 1972. A series of sudden flood disasters throughout the 1970s made flash floods the nation's number one weather-related killer. Unlike the great pestilences of the past, natural disasters are a phenomenon very much of the present, and certainly of the future. In most instances, their capability for destruction increases as the world becomes more highly developed, heavily populated, and interdependent.

[8]   Millions of persons in the United States alone—in fact, more than half the population—live in places that are highly susceptible to natural disasters. But no matter where you live, you are not safe from disaster's reach. Tornadoes have occurred in every state in the union, including Alaska. The devastating effects of hurricanes can extend far inland—Agnes is an example of that. The most pro-longed and violent series of earthquakes ever to hit the United States occurred not along California's San Andreas fault as we might suppose but in Missouri, 2,000 miles from the continent's main earthquake belt. Surprisingly, the worst and most consistent killer of all natural phenomena over the long range in this country is not, as we might think, tornadoes, hurricanes, floods or earthquakes, but lightning, which strikes at random and seldom receives the . . . national publicity accorded the more mass-destructive hazards. And lightning can strike anywhere. Lightning is not only a solo killer, it is a technological incapacitator. It is capable of knocking out computer systems our society has grown dependent upon or electrical power systems that we can go without even temporarily only at the risk of great social chaos—the lightning-initiated New York City power blackout in 1977, for ex-ample. . . .

[9]   Violent and destructive as they often may be, the extreme events of nature are not unmitigated evils. The hurricanes, typhoons, and tropical cyclones that can visit so much misery on the lands they touch also bring a large percentage of the needed life-nourishing rains to many regions of the world. An afternoon thunder-storm can bring damaging winds and devastating hail; more often it brings welcome and necessary moisture. Volcanoes can kill and destroy; they are also responsible for the existence of most of the oceanic islands of the world. Furthermore, they are the conduits through which escaped outward from the planet's interior the waters and gases that form today's oceans and atmosphere and thus can be said to be responsible for the development of life on earth. No small contribution.

Responses

1. In his introductory paragraph, Frazier divides the "awesome energies" into two groups—the first step in the classification. What are the two groups?
2. Which group is dealt with in paragraph 2? How many subdivisions are mentioned, and what are they? Which group is dealt with in paragraph 3? How many subdivisions are mentioned, and what are they?
3. Paragraph 6 is a definition paragraph. What is being defined? Write a class definition in your own words, using the information Frazier gives in this paragraph.
4. In paragraphs 7 and 8, Frazier gives a number of examples of natural disasters. Compare these examples with the list of "awesome energies" given in paragraphs 2 and 3. Is there a one-to-one correspondence? Is the order the same? If your answer to either of these questions is no, how can you explain what Frazier is doing here?
5. The transitions Frazier uses in this article seem so natural that many readers will not notice them at all. Pick any three adjoining paragraphs and trace how Frazier gets from one paragraph to the next.
6. How does paragraph 9 make this article sound finished? Do you consider the final "sentence" acceptable? Why or why not?
7. If you have had any experience with one of the "awesome energies" described here, write a short paper about it. In the paper make clear whether or not your experience would qualify as a natural disaster.

Taking It to the Streets

fiberists: people who work with thread, yarn, etc.
multiples: many copies of the same item
prestigious: having a high reputation

[1]   Traditional craft marketing techniques such as craft fairs will probably always be available for the fiberists who want to produce in multiples. But there are many other markets that are virtually untapped and a great resource. Before you jump off, contact a store, and get orders, one of the first things to do is to make sure that you are willing and able to produce in multiples and to fulfill your commitments. I've seen many, many craftspeople who have a difficult time surviving, not because they didn't have a market, but because they couldn't produce enough to

Noel Clark, "Taking It to the Streets," *Fiberarts*, September–October 1978, pp. 26–28.

meet a market demand. If you are a weaver, the concept of using a flying shuttle and other power assisted equipment to produce in larger volume should be something worth considering. . . .

[2]   Some of the best markets for selling are through your studio, craft shops, boutiques, gift shops, department stores, mail order catalogs, craft galleries (which in some cases are featuring wearable fiber), a sales representative, or selling at craft fairs.

[3]   Craft fairs are probably the most obvious market and a place where many fiberists do sell a good deal of their work. One of the important considerations, particularly if you are creating wearable fiber, is the time of year of the fair and the weather conditions. It is difficult to sell warm-colored wool ponchos and pillows if the temperature is 100 degrees outside. Most of the fiber people who do fairs find that one in the fall works best for selling ponchos because the weather is cool and people are thinking about warm garments. If you are doing a fair in the spring, or summer, consider lighter colors and more airy-type designs. . . .

[4]   People are interested in you at a craft fair. They're interested in your lifestyle, how your pieces are made, and technical things like where the fiber came from. You might provide a little biographical sketch so they can talk about the piece they bought and also talk about you, the person who made it. This is one of the advantages the public finds in coming to a craft fair—meeting the manufacturer.

[5]   Selling out of your studio can also be profitable, particularly for the craftsperson who is not working full-time or who has a limited supply of work to sell. An opening at the proper time of year (possibly spring or fall) and a show before Christmas might be enough to keep you working all year. You'll need to develop a mailing list, and a craft fair is a good place to do that. Send out invitations. If you are doing wearables, you might produce a small fashion show. Share the show with a friend who's a jeweler and whose work can complement yours. When selling out of your studio have someone else handle the money. It will be much more pleasant for you and more like a party if you don't have to be involved in taking the money from friends and acquaintances.

[6]   The first thing to do when selling to a craft shop is to go and look at the store and see if your work fits in with what is in the store. If it does, make an appointment (at that time or later by phone). Be on time for the appointment. If you get an order, ship on time. Price the work at what you consider to be the retail price, so that when the shop owner gets the box and opens it, the work is already priced. If you have a line of work, number it. (For example, poncho style #26.) This makes it easy for the shop to reorder. Make sure you include a packing invoice when you ship, and mail the bill at the same time that you ship. Don't wholesale things that aren't profitable. Follow-up is important. Call a month or so later and find out how your work is selling. Maybe your things are sold out and the shop hadn't realized this and your call reminds them to reorder.

[7]   The next possibility for marketing is selling to gift shops and boutiques. These are good outlets for the fiberist making pillows, bags and accessories. With the gift shop, you are moving up a notch in terms of volume. The instructions are the same as dealing with a craft shop, but you'll probably be dealing with people who are

less caring about whether or not the item is handmade and more interested in you being able to fulfill your commitments.

[8]   Department stores are the next notch up. Here accessories are the items that sell most successfully for fiberists. Rather than buy a complete line of work, department store buyers look at the holes in their merchandising and fill in those areas. Maybe they don't have really nice scarves or shawls (don't forget the men's department for scarves; the men's market is an important one that is grossly overlooked). This can be a very strong market. There are fiber people who are producing in gross lots for department stores. Also, department stores have specialty shops that are nothing more than small gift shops or boutiques. In these shops the volume is usually small and something that an individual craftsperson can deal with.

[9]   Mail order is another possibility, whether you do it yourself (which is more difficult) or sell to a large mail order catalog house. More catalog houses are starting to carry handmade items. The volume and inventory on this can be very large. There are smaller, more prestigious catalogs that might be similar to a department store. Write to the buyer of the catalog and send slides or samples of your work.

[10]   Dealing with art/craft galleries can be an excellent opportunity to try out new designs. There are some craft galleries now that are having shows in wearable fiber. This is a place for multiple work as well as one-of-a-kind pieces. Work is usually on consignment.

[11]   A sales representative is another marketing possibility. The representative will take between 10 percent and 20 percent of the wholesale value. (If you have an item that retails for $10 and you wholesale it for $5 the sales representative will take probably 20 percent, which is $1). There are advantages and disadvantages to dealing with a sales rep. Obviously, the percentage you pay the rep is a disadvantage, although on the plus side a sales rep may be able to get you higher prices which would more than cover the percentage you pay. The rep may also be able to get you into stores that would otherwise be difficult to get into on your own. A sales rep may take over your existing accounts and want a percentage of any accounts you establish yourself. The rep is not responsible for the store paying you—that's up to you. There are some craftspeople who have done extremely well using a sales rep, and there are some bad experiences too. So if you decide to try a sales rep check out his/her reputation before you sign a contract.

[12]   There are some methods of selling that are available to most people in almost any area. In terms of wearable accessories, pillows and lamps, there is the possibility of tying in with a charity and having a sale. The method here would be to have the charity pick the location and handle all the sales. You would consign a certain amount of work to the charity and agree to give them a percentage of your sales (25 percent is appropriate). The charity can get free publicity for the sale on the radio and in the papers. You end up creating a market and getting a lot of publicity. The charity ends up making money and everyone is happy. Another way of tying in with a charity is to have a fashion show and luncheon. You provide the clothing; the charity makes money by charging people to come to the fashion show and luncheon. This would be a good way to get publicity as a producer of wearable fiber. . . .

[13]   The future survival of the craft movement is going to be based partly on the reliability of craftspeople to supply work. There have been markets that are now difficult to open because in the past craftspeople have not filled their commitments. I feel the future for fiberists, as well as other craftspeople, is excellent: it is a matter of developing new markets and becoming professional and reliable.

Responses

1. Which of the following is the main idea sentence of this article: the first sentence of paragraph 1, the second sentence of paragraph 1, the third sentence of paragraph 1, or the single sentence in paragraph 2? How can you tell?
2. In the rest of the article, Clark does not follow the order of the list given in paragraph 2. Which markets are out of order? Can you see any justification for the rearrangement? If you can, what is it?
3. Does Clark discuss any markets that are not listed in paragraph 2? If so, what are they? Should they have been listed there? Why?
4. Clark mentions craft fairs again in paragraph 5. Is she getting the categories mixed up or letting them overlap? Explain the reasons for your answer.
5. In paragraph 11, Clark uses a slang term. What is it? Does it seem to you out of keeping with the rest of the language in the article? Why or why not? Do you think the readers of the article will be likely to object to the slang?
6. The readers of this article are obviously weavers who turn their weaving into garments or pillows. Considering only the list given in paragraph 2 as the plan for the classification, could a similar article be written for other kinds of craft workers? Who might some of the others be? What part of the advice given here could be used in a more general article on markets for craft workers?

Talking Dogs

anthropocentric: assuming that human beings are the most important part of the universe
quasi-: resembling something, but not really it
blatant: extremely obvious or offensive
exemplify: act as an example of something
nuances: subtle differences

Adapted from Thomas A. Sebeok, "Talking Dogs," *Animals,* February 1980, pp. 6–10.

[1]   Students of animal behavior usually distinguish between two sorts of communication systems in the domestic dog: intraspecific—used with other dogs; and interspecific—used by the dog when interacting with other species of animals, say, when working with sheep or when in social contact with human beings. These two sorts of codes might be dubbed canine communication of the first kind and of the second kind. The topic of this article will be communication of a third kind, that involving the very special anthropocentric phenomenon of the talking dog.

[2]   Reports about talking dogs fall into four distinct categories. The most ancient are clearly identified as belonging to folklore or mythology. There are countless North American Indian tales in which the talking dog appears as a truth teller, for instance, or as a tattler. In Ireland a talking dog is a sign of impending disaster, as it is among the Hupa and Yurok Indians of California, and elsewhere.

[3]   The second category features talking dogs in a quasi-literary setting, which may range from serious philosophical works to comic strips. It was Plato who, in *The Republic,* characterized the dog as the "philosophical" animal par excellence; the most celebrated contemporary philosophical dog is undoubtedly Charles Schulz's creation, Snoopy. There are many novels, short stories and fictive memoirs where all the action is narrated from the viewpoint of a dog hero: one thinks of Buck, in Jack London's *The Call of the Wild,* who converses with his fellows in "dog language," but is represented as thinking and dreaming in human terms.

[4]   A third, quaint category, described by Theodore Ziolkowski, has been fabricated by the dog food industry, which, in a blatant attempt to sell more of its product, "has populated our television screens with so many loquacious dogs."

[5]   In the fourth category belong reports of real dogs that are reputed to actually talk (or, in some instances, sing), and it is with these humanized creatures, belonging to the curious intermediate world Horace Walpole designated "dogmanity," that we are chiefly concerned.

[6]   Talking dogs in general exemplify the Clever Hans experimenter expectancy effects, which were named after an illustrious horse that tapped answers to questions posed by its operator. Many other so-called clever animals have been described, such as mice and rats, bears, cats, learned pigs, a goat of knowledge, sea lions and even a walrus, innumerable birds, the dolphins of the 1960s and three species of African apes in the 1970s. All talking dog cases of this kind fall into two broad classes: those involving intentional deception [hoax, fraud], and those affected by self-deception in varying degree, exemplifying the Clever Hans fallacy proper. . . .

[7]   A dog can readily be trained to bark in response to cues, imperceptible to human bystanders, emitted by its operator. Bernhard Grzimek—no mean observer of the nuances of animal behavior—witnessed one such performing dog barking "answers" to questions addressed to it by its master:

> The dog carried out its routine several times without Grzimek noticing any cues being given by the dog's master. Afterward, the trainer told Grzimek that his dog began to bark when the man shifted his weight from one foot to the other, and the dog ceased barking when weight was shifted back to the original foot. The begin-

ning and ending of barking series could be accurately controlled in this way. The trainer had also taught the dog other signs used to communicate commands. . . .

[8]   We might also examine the case of Rolf, the astounding Airedale terrier of Mannheim, whose wondrous reputation persists to this very day. Probably the most telling incident about Rolf was that he suddenly became ill shortly after the arrival of a Swiss psychologist, Professor Claparède, the scientist who was to have subjected Rolf's ability to a series of critical tests. This little detail is almost never mentioned in the many colorful yarns about Rolf; it reminds me of the refusal of a famous "psychic" to go onstage after receiving word that the front row was packed with magicians. He made up a story about a bomb threat and canceled his show. . . .

[9]   I should like to take a closer look at another sort of talking dog. Don, the dog that, by all objective accounts, barks, yet is widely believed to have spoken, will serve as the prototype. . . . As reported by Harry Johnson, the main act consisted of Don speaking (not tapping or typing) "if food was held before him and the following questions propounded: 'Was heisst du?' 'Don.' 'Was hast du?' 'Hunger.' . . . Moreover, he was set to answer categorical questions by 'Ja' and 'Nein'; and in reply to another question to speak the name, 'Haberland.' " Like the horse Hans, Don could be questioned in any language. Unlike Hans, however, he replied not in a sign language but in spoken German. One of Don's interlocutors chanced to be Oskar Pfungst, the same gifted psychologist who had figured out the correct solution to the Clever Hans problem, and who, of course, by no means shared the presuppositions of the general public. Pfungst thoroughly investigated, in part on the basis of a number of phonographic recordings, the dog's behavior. . . .

[10]   In the process of recording, a curious acoustic transformation occurred—or so it seemed. In place of the real Don's spoken German, the recorded Don produced only disyllabic and monosyllabic noises which, to disinterested hearers, i.e., those whose presumptions had not been doctored, sounded like nothing so much as ordinary barking. Pfungst quickly established that the dog invariably answered all questions with answers ordered in the same sequence—if the arrangement of the elements in the questioning changed, his responses turned out to be inappropriate or "ungrammatical"; and that Don learned nothing by observation and imitation.

[11]   Pfungst then decided, correctly, "that the speech of Don is therefore to be regarded properly as the production of vocal sounds which produce illusions in the hearer." Indeed, the uncritical "habitually ignore the important part which suggestion always plays in ordinary situations." The riddle of the talking dog thus stands fully explained: when the effect is not altogether imaginary, the underlying mechanism must either be intentional cuing (deception) or unintentional cuing (self-deception).

Responses

1. What does Sebeok accomplish in the introductory paragraph? Would the title of the article be confusing without this paragraph? Why or why not?

2. What is the main idea sentence of this article? Does it follow the advice given in the chapter? Does Sebeok do all his main idea sentence promises? Does he go beyond it? Be ready to defend your answer.
3. Fill in the classification chart used in this article. Does your chart follow the same order that Sebeok used in the article?

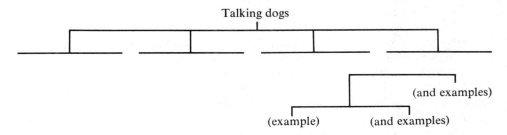

4. Write a paragraph classifying the kinds of communication used by some animal you have known. Or, if you prefer, write a paragraph classifying the kinds of communication used by a baby too young to talk.

Energy Alternatives

alternative: a choice
brokerage: an agency buying, selling, or arranging for somebody else
geometrical: increasing by multiplication rather than addition
inaugurated: began a system
hierarchy: a system of ranking things according to importance
populist: movement or ideas arising from people rather than laws

[1] Driving alone in a petroleum-burning vehicle isn't the only way to get where you need to go. You can ride with a few other people in a carpool, or with a lot of other people in a vanpool. You can use your own energy to pedal a bicycle. Or you can burn a different kind of fuel. Whatever method you may choose, if you decide to look for an energy alternative, you will be part of a nationwide search for ways to conserve energy in transportation.
[2] One of the most important of these ways, ridesharing, saves well over 100,000 barrels of gasoline every day and cuts down on both traffic congestion and air pollution. It costs little in terms of capital investment, since most ridesharers use vehicles that are already on the roads, and those roads have also already been paid for. Perhaps most significantly, ridesharing involves only slight changes in those

Mary Trullinger and Carol Sanger, "Energy Alternatives," *Transportation USA,* Fall 1979, pp. 10–14.

patterns of behavior that have made America—at least until now—the home of the "one person, one car" philosophy of transportation.

[3]   A second energy-saving strategy focuses on a form of transportation older than the automobile, but never so popular as now. Almost everyone has used it at one time, but more people have, inadvisably, given it up. It's one of the smallest, most maneuverable, most energy-efficient forms of transportation around: the bicycle. Even a small switch from cars to bicycles could save significant amounts of energy. As an example, diverting only ten percent of all short urban trips of less than five miles from cars to bikes would save about 30 million barrels of oil a year.

[4]   A third strategy revolves around alternative sources of fuel. The search has turned a lot of people to alcohol—not exactly the drinking kind, but fuel-grade alcohol, usually mixed 1 to 9 with gasoline into a concoction called "gasohol." Some are taking the idea even further and are experimenting with 100 percent alcohol fuels.

[5]   In addition to these three primary approaches—ridesharing, bicycling, and switching to gasohol—there is a slew of miscellaneous plans being tried that stand to save energy on a large scale.

[6]   Sharing a ride. It sounds so simple. It can be as uncomplicated as two neighbors riding to work together, or as complex as the ride-matching Knoxville Commuter Pool. The concept of the Commuter Pool was developed at the University of Tennessee's transportation center in Knoxville. The program was started in 1975 with grant money from DOT's Urban Mass Transportation Administration. The Knoxville plan involves a transportation brokerage system that matches an individual with the mode of transportation most efficient for his or her commute, be it carpool, vanpool, buspool, or whatever. Surveys of local employers provide the data for the match-up, though individuals may also call in directly to the Commuter Pool. . . .

[7]   For individuals, the savings from carpooling or vanpooling are considerable. When two people decide to carpool to work, they automatically cut their commuting costs in half. And the cost of riding in a vanpool for one week is about the same as driving alone one day. . . . From California to Maine, the country is full of ridesharing success stories.

[8]   California, home of ten percent of the nation's population, has strongly supported ridesharing. RIDES for Bay Area Commuters in the north and Commuter Computer in southern California offer matching services to individuals and work with area employers and local officials to help promote ridesharing. "There is a prevailing myth in this country that you can't separate Americans from their love affair with the automobile," says RIDES executive director Tobias Kaye. "We believe that if we provide attractive alternatives, people will go for ridesharing. And we are proving it. RIDES is the fastest-growing vanpool program in the U.S.; we've had a geometrical growth in the last six months." . . .

[9]   The 3M Company of St. Paul, Minnesota, has the oldest company-sponsored vanpool program in the country, begun in 1973. The company has saved $2.5 million from the reduced need for employee parking spaces, during a time when employment was increasing by 23 percent. The vanpool program has also saved an

estimated 1,165,600 gallons of gas between 1973 and 1979 and has significantly reduced tardiness.

[10]   One hundred employers in San Antonio, Texas, are involved in that city's ridesharing program. One insurance company, United Services Automobile Association, has gone for ridesharing and energy conservation in a big way. They switched to a four-day work week, thus eliminating 20 percent of their commuting, and inaugurated a carpool program. A year ago, they added a vanpool program, which has grown to include 81 vans. The combination of ridesharing and the four-day week saves an estimated 300,000 gallons of gasoline each year for USAA employees. . . .

[11]   At about the same time that the Knoxville Commuter Pool was being developed, the nearby Tennessee Valley Authority started a ridesharing program for its employees. Originally aimed at reducing congestion at TVA headquarters in the central business district of Knoxville, the TVA van program has been expanded to include transporting workers to isolated rural construction sites, to downtown Chattanooga, and to outlying power production facilities. TVA estimates a savings of $10 million by reducing the need for additional parking and highway facilities as a result of its vanpool and buspool programs.

[12]   In Vermont, the state energy office directs people interested in forming a vanpool to car dealers in the state who offer leases on vans. The vanpool members may even incorporate themselves to avoid individual risks on insurance. Members of one Vermont vanpool came up with a novel idea. Since they all worked a night shift, they decided to lease their van during the daytime to the Lamoille, Vermont, transit company for use by the elderly and handicapped.

[13]   Next door in Maine, the state department of transportation has purchased vans for a demonstration project of vanpools for their own employees. "We are a rural state with little mass transit," says Jamie Firth of the Maine Office of Energy Resources. "We expect ridesharing to spread like wildfire, but we are trying to avoid the impression that the state government is telling people how to behave. We are all in this energy crisis together."

[14]   Contrary to the uncomfortable image of six executives crammed into a VW (one in the glove compartment), ridesharing is quite popular with the participants. Ridesharers report that they appreciate the money and energy saved—and also enjoy the company of their fellow riders. More than 90 percent of current ridesharers say they intend to stay with it.

[15]   For too long, the bicycle has been seen as just a toy. Now, people are beginning to realize that the bicycle is a highly efficient, inexpensive, nonpolluting, and easily operated mode of transportation.

[16]   Bill Wilkinson of DOT's Office of Environment and Safety says bike programs are aimed at getting away from the "toy bike" mentality and concentrating on three areas of concern: making the highway environment suitable for bikes, educating riders and motorists to be aware of each other and of the basic techniques of safe bicycling, and making streets safe by enforcing traffic laws. "The skills of the successful cyclist on the road can be learned, making it possible to ride safely in traffic," Wilkinson says. "Too often in an accident involving a car and a

bicycle, the driver of the car will say, 'I didn't see the bike.' We hope to educate the public, to make the cyclist visible."

[17]   North Carolina has used a variety of federal-aid funds for its extensive bicycle program, administered by the state department of transportation. Headed by Curtis "Captain Carolina" Yates, the program gets high marks for its education and enforcement programs.

[18]   Yates feels that bicycles have to be better integrated into the transportation system, not isolated from it. "The cyclist and the automobile driver must be aware of each other. The law enforcement official must understand where the bike belongs in the highway hierarchy. Bike paths are not the total solution to the question of using bikes as transportation." Some of the recent programs around the country reflect this attempt to incorporate the bicycle into the total transportation system. In Denver, funds were obtained from a private foundation to begin a training program to teach people how to ride bikes in the streets. Washington, D.C., provides bike racks and lockers at some Metrorail stations. Santa Barbara and San Diego, California, make bike racks or trailers to carry bikes available on transit routes, allowing cyclists to combine bike and bus travel more easily. . . . Mayor Edward Koch of New York City has promoted city cycling with a new bike lane on the Queensborough Bridge and bike lanes on major avenues.

[19]   In Madison, Wisconsin, the police department has started a program to put police officers on bikes in the downtown area. Often, in the crowded city streets, the officer on a bike can make good time in the pursuit of crime without disrupting traffic patterns. In all these ways, the bike is just a toy no more.

[20]   At least part of the answer to America's energy needs can be found growing on top of the ground rather than buried underneath it. It's not such a far-out idea. In fact, harvesting energy from corn and grain fields instead of oil fields is already a grassroots reality throughout the Midwest and there are clear signs that this populist movement in the search for alternative energy sources is catching on nation-wide.

[21]   These alcohol fuels are not much different from that old-fashioned brew that for years was the bane of "revenuers" and the mainstay of the Hatfields and Mc-Coys. Alcohol fuels can be produced in mass quantities or in a backyard still (with proper permits) from such diverse by-products as crops that can't be marketed, corn stalks, wood chips, sugar beet residue, and even garbage. Already, more than 1,000 independent service stations from coast to coast are offering alcohol fuels to their customers in a blend of 10 percent alcohol and 90 percent gasoline called gasohol. The success of gasohol sales throughout the nation in the last year was enough to attract at least one major oil company, which is now test-marketing gasohol at its stations in several Midwestern states. "The public's reaction has been incredible," says Bill Gruppe, a gasoline distributor in Muncie, Indiana. "I'm supplying five stations right now, and the biggest problem is that we just can't get enough of it to meet the demand." . . .

[22] New Hampshire is one of a dozen states so far that have either reduced or eliminated entirely the state sales tax on gasohol. Congress, in legislation passed last year, eliminated the four-cents-a-gallon federal excise tax on gasohol in an effort to make it more cost-competitive with gasoline. As the price of gasoline con-

tinues to rise, gasohol—which averages around one to three cents a gallon above unleaded regular gasoline in most places—is becoming increasingly competitive in price, and its promoters predict that soon a gallon of gasohol will sell for less than a gallon of the cheapest gasoline. . . .

[23]   Tests on mileage, performance, and emissions for gasohol are being conducted in California, where a number of state vehicles soon will be running on gasohol; in New York, where the New York City Police Department is running several cars on various mixes of gasohol and ethanol/methanol alcohol; and in Marion County (Indianapolis), Indiana, where the sheriff's department has been experimenting with gasohol-powered patrol cars for several months. The 90-10 mix of gasohol being sold in the U.S. requires no engine modifications at all.

[24]   Reverse commuting, organized hitchhiking, and car-free transit malls are just a few examples of the sort of novel ideas that have been translated into transportation programs recently. And new approaches keep popping up all across the country.

[25]   The city of Hartford, Connecticut, was one of the first to work out reverse commuting. Many people in Hartford's inner city were unemployed, and many of the employers had moved to the suburbs. To help the two get together, the city set up a shared-ride taxi program to transport prospective employees out for job interviews. Those who need the service are matched, four to a cab, by route and destination. If the number of people needing a ride is too large for a taxi, vans are used for the trips. Once the reverse commuters are hired, subscription vanpools are set up. A local taxi company provides drivers, dispatchers, insurance, and so on through a semi-charter arrangement. If demand is large enough in a neighborhood, the city transit company will reroute express buses to meet the need. "Ninety percent of those now taking part in the reverse commute program had been on some form of public assistance," says program manager Helen Kemp. "Now, with a little help from the community, they can pay their way."

[26]   Out in Marin County, California, young executives step up to the curb, hold out an ID card, and hitch a ride to work with cars displaying similar cards on their sun visors. A program called Commuter Connection promotes organized hitchhiking to work. The drivers work out the cost-sharing with the hitchers, and they all take advantage of the reduced tolls and preferential carpool lanes on highways going into San Francisco.

[27]   These preferential lanes, also called high-occupancy-vehicle lanes, are another energy-saving transportation idea. An outstanding example of this priority treatment for carpools and buses is the Shirley Highway express lanes on I-395 from northern Virginia into Washington, D.C. During the morning rush hour, these two express lanes carry 70 percent of the passenger traffic coming into the city, an amount equal to the capacity of 14 normal freeway lanes.

[28]   In Portland, Oregon, Tri-Met, the transit company, also coordinates carpools and helps employers with transportation problems. They have developed bus pass subsidies for employers to encourage workers to use mass transit. A transit mall, designed to restrict automobiles and encourage pedestrians and the use of mass transit, has revitalized the downtown business district. In the downtown area, there are nearly 300 curbside parking spaces reserved for carpools, and free bus

rides are given in a 300-square-block zone. Fifty thousand people participate each day in some aspect of Portland's shared-ride program, making it one of the most successful in the country.

Responses

1. This article classifying energy alternatives could be divided into six parts. What is accomplished in paragraph 1? In paragraphs 2–5? In paragraphs 6–14? In paragraphs 15–19? In paragraphs 20–23? In paragraphs 24–28? On the basis of these divisions, make a short plan showing how the paper is developed.

2. Even though this article is quite long, the classification used in it is fairly simple. Make a chart showing what the classification includes, beginning with the title as the general class, using the information in paragraphs 2–5 as the first step, and using the information in paragraphs 24–28 as the second step. Compare your chart with those other students have made. How many items did you include in the second step?

3. Paragraph 6 begins with a fragment, followed by a very short sentence. Why do you think the writers deliberately used this fragment? Would you like it better if the first sentence of paragraph 6 read "Sharing a ride sounds so simple"? Why or why not?

4. In paragraphs 8, 13, 16, and 21, the quotations are all introduced by the verb "says," even though the speakers must have made their comments in the past, before the article was written. What is the effect of using "says" instead of "said"?

5. In several places, the writers use alphabetical abbreviations instead of names (see paragraphs 6, 10, 11, and 14). What is your reaction to these abbreviations? Did you have any trouble figuring out what the abbreviations stand for? Was it easier to figure out in paragraphs 10 and 11 than in paragraph 6? Why? Did knowing what agency published this article help you any? What about the abbreviation in paragraph 14?

6. The writers apparently believe that the country must save energy. Do they urge readers to adopt any of the methods classified in this article? If you think they do, find the places where they openly take sides. If you think they don't, discover how you get the impression that they favor using these methods.

7. Write a concluding paragraph that will make this article sound finished. Use any kind of conclusion you prefer, but make what you say fit with the introduction.

More Suggestions for Writing

Classify:

> the clothes you own
> doctors
> party refreshments
> furniture
> kinds of meat
> pleasure boats
> cars your family has owned
> grocery stores
> shoppers in a grocery store
> kinds of vacations
> garden plants
> bills
> household tools
> attitudes toward voting
> attitudes toward religion
> attitudes toward the younger generation

Chapter 6

Explaining: Analysis

The fourth method of explaining is analysis. Things that cannot be defined or compared or classified can often be explained by analyzing—explaining a whole by examining it piece by piece.

Although both classification and analysis deal with separate things that somehow belong together, with classification we begin with a group of things, divide it into parts, and then divide the parts again as many times as necessary; or we start with one thing and put it with a group of other things somewhat like it. Shawn Casey is classifying when she decides to keep her bread, crackers, and chips in the cabinet above the refrigerator and her canned goods in the pantry, separating the canned goods into meat, vegetables, and sauces. She is also classifying when she looks at a can of cream of mushroom soup and decides to shelve it with the sauces. With analysis, on the other hand, we begin with something we think of as a single thing and divide that thing into its separate parts so the parts can be examined piece by piece. Shawn can, if she's interested, analyze that can of soup and read its ingredients: chicken broth, mushrooms, water, preservatives.

Both classification and analysis can help us understand things and perhaps keep them under better control. And even though they are separate processes, we sometimes use them together. The lab technician working in a blood bank first *analyzes* a blood sample—looks at it under a microscope to see its separate parts—and then classifies it—labels it so it can be stored with other blood that belongs to the same type.

In ordinary life, most of us use analysis for two purposes: to explain *how* and to explain *why*. When Shawn Casey analyzed the soup to see what ingredients it had, she was curious about *how* the soup was made; when she looked at the price and realized cream of mushroom soup had gone up six cents in the past month she tried to analyze *why* the cost had risen. When your optometrist was going to medical school, she examined the parts of the human eye to see *how* a normal eye works. When she examines your eyes, she's trying to find out *why* you see two fuzzy letters where there's really only one clear letter. We call the first kind of analysis—looking at something to see *how* it works—*operational analysis*. Looking to see *why* something happened—the cost has risen, your vision is blurred—is called *causal analysis*.

Operational Analysis

Usually, operational analysis explains a process that works the same way over and over again. We use it to help ourselves understand, and we write about it to help our readers understand. We can best explain how this page in the book got printed by examining the relationships of the author, the editor, the artist, the typesetter, and the printer who actually put the words and art onto the paper by a mechanical process. We can explain how blood courses through the human body by analyzing the parts of the circulatory system: the heart, the arteries, the veins, and the lungs. We can explain how a college is governed by examining what the board of trustees does, and what the president, the deans, the councils, and the student government are supposed to do. In explaining any of these things—the publishing process, the blood system, or the operation of a college—our concern is not with whether they *should* work that way but simply with how they *do* work.

Main Idea Sentences for Operational Analysis

Main idea sentences for operational analysis are easy to write. They always start with the thing being analyzed (the whole) and end by mentioning the parts. If the thing is fairly simple, the main idea sentence can actually name all the parts. If the thing is complicated, the main idea sentence may merely mention how many essential parts there are.

> The publishing process (*the whole*) involves a writer, an editor, an artist, a typesetter, and a printer (the parts).
>
> The circulatory system (*the whole*) is composed of the heart, the arteries, the veins, and the lungs (*the parts*).
>
> College government (*the whole*) is made up of five separate groups, all of them making recommendations about changes in policy (the parts).
>
> All thermometers (*the whole*) have just three basic parts.

The plan for the paper follows naturally from the main idea sentence. If you have already named the parts, you will use one section—maybe a paragraph—to discuss each part, and you will follow the same order you used in listing the parts. The paper on publishing will begin with the writer and end with the printer; the paper on the circulatory system will probably start with the heart. If, as you write, you think of a better order, all you have to do is rewrite your main idea sentence. After you have explained all the parts, a final sentence or two of conclusion will let your readers know you have finished.

Examining a Paper of Operational Analysis

How a Thermometer Works

[1]   Every morning I get out of bed and look at the thermometer outside my window to check the temperature before I leave for school. I never gave much thought to how the thermometer works; I figured it was similar to the weatherman's instruments, but they seemed too complex and sophisticated to understand. However, I recently learned that all thermometers work on the same principle. Thermometers have a tube containing mercury and a chart to measure the mercury's movement.

[2]   First, there is a tube which holds the mercury. Most are made of glass because mercury cannot eat through glass, and glass can easily be made into a long, thin tube—just the shape used in thermometers. Also, glass can be seen through. The weatherman must be able to see the mercury in the tube to measure its movement.

[3]   Next is the mercury. In most cases the mercury is dyed red or some other bright color to make it easier to see. Mercury is used because it is a liquid that expands in heat and contracts in cold, but it will not freeze under normal freezing conditions. Therefore, it is a good element to use in an instrument to measure temperature.

[4]   Last is a chart which measures the expansion and contraction of the mercury. This chart is scaled in degrees—Fahrenheit, centigrade, or both. These charts are scaled in a room where the temperature is already known. For example, if it's 72°F in a room, the tube of mercury is attached to a chart and placed in that room. After the mercury has adjusted to the room temperature, that point on the chart would be marked 72°F; then the rest of the degrees could be added to the scale.

[5]   Thus, although the weatherman's instrument looks complicated, it works on the same principle as the $1.09 thermometer I bought at the hardware store and put up outside my window. Mercury in a glass tube reacts to temperature, and this reaction is measured on a scale. So what's the difference between my thermometer and the weatherman's? You'll have to ask the man who makes them. I don't see much difference.

Notice that although this paper explains the process by which any thermometer works, it does not tell readers how to build a thermometer or even how to read the temperature. If the paper had done either of those things, it would have been a paper of directions. The difference between analyzing and giving directions should be clear if you compare the second paragraph of "How a Thermometer Works" with this paragraph from a paper called "How to Build a Simple Thermometer":

> To build a simple thermometer you will need a thin glass tube, a small amount of mercury, a roll of clear tape, a heavy piece of cardboard, a felt-tip marker, and a room where you already know what the temperature is.
> The first step is to . . .
> Next you . . .

The first paragraph of "How a Thermometer Works" clearly states the purpose: to analyze a thermometer so as to explain how all thermometers work. The main idea sentence with which the writer probably started ("All thermometers have just three parts") has been broken up and made part of two sentences, but the whole idea is clearly there. Further, the main paragraph catches the reader's attention by telling why the paper is being written: to explain some of the mystery of thermometers.

Does the order of the parts analyzed seem clear? The parts are arranged in the order that they are needed: a tube to hold mercury, some mercury, a scale to measure the mercury's reaction. The order is made even clearer through the use of transitions. Notice the paragraph beginnings: "First . . . , Next . . . , Last . . . , Thus. . . ."

And the conclusion makes the paper sound finished, both by summing up the analysis and by referring back to the introduction and picking up the idea already introduced—that the principle applies to all thermometers. Further, the writer repeats the comparison of the hardware store variety and the weatherman's instrument. This repetition not only finishes the theme, it also ties the whole thing together very nicely.

Causal Analysis

When you want to explain not how something works but why something happens (or happened) the way it does (or did) the process becomes a bit more complicated. You still begin with the thing, the event:

There's no hot water when you turn the tap on.

An old friend is always busy when you ask her to dinner.

There is a massive migration of population from urban to rural areas.

Karen Henderson is failing biology.

The rate of inflation keeps increasing.

And then you go on to the parts. But whereas the parts in operational analysis are things that can be counted, all of them necessary for the whole to work, the parts in causal analysis are reasons, or possible reasons, that you are trying to discover.

If the event is fairly simple or fairly personal, you can probably list all the possible reasons and check them out one by one. Why don't you get hot water in the shower? Have two other members of the household just finished bathing? Is the washing machine going? Is your husband running the dishwasher? Has the old water heater finally stopped operating? Have you forgotten to pay the gas bill? You find the cause by a process of elimination. In an event as simple as this, it would be very bad luck to discover that the water heater had rusted out *and* the gas had been turned off, both at the same time; you will likely find there was only one cause.

It may be less simple to discover why your old friend is avoiding you. You can ask her, of course, the next time you telephone. But if her manners are good, she may say she isn't avoiding you at all; it's just that there's so much overtime at the office, she hasn't a minute to spare. When you try on your own to figure out why, you may not be able to think of any single reason, just an accumulation of small things that might have helped her decide that she's "terribly busy this week" and next week and the week after. When you have finished your list, you can go back and decide which things you think are most likely, which the least likely, to have annoyed your friend.

When you read in the newspaper that there is a massive migration of population from urban to rural areas, finding the reason involves a different kind of problem. First, you have to determine what the statement means, just as you did in your definition paper. You must decide what the article means by "massive"; massive migration by the population of Los Angeles would certainly be different from massive migration by the population of Lompoc. After you've determined these things, you can look around to see why people are moving from the city to the suburbs or the country. In your own neighborhood, you know of three families that have moved: one family went to the suburbs so the children could go to another school; one couple retired and moved to their cottage in the country to avoid high city taxes; one family, tired of seeing all concrete and no water, moved to a small coastal town. A specific cause isn't always easy to determine.

If Karen Henderson had the time, she could go to the counseling center and spend several sessions trying to determine why she's failing biology, and still not be sure. Or if she had the money, Karen might hire a tutor to analyze what she's doing wrong. This tutor might use another method of explanation—comparison—when making his analysis. He might ask what Karen is doing to prepare for the class and compare that with what an *A* student is doing to prepare for the same class.

As for inflation, since world-famous economists have not been able to agree on the causes, it's unlikely that we will do any better. Unless you're asked in a test for some other course to analyze the causes of inflation, you'll do better to leave that topic alone. Complicated events like inflation are influenced by too many uncontrollable—and often hidden—factors. If the question does come up in a test, the most sensible plan is to summarize the causes that have been discussed in class, remembering to add, in your mind at least, "according to some authorities. . . ."

Cause and Effect

The more complex an event is, the more most of us are tempted to oversimplify what caused it. Did inflation increase *just* because we had a Republican administration? Did inflation increase *just* because a Democratic Congress voted too large a budget? Is Karen Henderson failing biology *just* because she isn't studying enough or *just* because her professor talks fast? Are people moving out of the city *just* because it's noisy or *just* because taxes are high?

When we forget that most events have several causes, we tend to settle for simple and incorrect explanations.

Some events, of course, do have only one cause. The water wasn't hot because the heater was old and finally wore out. The picture didn't turn out because the film was in wrong. And a counselor may find that Karen's problems in biology stem from a weak background in science—she needs to take a more basic general science course before attempting biology. Before we can say there's only one reason, however, we need to make sure there are no other possible causes. Unless you can eliminate those other causes, you need to consider them in your analysis.

Another easy way to go wrong is to suppose that because one thing happened after another, the first thing caused the second. Perhaps you forgot to send your friend a birthday card. Are you justified in supposing that that's why she was so "busy" the next week? Or suppose that Raglan College does away with final examinations in the fall and in the spring enrollment goes up. Are you justified in saying that abolishing the exams caused more students to come to the college?

People who believe that walking under ladders causes accidents forget to ask themselves whether the accidents could have been caused by anything else. At ten o'clock Rupert walked under a ladder and a moment later he tripped over a paint bucket and sprained his ankle. Did walking under the ladder cause him to trip on the bucket? Tansy caught a bad head cold, sneezed miserably for six days, and on the seventh day tried the new cold pill she'd seen in a television commercial. In four days the cold was gone. Did the pill cure her cold or did she simply get over it?

Are overcrowded classrooms the only reason children can't read? One way to find out might be to check several overcrowded classrooms. If most of the children are poor readers, you might decide that overcrowding is at least *one* of the causes.

Before you decide that one thing caused another, you should always ask two questions:

1. Could there have been any other possible causes?
2. When the cause is there, does the effect always follow?

Main Idea Sentences for Causal Analysis

Main idea sentences for papers analyzing the cause of something always have two parts: the event and the cause or causes. Because it is often so hard to be absolutely sure what caused something to turn out the way it did, it's especially important not to overstate your case. Sometimes, as we've already shown, you can eliminate all other possible causes of some occurrence and be left with only one thing that could have caused it—a nail in a tire caused it to go flat, for instance, or falling out of the cherry tree caused Billie to break her arm. When events are this simple, however, you probably won't need to write a whole paper of causal analysis; a simple report will be enough. You are more likely to be writing about events that have, or might have, more than one cause, even though one of the causes may seem more important than the others—a "main cause." In dealing with these more complicated situations, your main idea sentence must show that there might be more than one cause or mention what some of the causes might be.

In planning the paper, you will probably want to list all of the most likely causes, even though you expect to show that some of these possible causes are not very important. When you actually write the paper, you will be explaining what the relationship between the cause and the effect is—or isn't, if you are discarding some of the causes you discuss. If you have a job as a refrigeration engineer, for instance, and you are assigned to discover why the college's air conditioning system isn't working, you will probably want to include in your analysis each of the possibilities you investigated, giving most of the emphasis to what you think the real difficulties are. If you are a political analyst trying to find out why the mayor wasn't re-elected, you may want to give almost equal space to all of the things the people you interviewed have told you. As a refrigeration engineer, however, you will probably want to avoid saying, "The *only* cause of this failure was the hot weather." And as a political analyst you won't want to say, "The mayor lost the election *only* because he has a beard."

Examining a Paper of Causal Analysis

Dear Editor:

[1]   Ever since *The Bulletin* published the national achievement scores for Sellwood Elementary School last month, the newspaper has been full of letters complaining that the schools don't teach children to read these days. There was even an editorial last week suggesting that if the teachers would worry a little less about getting a raise and a little more about what they were paid to teach, 50 percent of the fourth-grade students might not be reading at second-grade level. I used to be a teacher at Sellwood, and I'm a little tired of hearing nonsense like that. There are several reasons those scores were low, but lazy teachers is not one of them.

[2]   For one thing, there are forty fourth-graders in one room this year, thirty-two chairs, and twenty-five reading books. If eight students are sick on the same day, the rest of the class can sit down, but seven of them still won't have any books. If half the day is spent on reading—the teacher is supposed to teach spelling and writing and arithmetic and geography, too—there's

exactly four and a half minutes to spend helping each child read. With conditions like that, what do you expect?

[3]   Last year Sellwood furnished free hot lunches to children on welfare, but the legislature cut school lunches out of the budget this year—there are no more funds. How much would you care about reading if you came to school without breakfast and knew you'd only get a candy bar for lunch? Hungry children can't concentrate.

[4]   But that's not the worst of it. The readers being used this year were published in 1959. They tell about Bobby, who lives in a big white house with a huge green lawn and a lot of flowers. His father is a stockbroker and his mother spends her afternoons in a frilly white apron, baking cookies for the children. Bobby's sister Peggy feeds apples to her own fat little pony, and the whole family takes a nice airplane ride to visit grandma at the seashore.

[5]   Most of the children at Sellwood have never seen a lawn, except in the park, and they think flowers mean a funeral. They live in dilapidated apartments, and they play in the street. They don't know what stock is, much less a stockbroker. Most of them don't have fathers living at home, and their mothers are out cleaning from 9:00 to 5:00, or standing in line somewhere trying to get food stamps. These students have never seen a pony, and when they can rip off an apple they eat it themselves, fast. They stand a better chance of riding an elephant than an airplane. Why should these children care about ponies and planes? Why should they try to read about them?

[6]   Overcrowded classrooms, hungry children, and foolish books are just some of the reasons the reading scores at Sellwood are low. The main reason is that the standardized tests have a strong racist bias. The tests don't measure what the children at Sellwood know. The tests, like the reading books, were made for middle-class white children; and "fourth-grade level" means the scores that suburban white children got, and that's all they mean. More than half of the Sellwood students speak Spanish at home, and more than half the rest are black. But these tests don't have any Spanish words in them, or any black dialect, or anything about life in the ghetto. Instead, the children are expected to understand stories about things they've never seen and sometimes never heard of. If the students took a reading test *made for* Spanish children or Black children, the scores would look quite different. The white scores might look different, too, if the white children tried to take a test that wasn't made especially for them. The main reason for the low scores at Sellwood is not the teachers and not the students. It's the test itself.

Sincerely,
Julia M. Peterson
A retired schoolteacher

Although the first paragraph of this letter doesn't contain a main idea stated in a single sentence, all the information is there. Readers can easily reconstruct the sentence: "Sellwood reading scores on the national-achievement tests were low for several reasons." Actually, the letter writer accomplishes several things in her first paragraph: she gives the reason for writing the letter (she wants to explain the low scores to the people who have been complaining); she identifies both the situation and herself; and she eliminates one reason that she thinks is wrong (the teachers are to blame).

The plan she used (which may never have been written down) is equally easy to find. The writer gives four reasons:

overcrowded rooms and inadequate supplies
underfed children
unsuitable books
biased tests

Apparently she thinks the first three reasons are about equally important, and she deliberately saves the most important reason for last. Of the other three, probably she decided to begin with the overcrowded conditions because that is a good way to get the readers' attention. Probably she used the unsuitable books third because that reason is so clearly related to what she thinks is the real reason—it made a natural transition. It's interesting to notice, too, that she groups the first three reasons together because they are a bit different in kind from the last reason: the first three explain why the children might have difficulty in learning to read. The last, and most important, reason explains not why the children can't read well but *why the test scores are low,* and it implies that, in other circumstances, these children might be able to read quite well.

Do you see any changes that should be made in the letter? Maybe the pronouns used in the last sentence of paragraph 5 could be clearer—did you know who "they" and "them" were? The easiest thing to do here would be to omit that sentence altogether; the point is made without it. And what about the "they" at the end of the fourth sentence in paragraph 6? The problem could be solved by changing the sentence to read, "That's all *those scores* mean."

Do you find the conclusion satisfactory? The conclusion is the last sentence of paragraph 6. Would you find it more effective if the writer had begun a new paragraph there, instead of making her emphatic statement a part of the long sixth paragraph?

Notice that the letter does two things very well. First, instead of just listing the causes as a series of general statements, it helps readers see what the conditions in the school are like. Instead of just saying that the textbooks deal with a kind of life most of the Sellwood children are unfamiliar with, it clearly contrasts the experiences in the book to the experiences of the children who try to read the book, giving a paragraph (4) to the books and a separate paragraph (5) to the children's own lives. The paragraphs giving the reasons have all been carefully developed.

The second thing the letter does well is never lose sight of its purpose—*analyzing* the causes of the low reading scores. Although it seems pretty certain that the writer would like to see many changes—the district to adopt a smaller ratio of students to teachers, the children to get a hot lunch, the school to use more suitable readers—she does not actually argue for any of these changes. Nor does she urge the school to drop the test; she just says the test itself causes the low scores. Readers who would like to see the scores higher or the tests abolished and who agree with Ms. Peterson's reasons, can write to the legislature or protest to the test makers, but in this letter Ms. Peterson does not ask them to. She remembers that her purpose in writing is causal analysis, and she sticks to that purpose.

Key Words _____

Here are some of the important terms used in this chapter. See whether you can answer these questions about them.

1. How does **analysis** explain things?
2. How is **analysis** different from **classification?**
3. What does **operational analysis** do?
4. What is the difference between a paper of **operational analysis** and a paper **giving directions?**
5. What two things should be clearly stated in a **main idea sentence** for **operational analysis?**
6. What does **causal analysis** do?
7. What are two questions that should be asked in trying to decide on **cause and effect?**
8. What should a **main idea sentence** for **causal analysis** contain?
9. What is the difference between **causal analysis** and **argument?**
10. What is the best **order** for a paper of analysis?

READINGS
Analysis

Zip Fastener

divergent: separated
duct: tube or pipe that carries something
resilient: springing easily back to original shape

Main idea sentence

[1]   The main parts of a zip fastener are the two chains of teeth, which are attached to strips of textile material, and the slide, which opens and closes the fastener.

How the chains work

[2]   Each chain consists of a large number of teeth, usually of metal, which are provided with small protrusions on the top surface and with corresponding recesses on the underside (Fig. 1). The protrusion on each tooth engages accurately with the recess in the tooth above. The two chains of teeth are slightly staggered in relation to each other. To close the fastener, the two chains must be so brought into engagement that the teeth on the two chains can interlock in pairs. This

What the slide does

is achieved by the slide. At its upper end the slide comprises two divergent ducts, which join each other and merge into one duct at the lower end. The slide is so designed that the two chains of teeth are brought together at exactly the correct angle to make the protrusions interlock or one tooth engage with the recess on the opposite tooth (Fig. 2). At each end of the zip fastener are end pieces which prevent the slide from coming off. In some zips the two halves can be separated, in which case the bottom end piece is so designed

The Way Things Work: An Illustrated Encyclopedia of Technology (New York: Simon and Schuster, n.d.), Vol. I, pp. 396–397.

that one chain of teeth can be withdrawn from the slide, while the latter is retained by the other chain.

Various kinds of zippers

[3] Zip fasteners sometimes have plastic teeth (e.g., perlon), which are of a shape rather different from that of metal fastener teeth. The chains do not consist of individual teeth, but of loops formed by a spiral coil (Fig. 3). Fasteners of this kind have the advantage that, because of the resilient properties of plastic, they are not destroyed by tearing open. In addition to the types of zip fastener described above, there are many others, all of which operate on the same principle, however, and differ only in the particular form of the teeth employed.

Conclusion; referring to basic principle

Drawings to help readers see what zippers look like

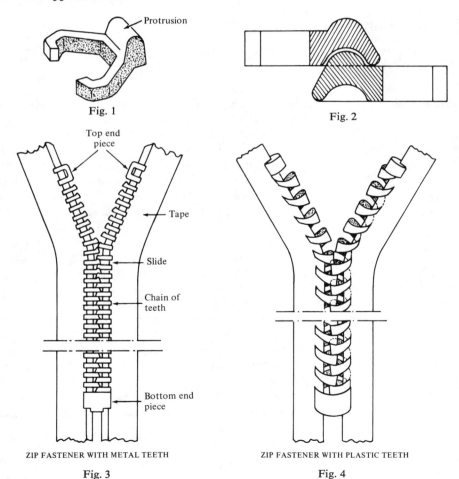

Fig. 1

Protrusion

Fig. 2

Top end piece

Tape

Slide

Chain of teeth

Bottom end piece

ZIP FASTENER WITH METAL TEETH

Fig. 3

ZIP FASTENER WITH PLASTIC TEETH

Fig. 4

Responses

1. Look at a zip fastener on one of your own garments to see whether it fits the analysis given here. Has anything been left out of the analysis? If so, what is it? Has anything unnecessary been mentioned? If so, what is it?
2. Why has the writer included the drawings—normally called figures when they are used to illustrate what's being said in writing? Could you have understood the analysis without the drawings? Why or why not?
3. Write a short paper explaining the operation of some simple device: a ball-point pen, a pulley, a coffee maker, an electric plug, a padlock, a cigarette lighter, or anything else with which you are familiar. If you think it would help readers to understand, you may include simple drawings of some of the parts.

The Course of a Bill

calendared: scheduled to be heard or discussed at a later date

[1]   The idea for a bill may originate with any citizen. But in almost all states, only a member of the House of Representatives or the Senate of the state legislature may officially introduce a bill by filing it with the clerk or secretary of his [*sic*] respective house. After the bill's title has been "read in" in open session, it is referred to an appropriate committee for consideration. When the committee (after hearing and debate) has finished considering the bill, it reports its decision and recommendations to the parent body. The bill and the committee report are read in and, upon a favorable vote, are referred to the Rules Committee to be calendared for a second reading.

[2]   Upon second reading the bill is subject to amendment, section by section. When no further amendments are offered, the speaker declares the bill has passed its second reading, and the bill is referred back to the Rules Committee for third-reading calendaring. Upon being brought back to the floor for third reading and final passage, the bill must receive a recorded vote in order to be sent on to the other chamber. When approved by the second chamber (through the same process), the bill is "enrolled" in the first chamber, where final processing takes place. The bill is signed by the presiding officer of the second chamber. Finally, the bill is sent to the governor for approval and signature. Only then is the bill ready to be filed permanently with the secretary of state and made part of the session laws.

Dorothy Smith, *In Our Own Interest: A Handbook for the Citizen Lobbyist in State Legislatures* (Seattle: Madrona Publishers, 1979), p. 13.

Responses

1. What is the process being analyzed here? How many steps are included in the process? What are they?
2. This analysis doesn't begin with a main idea sentence. If you think there is such a sentence anywhere in the article, what is it? If you think no main idea sentence is given, write one that would fit the article.
3. For what audience was this article intended? Does it contain all the information the expected readers would need? If you think the readers would need more information, what is it? Would examples have helped readers? Why or why not? Would drawings have helped?
4. The information given in this article might make a good answer to an examination question in a political science course. What would the question be?
5. When *"sic"* appears in backets, it means that the word or phrase just before the *"sic"* was exactly that way in the original, but that the person quoting or reprinting the article doesn't want to be responsible for the error, misspelling, or attitude implied by use of that word or phrase. Try to figure out why we have used *"sic"* here. Are all members of a state legislature men?
6. Why has Smith used quotation marks around "read in" in the first paragraph and "enrolled" in the second paragraph? What are the special meanings of these words as she is using them?
7. In two or three paragraphs, explain some process that must be followed on your campus or in your state. For instance, how can student government rules be amended or a student government officer be elected? How can somebody join a particular organization? What must you do to get a driver's license? Etc.

The Power Tower

parabolic: shaped into a geometric curve
thermal: having to do with heat or heat production
skepticism: being doubtful about something
rubric: general heading or group
prototype: an original or model
feasibility: likelihood of something working or being practical

[1]   High in the French Pyrenees sits a sparkling ten-story parabolic mirror that looks from a distance like an oversized diamond nestled in a sloping green valley. It is a 1-megawatt solar furnace—a power tower.

Modesto A. Maidique, "Solar America," in Robert Stabaugh and Daniel Yergin (eds.), *Energy Future,* Report of the Energy Project at the Harvard Business School (New York: Random House, 1979), pp. 202–204.

[2]   In 1977 this solar furnace, which lies near the town of Font-Romeu, was the only solar thermal electric system in the world that was pumping power into a conventional electric grid. Although the structure was designed primarily for achieving high temperatures for research purposes, the French tapped off some of the heat to prove a point: that solar energy could be used to generate conventional electric power.

[3]   The system works by reflecting the sun's rays onto the large parabolic mirror via an array of smaller mirrors perched on an adjoining hillside. The parabolic mirror focuses the incident light onto a small area where a boiler is placed. The steam produced by the boiler is piped down to a small building that contains a 100-kilowatt steam turbine-generator combination. "The French showed it works," one French energy official has observed. "But the Americans will commercialize it. We've worked for a decade with minimal budgets to get where we are. Yet the American solar thermal electric budget—for next year alone—is higher than the total we've spent thus far."

[4]   The budget for the U.S. solar thermal electric program is indeed growing rapidly. Despite criticism of the high costs of the program and skepticism about a centralized "technological fix" that has grown out of the nuclear experience, the solar thermal electric program, better known as the power tower, commands nearly a fifth of the entire federal budget for solar energy.

[5]   It is one of several large-scale methods that have been proposed for the centralized generation of electricity, all of which fall under the rubric of Big Solar. Some of the others are ocean thermal conversion, microwave space power satellites, and farms of large windmills (that can generate a hundred or more kilowatts of power). All involve complex high-technology systems. But farthest along technologically, the power tower is expected to continue to command a major share of the federal solar energy funds through the 1980's. For these reasons it best illustrates the problems, the costs, and the potential of Big Solar. Although the French official is right about American budgets, commercialization of the American system is still far from certain.

[6]   The U.S. power tower is a low-temperature system designed specifically to generate electric power. The giant parabolic mirror of the French tower is replaced by a concrete tower several stories high, which is capped by a steam boiler. Several acres of remote-controlled mirrors, or heliostats, capture sunlight and beam it to the boiler. The remainder of the system is similar to the French design.

[7]   The American power tower is presently at the prototype stage. Eighty percent of the cost of the early stages will be borne by the federal government; later, the participating utilities will increase their share to 50 percent. The first commercial station, a 100-megawatt system, is projected for the early 1990's.

[8]   The cost of the heliostats, or tracking mirrors, is the dominant element in power-tower economics, for at present, the mirror system accounts for up to two-thirds of the overall plant cost. The Department of Energy's goal is to reduce the present system's cost by one-tenth—that is, to $70 per square meter. But many in the industry doubt that the material-intensive costs of the heliostats can be reduced beyond $140 per square meter. At that level, a Jet Propulsion Lab analysis projects total plant costs of $2,000 per *peak* kilowatt, or about three times the plant cost of an *average* kilowatt of conventionally generated electric power. And the

plant's full output will be available only for a portion of the day—on certain days.
[9]   Balanced against this, however, is that the power is available when most needed in warm climates during hours of peak sunshine—and corresponding peak air-conditioning load. This fact, combined with the need for the direct light available on clear, sunny days, explains the choice of southern California and New Mexico as the first power-tower sites. If the power tower is analyzed as a backup system for conventional electric power generation, which is the way that it will be initially used, it becomes a more economic proposition. However, even the smaller, less efficient gas turbines presently used for peak power needs are more economical than the *future* cost of power towers, assuming there will be a reduction of heliostat cost to one-fifth of present levels, which is far from assured.

[10]   In addition to the economic hurdles, several technical obstacles remain. The maximum range at which the focusing mirrors can successfully operate has not been determined, nor is it known how difficult or costly it will be to keep the mirrors properly focused. Estimates for "maximum" size of an individual power-tower plant range from 10 to 100 megawatts, and some suggest that crews of hundreds of cleaning personnel will have to wipe the mirrors continually while scores of technicians adjust the heliostats to maintain the plant's power levels. Others have raised concerns about the blinding effect of hundreds of acres of mirrors on pilots flying over the area. Resolving these issues and proving commercial feasibility could take the rest of the century. Only then could commercialization begin.

Responses

1. What system is being explained in this article? Where does the explanation occur? What does paragraph 6 add to the explanation?
2. What does Maidique accomplish in paragraphs 1 and 2? in paragraph 4? in paragraph 5?
3. What is the transition between paragraphs 3 and 4? between paragraphs 4 and 5? between paragraphs 5 and 6?
4. Paragraphs 8, 9, and 10 could be called causal analysis—an explanation of why the American power tower is not in use and why it may not be used for several more years. What are the causes Maidique gives? How are these causes related to the operational analysis in the earlier part of the article?
5. Who are the readers of this article expected to be? What information will they already have? What is the evidence in the article for your answer?
6. Try to explain, in simpler language, how the American power tower works. You will need to combine the information about the French tower with the information about what is being done in the United States. As you write, assume that your readers are fourteen-year-olds, interested in energy but without the technical vocabulary to understand Maidique's article.

Why the Birds Cough

index: scale or measure
indices: plural of index
notorious: having a bad reputation
emphysema: serious lung disease
affinity: a natural attraction
acuity: sharpness

**Specific event—telling
what happened**

[1]　On the hot, muggy evening of August 28 last year, 30,000 people, mostly young, crowded onto the Boston Common, the big center city park, to hear a rock group named the Chambers Brothers. Many came in automobiles, which they parked beneath the Common in a three-tier, 1,500-car municipal garage built a few years ago.

[2]　In all, 1,300 cars were in the garage when the show was over. Much of the audience descended into the garage and, almost simultaneously, drivers turned on their motors and headed for the three toll-booth exits.

[3]　Within minutes youngsters began staggering out of the garage on foot, gasping and choking. Others passed out in their cars. Police carried at least twenty unconscious persons out of the garage. Ambulances took twenty-five persons to two hospitals, while oxygen was given to many other young people on the grounds of the Common. Fortunately, a quick-witted city official saw what was happening and ordered the toll-takers to stop taking tolls so that the garage could be cleared swiftly. Everyone recovered soon and went home. Twenty-four hours later the incident was nearly forgotten.

[4]　Yet the near-disaster at the Boston Common is an index to how air pollution from the auto has created a crisis in the nation.

[5]　There are other indices, some almost unnoticed.

Other examples

[6]　Los Angeles—"where the birds cough"—is notorious for its auto-produced smog. Indeed, wealthy Angelenos used to drive down to Palm Springs, a desert resort 110 miles away, to escape the Los Angeles smog. But last summer, for the first time, long fingers

William Steif, *The Progressive,* April 1970.

of tear-producing, yellow-gray smog appeared over Palm Springs.

Another example

[7]   Or consider the experience of the twenty-two men working the toll booths at either end of the Brooklyn-Battery Tunnel—all but one in their twenties and thirties. More than half were found to have dizzy spells from a higher-than-average concentration of carbon monoxide in their lungs. Over the one-month period in which the twenty-two were studied, five of the men had blackouts.

Factual statement, giving statistics

[8]   The death rate from bronchitis and emphysema in the United States today is nine times as high as it was twenty years ago. At the present rate of increase, 180,000 Americans will die of these lung ailments in 1983. . . .

Explanation—how the human body works

[9]   About thirty per cent of the oxygen inhaled by a person goes to the brain. Without it, the brain is fatally damaged within six minutes. The highly specialized tissue of human lungs—an evolution of millions of years —acts as a one-way screen, holding back the blood on one side but permitting the air's oxygen to make its way to the blood, where millions of red cells transport it to other body tissues and exchange the fresh oxygen for carbon dioxide, a waste which is conveyed back to the lungs and exhaled.

[10]   Almost everyone knows not to shut the garage doors when the auto's motor is running, but not many people know why.

Explanation—how internal combustion engines work

[11]   The reason is that the auto's internal combustion engine emits great quantities of carbon monoxide, a poison which has an affinity for the blood's hemoglobin—the red cells transporting oxygen—about 210 times greater than oxygen. Thus, relatively small concentrations of carbon monoxide can deprive vital body functions of an oxygen supply. The result, as recent studies have confirmed, can be headaches, loss of visual acuity, decreased muscular coordination, loss of energy, blackouts, damage to the central nervous system, and reduced chance of survival from heart attacks.

Cause and effect

[12]   Fresh air contains less than one-tenth of one part carbon monoxide for each million parts of air. The air in large American cities contains 100 times that amount of carbon monoxide. The bulk of it comes from the internal combustion engines of automobiles. . . .

More explanation of how car engines work

[13]   The engine burns its fuel within itself. Its carburetor mixes air with gasoline. The mixture is forced into combustion chambers (cylinders), where sparks explode the mixture intermittently, driving pistons. The power produced is transmitted to the wheels.

[14]   The problem is the intermittent explosion of the fuel—a process in which the fuel is never completely burned. . . .

Proposed changes

[15]   So far, the chief anti-pollution improvements on the internal combustion engine have taken two forms: Injecting air into the still-hot mixture going out the exhaust system, thus creating more thorough combustion, or regulating the carburetor jet or nozzle that mixes gasoline with air more precisely, so that less fuel goes into the mixture.

[16]   The latter method is used on about eighty per cent of new American cars because the former method requires an air pump and is more expensive. Using these two methods—and including the 1971 model year—total air pollution from automobiles will diminish somewhat in the 1970s, but by 1980, NAPCA says, it will be on the increase again because of the growing number of autos on the highways. . . .

A prediction

Comment from a car manufacturer

[17]   As for tests with such nonpolluting vehicles as the electric car, Henry Ford II said, in 1968: "We have tremendous investments in facilities for engines, transmissions, and axles, and I can't see throwing these away just because the electric car doesn't emit fumes." And when asked what his company's greatest problem was, Ford replied, "That's easy, making more money."

Responses

1. According to Steif, what causes air pollution that is damaging to humans? Does he say it is the *only* cause? How does he support his belief?
2. Why is the article called "Why the Birds Cough"? Do birds really cough? Would "Why People Cough" be a better title? Why or why not?
3. How effective are paragraphs 1, 2, 3, and 4 in helping Steif make his point? Why? How effective are paragraphs 9 through 13? Why?
4. Paragraph 12 probably comes closest to giving the main idea sentence of the article. What is it? After reading the whole article, can you produce the complete main idea sentence the writer probably had in mind? What was it?

5. Actually this article contains more than one cause-and-effect relationship. The first deals with the main cause of carbon monoxide pollution. What are the others? Look carefully at paragraphs 3 and 16. Which cause-and-effect relationships are best supported?
6. What is the effect of ending the article with paragraph 17?
7. In this article, which was written more than ten years ago, Steif repeats NAPCA's prediction that by 1980 air pollution from automobiles will be on the increase again. Was the prediction accurate? Write a short paper giving your answer and explaining it. If you think air pollution from cars has not increased, explain why the prediction was wrong. If you think it has increased, mention the causes, some of which are suggested by this article. But be sure that you have your own facts straight; you'll be able to get some information on this topic in your college library.

Trouble Diagnosis for Direction Signals

diagnosis: discovering and explaining some trouble
intermittent: stopping, then beginning again

[1]   Correct operation of the direction signal requires that the bright filament of the parking and tail lamps on the right or left side of car (depending on switch position) flash whether or not the head or parking, tail lamps, or stop lamps are "on." Note especially that when the stop lamps are "on," switching the direction signal "on" should cause the stop light on that side of car to blink while the stop light on the opposite side glows steadily.

[2]   If the direction signal is operating correctly, it will be indicated by a regular intermittent flashing of the red pilot light located on the speedometer dial. If either the front or rear lamp is not flashing, it will be indicated by the pilot light flashing once when the direction signal switch is turned "on" and then remaining off even though the switch is still in the "on" position. In this case the inoperative parking light or tail and stop lamp bulbs should be checked for a burned out bright filament. If this is not burned out, the circuit between the inoperative lamp and steering column switch should be checked. Note that if the stop lights work when brake pedal is depressed, lamp filament and wiring from direction signal switch to stop lamps is satisfactory.

[3]   If the direction signal is entirely inoperative, check fuse, flasher unit, and circuit from accessory fuse block up through steering column switch in the order named. Checking the flasher with a known good flasher is a simple operation, since the flasher is plugged into a 3-prong connector under the instrument panel.

Edward J. Mayo, *Automobile Accessories Repair Guide* (Chicago: Frederick J. Drake, 1958), pp. 67–71.

DIRECTIONAL SIGNAL INDICATOR DIAGNOSIS

1. Fails to operate
    a. Blown fuse
    b. All bulbs burned out
    c. Inoperative flasher unit
    d. Defective *manual* switch
    e. Inspect wiring harness for broken wires
    f. Check for loose socket connection, etc.
2. Lights burn—but *will not* flash
    a. Inoperative flasher unit
    b. Check for ground or short
3. Lights burn on one side only
    a. Bulb burned out
    b. Defective switch or wiring
4. Lights stay on
    a. Defective or disconnected wiring from manual switch to flasher or ignition switch
5. Improper cancellation
    a. Incorrect tension of switch hold down spring
    b. Poor or no contact between cancelling cam with cancelling pawls on manual switch

Responses

1. One of the reasons for knowing how something works is to understand the possible causes for its not working. What part of this article is operational analysis? Where does the causal analysis begin?
2. Sometimes there is a very thin line between analysis and giving directions, and the difference often depends on who the readers are expected to be. Who is the intended audience for this article? What sentences in the article sound more like giving directions than like straight analysis? Why?
3. Does the list at the end of the article help in understanding why direction lights might not work? If you think it does help, explain how. If you think the list is unnecessary, refer to the article itself to show where all the needed information has already been given.
4. In two or three paragraphs, first explain how some gadget works and then analyze the possible causes for its failure to work. You can either use some gadget you have not written about before, or you can begin with the operational analysis you wrote for response 3 on p. 175 and add a paragraph analyzing what could go wrong to make the gadget stop working.

If I'm So Smart, How Come I Flunk All the Time?

standardized: carefully controlled, kept within measurable limits
bias: inclination, established attitude
belligerent: aggressive, hostile
inadequate: not sufficient or suitable
image: appearance one creates for others

[1]   Can twenty flunking students of varying intelligence raise their math and English a full year's level in only thirty working days?

[2]   Dr. Lloyd Homme, chief of a special educational "fix-it" laboratory in Albuquerque, New Mexico, said yes and put teams of behavioral scientists together with the flunking students to work on the problem. Any available technology could be used—teaching machines, programmed instruction, computer-assisted methods—to cram a year's knowledge into the boys.

[3]   Were the experiments a success? The scientists said yes but the students said no. When grades were measured using standardized tests under strict laboratory conditions, marks went up more than one year on the average. Meanwhile, back at the school, the students were still barely passing, at best. "The experiment was fine for the scientists. They proved their theory on paper and made a name for themselves, but most of us were still flunking in class," remarked one seventeen-year-old.

[4]   The only clue to the mystery was this common remark: "The teachers ignore us—they've got it in for us."

[5]   At first the scientists on the team thought the complaint was just sour grapes and told the boys to work harder. When grades still failed to rise, the scientists felt there might be some truth in what the young team members were saying. Not that teachers were to blame, necessarily, but there still might be some negative bias. "You should see what goes on in class!" said the boys.

[6]   "The only thing to do was to take them up on it, go into the classroom with them and see what was holding back their grades," said Dr. Homme.

[7]   Hence, bearded behavioral scientists ended up in the back row of math and English classes and made observations about the behavior of students and teachers. Homme was surprised to discover that two simple actions made the difference.

[8]   "With few exceptions, our students acted like dummies," said Dr. Homme, "even though we knew they were ahead of the rest in knowledge. They were so used to playing the class idiot that they didn't know how to show what they knew. Their eyes wandered, they appeared absent-minded or even belligerent. One or two read magazines hidden under their desks, thinking, most likely, that they already knew the classwork. They rarely volunteered and often had to have questions repeated because they weren't listening. Teachers, on the other hand, did not trust our laboratory results. Nobody was going to tell them that 'miracles' could work on Sammy and Jose."

Charles W. Slack, "If I'm So Smart How Come I Flunk All the Time?" *Eye,* January 1969.

[9]   In the eyes of teachers, students seemed to fall into three groups. We'll call them: *bright-eyes, scaredy-cats* and *dummies.*

Bright-eyes had perfected the trick of:
1. "eyeballing" the instructor at all times, even from the minute he [sic] entered the room.
2. never ducking their eyes away when the instructor glanced at *them.*
3. getting the instructor to call on them when they wanted *without* raising their hands.
4. even making the instructor go out of his way to call on someone else to "give others a chance" (especially useful when bright-eyes themselves are uncertain of the answer).
5. readily admitting ignorance so as not to bluff—but in such a way that it sounds as though ignorance is rare.
6. asking many questions.

Scaredy-cats [the middle group]:
1. looked toward the instructor but were afraid to let him "catch their eyes."
2. asked few questions and gave the impression of being "underachievers."
3. appeared uninvolved and had to be "drawn out," so they were likely to be criticized for "inadequate participation."

Dummies (no matter how much they really knew):
1. never looked at the instructor.
2. never asked questions.
3. were stubborn about volunteering information in class.

[10]   To make matters worse, the tests in school were not standardized and not given nearly as frequently as those given in the laboratory. School test-scores were open to teacher bias. Classroom behavior of students counted a lot toward their class grades. There was no doubt that teachers were biased against the dummies. The scientists concluded that no matter how much knowledge a dummy gained on his own, his grades in school were unlikely to improve unless he could somehow change his image into a bright-eyes. This would mean . . .

1. Look the teacher in the eye.
2. Ask questions and volunteer answers (even if uncertain).

[11]   "Teachers get teacher-training in how to play their roles. Why shouldn't students get student-training in how to play bright-eyes?" asked Homme. Special training sessions were held at the laboratory. Dummies were drilled in eyeballing and hand-raising, which, simple as they sound, weren't easy to do. "I felt so square I could hardly stand it," complained one of the dummies. "That was at first. Later, when I saw others eyeballing and hand-raising and really learning more, I even moved my seat to the front. It flipped the teacher out of her skull. She couldn't get over it."

[12]   Those who found eyeballing especially difficult were taught to look at the instructor's mouth or the bridge of his nose. "Less threatening to the student," explained Homme. "It seems less aggressive to them."

[13]   Unfortunately, not all of the dummies were able to pick up new habits during the limited training period. Some learned in the laboratory but couldn't do it in the classrooom. These became scaredy-cats—at least a step up. But for the majority, grades improved steadily once they got the hang of their new techniques. The students encouraged and helped each other to hand-raise and eyeball.

[14]   Teachers' comments reflected the improvement. "There is no doubt that student involvement was increased by the program and as a result grades went up."

[15]   By way of advice to others wishing to improve their own eyeballing and hand-raising, student Jose Martinez suggests: "Don't try to do it all at once. You'll shock the teacher and make it tough for yourself. Begin slowly. Work with a friend and help each other. Do it like a game. Like exercising with weights—it takes practice but it's worth it."

[16]   Homme agrees. "In fact, results are guaranteed for life," he says.

Responses

1. No single main idea sentence is used in this causal analysis, although the main point is implied all the way through. Which of these statements comes closest to what you think is the main idea? Justify your answer by what the article says and by the way it begins and the way it ends.
   a. Students flunk because they know less than other students in their classes.
   b. Students flunk because teachers have it in for them.
   c. Students flunk because they want to.
   d. Students flunk because they don't look the teacher in the eye and don't ask questions or volunteer answers.
2. How does the title of this article help you decide what the main idea is?
3. In analyzing why some fairly well informed students get low grades, the writer uses two other writing purposes: classifying and giving directions. Find what is being classified, and make a chart showing the divisions the writer uses. Does this classification fit your own experience? Would you make a different classification of the behavior of the students in your own English class?
4. When do the directions appear? Why do you think the writer shifts from *telling why* to *telling how to do it?*
5. In several places in the article, the writer quotes exactly what people said, rather than telling us indirectly what they thought. In paragraph 4, for instance, the writer might have said, "The students thought the teachers had it in for them." Look at the other direct quotes, and decide what the change in effect would be if no direct quotes were used.
6. Think back over your own experience when you were in high school. Then write a short paper analyzing the causes for some end-of-term grade you

received, whether it was high or low. Try to avoid such obvious and probably inaccurate causes as "because I knew all the answers" or "because I was the worst in the class."

The Game

alternative: a different choice

[1]   JOHN (on the telephone): Are you busy tonight? How about going to a movie?

ALICE (hesitating): Well, I guess that's O.K. (She had been planning to go shopping after work and then go home and wash her hair.) Yes . . . that would be fun (weakly), I suppose.

JOHN: What would you like to see?

ALICE (softly): Oh, it really doesn't make any difference.

JOHN: We could see the new Fellini film downtown, or we could just zip over to the Varsity and see the western.

ALICE: Whichever you prefer. (She hates westerns.)

JOHN: I don't feel like driving all the way downtown, so let's go to the Varsity.

ALICE (long pause, followed by a sigh): Well . . . O.K.

JOHN: Are you sure that's what you want?

ALICE: It doesn't really matter that much—whatever you like.

[2]   Whenever we choose to stay uninvolved and give up our part in making choices, it is often because of the mistaken belief that expressing an opinion will antagonize others.

[3]   To avoid giving an opinion is to *avoid responsibility for the course that the action takes,* for any *conflicts* it may present, and for its *outcome.* "Don't blame me. I had nothing to do with it." "Everybody else was doing it." "I knew it would be a terrible movie, but *you* wanted to see it."

[4]   The deliberately uninvolved person is *never wrong*—and *never right*. She *never takes the risks* of being positive and using her power—and she never experiences the satisfaction of being responsible for getting what she wants. But in trying to avoid antagonizing others, she may end up irritating them even more than she would have by being straightforward.

[5]   A woman who wants to stay uninvolved may also rationalize away her wants by discounting their value. "Let Jack have the promotion. It's probably more important to him than it is to me."

[6]   The obvious alternative to staying uninvolved is to express one's own opinion,

Lynn Z. Bloom, Karen Coburn, and Joan Pearlman, "Be More Assertive," *New Woman,* May–June 1976.

directly and honestly. When John called, Alice could have admitted that she already had made plans to go shopping. She might then have listened to John's suggestions of movies, and have changed her mind if she honestly preferred the new possibility. If not, she could have thanked him for the invitation but said that she preferred to stick with her original plan. If she really wanted to see John at another time, she could have told him so.

Responses

1. Causal analysis is an attempt to find out why something *has* happened; it is closely related to prediction, which is an attempt to say, "if this cause is there, this effect *will* occur." In fact, one very ordinary reason for making a causal analysis is to help us control future events in the light of what we know about the past. Both causal analysis and prediction, in other words, deal with cause-and-effect relationships. How many of these relationships are dealt with in this article? Consider paragraphs 2, 3, 4, 5, and 6. How reliable do you think the relationships are? Why?
2. Try writing a dialogue between John and Alice at midnight that same night. You may use one of the *causes* suggested in paragraph 2, 3, or 4 as the basis for the dialogue, but your dialogue must show in the direct conversation what you think the *effect* will be.

More Suggestions for Writing

Operational analysis:

a weather vane
a compass
a doorknob
a water faucet
a poultry incubator
a subway turnstile
a pool table
a willow whistle
a flour sifter
a stapler
a churn
a thermos bottle
a dress pattern
a measuring tape
a padlock
a dictionary
getting a withdrawal slip from a class

opening a checking account
getting a credit card
leasing an apartment
registering to vote
ordering merchandise by mail
correcting a typing error
collecting unemployment insurance
using food stamps

Causal analysis:

bad dreams
insomnia
a broken leg—or arm, etc.
failing a test
a car that won't start
headaches
a fire department strike—or any other strike
a lockout
promotion on a job
a failure to be promoted
a flu epidemic—or any other kind
a letter lost in the mail
a fire
the collapse or destruction of a building
spelling problems
a team that has a losing season
an increase (or decrease?) in bus fares
a store losing customers
a house plant dying
differing scores on IQ tests
speech differences
lowered property values
a divorce
failure to enforce some law
decrease in fatal accidents

Chapter 7

Telling What Happened: Objective Reports

A report is an account of something that has happened, written in such a way that somebody who wasn't there can understand clearly just what did occur. Reports are usually not concerned with telling people how to do something or coaxing them to do it. Reports seldom bother with why an event occurred, and they don't praise the event or condemn it. They simply say that it happened. When you fill out your income tax report, for instance, you don't explain to the government why you made that much money (or that little). You don't, in the report at least, plead with the government to let you pay at a different rate or not at all. Instead, you tell the Internal Revenue Service how much money you earned, how much interest you paid on your house and your charge accounts, how many children you supported last year. Occasionally people who think the tax is unfair take the issue to the courts or don't make the report at all; but if they do make it, they stick to the financial facts.

Sometimes, of course, the term *report* is used more loosely than we are using it here. High-school teachers ask their students for "book reports" when the teachers actually want students to say what they think about the books they read. Government agencies issue "reports" on the health of Americans when they are actually analyzing why more cases of polio occurred this year than last. Stockbrokers print "reports" on whether the price of General Motors stock will go up or down when they are actually trying to predict the future—guessing about how many people will buy automobiles and for how much money. Looked at in one way, all these things do contain reports. In his paper, Edgar Lawson is telling his English teacher about one thing that happened (Edgar did read *Invisible Man*) before he goes on to say what he liked about the book. The government agency is telling about the number of people in the country who had polio last year before it speculates as to why the disease once again seems to be becoming a problem. The investment company is telling about what happened, too—how much the price of steel increased last year, how many auto workers went on strike, how severe the gasoline shortage was—and then making guesses as to how many cars will be sold. The prediction is based on a report of what has already happened. In this chapter, however, the term *report* will not include comments or analyses or predictions. It will just mean "an account of what has happened."

Everybody's life is full of reports. Your bank statement is a report of how many checks you wrote plus the number of deposits and withdrawals you made; and your telephone bill tells you not only that the basic rate has gone up again but that somebody used your phone to call Anchorage, Alaska, twice last month. When the college sends you a copy of your transcript, you are reading a report on the classes you took and the credit you received. When you glance at the front page of the *Evening Bugle,* you are reading reports of what happened today in the city, in the nation, and in the world.

Whatever your job is, you'll be writing reports as well as reading them. Some of the reports you write will be on ready-made forms that guide you in deciding what to say. An income tax form is one example of such a ready-made guide. An accident report form is another. If your Volkswagen slides into the back of a garbage truck, you'll have to fill in the blanks on a printed form. The form will remind you to tell the police, and probably the insurance company, where the collision occurred and when, how fast you were going, whether the streets were wet or dry. If you work in the admissions room of a hospital, you will probably use a form to report how many patients were admitted last night, who their doctors were, what rooms they were assigned to. If you are a teacher's aid, you'll probably have a form for reporting which children were absent, which ones came in late, which ones lost their lunch money. If you are a traveling TV repairman, you will have to fill in a form reporting what houses you called at, how many tubes you installed, how much time you spent doing it. All these forms help by reminding the writers what must be included in the report.

But other occasions require reports, too, and there are not always forms to act as guides. The secretary of the Gatewood Consumers Association writes the minutes of the November meeting—a report. A biochemist runs a series of tests on lung cancer in mice treated with nicotine and writes up the results of her experiment—a report. Two political science students spend a day with the city council and record what new regulations were discussed, what the mayor said, and how the council members voted—a report. A health officer investigates thirty children who got lead poisoning from flaking paint and turns the findings over to the housing bureau—a report. The housing bureau sends an inspector to examine the apartments where the children live—another report.

If these reports are satisfactory, they will have several things in common even though they deal with very different kinds of events:

1. Good reports are *precise;* they never leave their readers guessing.
2. Good reports are *orderly;* readers are never in any doubt about what happened first, what came next.
3. Good reports *stick to the subject;* readers are never left saying to themselves, "What does that have to do with it?"

4. Good reports are *complete;* they never cheat their readers by leaving out any part of what happened, even though the writer may not like it.
5. Good reports are *accurate;* they get the facts straight and present them to readers honestly and fairly.
6. Good reports are *objective;* they tell their readers what happened, not what the writer thinks about it.

Precision

Reports, perhaps more than most other kinds of writing, need to be precise. Precision means exactness. It means hitting the nail on the head—not half an inch to one side. In writing, precision means finding exactly the right word to tell what happened instead of settling for some other word fairly close to it.

The teacher's aide who writes "A few boys were absent" will not have a satisfactory report; the form must say "seven boys" and perhaps give their names. Nor can the TV repairman say "a battered old television set"; the report must say "a 21-inch Trutone Model X-489, with the picture tube gone." The biochemist must say "2 milligrams" instead of "a little bit"; and the housing inspector will write "lien against the property" instead of "the owner owes some money." The nurse may write "dysphasia" instead of "can't talk very well." In making all these choices, the writers want the exact wording—they want to be precise.

Nevertheless, before you choose an uncommon word in writing a report, ask yourself, "Does this word work better than a familiar, ordinary word? Is it more precise?" Part of your answer to that question will depend on the kind of report you are writing and who your readers will be. If you are writing a chemistry report instead of a recipe, you will need to say "sodium chloride," not salt. In chemistry there are many kinds of salts, and a good report will make clear which kind of salt you mean. If, on the other hand, you are reporting on conditions in the college cafeteria, it would be silly to say that some tables are supplied with pepper but not sodium chloride. And the nurse who writes "dysphasia" on the report is writing for doctors and other nurses, not for the worried parents of the child. When the doctor reports to the mother and father, she will try to use words with which they are familiar.

In reports, as in other kinds of writing, if there is a common, easily understood word for what you want to say, that word is usually the best choice. The word most people know is the word everybody is likely to understand. A teacher's aide who writes "The elementary educator operating in the learning situation to which I was assigned provided the students with assistance in philately" is merely showing off. "The sixth-grade teacher I worked under helped the children with their stamp collections" is a much better choice. "Sixth-grade teacher" is not only easier to understand, it's much more precise than "elementary educator." The political science students will say "the council members from wards 26 and 14" instead of "a couple of good old boys," which is vague, or "a duo of duly elected representatives of the people's will," which is pretentious.

Use ordinary words instead of fancy ones when the meaning is precise enough for the situation, but you don't have to stay with a "See Spot run" vocabulary. When you come across new words in your reading, don't ignore them just because they sound strange or new; but don't use them in your writing just for their fine sound, either. Examine them to see whether they are more precise than the common words they're replacing, and decide whether the audience you are writing for is likely to understand them. In writing reports, choose long or uncommon words only when you are sure that they are necessary for precision and that they actually do make your meaning clearer.

Order

Just as each word used in a report must be clear and exact, the order must be clear and exact, too. The best order for a report is like the order for giving directions. When you were telling someone how to do something, you began with the first step and went on to the next. When you are telling someone what *has been* done, report what happened first, what happened next, and how it all ended. Another way of saying it is that reports should be arranged in chronological order. The secretary of the Gatewood Consumers Association will have pretty unsatisfactory minutes if he writes them like this:

> Twenty-six members and four guests were present. Right at the end of the meeting Gertrude Abernathy announced that both branches of Best Brands Supermarket are going to begin unit pricing, and Ms. Abernathy was congratulated on what everybody agreed was a considerable victory. One of the guests was Peter Jones, vice president in charge of public relations for Gasco Company. Ms. Abernathy's committee has been working with the manager of Best Brands for two years, trying to get unit pricing put in. Bad news was that only ninety-five people have signed the petition protesting the increase in telephone rates. Early in the meeting the chairperson announced that the cost-of-living index has gone up two points this month and that the treasurer has moved to Colorado Springs. Another guest was Adeline Smith, secretary of the suburban consumer association in Little Rock. Unit pricing at Best Brands will begin fairly soon. We agreed to keep on trying on the telephone petitions.
>
> John H. Durham, secretary

Unless he wants the association to elect a new secretary, Mr. Durham will have to revise those minutes before the next meeting.

Sticking to the Subject

Another thing a report has in common with giving directions is that both kinds of writing must stick to the subject. Whenever the writer becomes sidetracked and gives readers a chance to say, "What does *that* have to do with it?" the report is off the subject. The political science students will not comment on the odd way the mayor's husband was dressed, even though they had trouble keeping their eyes off his flaming red tie and his purple and orange striped pants. The housing inspector will not comment on how big the philodendrons are or the number of comic books in the kitchen; he will confine his report to the flaking paint. When the secretary of the Gatewood Consumers Association improves those minutes by rearranging the order, the final result won't be very satisfactory if he adds details that have nothing to do with the meeting:

> At the November meeting, twenty-six members and four guests were present. It was raining hard in the morning, but by meeting time it had pretty much cleared up. One of the guests was Peter Jones, vice president in charge of public relations for Gasco Company, a very fat man with a walrus mustache. The other guest was Adeline Smith, secretary of the suburban consumer association in Little Rock. That's a new association that hasn't done much so far. The chairperson made two announcements. The first was that Casey Washington, treasurer of the association, has moved to Colorado Springs. My daughter says his children didn't want to go because the boy is a senior this year and didn't like changing schools. The second announcement was that the cost-of-living index has gone up two points this month. Kaye Underwood reported that only ninety-five people have signed the petition protesting the increase in telephone rates. My own telephone bill was five dollars higher last month, and I can remember when the whole bill was not much more than five dollars. Of course, that was for a party line. All the members agreed to keep trying on the telephone petitions. Finally, Gertrude Abernathy reported that both branches of the Best Brands Supermarket are going to begin unit pricing on March 14. Ms. Underwood made a motion congratulating Ms. Abernathy on a considerable victory, since her committee has been working with the manager of Best Brands for two years. The meeting adjourned at 5:00 P.M., and I was glad it wasn't raining.

Unless Mr. Durham can do better than that, the Gatewood Consumers Association certainly needs a new secretary.

Completeness

It is easy enough to see that the secretary included too much in his report. It is not nearly as easy to tell what he may have left out.

Perhaps Mr. Jones was invited to explain the way gas rates are determined and distributed a chart showing which rates apply to industrial users and which rates apply to householders. Those details belong in the report. Or perhaps the association agreed to organize a one-month boycott of beef products to protest the most recent price increase. Even though Mr. Durham disapproves of boycotts, voted against it, and has no intention of giving up his Friday night T-bone, he must include the resolution in the minutes.

As you can see, a report must be complete if it is to be honest, but completeness also affects usefulness. For example, the biochemist must make her report on the mice experiment complete if it is to be useful, either to her readers or for her own records. She cannot say:

> Last week I inoculated some mice with a nicotine solution in some sugar water. Now about half of the ones in the cage are still looking all right, but my brother hopes they will all die because he's afraid they'll get loose and come into the kitchen.

Such a statement is incomplete in two ways: it is inexact, and it does not contain enough details. For exactness, we need to know *when* the biochemist began the experiment, *how many* mice were inoculated, *how much* nicotine and *how much* sugar the solution contained, and what is meant by "about half" and "looking all right." And, of course, we don't care what her brother thought about it; his distaste for mice under the stove has nothing to do with the experiment. For completeness of details, we need to know what happened to the half that do not seem all right. Did they die? Did they sneak out through a hole in the cage and actually get into the kitchen? Have they been moved to another cage because they didn't look all right? Since the purpose of the report is to record what happened to the mice that were shot full of nicotine, a complete report must include several pieces of information not given here: What were the proportions of the solution? How many days have passed since the inoculation? How many mice were there? What, exactly, happened to each one of them?

The biochemist will help both her readers and her own records if her report reads more like this:

> On September 16, I inoculated twenty white mice with 10 milligrams of nicotine in a 2-percent sugar solution. On September 17, five of the mice refused to eat. On September 18, ten refused food and four would not move, although they were still breathing. On September 19, five mice were dead, seven refused food, and eight appeared to be eating and moving normally.

This report could be made even more complete. The biochemist could tell us at what hour the injections were given, the kind of food the mice were offered, and whether the mice that died on the nineteenth were the same mice that wouldn't eat on the seventeenth.

It would probably be a mistake, however, for her to spend much time and space recording just what kind of food was given, the time of day it was offered, whether it was warmed or very cold, and the type of dish the food was in. That the mice did not eat must be included in the report because loss of appetite is one of the symptoms of nicotine poisoning. But so is the lack of movement, and the biochemist will be overemphasizing the appetite loss if she gives lots of detail about the food and almost no information about the tails that didn't twitch or the mice that just lay there when she poked them gently with a stick. Complete reports give equal space to equally important elements.

In making out your accident report, for instance, you might decide that a complete description of your Volkswagen includes the information that it's pale yellow, that it has two bad tears in the back upholstery, that the cigarette lighter won't work. These details don't have much to do with the accident. It doesn't matter what color your car is. Even the insurance company, if your car was totaled, won't care much about the cigarette lighter or the condition of the back seat.

In deciding whether you ought to add more details to your report, ask yourself these questions:

1. Do the details have something to do with how the event turned out?
2. Am I giving too much information about one part of the event and too little about another?
3. Can the readers understand exactly what happened without the details?

Accuracy

A complete report will always include *who* and *what* and *when* and *where* and *how much,* unless the people who read the report will already know some of these things. A complete report will be exact in the details it gives and precise in the words it uses. But none of this completeness and precision will do much good unless the details are accurate. When the biochemist said "last week," and the secretary said "fairly soon," they were not being exact. When they made their reports more precise, we hope they made them accurate, too. September 16 and September 26, March 14 and May 14 are all *exact,* but only one of them is *accurate.* The manager of the Best Brands Supermarket will be justifiably indignant if customers complain on March 20 that there's no unit pricing on the shelves, when the date actually announced was *May 14,* not March 14. And the customers will be indignant, too, if the unit pricing says 4.6 cents an ounce for a one-pound package of soap flakes that costs 84 cents. The customers are likely to think they are being deliberately misled, and it won't improve Best Brands' business much for the manager to explain that it was just a careless mistake—the sign should have said 74 cents.

Whenever a report includes dates and numbers and quantities—and most of them will, for reports deal in exactness—the dates and numbers and quantities must be right. Guessing isn't good enough; the writer has to know. And what the writer knows is what must actually be in the report. The TV repairman can't say, "Installing the picture tube took quite a while." But if his report says, "Time: 12 hrs., 4 min.," Ms. Jones is likely to protest. She knows the repairman arrived at lunchtime and left just before dinner. If the repairman hastily removes the "1" so that the report reads, "Time: 2 hrs., 4 min.," Ms. Jones may be satisfied but the television company will lose money. What the report should read, to be accurate, is, "Time: 4 hrs., 12 min."

The newspaper that reports, "Cyrus P. Witherspoon, of 4612 East Main Street, was arrested Saturday night on suspicion of selling marijuana," when actually it was Cyril B. Witherspoon, who lives at 462 West Main, may find itself on the unpleasant end of a lawsuit.

Most of us trust the reports we read, just as we trust the manufacturers of yardsticks to make all their inches the same length, or the bus company to hire only bus drivers who have passed the driving test. Because most readers do trust reports, you have a special obligation to make sure the facts you give are exactly accurate.

Objectivity

Objectivity may be the most important characteristic of reports. *Objectivity* is the opposite of *subjectivity*. When you write *objectively* you keep yourself out of what you say; when you write *subjectively* you put yourself in. People who write subjectively see everything so much in relation to themselves that what they say is not of much use to anybody else. Of course, we all see things from our own point of view simply because it is physically impossible for us to *be* anybody else. It is possible, however, to remember this tendency and make a great effort to stay neutral. Unless you try hard to be neutral, you don't stand much chance of being objective.

To be objective means to keep opinions out of your report. But keeping opinions out involves more than remembering not to say "I liked it" or "I didn't like it." Some kinds of opinions are obvious: most of us realize that the TV repairman's report should not say Ms. Jones is a sloppy housewife; and that the newspaper reporter, when the Cyrus/Cyril apology is printed, should not tell readers that Cyrus Witherspoon is an upright citizen, who could never be suspected of breaking the law, whereas Cyril is a pretty suspicious character. Other kinds of opinions, however, are harder to recognize; in order to identify all of them, we have to know the difference between statements of fact and statements of opinion.

Fact and Opinion

A factual statement can always be checked, even though the person doing the checking may not share the writer's tastes and prejudices. If your son tells you it's raining outside, he has made a factual statement. What he says may not be accurate; maybe the rain stopped an hour ago. *But statements do not have to be accurate to be factual.* One advantage of factual statements is that they *can* be checked for accuracy. Unless you are sick in bed, you can go outside and see whether it's raining.

An opinion statement, on the other hand, lets the writer's judgment creep in, even though at first glance the statement may look factual. If your son tells you the weather is lousy, he has given you his opinion, and you cannot possibly check his statement for accuracy. Both of you mean the same thing by *rain,* but your son wants to play baseball and you want the garden watered. In the winter, when he wants to go sledding, he may think 45 degrees and bright sunshine make "lousy weather." You have made a factual statement if you tell your son that the temperature is 45 degrees—he can check the thermometer if he doesn't believe you. You have made an opinion statement if you tell him, "What a beautiful winter day!"

Perhaps you have read a report on Granite City, in which the writer refers to it as a large and prosperous town. Is that a factual statement or just the writer's opinion? Though "large and prosperous" may seem like facts, they are really opinion because the words *large* and *prosperous* depend on what the writer's experience has been. People who grew up on a farm where the nearest shopping center was a village of five hundred may think Granite City, with its five thousand inhabitants, is a huge place. But to people who grew up in New York or San Francisco, Granite City may seem very tiny. And people living where nobody can afford shoes for school and where having both bacon and beans at the same meal is a feast may think that owning three pairs of shoes at the same time or eating hamburger every night is the height of prosperity. People who never eat steak unless it's filet mignon and who give their shoes to Goodwill as soon as the toes are scuffed may see the ordinary citizen of Granite City as pitifully poverty-stricken.

All such words as *large, small, lousy, beautiful, prosperous, poverty-stricken,* are subjective. Such words depend on the writer's point of view, and we all have our own ideas of what they mean. No statements that contain such words can be checked. If you are thinking about moving to Granite City, a report that tells you it is large and prosperous won't help much. You need a report that says Granite City has a population of five thousand, that it has two grade schools and a consolidated high school, that the business section contains a movie theater, three groceries, two banks, and a tavern, all of which have been painted within the last two years. Then if you doubt the report, you can go to Granite City and count the people, count the schools and businesses, and look at the paint. While you are there, you will form your own opinion of Granite City's relative size and prosperity. But if you write a *report* for your employers, who are thinking of opening a branch there, you must include just the factual information and let your employers, in turn, form their own opinions.

Most of the knockdown, dragout arguments people get into could be avoided if we all remembered that some terms always rest on opinion. Are the Green Sox a *better* baseball team than the Blue Sox? Is baseball a *better* game than hockey? Are the teen-agers of this generation *worse* than their parents were at that age? Is the little boy next door *naughty* or *neglected?* None of these arguments can be settled until the people who are arguing decide what they mean by *better, worse, naughty,* and *neglected.* They must define their terms. Once they agree that *better* in baseball means home runs hit, bases stolen, games won, dollars earned, or fan mail received, they have something that can be checked. The sports section of the newspaper will tell them which team won the most games; and if they know a player on each team, they may be able to get an accurate report on the fan mail. In the same way, before we can decide whether teen-agers are *better* or *worse,* we have to decide what kind of behavior we want to consider. Do they get better grades in school? Are they arrested more often? Do they earn more money? Less money? Are we talking about everybody between twelve and twenty? Does the discussion refer to all the students in Overland High, all the kids on our block, or just the sixteen-year-old twins across the street? Until we make the discussion precise and until we produce the objective facts on which our opinions rest, the opinions aren't worth much.

The purpose of reports is to tell what happened, not to interpret the events. The teacher's aid who tells the school nurse, "Tommy's face is flushed and he has four red spots on his forehead. He has sneezed four times in the last five minutes, and his nose is running" is reporting. The teacher's aid who says, "Tommy doesn't feel very well" is interpreting. The first report includes only events that can be checked; the second tells what the teacher's aid thinks the events mean.

Slanting

Even when we try to report just the facts, our own attitude toward what happened tends to influence our choice of words. Getting rid of the opinions that sneak in with the words we use is sometimes very difficult. When we talk about people of other races, the words we choose often reveal more about us and our attitudes than about the people we are discussing. Whether white tenants call their Black landlord a "darky," a "colored man," a "nigger," a "Negro," a "spook," or a "Black man" has very little to do with the landlord; it has a lot to do with the tenants—how old they are, what magazines they read, what their prejudices are. In the same way, the Black tenants who call their white landlord "Mr. Charley," "whitey," "the man," "honky," or "sir" are not really discussing the man who collects the rent; they're discussing themselves.

Unfortunately, not all slant is that easy to recognize. If the local newspaper calls David Meddlar "a local businessman," we'll get quite a different impression than if he is called an "entrepreneur" or a "bookie." Whether Ms. Stevens is listed as a lawyer, a homemaker, or a women's liberationist will affect our vision of her—and may make the difference between Ms. Stevens getting elected to the city council or being defeated. The *referent* of the word (the actual thing or person the word refers to) hasn't changed at all. Ms. Stevens is still Ms. Stevens. She *does* practice law, she *does* mop the kitchen and get dinner, she *does* subscribe to *Ms.* and lecture in favor of the Equal Rights Amendment. All these terms are accurate enough in one sense, but they slant because, like stereotyping, they select just one part of Ms. Stevens's life and ignore the rest of her.

Suppose a headline in the *New York Times* said, "Jets Demolish Packers in Season Opener." As you read the article, you find out that the final score was 28–14—a fairly large point spread but not exactly demolishing. You keep reading and discover that Green Bay led the Jets 14–7 at the end of the third quarter. In the first play of the fourth quarter, the Packers' defensive tackle, who had been blitzing the Jets' quarterback all evening, was injured. Then the Jets completed several crucial passes and won the game 28–14. A turn of events seems to have helped the Jets win; the only thing that was demolished about the Packers was their injured tackle, and he was just injured, not demolished. That headline, which might seem objective at a glance, is actually full of slant and inference *against* the Packers.

But it's also possible to slant *toward*. Green Bay's headline might have said, "Injury Lets Jets Slip by Packers." Green Bay feels that they surely would have won the game if their tackle hadn't been injured. They didn't consider the possibility that the Jets' quarterback could have gotten hot and might have completed those passes with or without the Packers' blitz. Green Bay downplayed the fact that their offense failed to get a single first down in the fourth quarter. The facts are: the Packers led the game 14–7 at the end of the third quarter; the Packers' tackle was injured on the first play of the fourth quarter; New York's quarterback completed five passes in the fourth quarter; the Jets won the game 28–14.

An objective report would merely include these facts and draw no conclusions about cause and effect or what might have happened.

Good reports avoid slanting, either for the subject or against it. They neither purr nor snarl. *"Purr" words,* according to S. I. Hayakawa, who invented the term several years ago, are words that express our approval; *"snarl" words* express disapproval. In writing reports, talk about "a woman about seventy years old" instead of "an old hag" or "a sweet little old lady." Say "The car went through the intersection at twenty-five miles an hour," not "The car tore recklessly down the street" or "The car crawled along at a snail's pace." Say "came noiselessly" rather than "sneaked," "said" rather than "boasted" or "whimpered," "walked unevenly" rather than "staggered." If you give readers the facts in neutral terms, they can make their own interpretations.

Main Idea Sentences for Objective Reports

For some of the reports you make, you don't have to develop a main idea sentence; the form itself provides it, and all you have to do is furnish the details. The main idea sentence for an income tax report, for instance, is "We, _____ and _____, who live on _____ [street], in _____ [city], are reporting to the federal [or state] government how much money we made, and some of what we spent, last year." The main idea of an insurance-report form is that you, the insured, are reporting a loss and asking the company to reimburse you for it. The main idea of a job-report form is that the employee, a painter, for instance, spent four hours on Wednesday sanding the ceiling. There are many kinds of report forms. Some of them, such as IRS form 1040, are complicated; and some of them, such as a telephone bill, are simple. In filling out these report forms, writers need to be precise and accurate, complete and objective, but the forms do the rest of the work for them. Forms provide the main idea and a ready-made plan, and, through the kind of information they ask for, nudge the writer into sticking to the subject.

Other kinds of reports, however, leave us on our own. We must provide our own main idea sentences and our own plans. Writing a good main idea sentence will not insure that your report is complete and orderly, but, as usual, it will help. If your main idea sentence is objective and straightforward, it will be easier to keep the rest of the report objective and straightforward, too.

The main idea sentence for a report should make clear what event is being reported, when the event took place, and unless it would be obvious to readers of the report, where. The main idea sentence should tell who (and what) took part in the event. Here are some main idea sentences for several different kinds of reports:

> The regular meeting of the Gatewood Consumers Association took place on November 18, 1976, in the auditorium of the Gatewood Branch Library.

> On September 16, 1975, twenty white mice were inoculated with 10 milligrams of nicotine in a 2-percent sugar solution.

> During January, 1974, thirty children under the age of five were diagnosed as suffering from lead poisoning.

> On March 1, I inspected all eight apartments in the multifamily dwelling at 798 Chevy Chase Avenue, known as the Grand Ronde Hotel, checking for the type of paint used in the living quarters.

> Cyril B. Witherspoon, 462 West Main, was arrested Saturday night on suspicion of selling marijuana.

> Ms. Margaret Stevens, who has been called the city's leading exponent of women's rights, lectured at Raglan College yesterday on the effects of the Equal Rights Amendment.

Notice that all these main idea sentences give exact details; they include names, addresses, dates, and numbers. With one exception, they avoid using opinion words, and even that one—the sentence about Ms. Stevens—uses the opinion words "leading exponent" indirectly by claiming that somebody else said it. If the sentence had said, "Governor Arkwright called her the leading exponent of women's rights," it would be clearly factual; we could check to see whether Governor Arkwright had expressed that opinion.

In the third main idea sentence, "suffering" is probably not an opinion word. As medical people use the term—*"suffering* from the mumps," for instance—*suffering* means "has the mumps" or "sick with the mumps." In more ordinary usage, *suffering* does express opinion, or at least inference: "Take that ribbon off that cat! Can't you see the poor thing is *suffering?"*

Introductions and Conclusions

Most of these main idea sentences might serve as the first sentence of the report itself. Reports need much less introduction than other kinds of writing because reports are usually written for a special audience. Probably nobody except the members of the Gatewood Consumers Association will read the secretary's minutes. Only the biochemist's teacher will read the report of her nicotine experiment, unless there is something so unusual about the mice's reaction that she sends the report to a professional journal. The health inspector's report is written for the city council, and the building inspector's report will go back to the health department. The last two main idea sentences will introduce newspaper reports, but even in those reports readers who don't know the Witherspoons or who aren't interested in the Equal Rights Amendment are not likely to read much further.

Since you have a ready-made audience for your reports, there is less need to try to interest people in what you are reporting. The purpose of a report is to give information, and people who do not want to be informed about what happened will not read your report anyway, no matter how intriguing you try to make it. Fancy attempts to arouse interest will only annoy readers who want information. Stick to the facts, and the interest will take care of itself.

Just as reports don't need much introduction, they don't need very elaborate conclusions either. A good main idea sentence will have made clear the limits of the event you are covering. When you come to the end of the event, you have come to the end of the report:

The meeting adjourned at 5:00 P.M.

By Saturday, September 21, all twenty mice were dead.

Fourteen children were treated and released, fifteen are still in City Hospital, and one child died.

Lead-based paint was found in all but one of the apartments, where the tenant herself had scraped and repainted.

Mr. Witherspoon was released on a recognizance bond.

Ms. Stevens concluded by urging students to sign the petition available in the Student Center.

It's always a temptation to use the conclusion of a report to interpret the events, especially if you feel strongly about the subject. But just as the secretary should not end his minutes by remarking, "That was the dullest meeting I ever attended," so the biochemist must avoid saying, "This experiment proves that nicotine is terrible," and the building inspector must not say, "That landlord ought to be jailed."

Reports can be used to support arguments, of course, and very often are. In fact, the best and most successful attempts to persuade are always supported by facts. The local newspaper may run a series of editorials about the disgraceful conditions in the Grand Ronde Hotel, and argue that the city ordinances must be more strictly enforced. The editorial writer will probably use the health inspector's report and the building inspector's report as the basis for the argument. But the argument will be stronger if the report on which it is based is completely objective.

Examining an Objective Report

Memorandum

TO: Bernie Green, Chief of Parties
FROM: Joe Dawson
SUBJECT: Travel Report, Surveyors' Short Course, February 4–5, 1979.

[1]   As you requested, I am submitting this report of the Surveyors' Short Course held February 4 and 5, 1979, in Omaha, sponsored by the Nebraska Engineering Extension Service.

[2]   The conference opened with a buffet Friday evening. Charles Stacy, Professor of Engineering at the University of Nebraska, was the keynote speaker. As well as being a licensed surveyor, Stacy is a lawyer. He emphasized the need for surveyors to be legally accurate in their work and stressed the importance of upholding all ethical standards set forth in our canon. With today's increasing demand for real estate and with a rise in not-so-ethical practices in real estate, Stacy encouraged surveyors to maintain a high standard of professionalism.

[3]   Saturday morning's session helped reinforce what Stacy had said. John Bartholemew, Extension's vice president in charge of administration, proposed that surveyors consolidate efforts to make all field notes consistent. Currently most surveyors have their own form of abbreviations, which they use in their field notes, since they have no standard to follow. This inconsistency, Bartholemew suggests, could cause legal problems of interpretation.

[4]   Saturday afternoon I examined exhibits of the latest developments in surveying equipment. The new electronic distance meter (available from Surveying Supply Services, 1036 North Main, Omaha) should be useful in our company since most of our surveying is in large, open fields—the meter is not effective in obstructed areas. Other equipment, although fascinating, did not seem feasible for our company. For instance, the new WING computer can draft plots; however, the expenses of the computer ($60,000) and a programmer do not seem efficient for Holland Consultants right now. Brochures of the equipment I examined are attached.

[5]   The conference ended with a special session for Chiefs of Parties, which I did not attend since I am not a member of that group.

[6]   My expense account is attached.

Expenses for Joe Dawson
Surveyors' Short Course
Omaha, Nebraska, February 4–5, 1979

Travel, personal car from Lincoln to Omaha @ 20¢ per mile	$40.00
Cornhusker Hotel, 1 single room, 1 night (receipt attached)	23.00
Conference registration (buffet included)	19.75
2 meals (breakfast and lunch Saturday— receipts attached)	9.46
	$92.21

The introduction to this report is very short, containing only the main idea sentence. The report gives exact details—names, addresses, dates, numbers—and in general it uses ordinary, easy-to-understand words. There is one specialized term, "electronic distance meter," but since the report is written for a man in the surveying field, he'll know what this instrument is. The order is clear and chronological: what happened on Friday, what happened on Saturday. The report sticks to the subject—what happened at the conference. Joe Dawson may tell his family about the roaring party he attended Friday night and the interesting gossip he picked up, but he has very sensibly omitted that part of his activities from his report.

It's impossible to judge whether the report is complete and accurate. We guess that it's complete, since it even discusses the WING computer that wasn't suitable for Holland Consultants; but it's always possible that there was a session on unions for surveyors with which Dawson so strongly disagreed that he left it out. We also trust that the report is accurate. If the Chief of Parties wants additional information on the electronic distance meter, he can write the supply company; and if there's any question about the travel expenses, he can always check the mileage and hotel rates.

Most important, the report is objective. It does not comment that Charles Stacy was a typical professor who didn't know a thing about what was going on in the field, and it does not gush about how grateful Dawson was for a chance to take the trip. The report does contain opinion words: "not-so-ethical" in paragraph 2; "useful," "not effective," and "fascinating" in paragraph 4. When the report uses "not-so-ethical," however, it is stating what Stacy, the keynote speaker, said. When Dawson starts *evaluating* the new equipment (in paragraph 4), notice how he uses more opinion words. The report would be more objective if it said, "The equipment I saw included a new electronic distance meter, a WING computer which does drafting. . . ."

Key Words

Here are some of the important terms used in this chapter. See whether you can answer these questions about them.

1. What is the difference between **reports** and **directions?** In what ways should they be alike? In what ways are they different?
2. Why should you bother to learn new words if ordinary words are usually better? What is meant by **precision** in deciding which words to use? When are unusual words better than ordinary words?
3. Is the **order** of a report more like the order of a paper of directions or the order of a paper of explanation? What should the order be?
4. Explain what is meant by a **complete** report. How can you tell whether your report is complete enough and at the same time make sure it **sticks to the subject?**
5. What is the difference between **exactness** and **accuracy?** Is it possible to be **accurate** without being **exact?** Is it possible to be **exact** without being **accurate?** If your answer is yes, give two or three examples.
6. What is the difference between **objectivity** and **subjectivity?** Can people ever be completely **objective?** Can they ever be completely **subjective?**
7. Distinguish between **factual statements** and **opinion statements.** Do statements need to be accurate to be **factual?**
8. What are **"purr" words** and **"snarl" words?** What do these words have to do with **slanting?**
9. What should the **main idea sentence** of a report contain?
10. What should the **introduction** of a report contain? The **conclusion?**

READINGS
Objective Reports

What You Expect Is What You Get

phenomenon: an observable occurrence
hypothetical: supposed, made up
punitive: intended to punish
inevitable: something which can't be avoided

Main idea sentence; what the report covers

[1] The fact that a person is likely to find what she or he expects to find—a phenomenon more elegantly expressed as "the self-fulfilling prophecy"—has been studied again by three researchers from the University of Oklahoma Health Sciences Center. John Garfield, Steven Weiss and Ethan Pollack asked 18 elementary-school and special counselors to evaluate a hypothetical case: a nine-year-old boy described as defiant, dis-

The experiment described

ruptive, aggressive and a poor achiever. All counselors received the same set of facts, with one difference: half heard that he came from an upper-middle-class family with an income of $24,000 per year; the others, that the total family income, including Aid to Families of Dependent Children, was $320 per month.

Results from the first group

[2] In the case of the upper-class child, the counselors expressed the desire to visit him at home, talk to him personally, and generally become involved with him. With the lower-class child, the counselors took a more punitive attitude and suggested that he be retained in his present grade.

Results from the second group

[3] They were generally pessimistic in their predictions for the future of the lower-class child. They con-

Steven Weiss, *Psychology Today,* July 1973.

sidered delinquency and "dropping out" inevitable, even if the child received adequate help. The researchers also noticed differences in counselor behavior: "In the low-status group, frequent head shaking and sighing by the subjects were observed as the case was presented. None of this behavior was observed in the high-status group."

More details

[4]   Garfield, Weiss and Pollack reported that in the case of the high-income child, the counselors expressed a desire to pursue the facts further before drawing any conclusions. Their response to the lower-class child, in contrast, was resignation and apathy. They apparently saw the upper-class boy as being more important and more worthy of help. Statistically, lower-class children do stand a better chance of becoming delinquent, but the authors felt that "by passively accepting the expect-

Conclusion

ancy of unfavorable outcome, the counselor all too fre-quently contributes to the 'inevitability' of events"—a clear-cut example of the self-fulfilling prophecy in ac-tion.

Source of information

[5]   The article appeared in the *Journal of Counseling Psychology,* Volume 20, Number 2.

Responses

1. The event being reported in this article is research conducted on the self-fulfilling prophecy. What usual information (*who, what, when, where*) are you *not* given? Does the omission matter? Why or why not?
2. What is the effect of saying "described as" in the second sentence of para-graph 1? Who did the describing? Do you care whether or not you are told?
3. This article uses a number of opinion words that make a judgment—"pes-simistic" in paragraph 3, for instance, and "resignation and apathy" in paragraph 4. Are these judgments supported by factual statements? If you think they are, explain how.
4. This report does include an interpretation. What is it and where does it appear in the report? Do you think the interpretation is justified by the factual statements given? Why or why not?
5. Actually this report is a summary of a longer article that appeared in the *Journal of Counseling Psychology.* Who seems to be responsible for the interpretation, the person who wrote this article, or the three men who made the survey?
6. If you are taking, or have recently taken, a laboratory class, write a short report of one of the experiments you performed. If you have not taken

such a class, write a report of some article you have read recently, being careful to include just the information that appeared in the article without adding your own opinion. Or write an objective report of some situation where expectations influenced the outcome.

An Old-Fashioned Conservatory

coincident with: happening at about the same time
plethora: a great many
ramification: an extension or result of something else
rococo: highly decorated
noxious: poisonous
opulent: very rich
progeny: offspring

[1]   The concepts of indoor gardening were heralded 150 years ago by a blade of grass and a tiny fern which accidentally germinated in a large glass bottle. Dr. Nathaniel Bagshaw Ward, a London physician and amateur naturalist, had shut up a hawk moth chrysalis in a closed container and set it on a window ledge; he was intrigued to later observe two plants growing from dirt in the bottom of the jar.

[2]   Contrary to his expectations, they survived even when the bottle was placed outside, and Ward, a man of keen scientific curiosity, was quick to experiment by planting in sealed glass vessels a variety of species—they all flourished without attention. He therefore had built a series of tightly glazed miniature greenhouses, the prototypes of what would become, under the name Wardian Cases, "elegant and pleasing additions to the most tasteful and elaborately furnished drawing room."

[3]   Coincident with Ward's discoveries there developed in England an interest in ferns, a botanical family previously ignored even by scientists. Revolutionary advances in printing and the arrival at leisure and affluence of a whole new class of readers sparked a plethora of richly illustrated books on the subject. It became a demonstration of culture to raise ferns, whose "extraordinary exactitude of . . . ramifications" suited the Victorian delight in rococo, and the appreciation of whose subtle foliage distinguished those of taste from the lower classes, who preferred "mere gaudy flowers."

[4]   As knowledge of Ward's cases slowly became public, they were seized as the perfect vehicle for indoor ferneries: they provided an undisturbed climate of even temperature and high humidity, protected from the noxious gases of coal fireplaces and gas lighting; their frequent placement away from windows meant that the interior light levels were low. No other family of plants more fully appreciated such

Ron Goldstein, Habitat Institute for the Environment (Belmont, Mass.: March 1980).

conditions, and with the lifting of the onerous British excise tax on glass, fern-filled Wardian Cases became one of the great Victorian passions.

[5]   It was natural that this mania would lead to a desire to cultivate indoors all types of tropical plants in a variety of bizarre configurations. Contemporary publications illustrate such scenes as a parlor sofa surrounded by an ivied arbor and picture frames encumbered by vines growing from small pots behind the canvas. The opulent taste of post–Civil War America and the new prosperity which came with industrialization likewise adopted indoor gardening as hallmarks of wealth and gentility.

[6]   Contemporary hanging baskets and window gardening are both descendants of Victorian indoor horticulture, just as today's terrarium is the progeny of Dr. Ward's bottle.

Responses

1. This article is a historical report; that is, it tells what happened in the development of indoor gardening during the last 150 years. Is the report precise? What exact details does it give?

2. Can you tell whether the report is complete? Whether it is accurate? If you are not sure, how could you go about checking?

3. What is the order used in this report? Is the order suitable for what is being reported? Why or why not?

4. Does the writer stick to the subject? If you think unrelated information or comments are included, what are they?

5. Is the report objective? If you think opinion words are used in the article, what are they? Do you get a feeling that the writer either favors or opposes indoor gardening? What in the article accounts for that feeling?

6. What cause-and-effect relationships are mentioned in the article? How do they help you understand the development of conservatories?

7. Write a short paper reporting on the development of some hobby or craze that interests you. If you don't know what the background is, look it up in the library, but be sure to say where you got your information, as this writer does *not* do.

Doublespeak Award Goes to Nuclear Power Industry

lexicon: a collection of words on a certain subject
euphemism pleasanter sounding term for something unpleasant
aberration: a deviation from what is normal or right
nomenclature: a group of words used to name parts of a system

Councilgrams, National Council of Teachers of English, January 1980, p. 16.

[1]   The 1979 Doublespeak Award went to the nuclear power industry for what William Lutz, chair of the Committee on Public Doublespeak, called "a whole lexicon of jargon and euphemisms used before, during, and after the Three Mile Island accident and serving to downplay the dangers of nuclear accidents."

[2]   "An explosion is called 'energetic disassembly,' " Lutz said in his presentation at the Board of Directors meeting [of the National Council of Teachers of English] in San Francisco, "and a fire, 'rapid oxidation.' A reactor accident is an 'event,' an 'incident,' an 'abnormal evolution,' a 'normal aberration,' or a 'plant transient.' Plutonium contamination is 'infiltration,' or 'plutonium has taken up residence.' "

[3]   The Committee on Public Doublespeak gave second place to Kentucky State Representative Dwight Wells, who, on the statehouse floor, told news media reporters to tell Kentuckians only what they want to hear. The magazine *Mother Jones* quoted Representative Wells as saying, "When you start to write, read, or act, you can ask yourself, 'Is what I'm doing . . . uniting the people of Kentucky and helping them to stand and be great?' You are to the people of Kentucky what a parent is to a child. When the truth is harmful and detrimental to the people of Kentucky, you should not only not tell them the truth, but you have a duty to see they do not know the truth."

[4]   Colorado State Representative A. J. Spano came in third with a set of euphemisms meant to downplay Denver's rating as "the city with the second-dirtiest air in the nation." According to the *Denver Post,* Spano "introduced, and the House Transportation Committee passed last May, a bill to change the nomenclature of the state's air-quality scale. The level of pollutants called 'hazardous' by the federal government would now be called 'poor,' 'dangerous' would become 'acceptable,' 'very unhealthful' would become 'fair,' 'unhealthful' would become 'good,' and 'moderate' would become 'very good.' "

[5]   The committee made a special award this year for the most conspicuous example of doublespeak from a foreign source. It cited General Joao Baptista Figueiredo, who, on his election as Brazil's next president, told reporters, "I intend to open this country up to democracy, and anyone who is against that, I will jail, I will crush."

Responses

1. Do you find any evidence that the writer of this article has slanted the report either in favor of or against the doublespeak awards or the committee that made them? If so, what is the evidence?
2. Is the conclusion to this article appropriate? If so, explain why. If it isn't, write what you think would be an appropriate conclusion.
3. The term "doublespeak" was invented by George Orwell in his novel *1984.* Judging either from what you know about that novel or from what you gather from this report, explain what "doublespeak" means.
4. The punctuation used in this article provides some information. What is the writer telling you by using single quotation marks in paragraphs 2, 3,

and 4? What do the three periods in the middle of a sentence in paragraph 3 indicate? Can you explain the use of brackets in paragraph 2?

5. Make a list of all the euphemisms you can think of for death and dying, and for mental unbalance. Then compare your list with those other students have made.

6. Write a short paper reporting on euphemisms you have heard from friends or politicians or discovered in your reading. Try just to report the euphemisms, without commenting on them.

Novels Barred from Course at Kentucky

acrimonious: bitter, angry
demeaned: belittled, put down
vehemently: vigorously
explicit: clearly stated, leaving almost nothing to imagination

[1]   The barring of several novels from the syllabus of a freshman composition course at the University of Kentucky has led to an acrimonious confrontation between the chairman of the English department and teaching assistants. Among the works that chairman Joseph A. Bryant deemed inappropriate for the course are Henry Miller's *Black Spring,* William Faulkner's *Light in August,* Bram Stoker's *Dracula,* and translations of the satires of Juvenal and several plays by Molière.

[2]   Graduate students in the English department charged that Mr. Bryant had demeaned teaching assistants. Some critics charged that Mr. Bryant's actions constituted censorship, an accusation that he vehemently denied. Mr. Bryant, who is an ordained Episcopal minister, is in the second year of a four-year term as department chairman. He said the books had been "disapproved" because they "did not seem appropriate for a course in English composition." The course, he said, was focused primarily on composition and used literary texts only near the end of the semester. Students in the course had had little exposure to literature and did not have time in the composition course to understand more difficult or controversial works, he said.

[3]   The conflict between Mr. Bryant and the teaching assistants began after the father of a freshman in the composition course charged that his son had been forced to write a theme on *Black Spring* and had been repelled by the novel's explicit language and treatment of sex. The parent who complained—Eugene Goss— is a lawyer and former trustee of the university who served as state Commissioner of Economic Security in 1968–69 and as Commissioner of Highways in 1969–70. Mr. Goss contended that *Black Spring* had offended his son's religious and moral convictions.

[4]   In a telephone interview last week, Mr. Bryant said Mr. Goss had complained that his son had received an unfair grade in the course because of his objections to

the book. The graduate student teaching the course—Betty Jean Gooch—denied those charges, and Mr. Bryant said his review of the case had led him to conclude that the grade was fair. However, he said, in investigating Mr. Goss's complaint he "discovered" that the process by which books were being chosen for the composition course was not adequately supervised. He then ordered stricter procedures for approving books for the course and specifically "disapproved" several, he added.

[5]   In an interview with the student newspaper, Mr. Bryant was quoted as saying that teaching assistants lacked the competence to choose works for the course. Following those statements, the English graduate student organization called for Mr. Bryant to resign and to apologize for "undermining" undergraduate students' "confidence in their teachers." Mr. Bryant said he did not plan to resign unless the university administration instructed him to do so. Ms. Gooch, the teaching assistant who assigned the book in the first place, indicated that she planned to leave the university and pursue graduate training elsewhere.

Responses

1. What opinion word appears in paragraph 1 of this report? Do you think the opinion is backed up by the rest of the article? Be ready to explain your answer.
2. Is this article slanted—that is, can you tell from any words or statements in the article whether the writer wants you to sympathize with any of the people mentioned? If you think you can tell, how?
3. Does the article omit any information you would like to have in understanding what happened at the University of Kentucky? If you would like to have more information, what would it be?
4. If you know of any argument over what should be taught in the schools, what books should be used, or how the material should be taught, write a brief report of what happened. Show your report to other students to see whether they can tell which side you are on. If they can tell, rewrite the paper so that it is a straight report.

The Myth of Indian Land Gains

sovereignty: final authority or power over an area or a people
litigation: law cases
expedient: something to help somebody get what they want
aboriginal: belonging to the first inhabitants
encroachment: moving in on something
extinguishment: wiping something out

Jon Stewart and Peter Wiley, Pacific News Service.

[1]   To many Americans, the recent spate of huge Indian land claims and a number of favorable court decisions on Indian resource rights suggest that the once great Indian nations are making a comeback. Indians have gone on the "lawpath," say the headlines, to win back their sovereignty and their land, including huge portions of some states. But a review of actual Indian land disputes in recent years reveals a much more somber reality. With one exception, the actual amount of land that has been regained by Indian tribes is hardly enough to constitute a medium-sized city park.

[2]   "You will find a great deal of litigation" concerning land claims, says Steven Tullberg, an associate of the Indian Law Resource Center in Washington, D.C., "but not much in the way of victory." Tullberg's colleague, Center director Tim Coulter, adds: "All the media stories in the last few years about Indians taking over the state of Maine and half of New York have given a false impression. There have been no meaningful victories in the field of Indian affairs."

[3]   Government statistics bear this observation out. The American Indian Policy Review Commission in 1977 found that over the preceding forty years the government had spent $5 million to acquire 500,000 acres for Indian tribes. But during the same period, tribes lost 1.8 million acres for a variety of reasons. According to Lou White of the Bureau of Indian Affairs' real estate office, tribal land holdings as of the end of August 1979 totaled about 41.5 million acres, plus nearly 10 million acres held by individual Indians and in Indian trust. That is roughly 1 million acres less than Indians held in 1934, at the dawn of President Roosevelt's "Indian New Deal," a series of programs that were supposed to consolidate and expand Indian land.

[4]   The land base, said White, has been "fairly constant": "It fluctuates with the policy of the times. Now the policy is to help Indians acquire land." That may be the policy, but the reality has yet to show it. Aside from an 1,800-acre parcel awarded this year to the Narragansett Indians in Rhode Island, the only sizable Indian land victory has been the 44,000 acres returned to the Taos Indians of New Mexico in 1970.

[5]   Whatever the stated policy of the BIA, the government remains determined to "buy out" Indian land claims with cash settlements which reflect a mere fraction of the modern value of the land. "The basic way the U.S. has operated is to extinguish aboriginal title by purchase," said Kirk Kicking Bird, counsel for the Indian Policy Review Commission and author of a book on Indian lands. "This is more expedient and costs less than war."

[6]   But the problem, for the government, is that increasing numbers of tribes are no longer willing to accept the cash settlements. Traditional Indian leaders, particularly, are winning wide support among their tribes for the notion that Indians have a sacred responsibility to hold and protect the land for future generations. "If we give up our land, we are giving up ourselves as a tribe," said Thomas Banyacya, spokesman for the traditional Hopi leaders of Arizona. Other Indian leaders, less spiritually inclined, argue that there is vast wealth in uranium, coal, and other ores, including gold, under much of the aboriginal land. One Sioux leader in South Dakota recently suggested that Indians there should have a share in the gold profits coming out of the Black Hills, where Homestake Mining Company operates the

largest gold mine in the Western Hemisphere on land taken illegally from the Indians by General Custer.

[7]   The Sioux claim is one of the largest land claims ever filed. The government has acknowledged that the various Sioux tribes have a rightful claim to some 55 million acres, including the Black Hills, and has offered a cash settlement totaling $149 million. But so far, the tribes have refused to accept the payment. Elections among the tribes will be conducted soon to settle the question, but opposition appears to be running high. The Department of Interior recently released documents under a Freedom of Information suit revealing that at least seventeen other tribes are currently resisting buy-out efforts involving hundreds of millions of dollars. Like the Sioux, the tribes want their land, not the money.

[8]   The best-documented example of how the government has dealt with Indian land claims is the case of the Hopis. The Indian Law Resource Center recently completed a study of Hopi traditional leaders' efforts to regain land guaranteed to the tribe by an 1882 treaty. The tribe had suffered the loss of millions of acres of their original reservation by the gradual encroachment of white settlers and their more numerous Navajo neighbors. In the early 1950s the tribe was persuaded by its attorney, John Boyden, to file a claim for their lost land. Boyden suggested that they could get some land restored, as well as monetary compensation for the rest. But Boyden, an accomplished lawyer in Indian affairs, knew that the government mechanism for settling the claim, the Indian Claims Commission, was not empowered to return land to Indians. By federal law, which Boyden's former partner, Ernest Wilkinson, had helped to write, the Commission could only buy out land claims with cash settlements. Typically, the prices, which were determined by the Commission, reflected the value of the land at the time it was "lost," usually in the nineteenth century. Consequently, the Hopis, who had expected to win back some land, instead had to settle for $5 million for the 4 million acres they lost, much of which is known to contain valuable mineral deposits.

[9]   The claims law also calls for the tribe's legal counsel to receive up to 10 percent of the land settlement, meaning that Boyden received $500,000 for, in effect, persuading the Hopis to sell their claim. According to a conservative estimate by the Indian Law Resource Center, Indian claims lawyers—all of them white—have netted some $60 million in legal fees for their roles in "extinguishing" land claims. This earned the claims law the epithet "the Indian Lawyers' Welfare Act." "The law became an incentive for lawyers to prove how much the Indians no longer owned," commented an attorney who has represented two tribes in efforts to avoid the government buy-out. In a claim case involving the Goshiute Indians in Nevada, tribal leaders who opposed accepting the claim fired their attorney and refused to take the money. Nonetheless, the attorney was paid his share of the settlement by the government, though no money has yet been paid to the unwilling tribe. A similar situation persists among Nevada's Western Shoshone, who refuse to accept payment for land on which the Pentagon is reportedly eager to build MX nuclear missile sites.

[10]   The claims formula—the extinguishment of title by cash buy-outs—has in most cases proven successful from the government point of view. During the thirty-two-year lifetime of the Indian Claims Commission it paid out some $800 million

for Indian land claims. Attorney Kicking Bird estimates that 95 percent of the public domain lands were purchased from Indians, much of it through the Claims Commission extinguishments.

[11]   The track record of the Commission on obtaining title to Indian lands has led a new generation of claims attorneys to consider trying a similar approach to getting rights to Indian water, the key to future energy development in the West. But the growing opposition to accepting payments for land or water among many tribes could create a sizable quandary: Can the government buy out a claim that Indians say is not for sale?

Responses

1. What is being reported in this article—a single event, a series of events, or a generalization about those events? If you think it is a single event, what is it? If you think it is a series of events, what do they have in common? If you think it is a generalization, do the writers give enough examples to support the generalization?
2. How much of this report seems to come from the writers' own knowledge? How much is a report of what other people have said? When the writers make statements of their own, how are those statements backed up? Can you find any statements made by the writers that are given no backing? If so, what are they?
3. What is the order followed in this report? Does the order seem appropriate? If you think it isn't, how would you rearrange the information?
4. What evidence can you find in the article that makes the information seem precise? What evidence is there that facts have been interpreted?
5. What is the effect of ending this article with a question? Has the article answered the question? How? If you think the question has not been answered, who is supposed to answer it?
6. Select one of the tribes mentioned in this report, and investigate their present situation, using the information you can find in the college library. Report what you discover in two or three paragraphs, giving the source for any general statements you make in the report.

Police Test Made More Realistic

disproportionate: out of proportion; unfair or unjust
devised: made
validated: tested, proven reliable
pictorial: containing pictures

Robert L. Joiner, *St. Louis Post-Dispatch,* September 22, 1975.

[1]   Assume that it's last year, you're a high school graduate, Black and want to become a St. Louis policeman. You're fairly intelligent and healthy; your afro is short enough, and you've never been busted on a marijuana charge. In effect, you're a pretty good prospect. You go down to take the Police Aptitude Test, and while you're listening to the instructions, you get this uneasy feeling in your stomach because you don't know what might be included in the exam.

[2]   Start: Gee, this ain't bad at all, you say as you breeze through a few questions and wonder why there has been so much fuss over the contents of this test. You find out why in the next question: "The federal statute relating to the transportation from one state to another of stolen automobiles is the (A) Harrison Act; (B) Wright Act; (C) Dyer Act; (D) Sheppard-Towner Act." Whew! Not only do you not know the correct answer (the Dyer Act), you've never heard of any of the possible choices. And you begin to wonder, like many applicants before you, what the question has to do with becoming a good police officer.

[3]   Anyway, skip it. You're wasting time. Then comes another item: "Arson is most closely related to (A) Incendiarism; (B) Poison; (C) A storehouse for weapons; (D) Person who sets a fire." Back in the ghetto, not too much was said about incendiarism, the proper answer. But you do know that arson has something to do with fire, so you check answer D. After the test, you go home, check the dictionary and realize that you don't have much of a chance of becoming a police officer.

[4]   Until April, that's the predicament that many Black prospective policemen found themselves in when seeing items like these from the entrance examination. But in April, the Police Department stopped using it because some believed it was unfair to Black applicants. The critics were right if they based their view on the Equal Employment Opportunity Commission's guideline for what constitutes an unfair test. The federal agency says that any employment test that tends to eliminate a disproportionate number of persons from a single racial or ethnic group is discriminatory. Police Department figures show that 62.2 per cent of the Black applicants failed the old test through last September. By contrast, 91 per cent of the whites passed it.

[5]   The test, which had been devised here, is being replaced with one devised by Educational Testing Service of Princeton, N.J. The new test was developed under contract for the International Association of Chiefs of Police. One of the Educational Testing Service experts who helped to make up items for the new test said that the new examination would be both job-related and culturally fair. The old test was often criticized on both counts.

[6]   "The old test is more of a police elimination examination than a police selection test," says Robert Williams, a psychologist here. "The test was not properly validated against job performance of a policeman. It didn't predict how well an officer would perform on the job. But it did a good job of screening out people. A number of the questions asked for information that a policeman would need to know after actually becoming an officer—things he could learn while in the academy. Others were not job-related and had nothing to do with the duties that are involved in being an officer or the skills needed for a person to carry out his job as an officer.". . .

[7]   Richard Thornton, a psychologist with the Educational Testing Service,

helped to devise the test that the Police Department will begin using later this year. He said the new test would do all the things that Williams said a test should do. "What we did was made a survey of on-the-job police material, and we found that on the average the material is written at the tenth-grade reading level," Thornton said. "The reading level of material in some of the old test is discriminatory either by race or sex, but the new test didn't make the reading level higher than what's required on the job." Only knowledge actually required on the job would be included in the new test, he said. "For instance, there's no math in the test," he said. "By and large, we found that the policeman isn't required to do math, although many old police tests do contain it."

[8]   He said also that, unlike old tests, the new test would feature a preexamination booklet to be passed out to applicants well in advance of the examination. "Samples of every type of question that's in the test are contained in the pretest booklet," he said. "We have a list of police-related words, and candidates would have several weeks to study their meaning. We can't go back and change the results that possibly happened in the educational system over 12 years. But instead of telling people to study the *Seventh Collegiate Dictionary,* we say, 'Study these 150 words. They're going to be in the test.' "

[9]   He said that the test would be highly pictorial and would consist of 12 sections, would contain about 100 items and would take about three hours. He said that he and another psychologist were completing validation studies in four cities, including St. Louis. The test should be ready for distribution before the end of the year, he said. The only drawback of the new test, Thornton said, is that it was not validated on women because a large enough sample of women officers could not be found.

Responses

1. This account is a mixture of "feature article" (piece of writing deliberately intended to be interesting rather than informative) and objective report. Where does the report part of the article begin? How can you tell?
2. What is accomplished in the first three paragraphs? Would the article be more or less effective if these paragraphs were left out? Why?
3. Using your own words, write a main idea sentence for the article. Be sure to include *who, what, where,* and *when.* Then compare your sentence with those other students have written. How many of you have included *why* in the main idea sentence? Does the *why* belong there? Explain your answer.
4. What is the effect of the long quotations included in the last part of the article? Do they make the report seem more or less factual? Why?
5. Can you tell what Joiner's attitude toward the old and the new police tests is? If you think so, find the places in the article that let you know how he feels.
6. Have you ever taken a test that seemed to you unfair? If so, write a short report that lists the unfair questions, but try to avoid saying that they were

"unfair"; instead, give a specific account of the things in your background or experience that made you unable to answer the questions. Then see whether other students in the class agree that the questions were unfair for you.

7. Or write a combined feature article/report of some recent event on your campus. Let other students in the class deside which parts of your article are "report," which parts "feature article."

Battered Grandparent Issue out of Closet

ombudsman: a person appointed to hear and investigate complaints; the person is not connected to either side in a dispute

[1]   A national problem little known to most Americans—and thus getting little attention from government or private agencies—is that of the battered grandparent. Most attention regarding violence in the family has focused on child abuse, or more recently on spouse abuse (previously tagged wife abuse but now including abuse of husbands). What notice there has been of physical abuse of elder persons has centered mostly on those living in nursing homes or other institutions. But University of Rhode Island sociologist Richard J. Gelles, who recently completed a national study of violence in the American family, estimates that each year at least 500,000 persons age 65 or over who live with younger members of their families are physically abused by them. The problem is not new, Gelles suggests, just little-documented until now.

[2]   Interviews with more than two dozen social-service professionals, researchers, government officials and others across the United States indicate that:

—Abuse of the elderly by younger family members living with them is occurring in all parts of the country.

—The most common physical abuse is beating or punching, although scalding, burning with cigarettes and starvation are among the most severe forms of mistreatment.

—Most commonly, the abuse occurs when younger family members feel burdened by financial or emotional demands on them from the elder family member living with them.

—Little is being done in response to the problem. Public and government awareness of it is very limited. But there is a growing realization that more needs to be done.

[3]   "I know there's a need," says June Zeitland, head of the new Office of Domestic Violence in the U.S. Department of Health, Education and Welfare. But her

Robert M. Press, Christian Science Monitor News Service, reprinted in *The Columbian,* January 9, 1980.

small staff is focusing primarily on abuse between spouses and has "no immediate plans" to address the battered grandparents question, she says.

[4]   "At least as common as physical abuse is neglect of grandparents," experts say. This typically involves denial of adequate food or medical attention or just being socially ignored for long periods, they explain. "The consequences of verbal, emotional or even unintentional neglect can be just as fatal as physical abuse," says Richard Douglass of the Institute of Gerontology at the University of Michigan.

[5]   Some specialists see the problem of abuse of older persons increasing as more of them are obliged to live with younger family members. As Americans are living longer, these specialists point out, the price of separate housing and nursing-home care continues to climb rapidly, and even if affordable, some of the best nursing homes have long waiting lists. Abuse of grandparents is "very much hidden," says John Von Glahn, executive director of the Family Service Association of Orange County, Calif. "Often the grandparent is dependent on those children. If the grandparent reports abuse, he or she is probably going to be cast off," he says. And, he adds, today's grandparents grew up in an age when you "didn't go outside the family" to solve a problem.

[6]   Yet, increasingly, cases of abuse of older persons are coming to light. In the past two years 30 cases of battered grandparents have been referred to United Charities of Chicago—"a significant increase over past years," executive director Gerald Erikson says. "We feel the violence we're seeing is just the tip of the iceberg," he says.

[7]   A recent study of abuse of older persons in Massachusetts found that 70 percent of the cases reported were detected by nonfamily members. The researchers assume that many more cases remain undetected. The typical victim was 75 or older, a woman and "frail," says Helen O'Malley, who directed the study by Legal Research and Services for the Elderly in Boston. Eighty-four percent of the abusers were relatives, and 75 percent of the victims lived with their abusers, she says. Three-quarters of the victims had physical or mental disabilities, she adds.

[8]   "The hale and hearty grandma" is not so likely to be abused, says Suzanne K. Steinmetz of the University of Delaware, who has done research on the problem. Often, the more dependent the elder family member is, the more pressured younger family members feel, she says. A couple in the mid-50s, perhaps with their children still in college, may suddenly find themselves housing an 80-year-old who requires considerable attention and financial support, she says. It's a "middle-age crunch" that some people can't cope with, so they turn their frustrations into violence against the older family member, she adds.

[9]   In cases where an elderly relative really is not wanted at home, a nursing home may be a better answer, says Douglass of the University of Michigan. Housing an elderly family member but making the grandparent feel resented—letting him or her know, for example, "that the kids really want their room back"—is devastating, he says.

[10]   In addition to honest appraisals by families of what is involved in caring properly for an elder family member, specialists suggest the following:

—Greater awareness. Responding to a nationwide spot telephone survey of social-service agencies, professionals in some cities expressed no familiarity with the problem of elder abuse. Yet, in the few states where even an initial statewide assessment of the problem has been made (such as Pennsylvania and Massachuetts), the results indicate the problem is much more prevalent than previously assumed.

—Elder abuse reporting laws. Connecticut's law probably is the nation's most complete, says Jacqueline Walker, ombudsman for elder affairs in that state. Physicians, clergy, coroners, social workers and certain others are required to report detected abuse cases within 72 hours (or sooner in case of emergencies). Social-service investigators then visit the home concerned. If needed, homemaker services are provided to relieve family tensions. If appropriate, alternative living arrangements are made for the abused.

—Temporary care. In Denver, the York Street Center provides abused persons, including the elderly, with referrals to temporary housing, emergency food and family counseling. Also needed, Denver social worker Katherine Saltzman suggests, are daytime nursing homes (which would be much cheaper than 24-hour care) where the elderly could get proper care while younger family members work.

—Arresting the abuser. Atlanta social worker Jack Mallory or one of his seven staffers accompanies local police on domestic violence calls. He urges the elderly to file arrest warrants if they are physically abused by a grandchild. This, he says, will help the older person reassert some authority in the family. Others caution against filing criminal charges against the abuser (especially if the abuser—the son or daughter—is the homeowner) because it might leave the elderly person with no place to live in but an institution.

Responses

1. Strictly speaking, "battered," "abused," and "neglected" are all opinion words: they express the writer's judgment about a situation, rather than making a factual statement that could be checked. Find at least two factual words in this report that could be used to back up each of these opinion words.
2. Which paragraphs attempt to give reasons (find the cause) for the situation? How convincing are the reasons? Why? Can you think of other possible reasons? What are they?
3. Paragraph 2 and paragraph 10 are both in the form of a list, instead of an ordinary paragraph. Why do you think Press used this method? What is the difference between the two lists? If one list seems more appropriate or useful than the other, explain why.
4. Almost all of this report is based on information supplied by people other than the writer. Who are these other people? How are they identified? Are some identifications more useful than others? Why?
5. Write an imaginary report, giving the details of some situation in which a

child, a spouse, or an elderly person has been abused. Give made-up names, dates, and specific details, but let the situation speak for itself; keep your attitude and reactions out of the report. Your intended readers may be a social-service agency, a law court, or the general public.

6. Locate somebody who has information about some subject that interests you, and conduct an interview with that person. Before the interview, prepare some questions you want to ask, but add other questions as you talk to the person. Take notes whenever the person says something you think should be quoted exactly. Then write a report of the interview, using quotation marks when you repeat the exact words of the person you were interviewing.

Jojoba: One Important Bean

ingested: taken by mouth
agronomist: specialist in soil management and field crops
perpetuate: make permanent
labyrinthine: like a maze

[1]   Can a scraggly-looking desert bush long overlooked and little understood save the whale, replace petroleum and keep 20th century man's machines from grinding to a halt? Yes, say a handful of enthusiastic California scientists, farmers and businessmen. Yes, says Governor Jerry Brown, who has made the humble plant an integral part of his statewide energy resources policy. Yes, say several thousand California and Arizona Indians who view the lowly bush as their economic messiah.

[2]   The subject of all this attention and enthusiasm is a drab, bean-bearing shrub called jojoba (pronounced ho-ho-bah). For centuries it has grown obscurely in the deserts of southern California, Arizona and Northern Mexico—and nowhere else. Hardly anyone gave it a second glance. True, the Apache Indians used the rich golden oil squeezed from its acorn-sized beans to treat skin ailments and oldtimers discovered that their sheep and cattle liked to nibble the bush, prompting them to call it "goatberry" and "sheepnut." But serious research into the jojoba didn't begin until 17 years ago, and only in the past five years has it managed to generate what has come to be called "jojoba fever."

[3]   At first the story of the jojoba sounds almost too good to be true. Scientists from Peoria to Palo Alto have come up with an almost inexhaustible list of applications for the oil it produces (actually, a liquid wax), which makes the plant sound like some kind of miracle shrub. In addition to the fact that jojoba oil is one of the finest grade lubricants ever discovered, Wyeth Laboratories has found

Ronald Yates, *Air Illinois,* January–February 1980, pp. 21–25.

that jojoba oil is superior to any known anti-foaming agent used in the fermentation of penicillin and tetracycline. Westinghouse Electric Corp. will use jojoba oil as the sole lubricant in an implantable artificial heart it is designing, and the cosmetics industry has discovered that jojoba oil is the perfect "natural" oil base for products ranging from shampoo to make-up remover. Researchers have found that when jojoba oil is used in cars and trucks, fuel economy increases as much as 20 percent and engine oil need only be changed every 20,000 miles. Industry can use jojoba oil to lubricate everything from expensive high-tolerance machinery to clocks, fishing gear, locks and sewing machines. The oil will renew shoes, baseball mitts and briefcases; polish furniture; wash clothes; cure acne; wax your car; treat baldness; protect you from the sun; and coat your pills. It can be used to manufacture chewing gum, printing ink, linoleum and plastics. It can even be put on salads; and the bean, when ingested, acts as a powerful natural appetite inhibitor.

[4] "Jojoba is a crop whose time has come," says an enthusiastic Professor Demetrios M. Yermanos, an agronomist at the University of California, Riverside. Yermanos began working with jojoba in 1961 and has seen it evolve from "just another bush" into a plant on the brink of exploding into a world-wide industrial crop. "When we started working with these desert bushes, people laughed at us," recalls Yermanos. "They aren't laughing anymore, not when they see me putting jojoba oil into my Volvo."

[5] If Danny Christoferson had his way, everybody would be pouring jojoba into their crankcases, transmissions and differentials. Christoferson, president of Alaskan Brand Engine Coolant of Los Angeles, is convinced that next to the little old lady from Pasadena who only drives on Sundays, jojoba oil is a car's best friend. "Jojoba oil by itself won't work," says Christoferson. "It has to be mixed and blended with a regular high grade oil. But when it is, the results are amazing." For example? Well, says Christoferson, there was that test back in New Jersey not long ago on a 1977 Pontiac. A 15-ounce bottle of the specially blended motor oil was put into the motor, the transmission and the differential, and after 5,000 miles fuel economy increased 26 percent in the gas-guzzling V-8. "We know that hot spots in an engine drive oil away," Christoferson explains. "But jojoba is a heat seeker. It helps reduce engine heat, reduces drag and helps seal the rings. . . . We've run cars with jojoba oil for 25,000 miles without an oil change. . . . Truckers have written me telling about driving 90,000 without an oil change after putting it into their diesel rigs."

[6] So far, Christoferson and another firm in Santa Fe Springs, California, called Key Oils and Lubricants, have confined the marketing of their unique motor oil to the West Coast. But now, says Christoferson, the oil will be made available nationally. It will also go on sale soon in Canada, Japan and South Korea. "Nobody laughs at the jojoba anymore," says Christoferson. "It's here to stay."

[7] Indeed, how can anybody laugh at a plant which produces a lubricant which, unlike sperm whale oil (its closest counterpart) needs no refining? "But the greatest thing about jojoba oil is that, unlike sperm whale oil, it is a renewable natural resource," says Jim Trotter, former marketing director for Jojoba International, Inc. of Carpinteria, the largest of five corporations which have gotten in on the ground floor of the jojoba boom. "The world kills its limit of 6,000 sperm whales

each year for the same amount of oil that 200 acres of fully matured jojoba beans can produce," says Trotter, who is now an independent consultant on renewable resources. "And jojoba oil is better than sperm whale oil for several reasons. First, it's legal (the importation of sperm whale oil and products made from it was prohibited by the 1971 Endangered Species Act), second, it's a vegetable product and therefore smells better than whale oil, and third, it is purer than sperm whale oil, which contains 25 percent glycerides and acids and, therefore, must be refined."

[8]   It was precisely those arguments which Governor Brown used in a Save The Whale Day speech two years ago when he pledged to use every government resource available to him to perpetuate jojoba cultivation in California. Governor Brown even went so far as to order that jojoba plants be used to landscape the state's labyrinthine freeway system after tests by Professor Yermanos showed that the hardy bush was the last plant to die in a smog-tolerance experiment. In fact, the only enemies of the jojoba are the four-footed critters which like to graze on it. It can survive temperatures as low as 23 degrees and as high as the desert can dish out. It needs only five to 10 inches of rainfall every year (its waxy leaves hold in every drop of moisture) and it will bear fruit for 150 years—all the while requiring a minimum of care.

[9]   "It takes an initial investment of about $1,500 an acre to get started in this business," says Trotter. "Then you have to wait five years for your first crop. Your first harvest would be about one pound of beans per bush, or about $2,000 profit an acre. But the yield increases by a pound a bush every year thereafter, until they reach a maximum of 10 to 15 pounds when the plants are 10 feet high. That means at maturity you could earn anywhere from $20,000 to $30,000 per acre at current prices." "This is obviously no get-rich-quick scheme," Trotter adds. "You have to have patience. We figure by the sixth or seventh year jojoba farmers will experience economic turn-around. A family of four could support themselves on 15 acres, but if you only had two acres, that's enough to provide a good supplemental income— enough to buy a new car every year."

[10]   Jojoba International, which operates from a small building on Linden Avenue in Carpinteria, has shifted its emphasis away from strictly selling the oil to marketing parcels of land planted in jojoba bushes, says Kelley Dwyer, the firm's vice president in charge of sales. "During 1979 we will be selling 10-, 20-, and 40-acre fully developed jojoba bean farms," says Dwyer. The cost, he adds, is $9,300 per acre—which includes the plants, irrigation system and a mobile home. Without the mobile home the farms will run $7,500 per acre. "We are attracting a lot of retirees who see this as a way to live in the country and yet not atrophy because of inactivity," Dwyer says. In one year sales at Jojoba International have more than tripled, from $110,000 in 1977 to $400,000 last year, indicating that the rush to jojoba is on.

[11]   So far, no commercial jojoba crops have been harvested in the United States because most weren't planted until four years ago. Dwyer estimates that there are anywhere from 3,000 to 4,000 acres of jojoba planted in California and that 1,000 acres of that will be harvested this fall. However, in order to supply the domestic needs of the United States, 150,000 acres of jojobas are needed. To supply the

world's needs, more than one million acres would have to be planted. Today's commercial needs (about 50,000 pounds a year) are met by beans plucked from wild jojoba bushes by American Indians. Because the supply has been erratic, cosmetics firms, oil companies and other industries have been reluctant to sink much manpower or money into jojoba oil development.

[12]   "But all that will change when there is a steady, predictable supply of oil," says Trotter, who adds that between 1982 and 1993 the market demand for jojoba beans will be more than 570 million pounds. That demand, says Trotter, will more than likely be met by small jojoba farmers with high-yield bushes. Planted at intervals of three to five feet in rows 10 feet apart, one acre of desert land can support anywhere from 800 to 1,400 plants. Jojoba is also an excellent alternate crop for farmers whose soil is infested with avocado root rot.

[13]   Like most plants, jojoba bushes come in two sexes—male and female, and until the 18th month they look identical. However, only the female produces seeds, so excess male bushes are usually removed (one male bush can produce enough pollen to pollinate 10 to 15 female plants). Once pollinated, the leaf-like flowers on the female bushes begin forming green, olived-sized fruit. Once the beans mature, they dry out and drop to the ground—usually between August and October. "You can harvest jojoba beans with a vacuum cleaner if you want to," says Dwyer. "Just shaking the bush does the trick."

[14]   What do you do with the beans after you've harvested them? Well first, says Dwyer and other jojoba enthusiasts, there is never time to contemplate that question. "The beans are snapped up immediately—demand for them is incredible," says Dwyer, who adds that Jojoba International will purchase every harvest it can find.

[15]   "We are witnessing the birth of a new industry here," says Prof. Yermanos. "Right now prices are high ($65 for a gallon of pure jojoba oil), but then the very first pair of nylon stockings cost $156,000 to produce and now they sell for only 50 cents. Prices will drop as demands are met, and jojoba oil will touch every American in some way some time."

Responses

1. This article, which first appeared in a magazine produced by an airline for free distribution to its customers, was obviously written for the general public. What evidence can you find that the writer was trying to arouse interest as well as provide a report on a new industry?

2. What information is given to back up the opinion word "inexhaustible" used in paragraph 2? Do you think the opinion is justified? Why or why not?

3. Rewrite this article in the form of a straight report, leaving out all the opinion, whether the opinions are expressed by Yates or by the people he quotes, and leaving out all the "interest-getting" parts of the article. Your rewrite should be considerably shorter than the original, but it should in-

clude all the factual information. You may use some of the sentences from the original article, but you are also free to change the wording whenever it seems necessary to keep the report objective.

More Suggestions for Writing

If you write any of these reports, be sure to keep in mind who the readers (or reader) of the report will be.

an accident
a fire
a power failure
a burglary
unemployment conditions in your area
a survey on almost anything: attitudes toward the school cafeteria; preferences in fast food stores; how students will vote in the next election; opinions on ERA; the favorite TV programs of the people in your dormitory or your class
a single day on your present job or any job you have held
an interview with a professor, a politician, or a business person, on any subject that interests you
air pollution in your area
current grocery prices
volcanic activity in the United States—or anywhere else
job possibilities in your chosen field
the drop-out rate in the college
the minutes of a meeting you have attended

Chapter 8

Telling What Happened: Personal Experience

A good essay about personal experience does both more and less than simply tell what happened. It not only gives the details that make the telling vivid, it also leaves out the details that don't relate directly to the *significance* of what happened. Writing that tells what happened, without any awareness of its significance, tends to go on and on:

> I got up early in the morning, I ate my breakfast, I packed the car, I drove there, I set up camp, I ate my dinner. I went to bed. I got up early in the morning. I ate breakfast. I washed the dishes and put the fire out. The country was very pretty. I almost shot the biggest deer I ever saw, but I didn't. We got home very late and very tired, and we all agreed it was the best hunting trip we ever had.

Someone who loves the author dearly might be able to read such stuff through to the end. Anyone else would probably put it down before finishing the second sentence. The writing is dull. Too many bare events are listed, but there are no details that help the reader visualize what it was like. Even more serious, the writing *makes no point*. One thing happens, and another, and another, and soon our attention drifts and wanders. We simply stop caring. We say "So what?" and look for something more engaging to read.

When you are writing just for yourself, the kind of private writing you do in a diary or a journal, naturally you can write anything that satisfies you any way that satisfies you. But when you write in order to share your personal experiences with others, you'll want to have a definite reason for telling those experiences, and you'll want to make that definite reason clear to your readers. Unless your writing makes a point, it will not be interesting no matter how exciting the experience was for you. In that respect, writing about personal experiences is quite different from factual reports. In factual reports, you avoided interpretation; in writing about your personal experiences, you must interpret, find what is meaningful in them. You can convince your readers that what happened to you is significant not only to you but to them. And that means doing more than rambling on and on—a lot more.

What to Write About

There are at least two ways of finding a topic for a paper of personal experience. One is to find a significant event and begin writing. The other is to examine experiences for their significance. What's the difference? In the first, you know what the significance is and you're on your way. In the second, you begin with the experience and work into it until you discover why that experience is important enough to remember. And it's nearly always true that if we remember a thing, there's a good reason why.

Many people start by saying, "I don't have any significant experiences. Nothing important ever happens to me." That is somewhat like the man who walked through the woods all day long before he saw "scenery." The scenery was there all the time, everywhere, but he was looking for a special kind and so failed to see what was in front of his eyes. If he had not had such a narrow idea of "scenery," his walk would have been much more pleasant and much more memorable, too.

So how does this apply to you? Most of us have had significant experiences with the really big things of life: the birth of a first child, the death of a close friend or relative, a wedding, or a divorce. In a sense, those are the kinds of "scenery" that happen to us only occasionally. But there are thousands of other events that we remember in vivid detail, and those are also important. You can write about any of those thousands; and if you catch the significance of the event, you can share it with other people. The words you use and the details you give will force readers to see why the event seemed important. In other words, you can write about even "little" experiences so your readers will find them interesting.

You don't have to wait for a thing you recognize as an "experience." It's there, right now, in your memory. You just need to look at it. Pay attention to what you see and what you do. Pay attention to what you remember. As you work on discovering the significance of those experiences, you may discover that exploring your mind is as exciting as exploring Antarctica. At least there's a much more varied horizon and more hospitable climate. And if Admiral Byrd can move millions of readers with his account of what happened in such a boring place as the South Pole, imagine what you could do with your own, much richer resources.

Main Idea Sentences for Personal Experience

For this kind of writing, the main idea sentence is particularly useful, whether or not you ever use it in the paper. It is the process of arriving at the main idea sentence that sharpens your perceptions and your purpose. You can see for yourself how it works. Suppose you want to write about the night the hurricane came, mainly because you remember so many vivid details from that night.

Obviously, the main idea sentence must be more than just a statement of what happened. "Last November we had a hurricane" will not do. The sentence fails to say why the hurricane was important or what you learned from it. Such a sentence may lead to one of those on-and-on-and-on strings of dull details. The topic is fine, and the details you remember vividly are probably important; it's a better main idea sentence we're after, not a better experience.

You might start again by writing "I want to write about the night the hurricane came." But by now you know that the word "about" is a tip-off that more work needs to be done. "It was very exciting the night the hurricane came." Okay, that's better. But *what* was exciting about that night? And *why* was that night important? "There was lots of wind and noise and the lights went out and so did the furnace and the electric range and the phone and the driveway was blocked with fallen trees and we couldn't get in or out and there wasn't any help." Excellent! The details are coming along nicely, and the focus is shaping up, too. Ask yourself what you learned from that experience. What *did* you learn? "I learned that even when everything got shut off, I could get along and not panic." Aha. There's the focus, and you're ready to write.

It may help to see this kind of main idea sentence as a two-part pattern. Put the event or experience into the first part of the sentence. Then ask yourself what you found out during the experience, and fit the significance into the second part. Part one is the event; part two is the significance.

Event	*Significance*

(1) On a hunting trip last fall, (2) _____

(1) During the hurricane last year, (2) _____

(1) When we went to the beach for the weekend, (2) _____

Even though many kinds of discoveries will fit into the second blank, you will not be able to use them all. "On a hunting trip last fall, I discovered that it is 110 miles from my front door to Route 66" is useless for two reasons. First, it is a "so what?" discovery. Nobody except your family or possibly a prospective buyer of your corner lot cares how far it is from your house to the highway. But even supposing there were readers who would find this fact meaningful, what else can you say about it? Once you have said how far it is, you are through. "When we went to the beach for the weekend, I discovered that the tide goes out and comes in every twelve hours" is not very useful either, if you want to tell about your trip to the beach. If, on the other hand, you want to write a paper of *explanation,* telling about the behavior of the tides, "The tide goes out and comes in every twelve hours" might be a good main idea sentence. Notice, however, that your weekend at the beach has faded completely out of the sentence; the tides come in and go out whether or not you are there. If you got stuck on the fishing rocks and had to wait twelve hours before you could get off, you have a different kind of significance, and it might make a fine paper. Remember, there's nothing magic that guarantees one topic is better than another. It's your performance as "significance finder" that makes your writing memorable.

The kind of discovery you are looking for must grow out of the event you are telling about, and it must have a meaning that will carry over into other experiences. Your common sense is guide enough on that. A discovery that applies only to you, only to that time, only to that event, is less likely to interest your readers than a discovery that has wider importance. For example, when you took that hunting trip, did something happen to remind you that safety is important? (If so, what you learned will carry beyond that particular experience.) Did you learn that inexperienced campers get into trouble? Did you come face-to-face with a deer and find that the trusting look in those liquid brown eyes made you unable to pull the trigger? Did you discover, in the strain of sharing camp chores, that the football hero you had always admired was a lazy, no-good slob?

These ideas may not be the kind of earthshaking thing we usually think of as "significant," but they all have two things in common: (1) they can be formed into good main idea sentences for thoughtful and interesting papers, and (2) they clearly show why the hunting trip meant something to you. If it meant something to you, it's more likely to mean something to your readers, too. Probably the main idea sentence you write will not appear in the finished paper at all; if you make the significance clear, it won't need to. But you, as the writer, must know what it is; and if you write a good paper, your readers will be able to figure out what it was.

Selecting Significant Details

Just as in any other kind of writing, the main idea sentence for a paper of personal experience should serve as a guide to what is included in the paper. If your main idea sentence reads: "On a hunting trip last summer, I discovered that I don't really like killing animals," you must put into the paper only the details and events related to your discovery that you are more humane than you had thought you were.

It would be a waste of time to check the account of the hunting trip given at the beginning of this chapter for the relation between its details and its discovery. Besides being pointless, the story also is completely without specific detail. What is "early" in the morning? Four o'clock? Seven-thirty? Half-past ten? Did "breakfast" consist of five slabs of bacon, four eggs, half a dozen biscuits, and a pint of orange juice, or was it a bowl of stale dry cereal and a crust of leftover toast? The writer says the country was "very pretty," but fails to tell the reader what it looked like. Is "pretty country" flat brown fields, neatly divided by painted white fences? Is it miles of sand and sagebrush, with nothing else in sight except the horizon? Is it towering white mountains or restless green water? The writer must make you see it for yourself so you can make your own decision as to whether it was "very pretty."

When you write a personal experience paper you must interpret the meaning of your experience, but you must not fog the experience itself in so many vague generalities that there's nothing left to interpret. Instead, you must make your readers share the experience with as much vividness as possible, in the hope that shared experience will lead to shared interpretation. Specific details are as important in writing about personal experience as they are in report writing; it's just that the *kinds* of details you use are different. Writers who do a skillful job of selecting details may not only get you to see the same meaning in their experiences as they saw, they may also make you aware of beauties in sagebrush and sand that you never dreamed were there. They can enlarge your experience by letting you share theirs.

Showing the Significance of Events

All successful personal experience writing offers its readers this kind of vicarious experience. If your account of what happened to you is to succeed beyond your immediate circle of close friends, you must start with details, but you cannot stop there. Even though the following version of the hunting paper has been stuffed with specific details, it is not much better than the earlier version:

> I got up at four-thirty in the morning. I ate a slice of ham, a boiled egg, two and a half biscuits, and a glass of milk for breakfast. I put three cans of pork and beans, a loaf of bread, my old brown suede jacket, Mary's torn sleeping bag, and my new shotgun into the back of my 1956 Dodge sedan. I drove 183.7 miles due north to Ogden's Woods. Natty came with me. We decided to make camp on the edge of a lake that is about half a mile from shore to shore. First we opened the trunk and laid the tent stakes in a pile on the ground. Then we. . . .

This paper is about as lively as a telephone directory. Too many unselected details can be almost as bad as no details at all. Whatever specific details or events are included, it is the writer's job to show their significance. Does getting up early in the morning have anything to do with reluctance to shoot the deer? Does what was served for breakfast, or even eating at all, really matter? What about stuffing the car with extra clothing, cans of pork and beans, and the sleeping bag? Was the unwillingness to shoot the deer connected with the decision to pitch camp near the lake?

In these two pointless accounts of a hunting trip, the writer has failed to relate the details and events to the main idea. The writer did things or saw things and simply wrote them down without asking what significance, if any, they had. If the significance of events and details can't be shown, they must be firmly discarded.

But if you discard events and details at this rate, you may ask, what will you have left to write? The answer, of course, is that you don't discard everything that happened. Rather, you re-examine events in the light of what you discovered. As the writer stumbled out of bed at four-thirty, were the thoughts of the venison steak she could eat next winter comforting? Did she tell her family, as she loaded her plate with fresh slices of ham, that they could stop worrying about the high cost of meat? As she rode out to camp with her friend Natty, did she keep boasting about the sureness of her aim and the steadiness of her finger on the trigger? As she helped to put up the tent, did she see herself as the Great American Hunter, a kind of twentieth-century Daniel Boone, complete with everything except the coonskin cap? In other words, did the magnitude of her expectations before she met the deer face to face in the brush contrast with the smallness of the way she felt when she discovered she could not bring herself to shoot it? If what went before relates to what went after, it belongs in the paper; but the relationship must be clear.

The author can also use what she saw and did after her meeting with the deer, as long as she uses the same test. She can record an apparently aimless conversation with Natty, but she must make it clear that her hesitation in answering no to his question "See any deer?" was because she couldn't decide whether to tell him what she had found out about herself. She can include what she had for supper if she emphasizes that her appetite for pork and beans was greatly increased because she had not killed the pig. She can describe the beauty of the pointed fir trees against the drab gray sky or the quiet splash of lake water against the rocks if she pauses to remember that her camp is deer country, not man country, and that the great stag she did not kill is alive to drink from the lake after she has gone home.

This particular treatment of a hunting trip may strike some readers as sentimental or silly—especially if they are the first ones in town to fill out their deer tags. But even if they're scornful of the writer's discovery, at least they're not saying "So what?" The writer has at least made them see what she saw and understand how she felt about it, even though they may not be sympathetic. She has made her point.

Using Natural-Sounding Language

In all the writing you do, the more natural you sound, the better, and the more comfortable your readers will be. You already know that if an ordinary word is just as precise as a long, unusual word, the ordinary word is the better choice. That rule is especially important in personal experience writing, where the style should be more informal than in explanations or objective reports. After all, you are writing about your personal life; it makes sense to use a personal style. Moving to the big city, having a baby, shopping at a co-op—all are more convincing and more interesting if they sound as though they were written in the language of conversation. Stilted and pedantic language can only bore the reader:

> Shortly after I had, for the first time, assumed the vestments of an on-duty police officer, I encountered an individual who seemed to take exception to my occupational role. He spoke to me in abusive and disrespectful language, even though we had never seen each other before.

Such writing is fine for parody, awful for naturalness. Any reader would be quick to recognize that "vestments" is a most unordinary word for "clothing." In fact, "vestments of an on-duty police officer" can be boiled down to "police officer's uniform," converting seven words to three, and improving the naturalness, too. The "individual who seemed to take exception to my occupational role" could probably be translated into "a man who didn't like the police"—and that's the way most of us would say it if we were talking to a friend. And what did the "individual" say? We are told it was "abusive and disrespectful," but the actual words spoken would be more detailed, more lively, and certainly more accurate. The word order, too, is strained. If the writer is talking about his first day on duty he should say so, not mess around with "shortly after I had, for the first time, . . ." Redone, it might sound like this:

> My very first day in uniform, I ran into a man who just plain didn't like the police. Although I'd never seen the man before, he walked up to me, called me a dirty copper, and asked how many children I'd shot.

The changes in wording and word order transform a bloated and stilted style into a swift-moving and persuasive story.

When you've finished writing, you should read your paper aloud to see if your voice can follow what you've written. If you falter or pause to figure out what you "meant," you might experiment with saying it more directly, then rewrite it the way it sounds most natural. In informal accounts of your experience, if you would feel silly saying it, don't write it.

Talking and Writing

Though the language in papers of personal experience should sound natural, it can't be *exactly* like conversation. For one thing, we have to be clearer in writing, since the reader can't interrupt or ask questions or give us a puzzled look or a despairing gesture. When we talk, we rely on feedback to tell how we're doing; when we write, we've got to do it without any help from our readers. A sentence may be quite clear in conversation but rather muddy when it's written. "When the people come for their cars, be sure that they're clean." In conversation, you would know whether the cars or the people were supposed to be clean, but in writing there's not much way of telling. What do you mean by *this* and *it?* In writing, the reader needs to know what your pronouns are pointing at. (If this discussion seems familiar, perhaps you remember a similar discussion about pronouns from an earlier chapter.)

Another difference between talking and writing is the number of fragments or incomplete sentences we use in talking. We say a word or two here, a phrase there, and let the rest of what has been said help us out. A perfectly normal conversation between high-school students might go something like this:

"Coming?"
"Guess not."
"Oh, gee. Why?"
"Mom won't let me."
"What's the matter? Worried about you or something?"
"A fussbudget, that's what she is."
"Will she ever let you?"
"If my dad says."
"Will he?"
"Nope."

To the speakers, such fragments are probably perfectly clear, but written down just as they were spoken, the effect is somehow incomplete. We saw earlier, with the example of the police officer's first day in uniform, that telling what was said added to the impact and accuracy of the narrative. But we must be selective about the conversation we do include.

When we talk, we not only use fragments, we often repeat ourselves without any awareness of sounding like a stuck phonograph record:

"My, this is a good dinner. This is one of the best meals I ever ate. My, this is good. I was just telling Angie that I sure like the way Aunt Mary fixed this meat. It tastes awfully good. Henry, don't you think this is good? I think this is the best meat I ever tasted. It's sure good."

If everybody is enjoying the dinner, probably nobody will find this series of remarks very repetitious, and Aunt Mary will be pleased about the whole conversation. But written down, the repetition is too much. An excess of fragments and repetitions can take the edge off.

When you are writing your experiences, you may, if it is easier for you, first write them *exactly* the way you would talk; but before the paper is finished, you must go back and check the fragments and repetitions. Even if you are quoting what someone said, leave in just enough repetition and just enough fragments to make the conversation sound natural. Don't overdo it.

Using Better Connecting Words

You have probably also noticed that in talking, many people string their sentences together, using almost no connectors except *and* and *so*. Even in conversation the effect is a kind of breathlessness, a headlong dashing on and on, a seeming unwillingness to pause enough to let someone else speak. But at least in conversation the competition for dominance gives a bit of drama to the situation. If you're bored with "and" talking, you can always devise ways of breaking into the nonstop stream and thus keep some interest going. In "and" writing, though, readers are helpless to interrupt; all they can do is stop reading. Here's some "and" writing. What effect does it have on you?

> I was telling my wife about how hard my job was in the cannery and how long the hours were and how hot and steamy it was and how the floor shook and how the place smelled, and she said to me, "Well, how long ago was that?" and I realized it was nearly fifteen years ago, and she kind of smiled and then laughed and said, "Well, it sounds like you worked a full shift yesterday," and I smiled back and laughed a little and said, "Yeah, I guess I better get over that," and I realized that fifteen years is long enough to complain about a job.

Are you still there? Actually, it's not bad, and there is a discovery at the end. Nevertheless, any "and" writing can be made smoother once the writer gets rid of the stringy effect by using words that show more precise relationships: *nevertheless, in spite of, although, before, while,* and a good many others.

> *As* I was telling my wife about how hard my job at the cannery used to be, I really got into it. *"Even though* you'd think the twelve hours a day were the worst part, they weren't. It was one hundred twenty degrees in there, and so much steam you couldn't see across the room. *On top of all that,* the machinery smelled awful and the floor never stopped vibrating."
>
> *When* I stopped for breath she looked up and smiled. "How long ago was that?" she asked.
>
> *Because* I had been so involved in my story, her question really bought me up short. "Fifteen years ago," I said.
>
> She smiled a little more, *then* laughed. "Well, it sounds like you just worked a full shift yesterday."
>
> *In spite of myself,* I had to laugh, too. "Yeah, I guess I'd better get over that. Fifteen years is long enough to complain about a job."

In this revised version, the sentences are more normal in length and the connectors are varied. The reader still gets the point, yet with more ease and, surprisingly, more naturalness.

Slangin' 'n Swearin' 'n Stuff Like That There

"Well, like, y' know, man, today's *hip* is yesterday's *groovie,* and who wants to get stuck with *twenty-three skidoo,* you dig? Like, I mean, really. Y' know?"

Which is to say that the chief characteristic of slang is that it is either current or dated, and you'd better be sure or else you'll look silly. *Right on* was yesterday's rallying cry, today's yawn. A bit of slang gives dash and movement, but too much is too much (as too much so often is). Usually, slang words or expressions are developed because there are no equivalents in "ordinary" words that are quite as lively or as accurate or as much fun to use. But a lot of slang expressions are not lively at all—they are as worn out as old Kleenex, and just about as deadening to thought. The words *marvy, groovy, far out, heavy,* and *bad* all mean about the same thing even though they span decades. All these words do is express approval; all they convey is, "I like it." When you are tempted to use this kind of slang, ask yourself, "Okay, so what's so *bad* about it?" and fill in the blanks. Then readers will know not only what you think—your opinion—but also why you think so— your reasons.

As for swearing, there's only one problem, and it has always been the same problem and probably always will be. No words are "bad" in themselves, but because some people *think* some words are "bad," using those words will turn those readers off and destroy the effect of whatever else you are saying. We all know what the words are, and we know when we can and cannot safely use them (and where, and with whom). Robert Louis Stevenson said the hardest thing about writing *Treasure Island* was to create convincing pirates who didn't swear. But he succeeded so well that most of us don't even miss the profanity; we take "Shiver me timbers" and "Avast thar, matey" as powerful oaths.

Terrific court battles have been fought, as far up as the Supreme Court, about words that can be printed without fear of arrest. The fact remains, however, that there just isn't any single all-time, all-place, all-audience rule about what "obscene language" is and what "art" is. If you have strong convictions about using the commoner words for bodily elimination and procreation, then you may want to remember that your convictions are *yours,* not everybody's. Even though most of the people you know may share your convictions, there are probably at least as many people who disagree vigorously. If you don't care whether such readers are offended, use whatever words you please, but do it with a deliberate consciousness of what the effect will be.

Profanity and slang, carefully used, may give flavor to your writing in much the same way that pepper flavors a roast. Tastes vary as to how much is acceptable. Whatever your own taste is, remember that though a careful sprinkling gives spice, dumping in great quantities to conceal the absence of thought is like pepper used to conceal the fact that the meat is spoiled. (How is *that* for bad taste!)

Planning Personal Experience Papers

In organizing papers that tell what happened to you, there are two things you should keep in mind. First, the order is usually not as straightforward as it is in reports or explanations. Certainly personal experience papers do have introductions and conclusions, but the introduction sets the scene for the experience rather than serving as an unmistakable contract. After your readers have finished the whole paper, they should be able to go back to the introduction and see how it prepared them for what happened; but on a first reading they might not be able to guess what the point is going to be. In giving directions, in explaining, in reporting, your main idea sentence usually appears in the introduction, often as the first sentence in the first paragraph. In papers of personal experience, it may not appear at all. Even though you must know before you begin to write that your main idea is "During my hunting trip last summer, I discovered that the football hero I had always admired was a lazy, no-good slob," you will probably not begin your paragraph with that discovery. Instead, you may start with something like this:

> Last summer, when Tarzan Peterson invited me to go elk hunting with him and his cousin, I couldn't have been more flattered. I had known Tarzan for nearly ten years, first as the second-grader who could chin himself more times than any other kid in school, then as the junior-high-school strong man who claimed he could lick anybody in school, the teacher included, and finally as the star halfback of Podunk's winning team, the big shot that all the prettiest girls mooned over and all the fellows envied. I thought he was a real hero.

What this paragraph is doing, of course, is building Tarzan up so that when you show him for the slob and no-good he is, you can knock him down effectively.

Just as the introduction in personal narrative is less direct than in other kinds of writing, so is the conclusion. Your new view of Tarzan as a quite unheroic hero may not be clearly stated until the end of the paper, and maybe even then it will be only implied: "That fall, when the adoring crowd of seniors made themselves hoarse shouting Tarzan's praises, my shouting was pretty restrained. I'm not sure I even whispered."

Using Personal Experience for Other Purposes

The ability to find the significance in what has happened to you will make you much more skillful in at least two other kinds of writing: explaining and convincing. If you can add some personal experience to those other writing purposes, you will probably make your explanations and arguments more detailed and convincing. Practice in blending purposes will make it easier to keep one purpose, whatever it is, subordinate to your main purpose, whatever that is.

You have already had some practice in blending purposes. When you wrote a definition paper explaining what you meant by "gifted child" or "prejudice" or "success," you were using what had happened to you or someone you knew. The difference between that use of personal experience and what you are doing now is just a simple turnaround. In papers of explanation, you began with the meaning and looked for an experience that would illustrate it. Here, you begin with the experience and arrange it and select the details of it in such a way that the meaning becomes clear.

It sounds like a tall order to write personal experience papers that make a point, use significant details and events, and sound natural. Such papers do take more thinking out than a series of generalizations or a catalog listing of details. But they are certainly a great deal pleasanter to read, and they do provide you with excellent opportunities for examining the meaning of your own experiences.

Examining a Sample Personal Experience Paper

Here's the first version of a personal experience paper:

My Real Uncle Fred

[1]   When I was a little kid, I thought my Uncle Fred was about the greatest thing on wheels. He wasn't my real uncle. He was one of those adopted uncles. But I couldn't have been fonder of him if he'd been a blood relation. He was really great to me when I was little, and it was always fun to see him. Even When I was little we'd wrestle and play, and when I got older he taught me about fishing.

[2]   After he and Aunt Ruth moved out of town, one of my biggest treats was to spend time with them. He owned a department store in a small town, and my first work experience was with him. And although I often goofed off a lot, he never was too hard on me.

[3]   When I started high school I got my first real job. Now I was expected to be very grown-up and responsible. No more kid stuff. So I pretty much behaved myself. One day in the store I mentioned my Uncle Fred. One of the men said, "Oh yeah, that little skinny, funny-looking guy."

[4]   I tell you I was knocked out by that. But I had to agree, once I thought about it, that he was only about five foot one or two, that he was bald, wore thick glasses, and walked kind of funny. His ears stuck out, too, and weren't quite right.

[5]   It's funny that I never thought about that before. I guess I was too fond of him to see him that way.

This paper clearly has some strengths, but it also has some problems. Though the language is natural sounding, a lot of it is not very precise. What kind of "goofing off" did the writer do? What responses did Uncle Fred make that she thought were "never too hard"? The details about Uncle Fred's appearance help, but even they are not precise. What was "kind of funny" about his walk, and what wasn't "quite right" about his ears?

Adding specific details would help readers considerably. As it was first written, the paper seems lifeless and unconvincing. Most disappointing of all is the conclusion, which fails to show why the writer found the event significant. What was important about this experience? Why were we told about it? Did the writer change her opinion about Uncle Fred? Or was she just surprised or puzzled or angry?

Even the title is a bit confusing: Does it mean that Uncle Fred is a blood relative, rather than an adopted uncle?

Here's a revision that works much better:

The Eye of the Beholder

[1]   When I was a little kid, I thought my Uncle Fred was about the greatest thing on wheels. He wasn't a blood uncle—I had just adopted him and

"made" him my uncle, but I couldn't have been fonder of him if he'd been an actual relation.

[2]   He was really great to me when I was little, and it was always fun to see him. When I was just a baby we'd have a tremendous time wrestling. He'd make scary grunting noises, puff through his nose, and turn red with the strain of twisting my arm, and when I'd push back he'd go rolling across the room and crash into the davenport, completely overcome. Then we'd both laugh at how silly we were being. As I remember him, he was always ready for a romp, riding me piggyback or coming into my room to admire the tepee I'd made from bedsheets.

[3]   When I was old enough to have a BB gun, he'd stalk water rats with me by the hour. He never seemed to notice that we never shot one. Each time he was as serious as I was, and as stealthy. He was a splendid pal, and my mother said he was turning me into a tomboy.

[4]   He also taught me about fishing, the thing he really loved to do. I'd spend hours in his basement watching him tie flies, and he'd patiently tell me the names of the colorful and exotic creations and sometimes would let me wrap my own. He taught me how to fish for salmon, what kind of plug to use, and how far down to set it. He taught me how to love fishing, whether or not we caught fish.

[5]   After he and Aunt Ruth moved out of town, one of my biggest treats was to spend time with them. He owned a department store in a small town, and my first work experience was with him. I was in grade school at the time, and I was supposed to empty the wastepaper baskets and straighten the shirt displays. Occasionally, I'd recommend a purple shirt to an old man or shoot a clerk with a spitball, just to make things interesting. Uncle Fred never overlooked those pranks, but he also never lost control because of them. He'd talk to me as though I were grown-up enough to realize the long-range effects of my acts. "That old gentleman might not come in again, and we'd lose his business," or, "Mister Lucas told me you shot him with a spitball. He's worked here twelve years, and I'd sure hate to have him quit or be unhappy. He's first-rate help." I got the message.

[6]   When I started high school, I got my first "real" job at another store. I was expected to act very grown-up and responsible, and I really believe that I did all right, mainly because of my Uncle Fred's gentle guidance. In fact, one day in the store I mentioned my uncle, since he had managed a store in the same town years ago. One of the men said, "Oh yeah, that little skinny, funny-looking guy."

[7]   I was really thunderstruck. But I had to agree, once I thought about it, that he was barely five-feet tall, weighed about 110, was bald, and wore thick glasses. He walked kind of sideways, and his ears stuck out and weren't the same height or size.

[8]   At first I was angry that my friend had such a low opinion of Uncle Fred. Then I was amazed that I'd never seen him the way other people did, "objectively." I was sad for a while, thinking that the reality wasn't as big as my dream. Then I finally figured it out. The Uncle Fred of my childhood was

indeed very, very real. What we'd done together was real. What I'd learned from him was real, and my love for him was real.

[9]   I felt a whole lot better. I hadn't been blind to Uncle Fred's appearance, not at all. I just had so much more to know about him that his looks were hardly important. If the guy at work judged him by appearance alone, too bad. It was a case of "objectivity" that was only partly informed. If he thought my uncle looked funny, that was his problem, not mine. I knew otherwise.

This revision is a much improved example of "public writing" based on personal experience. It stays with the event, a chance remark by a fellow-worker, but works out the significance. The new title helps to focus the message. The language still sounds natural but gains considerably in precision and detail. Compare the difference between just saying "we'd wrestle" and saying "He'd make scary grunting noises, puff through his nose, and turn red with the strain of twisting my arm, . . . go rolling across the room and crash into the davenport. . . ." In the same way, "riding me piggyback" and "admire the tepee I'd made from bedsheets" make the very general word "play," in the first version, come alive. Paragraphs 3 and 4, which are almost completely new—these ideas were covered in the first version by the single phrase "taught me about fishing"—provide more pictures of what it was like to grow up with Uncle Fred around. If you look carefully at the two versions, you can see other examples showing how the writer has changed general statements to more specific "pictures."

The conclusion is more satisfying, too. Where the first version left us uncertain about what the writer's current attitude toward Uncle Fred is, the revised version makes clear that the writer's main idea sentence was probably something along these lines: "When another person made a disparaging remark about a person I loved, I realized that outside appearances didn't show the 'real' person." One problem with that first version may have been that the writer hadn't actually worked out a main idea sentence; sometimes the process of writing and rewriting clears up our thoughts and helps us produce new ideas.

This rewritten paper, which is more than twice as long as the original, shows that usually you don't have to add more *events* to a paper; you just have to dig in and make the material you already have more vivid. This new version of the paper does succeed in showing readers the significance of an "ordinary" event.

Key Words

Here are some of the important terms used in this chapter. See whether you can answer these questions about them.

1. What is the difference between telling what happened in an **objective report** and telling **what happened to you?** How are they alike?
2. Explain the difference between looking for a **significant event** and looking for the **significance of an event.**

3. What are the two parts of a **main idea sentence** for a **paper of personal experience?** Why are both parts necessary?
4. In writing a paper of personal experience, how do you use the **main idea sentence?** Does it have to appear in the paper? Why or why not?
5. What is a **"so what"** paper? How can you avoid writing one?
6. Why is it important to include **specific details** in personal narrative? How can you tell which details are **significant?**
7. Explain how **fragments** and **repetition** work differently in **conversation** than they do in **writing.**
8. How does **word order** make your writing sound natural or unnatural?
9. How does **"and" writing** improve when you use a **variety of connectors?**
10. Is it always wrong to use **slang** or **swear words** when you're writing personal narration? Why or why not?
11. How does the **first paragraph** introduce a paper of personal experience?

READINGS
Telling What Happened
Personal Experience

Cats Past

mastitis: inflammation of a cow's udder
deterred: discouraged or prevented
Don Juan: an imaginary Spanish hero, famous for his affairs with women
progeny: offspring
reminiscence: memory

First paragraph shows how important cats were

[1]   The day my aunt died, I climbed the ladder to the hayloft in the horse barn and sought comfort with Spotty and her kittens. Spotty, mostly tame, and her kittens, mostly wild, were part of my growing-up years, as integral a part of a farm childhood as the cows in the barn and potatoes in the field.

Number of cats and details of how they were treated

[2]   We always had cats—dozens of cats—in our barns. They had arranged among themselves a distribution of accommodations, some taking the lofts in the larger cow barn and others establishing themselves in the cozier confines of the adjacent horse barn. All met in the milkhouse under the comforting roar of the milking machine motor at 4:30 A.M. and 4:30 P.M., when my father would pour fresh warm milk into miscellaneous battered containers. He also served up the paper strainer from the milking machine, a delicacy to be sucked but not swallowed, and milk from cows newly calved or suffering from mastitis. His special favorites received shots straight from the teat, a treat

Susan Burns, *Animals,* February 1980, pp. 25–26.

that tested his aim and the cats' patience to the delight of a childish audience.

Details about kittens

[3]   In the spring the deep lofts in the cow barn were cavernously empty, their stores of hay depleted by the usually long Vermont winter. Beams and cross boards on the unfinished walls of each loft created hundreds of cozy boxes suitable for raising a family of kittens. When the lofts were filled with hay, the mother cats tunneled among the bales to reach the nesting boxes, now even more secure from prying children.

[4]   The degree of wildness attained by the kittens was directly related to our access to them. We loved the tiny bundles of fur and made every effort to locate, fondle and play with each litter. Some wily mothers, however, managed to raise their families undisturbed, and these kittens grew to be wild indeed. Not that this deterred us; I remember that my arms and hands seemed always to bear the scratches of my latest convert to pethood.

Female and male cats

[5]   Several female cats formed the core of the barns' feline society, with various large and scar-faced toms making frequent appearances. Winter mornings would find fresh tracks in the night's snowfall, evidence of another visit from these wandering Don Juans. Most barn toms sported ragged ears, badges of hardwon honor in the battle between the sexes. Local farmers swapped stories about "their" toms and the number of look-alike progeny in residence at their neighbors' barns. Completing the barn cat demographic picture were the throwaways, hapless kittens tossed from the briefly pausing cars of town dwellers who used this means to clear their consciences about unwanted pets.

Cat names

[6]   Like all of our cows, all of our cats had names. Barn cats of our childhood were given such obvious and descriptive names as Spotty and Blackie and Pinky. Our few house cats, by contrast, received more sophisticated names: Tinkerbell, Slippers and Traggy (namesake of Lieutenant Tragg of the "Perry Mason" program). When Tinkerbell's offspring threatened to overwhelm the household, they became barn cats, but none were as successful as those kittens born to the barn.

Barn cats

[7]   The purpose of barn cats, other than to amuse the farmer's children, is to control rat and mouse populations, especially in the vicinity of the grain bins. Our cats also pursued barn swallows, moles and field mice. Summer sunsets silhouetted mother cats leading their

kittens around bales of hay in the fields, teaching them the timeless arts of pursuit and capture. They also chased our dogs, much to the chagrin of these macho personalities.

What happened to the cats

[8]   The fate of most barn cats, however, makes a more bittersweet reminiscence. They died young: some after being crushed by the cows they snuggled up to seeking warmth on a bitter night; some of exposure, inadvertently shut out of the barns; many of disease— respiratory infections, pneumonia, leukemia. All were beseiged by fleas and internal parasites. Medical care, even the most routine shots, was unthinkable for so many cats, spaying or neutering not even considered. The cats were viewed not as pets, exactly, but more as animals that did the farmer a favor (rodent control) in exchange for milk and a warm place to stay. That they became objects of our childish affection did not alter the terms of this agreement. We mourned these cats as we mourned the cows sent away in Mr. Herman's big red truck, but like the cows their passing was a fact of farm life.

Conclusion

[9]   There are no statistics on barn cat populations, or on how many are well cared for in those barns, how many not. We can say that it is not an easy life—those city folks who left their kittens in the country can rest no easier for it. Mostly the farmers are well-meaning, usually their children are, but it cannot be denied that the barn cat who attains house cat status is a very lucky fellow indeed.

Responses

1. If you read only the first paragraph of this article, what do you expect the experience being written about to be? Burns' aunt? the sadness of a death? barns? kittens? a farm childhood? cows and potatoes? What is there in the first paragraph that helped you decide?
2. Which of the following would make the best main idea sentence for this article?
   a. When my aunt died, I discovered that kittens were a comfort.
   b. When I remember my childhood, I realize that the barn cats were an important part of it.
   c. House cats are better off than barn cats.
   d. When I think about barn cats, I can see that they have an important job on the farm.
   e. When my father milked the cows, he was always kind to the cats.
   Give reasons for your choice.

3. What specific details in paragraph 2 help you to get a picture of the scene in the barn?
4. How does the conclusion relate to what's been said earlier in the article? Look at each sentence in paragraph 9, and find the place in the article that justifies each concluding comment.
5. Burns is not writing much about herself in this article. Instead, she uses one event as a starting place for examining more general childhood memories, all tied to cats. Think back to your own childhood and find something that had a permanent place in your life. Then write a short paper making clear what that thing meant to you.

Speaking of Children . . .

appendage: something permanently attached, like an arm or leg
converse: talk
ominous: threatening disaster
doltish: dull or stupid

[1]   One child is an appendage. More than one is a way of life.

[2]   One child is outnumbered. You can brainwash it. You can make it do what you want it to do, carry it to parties and toss it on the bed with the coats, lug it in a backpack through the Adirondacks, teach it to say "How do you do?" and pass the hors d'oeuvres. Plural children are a counter-culture in the house. You and your husband are outnumbered. A creeping, irresistible tide of Leggos and Lincoln Logs and doll clothes and Matchbox cars seeps into the living room and cannot be turned back. You no longer go to New York for the weekend, you go to Disneyland instead, and dine at six instead of seven or eight. You pack up everything and move because the schools are better somewhere else. You spend long hours in social converse with people you would never otherwise have met at all, because your children know their children.

[3]   Relentlessly, year by year, you are pushed backward, shouting helplessly, from your own life into theirs. Your own errands are wedged into the time left over after you've taken the children somewhere and brought them home again. When they get older, you're lucky if you get to use your telephone one try out of six. With one child, you and your husband are still yourselves; you have merely acquired an extra thing, like a Yorkshire terrier or an electric toothbrush. More than one and you're a family, and the piano keys are covered with jelly and whenever you try to talk to each other somebody says, "Who's he? Do I know him? Why is she going to divorce him, doesn't she like him any more?" and after a while you give up.

Barbara Holland, *Mother's Day or the View from in Here,* (Garden City, N.Y.: Doubleday, 1980), pp. 52–54.

[4]   I have read that it's terribly important to a healthy marriage that the wife set aside some quiet private time to chat with the husband, preferably when he gets home from work, or they get home from work. Just half an hour. Peace, privacy, a couple of martinis, and "How was your day, dear? Is the new man working out all right?"

I would like to get my personal hands on the people who keep suggesting this, and find out how I'm expected to manage.

"Now, I want everyone to play quietly and nicely in your rooms for half an hour, while Mommy talks to Daddy."

"I want to talk to Daddy too!"

"Later, sweetie. Right now is going to be our private time together, and then later you can have a private time with him, okay?"

"What are going to talk about?"

"Oh . . . I don't know. Things. Now you play nicely and don't interrupt us, all right?"

"What if it's something important?"

"It better be terribly important."

Peace. Privacy. The well-chilled martini.

"And how was your day, dear?"

"Well, as a matter of fact—"

An ominous splintering crash overhead, and you both glance apprehensively at the ceiling. Silence.

"As a matter of fact, something rather interesting seems to be brewing. Scott was saying—"

Feet on the stairs. A child, and another child behind it.

"I said not to interrupt us."

"You said if it's important. It's important, I have to ask you something."

"What? Ask, and leave."

The eyes unfocus, the face blurs, the sneakered toe traces a pattern on the carpet. "I'm trying to remember . . ."

"Hurry up. Mother and I were talking."

Theatrical hand on brow. "I can't remember. I've forgotten. It was important, though. Can I taste your drink?"

"No. Go back to your room."

"Just a tiny *taste?*"

"Go upstairs and play!"

Bitter looks. Feet stomp halfway up the stairs and then stop; silence, not even a breath, in case of missing a single word from below.

"Yes, well, you were saying?"

"I forget. Well. Did *you* have a nice day?"

Muted scuffling on the stairs.

"Oh yes. Very nice."

You gaze at each other, paralyzed with self-consciousness, each wondering how you came to get stuck with this doltish stranger. Besides, it's time to start the water for the spaghetti.

There's always bed, of course, but mothers of more than one child fall asleep with startling suddenness and finality.

You could write each other notes. At least until the children learn to read.

Some parents communicate in high school French, but my husband took German instead.

We take to calling each other at our offices when we have anything to say.

Responses

1. The main idea sentence of this article—or the last half of a main idea sentence—is clearly stated in the first sentence. (Using the pattern given in this text, the whole sentence would probably be "When I had two children, I discovered . . .") Where else in the article is this idea repeated in slightly different words? How does this repetition serve as a transition to the rest of the article?

2. Almost half the article consists of conversation, directly quoted. What makes the conversation sound natural? Holland never identifies the speakers—never writes, "The child said . . ." or "I said . . ."—but it's not hard to decide who the speakers are. How can you tell?

3. Beginning with paragraph 4, Holland deliberately uses a number of what would normally be considered sentence fragments. Why are they appropriate to this article? What effect do they create?

4. The paragraphs in the last half of this article are all very short, too short to number for your convenience in talking about them. After paragraph 4, they seldom contain more than one sentence. Quoted conversation is always given a separate paragraph for each speaker. But what is the reason for the four single-sentence paragraphs at the end of the article? Would you like it better if these four sentences were combined into one paragraph? Why or why not?

5. Write a short paper in which you show a siutation or event by quoting what people say. Try to make at least a third of your paper direct quotation.

On the Way to the Wolf Den

doughty: brave and strong
expedient: means used in a desperate situation
ensuing: following
traumatic: shocking
nocturnal peregrinations: night wanderings
callously: without sensitivity
engender: bring forth
affinity: feeling of closeness

Farley Mowat, *Never Cry Wolf* (Boston: Little, Brown, 1963).

[1]   It is a long way in time and space from the bathroom of my Grandmother Mowat's house in Oakville, Ontario, to the bottom of a wolf den in the Barren Lands of central Keewatin, and I have no intention of retracing the entire road which lies between. Nevertheless, there must be a beginning to any tale; and the story of my sojourn amongst the wolves begins properly in Granny's bathroom.

[2]   When I was five years old I had still not given any indication—as most gifted children do well before that age—of where my future lay. Perhaps because they were disappointed by my failure to declare myself, my parents took me to Oakville and abandoned me to the care of my grandparents while they went off on a holiday.

[3]   One hot summer day I was meandering aimlessly beside a little local creek when I came upon a stagnant pool. In the bottom, and only just covered with green scum, three catfish lay gasping out their lives. They interested me. I dragged them up on the bank with a stick and waited expectantly for them to die; but this they refused to do. Just when I was convinced that they were quite dead, they would open their broad ugly jaws and give another gasp. I was so impressed by their stubborn refusal to accept their fate that I found a tin can, put them in it along with some scum, and took them home.

[4]   I had begun to like them, in an abstract sort of way, and wished to know them better. But the problem of where to keep them while our acquaintanceship ripened was a major one. There were no washtubs in Greenhedges. There *was* a bathtub, but the stopper did not fit and consequently it would not hold water for more than a few minutes. By bedtime I had still not resolved the problem, and since I felt that even these doughty fish could hardly survive an entire night in the tin can, I was driven to the admittedly desperate expedient of finding temporary lodgings for them in the bowl of Granny's old-fashioned toilet.

[5]   I was too young at the time to appreciate the special problems which old age brings in its train. It was one of these problems which was directly responsible for the dramatic and unexpected encounter which took place between my grandmother and the catfish during the small hours of the ensuing night.

[6]   It was a traumatic experience for Granny, and for me, and probably for the catfish too. Throughout the rest of her life Granny refused to eat fish of any kind, and always carried a high-powered flashlight with her during her nocturnal peregrinations. I cannot be as certain about the effect on the catfish, for my unfeeling cousin—once the hooferaw had died down a little—callously flushed the toilet. As for myself, the effect was to engender in me a lasting affinity for the lesser beasts of the animal kingdom. In a word, the affair of the catfish marked the beginning of my career, first as a naturalist, and later as a biologist. I had started on my way to the wolf den.

Responses

1. In your own words, write what seems to be the main idea sentence of this article, using the pattern "When I _____, I discovered _____."
2. Mowat is a well-known expert on wolves, so this event in his life is prob-

ably of interest to people who know about his work. How has he made the experience interesting to people who don't know or care much about wolves?

3. This article is not about a "big event" in the usual sense—it doesn't deal with marriage or divorce, birth or death. Does Mowat show you why it was important to him? Does it remind you of similar experiences in your own life? What are they?

4. Part of the effect of this essay is the unexpected contrast between wolf dens and Granny's bathroom. List some similar unexpected contrasts that fit the experiences you thought of in answering question 2.

5. Paragraphs 5 and 6 describe what happened when Granny went into the bathroom, but the telling is extremely vague, so you are left to imagine most of the details. Would you like it better if the details had been given? Why or why not?

6. In paragraph 6, the language becomes quite formal, using words like "traumatic," "ensuing," "nocturnal peregrinations," "callously." Does this more formal language fit the event—an old lady's surprise when she discovers catfish in her toilet in the middle of the night? What would be the effect of using coarser language and more details? Try rewriting this section, giving more details; then compare your version with those other students have written. Which do you like best—some of the student versions or the one Mowat wrote?

Home

compote: fruits cooked in syrup
dexterous: skillful with the hands
dissension: strong disagreement

[1]   Home always warmly awaited me. Welcoming, enveloping. Home meant a quick-walking, careful, Duty-Loving mother, who played the piano, made fudge, made cocoa and prune whip and apricot pie, drew tidy cows and trees and expert houses with chimneys and chimney smoke, who helped her children with arithmetic homework, and who sang in a high soprano:

"Brighten the corner where you are!—
Br-rrr-righten the corner where you are!—
Some one far from harbor you may guide
     across the bar—
Brigh-TEN the cor-nerr—
       where
            you
                 are."

Gwendolyn Brooks, *Report From Part One* (Highland Park, Michigan: Broadside Press, 1972).

[2]   Home meant my father, with kind eyes, songs, and tense recitations from my brother and myself. My father seemed to Gwendolyn and Raymond a figure of power. He had those rich Artistic Abilities, but he had more. He could fix anything that broke or stopped. He could build long-lasting fires in the ancient furnace below. He could paint the house, inside and out, and could whitewash the basement. He could spread the American Flag in wide loud magic across the front of our house on the Fourth of July and Decoration Day.

[3]   He could chuckle. No one has ever had, no one will ever have, a chuckle exactly like my father's. It was gentle, it was warmly happy, it was heavyish but not hard. It was secure, and seemed to us an assistant to the Power that registered with his children.

[4]   My father, too, was almost our family doctor. We had Dr. Carter, of course, precise and semi-twinkly and effective—but it was not always necessary to call him. My father had wanted to be a doctor. Thwarted, he read every "doctor book" (and he remembered much from a Black tradition) he could reach, learning fine secrets and curing us with steams, and fruit compotes, and dexterous rubs, and, above all, with bedside compassion.

[5]   "Well, there, young lady! How's that throat now?"

[6]   "Well, let's see now. This salve will take care of that bruise! Now, we're going to be all right." In illness there was an advantage: the invalid was royalty for the run of the seizure.

[7]   And of course my father furnished All the Money. The "all" was inadequate, felt Keziah Wims Brooks: could he not leave the McKinley Music Publishing Company, which was paying him about twenty-five dollars a week (from thirty to thirty-five when he worked overtime)? Uncle Paul, her sister Gertrude's husband, worked at City Hall—had a "snap" job—made *fifty* dollars a week . . . True, during the bad times, during the Depression, when McKinley, itself stricken, could pay my father only in part—sometimes eighteen dollars, sometimes ten dollars—our family ate beans. But children dread, often above all else, dissension in the house, and we would have been quite content to entertain a beany diet every day, if necessary, and *not* live in Lilydale as did bungalow-owning Aunt Gertrude and Uncle Paul, if only there could be, continuously, the almost musical Peace that we had most of the time.

Responses

1. How does the quotation at the end of the first paragraph add to this essay? What if the writer had ended the paragraph without it?
2. What details does the writer select to show the qualities of her mother? of her father?
3. In paragraph 7, the writer mentions the Depression. What other clues does she offer that help to establish the time of this recollection?
4. The last sentence points up the significance of the experience. What details has Brooks used to emphasize the peacefulness of her childhood

home? Do you agree that "children dread, often above all else, dissension in the house"? Give specific examples that support your answer.

5. Paragraph 7 seems to say that there's a choice that must be made between eating beans and having dissension in the house. Do you think that's a fair statement? Why or why not?

6. Gwendolyn Brooks is a famous and honored American writer. How does that information affect how you react to her writing—or does it?

7. Write a paragraph or two that makes clear how you remember your father —or mother—when you were about ten years old. Try to make whichever parent (or substitute parent) you write about come alive by using quotations and specific details.

The Labor Market

dispersed: scattered, went away
palpable: plain to see

[1]   In the dark beneath the overpass, the men stood in loose lines on either side of the street. Above, a solitary truck passed on the expressway, disrupting the early quiet of downtown San Antonio. Some of the men stood alone; others stood talking in small groups. A white panel truck pulled in beneath the overpass, rolled to a stop, and the men rushed it. They swarmed the truck, trying to get the drivers' attention. After a few moments' haggling, one of the men climbed in, the truck drove off, and the others drifted back to their places.

[2]   Across the street from me, I could make out two men in cowboy boots, hats, and jeans who appeared to be *rancheros* from Northern Mexico. There was also an older man in straw sombrero and sandals. They were standing among men who were either Mexican-Americans or urban Mexicans. When I started across the street, they floated down the sidewalk out of range.

[3]   The men had come to what economists call a shadow labor market. Each morning, the market forms beneath the expressway that divides the commercial center of San Antonio from the west-side slums. Mexicans without legal documents and Mexican-Americans on unemployment look for work. Small contractors who don't want to pay minimum wages or bother with Social Security look for workers. It is an old San Antonio institution that used to take place next to the farmers' market before it was renovated and turned over to tourists. I went there thinking I could stand in one of the lines, start a conversation with some of the men, and explain that I was a journalist who wanted to find out about wetbacks in San Antonio. Having a beard and wearing blue jeans, I hadn't worried about being mistaken for an immigration officer. But beneath the overpass, being Anglo was cause enough for suspicion.

John Davidson, *The Long Road North* (New York: Doubleday, 1979), pp. 10–13.

[4]   A succession of panel trucks and pickups came. The lines dwindled as the sound of traffic above increased and the light grew. Each time I walked toward any of the men, they faded away before me. If I started across the street toward a group, they dispersed, acting as if they neither saw nor heard me. The only time I got near was when I would follow to the stopped vehicles where I could hear the bargaining over hours and wages.

[5]   When the traffic above reached its rush-hour roar and the sun rose high enough to dispel the shadows, the pickups and panel trucks stopped coming. Among the men left waiting, there was a palpable air of disappointment as they realized the market was over and they hadn't been chosen. They stood for a while, then started drifting away. Disappointed myself, I picked out a young Mexican who was heading back into the slums and started after him. He walked slowly until he realized he was being followed, then increased his pace. I called to him in Spanish and walked faster, but he hurried on, refusing to look back. Grim yet amused at the idea of a chase, I lengthened my stride and was beginning to gain on him when I thought of how his heart must be beating. I stopped and watched him hurry down the street and disappear behind an old warehouse.

[6]   After a week in San Antonio looking for wetbacks, illegal aliens, undocumented workers, or whatever the appropriate euphemism happened to be, I had yet to talk to a Mexican without legal papers and was beginning to feel mildly frustrated. I had gone to San Antonio with the plan of making friends with wetbacks, establishing connections with their village in Mexico, and going there to make the trip north with the next group that came. Each day the plan seemed less realistic.

[7]   My main contact in San Antonio was a man I'll call Guillermo. I met him while working on another story about farmworkers in the Rio Grande Valley, where he told me that he himself had come to the United States as a wetback and was "King of the Wetbacks" in San Antonio. Graying, handsome, Guillermo worked as a union organizer and had a distinct rotten-tooth charm. Each morning when I went by his house to pick him up, he would appear unwashed and unshaven, drinking his first quart of beer. He had an anemic-looking, cowed young wife and several sickly children depressingly close in age.

[8]   Throughout the morning, Guillermo and I would make the rounds to the various minor politicians in the Mexican-American community. After long preludes of small talk and measured beer drinking, Guillermo would tell them what I wanted and they would say that of course they knew wetbacks, that the city was filled with wetbacks, but that they couldn't think of any right off. They would then give me the names of community workers—priests, nuns, social workers—and I'd take Guillermo home and spend the rest of the day looking up the new leads. The leads usually gave me the same response as the politicians, or, as one nun, Sister Somebody, did, would promise me I'd never find an illegal alien who would talk to an Anglo reporter. If the community workers had access, they guarded it closely; the politicians I began to think of as ducks floating indifferently on currents of hardship and poverty.

[9]   The absence of visible wetbacks combined with the official estimates that 40 per cent of San Antonio's unskilled labor force was undocumented fostered in me

an uncomfortable sense of bewilderment. If the facts were accurate, where were the wetbacks? As with previous reporting excursions into subcultures that exist outside the law and are thought to represent an "underworld," I was struck by how well such groups of people blend into their environment and by how little appearances reveal. I was able to see only when I stopped worrying about the facts and stopped anticipating. Then it was possible to begin the leap from culture to culture, reality to reality.

Responses

1. Davidson never defines such terms as "rancheros," "wetbacks," "Anglo," etc.; does he make clear from the context what the words mean? If you think he does, give a definition of these three terms in your own words.
2. What verbs does Davidson use to describe the men's departure (see especially paragraphs 2, 4, and 5)? How do these verbs help establish the idea that the men didn't want to talk to Davidson?
3. What is a euphemism? Why does Davidson use the word in paragraph 6? How do euphemisms fit the situation Davidson is describing?
4. In paragraph 7, Davidson first uses the general term "handsome" to describe Guillermo, then follows it with a few specific details about his appearance. What are those details? How do they give you a picture of Guillermo? Do the details fit your idea of "handsome"? Why or why not?
5. Davidson ends paragraph 8 with a comparison. Do you think the comparison fits the situation? Write a paragraph or two of your own, beginning with "According to Davidson, the politicians behaved like. . . ." Then go on to explain why the comparison does or doesn't fit.

An Open Letter to Consumer Reports

knead: to punch, pound, and press, as in making bread
consistency: degree of firmness
ensue: come after

Dear *Consumer Reports:*
[1]   Just reading *Consumer Reports* fills my window shopping needs and makes me feel practical and economical, but this isn't my annual fan letter. Right now I want you to go bail for me.

Betsy Cochran, *The Cape Codder.*

[2]   I set out for the January sales with your new Buying Guide Issue under my arm, love in my heart, and a wallet in my jeans that was nicely filled out with Christmas bonuses. I never thought of Boston as a hostile town, yet here I am in the hoosegow, and no one seems to care or understand. I am writing you because I feel perhaps you will understand, and in the hope that you will care.

[3]   What happened is this: I headed for the department store area with two particular items in mind—molded luggage, and bed pillows. First the luggage. I found stacks of it taking up half a room in the first store I tried. Whipping out the Guide, I followed its instructions:

[4]   ". . . Check the frame's sturdiness by opening the case ninety degrees and seeing how hard it is to flex the edges; pull the lid sideways to see how readily it tends to deform. . . . Try the handle for size and comfort. Pinch the lining in several places to see how firmly it is glued down. . . ."

[5]   It was while I was still pinching the lining of a $45 twenty-six-inch case that the salesman accosted me. "Can I help you?" he asked between clenched teeth.

[6]   "Why no," I said, "as a matter of fact I find the linings of your cases are not well glued, and the lids don't stay open the way they should, so I shall have to look elsewhere."

[7]   He accompanied me to the elevator and pushed the button. My next quest before I left the store was for bed pillows. I had read all you had to say about shredded foam and waterfowl down, so when I approached the generously stacked counters I knew just what to do. I compared them for resiliency by placing them on a flat surface (the only one handy was the floor) and compressing them to about half their original thickness. I made sure the openings used for inserting the filler were well-closed with both ends of the seam back-stitched (and not all of them were). I made it my job to "knead a synthetic fiber or feather-down pillow to determine whether its fillings had uniform consistency," and at this point I was approached by the floor manager. He did not ask if he could help me.

[8]   "Watcha doing to our pillows?" he asked, his face flushed. In truth, the display case was in some disarray, and a few tiny goose down feathers were gliding softly between us.

[9]   "I was only giving them the necessary tests," I replied with hauteur. "They don't all measure up," I added. I balanced a couple of them on my arm, as you suggested, to see if the corners drooped, and then held them by the ends and shook them.

[10]   "See here," said the manager, "quit it!"

[11]   Indignantly I pointed to the section of page 96 of the Buying Guide that was giving me my instructions. "We must now fluff the pillows to see if they have good dome-shaped crowns," I pointed out, "and unzip the foam rubber ones to see if the filling is in one piece. We must make sure that zipper tapes are attached with two rows of stitching, tap and fold the ticking to see if it is heavily treated with sizing material, punch it and watch for signs of dust, and bury our face in it and sniff to see if the filler has been cleaned properly."

[12]   "Must we indeed," he said, "we'll see about that." I turned away from him and began to fluff and punch. "I'll bury your face in them for you," he shouted, and we soon had a brisk pillow fight on our hands (another effective test), until

stronger authorities intervened. It seems the law was on his side, though Virtue and Righteousness were on mine.

[13]   This brings me to the spot where I now languish. I can only hope that the lawsuits which will ensue will turn out to be a Best Buy.

[14]   Please get me out of here.

Faithfully yours,
B.C.

Responses

1. Why is this article written in the form of a letter to *Consumer Reports* (a magazine that tells subscribers how to check the quality of merchandise)? Do you think it was ever sent to the magazine? Why?

2. Does the writer apparently keep on believing in the advice *Consumer Reports* gives? Look especially at the end of paragraph 12, paragraph 13, and the closing of the letter.

3. Why does the writer quote the exact directions the magazine gives for testing suitcases and pillows?

4. How is the price of the suitcase in paragraph 5 related to the point of this essay? How is the fact that not all the pillows had backstitched seams related to the point?

5. Would this story be as funny if the writer had first tested the pillows and then been jailed after testing the suitcase? Why or why not?

6. At first reading, you might think that the main idea sentence of this article is "When I tried to follow the directions in the Buying Guide, I discovered I was in trouble." But is the point of the essay that she got into trouble, or is the story really saying something about the directions themselves? What would be a better main idea sentence?

7. Make up an accident or an embarrassing situation that could have resulted from purchasing some faulty merchandise. Then, using Cochran's letter as a kind of model, write a letter to the store asking for help or guidance.

Making Room in the Inn

vise: a tool that clamps things immovably together
neutralize: destroy the damaging effects of something

[1]   I couldn't forget that day in Arlington Cemetery. After all, President Kennedy had challenged all Americans to ask themselves what they could do for their

Dick Gregory, *Up from Nigger* (New York: Stein and Day, 1976), pp. 20–24.

country. I knew one thing I could do, that I *had* to do, was to continue to put my career, my body, and my life on the front line in the struggle for civil rights.

[2]   There is a strange thing about the course of human events. A beautiful or courageous human action can have the effect of raising the consciousness level of the entire nation. On the other hand, a horrible act often has the reverse effect, and the consciousness level of the nation is dulled.

[3]   The assassination of President Kennedy seemed to have a deadening effect, as though a drug had been injected into the main artery of national feeling. The nation was dumbfounded. The tragic circumstances under which Lyndon Baines Johnson became president of the United States seemed to create a moral vacuum and a crisis of conscience. There was a tendency to put protest aside for a while, to give the new president a chance, check out his intentions, and let him chart a clear course for the future.

[4]   For a month or so after the assassination, it seemed as though the civil rights movement had been wiped out. There were no demonstrations. Leaders seemed to be caught in a vise of indecision. Something was needed to jar the nation's sensibilities, to free the national conscience from its temporary moral paralysis.

[5]   One day I got a phone call from the SNCC kids (Student Nonviolent Coordinating Committee) in Atlanta, Georgia, telling me about a particularly touchy situation there. Although the city of Atlanta had a public accommodations law, it was neutralized and protected from implementation by Georgia state law. State law stipulated that anyone who refused to leave a place of business after having been asked to leave by the owner in the presence of a police officer, could be arrested for trespassing. Every time demonstrators tried to integrate restaurants in Atlanta, they would be arrested under Georgia state law. The city of Atlanta, much like Pontius Pilate, would wash its hands of responsibility. City officials insisted that nothing could be done until the state law was changed.

[6]   Lil and I talked about the problem in Atlanta, as well as the need for a dramatic national reminder that the civil rights issue was still very much alive. Lil was pregnant with our twin girls at the time. We decided that the pregnant wife of a national celebrity in jail on Christmas Day, while daddy was at home with the other two kids, Lynne and Michele, would be an appropriate and dramatic Christmas reminder that there was still no room for Black folks in the inns and restaurants of Atlanta. We decided that Lil should go to Atlanta and get arrested on Christmas Eve. And if she participated in the demonstrations, there was no doubt she would be arrested!

[7]   Lil went to Atlanta. She didn't want to go. She didn't want to be away from our other two girls on Christmas. But Lil's humanitarian impulse took over from her motherly instinct. She took part in a sit-in demonstration at one of the Dobbs House restaurants. The white folks didn't let us down! The state law was invoked, Lil and many others refused to leave, and they all went to jail.

[8]   I sent a telegram to Lil at the jail on Christmas Eve. It was released to the press on Christmas Day. I said that the kids were all right, but they missed their momma, and I thanked her for being willing to give up her Christmas so that one day all folks in America might have something to celebrate. I added a line which got a lot of coverage in the press, "If they had found as much room in the inn two

thousand years ago for a pregnant woman named Mary as the Atlanta police have found in their jail for you, maybe none of us would be celebrating Christmas today."

[9]   Lil became a symbolic reminder that the civil rights struggle was not over. Three days later I joined the Atlanta demonstrations. They had grown to huge proportions, with hundreds of people arrested each day.

[10]   I had noticed that Dobbs House and Toddle House were on the New York Stock Exchange. I received a sudden inspiration about how to beat the Georgia state law. I bought two shares each of Dobbs House and Toddle House stock. Then I went back to demonstrate.

[11]   The manager came over with the required cop as a witness and asked me to leave the premises. I said, "I happen to own stock in this business. Do you?" Of course, I didn't say *how much* stock I owned. It was a great example of how to use an image. Everybody knew I was a big entertainer and assumed I made big money. Their assumptions inflated the value of my stock holdings!

[12]   The manager admitted that he wasn't a stockholder. I shook my head and said, "Well, under these circumstances, it appears that I represent more ownership than you do. So I'll have to ask you to leave my premises. Officer, do your duty!"

[13]   The manager requested an immediate stockholders' meeting, so we huddled in the corner. He explained the integration problem. There were a number of similar restaurants in Atlanta owned by a man named Charlie Loeb. A Loeb establishment was right across the street. The manager said it wouldn't do any good to integrate his place because white customers would simply boycott and go to the Loeb establishment. I indicated that we'd deal with Loeb after Dobbs and Toddle Houses were integrated.

[14]   We won that battle, and the Dobbs and Toddle Houses of Atlanta soon were integrated. But integrating the Loeb establishments was much harder. We met with strong resistance. I wasn't a stockholder, so I didn't have the negotiating power. We kept on demonstrating, going to jail, and it seemed as though we were going nowhere.

[15]   One day, while I was in jail, I read a newspaper quote which hinted that Charlie Loeb wasn't the "tyrant" other statements had made him appear to be. As soon as I was released from jail, I decided to try some personal negotiation. I went by Charlie Loeb's house. It happened to be his birthday, and there was a party going on. We went into a side room and I told him, "I've read some statements you've made to the press. I get the feeling there's more to your resistance than shows on the surface. What's the real problem?"

[16]   He said, "You're right. There are two problems. I'm getting ready to sell my restaurants, and it's very difficult for me to integrate before I sell. The buyer will think I'm doing it just because I'm getting out."

[17]   I could understand that problem, but the second one caught me off guard. Charlie Loeb told me why he had refused to let Harry Belafonte into his establishment. The mayor had brought Harry by after giving him the keys to the city.

[18]   Loeb insisted that the incident didn't have anything to do with Harry's being Black. But every time a white person was given the keys to the city, the party was held at the country club. Loeb felt Harry was being brought to his place, in-

stead of to the usual country club affair, because Loeb was Jewish. I wasn't ready for that one! Loeb was on the same side we were. He was protesting discrimination!

[19]   We made a deal. We would call off the demonstrations if Loeb would agree to have his restaurants sold within sixty days and would also get city officials to drop all charges against arrested demonstrators. He agreed.

[20]   I couldn't help thinking of Lil's contribution. Not only had she helped to open the restaurant counters in Atlanta to Black folks, but she had unconsciously exposed discrimination against Jews. I wondered if that was why there was a no vacancy sign on the Bethlehem inn that night two thousand years ago. Would they have put a pregnant mother out in the stable if she hadn't been Jewish?

Responses

1. Which of these sentences comes closest to expressing the main idea of this article?
   When I tried to integrate the restaurants in Atlanta, I discovered that
   a. being famous gets more publicity.
   b. a trick will sometimes work when persuasion won't.
   c. it helps to involve pregnant women.
   d. some unexpected people were fighting for the same thing I was.
   Defend your choice by referring to what Gregory says in the article.
2. The personal events covered in this article begin with paragraph 5. What does Gregory accomplish in the first four paragraphs? Would you like the article better if it began with paragraph 5? Why or why not? Is anything that Gregory says later in the article related to those first four paragraphs? If you think there is a relationship, what is it?
3. Explain the phrase "much like Pontius Pilate" in paragraph 5. How is that reference connected to the title of the article and the conclusion?
4. Why does Gregory say, in paragraph 7, "The white folks didn't let us down!" Does he mean that in general the "white folks" were on his side? If not, what does he mean?
5. Write a paper telling what happened when you misjudged somebody's motives, or somebody else misjudged yours.

In Search of Our Mothers' Gardens

fidelity: faithfulness
legacy: an inheritance

Alice Walker, in Sara Ruddick and Pamela Daniels (eds.), *Working It Out* (New York: Pantheon, 1978), pp. 97–101.

[1]   Black women are called, in the folklore that so aptly identifies one's status in society, "the *mule* of the world," because we have been handed the burdens that everyone else—*everyone* else—refused to carry. We have also been called "Matriarchs," "Superwomen," and "Mean and Evil Bitches." Not to mention "Castraters" and "Sapphire's Mamma." When we have pleaded for understanding, our character has been distorted; when we have asked for simple caring, we have been handed empty inspirational appellations, then stuck in the farthest corner. When we have asked for love, we have been given children. In short, even our plainer gifts, our labors of fidelity and love, have been knocked down our throats. To be an Artist and a Black woman, even today, lowers our status in many respects, rather than raises it; and yet, Artists we will be.

[2]   Therefore we must fearlessly pull out of ourselves and look at and identify with our lives the living creativity some of our great-grandmothers were not allowed to know. I stress *some* of them because it is well known that the majority of our great-grandmothers knew, even without "knowing" it, the reality of their spirituality, even if they didn't recognize it beyond what happened in the singing at church—and they never had any intention of giving it up.

[3]   How they did it: those millions of Black women who were not Phillis Wheatley or Lucy Terry or Frances Harper or Zora Hurston or Nella Larsen or Bessie Smith—nor Elizabeth Catlett nor Katherine Dunham, either—brings me to the title of this essay, "In Search of Our Mothers' Gardens," which is a personal account that is yet shared, in its theme and its meaning, by all of us. I found, while thinking about the far-reaching world of the creative Black woman, that often the truest answer to a question that really matters can be found very close. So I was not surprised when my own mother popped into my mind.

[4]   In the late 1920s my mother ran away from home to marry my father. Marriage, if not running away, was expected of seventeen-year-old girls. By the time she was twenty, she had two children and was pregnant with a third. Five children later, I was born. And this is how I came to know my mother: she seemed a large, soft, loving-eyed woman who was rarely impatient in our home. Her quick, violent temper was on view only a few times a year, when she battled with the white landlord who had the misfortune to suggest to her that her children did not need to go to school.

[5]   She made all the clothes we wore, even my brothers' overalls. She made all the towels and sheets we used. She spent the summers canning vegetables and fruits. She spent the winter evenings making quilts enough to cover all our beds.

[6]   During the "working" day, she labored beside—not behind—my father in the fields. Her day began before sunup and did not end until late at night. There was never a moment for her to sit down, undisturbed, to unravel her own private thoughts; never a time free from interruption—by work or the noisy inquiries of her many children. And yet, it is to my mother—and all our mothers who were not famous—that I went in search of the secret of what has fed that muzzled and often mutilated, but vibrant, creative spirit that the Black woman has inherited, and that pops out in wild and unlikely places to this day.

[7]   But when, you will ask, did my overworked mother have time to know or care about feeding the creative spirit?

[8]   The answer is so simple that many of us have spent years discovering it. We have constantly looked high, when we should have looked high—and low.

[9]   For example: in the Smithsonian Institution in Washington, D.C., there hangs a quilt unlike any other in the world. In fanciful, inspired, and yet simple and identifiable figures, it portrays the story of the Crucifixion. It is considered rare, beyond price. Though it follows no known pattern of quiltmaking, and though it is made of bits and pieces of worthless rags, it is obviously the work of a person of powerful imagination and deep spiritual feeling. Below this quilt I saw a note that says it was made by "an anonymous Black woman in Alabama, a hundred years ago."

[10]   If we could locate this "anonymous" Black woman from Alabama, she would turn out to be one of our grandmothers—an artist who left her mark in the only materials she could afford, and in the only medium her position in society allowed her to use. . . .

[11]   And so our mothers and grandmothers have, more often than not anonymously, handed on the creative spark, the seed of the flower they themselves never hoped to see: or like a sealed letter they could not plainly read.

[12]   And so it is, certainly, with my own mother. Unlike Ma Rainey's songs, which retained their creator's name even while blasting forth from Bessie Smith's mouth, no song or poem will bear my mother's name. Yet so many of the stories that I write, that we all write, are my mother's stories. Only recently did I fully realize this: that through years of listening to my mother's stories of her life, I have absorbed not only the stories themselves, but something of the manner in which she spoke, something of the urgency that involves the knowledge that her stories—like her life—must be recorded. It is probably for this reason that so much of what I have written is about characters whose counterparts in real life are so much older than I am.

[13]   But the telling of these stories, which came from my mother's lips as naturally as breathing, was not the only way my mother showed herself as an artist. For stories, too, were subject to being distracted, to dying without conclusion. Dinners must be started, and cotton must be gathered before the big rains. The artist that was and is my mother showed itself to me only after many years. This is what I finally noticed:

[14]   Like Mem, a character in *The Third Life of Grange Copeland,* my mother adorned with flowers whatever shabby house we were forced to live in. And not just your typical straggly country stand of zinnias, either. She planted ambitious gardens—and still does—with over fifty different varieties of plants that bloom profusely from early March until late November. Before she left home for the fields, she watered her flowers, chopped up the grass, and laid out new beds. When she returned from the fields she might divide clumps of bulbs, dig a cold pit, uproot and replant roses, or prune branches from her taller bushes or trees—until night came and it was too dark to see.

[15]   Whatever she planted grew as if by magic, and her fame as a grower of flowers spread over three counties. Because of her creativity with her flowers, even my memories of poverty are seen through a screen of blooms—sunflowers, petunias, roses, dahlias, forsythia, spirea, delphiniums, verbena . . . and on and on.

[16]   And I remember people coming to my mother's yard to be given cuttings from her flowers; I hear again the praise showered on her because whatever rocky soil she landed on, she turned into a garden. A garden so brilliant with colors, so original in its design, so magnificent with life and creativity, that to this day people drive by our house in Georgia—perfect strangers and imperfect strangers—and ask to stand or walk among my mother's art.

[17]   I notice that it is only when my mother is working in her flowers that she is radiant, almost to the point of being invisible—except as Creator: hand and eye. She is involved in work her soul must have. Ordering the universe in the image of her personal conception of Beauty.

[18]   Her face, as she prepares the Art that is her gift, is a legacy of respect she leaves to me, for all that illuminates and cherishes life. She had handed down respect for the possibilities—and the will to grasp them.

[19]   For her, so hindered and intruded upon in so many ways, being an artist has still been a daily part of her life. This ability to hold on, even in very simple ways, is work Black women have done for a very long time.

[20]   This poem is not enough, but it is something, for the woman who literally covered the holes in our walls with sunflowers:

> They were women then
> My mama's generation
> Husky of voice—Stout of
> Step
> With fists as well as
> Hands
> How they battered down
> Doors
> And ironed
> Starched white
> Shirts
> How they led
> Armies
> Headragged Generals
> Across mined
> Fields
> Booby-trapped
> Ditches
> To discover books
> Desks
> A place for us
> How they knew what we
> *Must* know
> Without knowing a page
> Of it
> Themselves.

[21]   Guided by my heritage of a love of beauty and a respect for strength—in search of my mother's garden, I found my own.

Responses

1. If you don't recognize at least two or three of the women listed in paragraph 3, look them up in the library. What do they have in common? What point is Walker making by mentioning them here?

2. Read the fourth and fifth sentences of paragraph 1 carefully. How are these sentences alike? What effect is created by reading the two sentences together? Is the effect made greater because the fifth sentence is shorter than either piece of the fourth sentence?

3. Instead of talking about her own experiences in paragraphs 2 and 3, Walker gives the background of her thinking and, indirectly, her reasons for writing this article. What are those reasons? How are they tied to the rest of the article?

4. On the basis of what Walker says in this article, can you give her definition of "creative spirit"? What would it be?

5. In paragraphs 8 and 9, Walker seems to stop talking about her mother, then comes back to her in paragraph 11. Does this interruption bother you? What do you think the purpose was?

6. How is the poem Walker wrote for her mother connected to the main point of the article? Does the last line of the article mean that Walker is a gardener too? If not, what does it mean?

7. Do some of your attitudes reflect the attitudes of the person who brought you up? How is the similarity shown? Write a paper explaining the similarities (or differences if you prefer), but don't just make general statements; give details and create a picture of behavior.

More Suggestions for Writing

the first time you were punished
when a friend let you down
when a stranger gave you some help
when you had an accident
a time you were greatly embarrassed
moving away from home
quitting a job
getting a job
campaigning for a school office
a party that failed
when you spent a sleepless night
when you were overcharged at a store
when you lost your money or had it stolen
when the police stopped you
a day you went hungry
a quarrel
the death of someone you knew or loved
a serious illness

Chapter 9

Writing to Persuade

Persuasion, and attempts at persuasion, go on all around us all the time. Other people try to persuade us, and we try to persuade them. We have been using persuasive techniques since we were born, and we'll keep using them till we die. Babies bawl for the breast or the bottle; children scream and stomp, smile and coax; adults argue, plead, and sometimes slaughter each other. All these kinds of behavior—bawling, begging, and battering—have one thing in common: they are attempts to get other people to give us what we want, to do what we want them to do.

Between the methods of the baby and the methods of the businessman, bus driver, or bureaucrat, however, there are some important differences. A new infant's crying is instinctive—a reaction to hunger and discomfort. But soon instinct turns to calculation. Even very small children's attempts at persuasion have become emotional: anger makes them holler and hit, and if their parents are tired enough or the other child is small enough, anger can be a successful technique. Observant children, though, learn early that anger doesn't always work, and they develop new ways of persuading. They discover that sometimes a smile and an appealing glance, a muttered "Momma, I love you," get them further than temper tantrums do. These children are learning to play on other people's emotions, not just to indulge their own. Many of them discover that personal charm can take them a very long way toward getting what they want.

And some adults don't go much beyond these elementary methods of persuading. They rely on anger, cursing and condemning ideas they don't like. Or they gamble on our emotional reactions, pleading for our pity, flattering our egos, and coaxing us so enchantingly that only real curmudgeons can avoid saying, "Of course, of course." Such emotional methods do work, especially in face-to-face situations. The wife who can aim a skillet accurately enough usually gets her husband's attention without much delay. The husband who can shout obscenities loud enough can usually cow his wife. Lovers respond to soulful eyes and tear-streaked faces. Employers promote stock clerks who make ordinary supervisors feel like vice presidents. A candidate who appears on television with a lock of hair carefully disarranged and with a shy, engaging grin can win elections.

Beyond instinctive reactions and emotional appeals, however, is another, more adult method of persuasion, sometimes called rational argument. Rational argument relies on reasons, not just emotions, for getting people to do one thing rather than another. The emotional appeals that work when people deal face-to-face with one another often fail when people are separated in space or time. Readers can't see that drooping mouth, that worshipful look, that engaging grin—all they can see are the words on the paper. Good readers demand reasons, and successful written persuasion must produce those reasons. In writing, as in talking, you succeed if you are a skillful persuader; but you must persuade through sound performance, not merely sound.

Discovering a Topic

In an ideal world, all persuasive writing would represent the writer's honest convictions. No writer would try to convince readers about anything the writer didn't really believe in. Unfortunately, in the actual world that isn't always true. Advertising agencies are hired to convince the public that one headache pill is better than another. Editorial writers are told whether to be for the new airport site or against it. Public relations departments, and sometimes ordinary employees, are forced to support their employer's point of view. A public relations woman who puts out a release showing that her university is not trying very hard to meet affirmative action goals or a public relations man who hints that half the dollars collected in the arthritis campaign were spent on champagne dinners will both be looking for new jobs rather suddenly.

As a writer, you may occasionally find yourself in a situation where you have to argue for or against a belief you don't care much about. Perhaps you have a job that requires you to take a stand you don't really believe in. Or you have a teacher in college who assigns a paper contrary to your convictions. When that happens, you will of course put your own beliefs to one side and do the best you can. Most of the time, however, nobody will tell you what to believe in or what side to support. You won't be asked to change your opinions as easily as you change your clothes. Instead, you will be asked to examine your own opinions and your own convictions and choose a topic that seems to you really worth writing about.

As you try to decide which of your beliefs you will use for your paper, remember that your aim is to get your readers to do something or believe something. If your paper succeeds, it will result in either changed actions or changed attitudes. So now you have two things to consider: what you believe yourself and what you want your readers to believe. Advertising agencies and public relations experts to the contrary, writing that really convinces usually comes from writers who are themselves convinced; and unless you are writing about something you care about, you will find it very hard to make your readers change either their behavior or their minds. But unless you are writing about something your readers care about, too, you will find it even harder.

Suppose you begin by listing some of your genuine beliefs. You're against inflation, and you think murder is wrong. You believe in love and brotherhood. You are strongly convinced that the man next door should keep his poodle out of your petunias, that the college cafeteria ought not to charge eighty cents for a cold hot dog, that your history teacher shouldn't force you to take a final exam. All these convictions meet the first test: you believe in them. How many of them meet the second: will your readers care?

Probably most readers do care about inflation and murder. Like you, they're against them. No matter how vigorously you maintain that inflation is a bad thing and that the government should *do something,* no matter how often you assert that killing other human beings is terrible, you won't change any minds because your readers already agree. Do you know anybody who likes inflation or who argues that murder is right? Readers care about brotherhood, too. They're for it, although they may be against bussing or against welfare or against the Chinese. The trouble with being against inflation and murder or in favor of brotherhood is that these beliefs are too broad. They're too general and too widely accepted. Arguing for them is a waste of your time.

If, on the other hand, you can bring these beliefs down to size, if you can center in on these topics at a level where there is some disagreement, you may change people's minds. There is disagreement about the causes of inflation, and if you have a wide knowledge of economics and lots of time, you may be able to present a sound argument showing that a new policy of international exchange will cause prices to go down. Even economists, however, can't do it without presenting a lot of statistics, without writing several thousand words. Nobody can do it in a short paper; and most readers, unless they are economists themselves, will have trouble following the argument. In the same way, you might be able to trace people's attitude toward killing through several different cultures, from the beginning of civilization, and come up with a clear distinction between acceptable and unacceptable forms of human slaughter; but that's a semester's project. If you want to deal with either inflation or murder, you will need to narrow your topic a bit more, to find a place where it touches your readers' lives more closely. Should the local gas company be allowed to double its rates? Should the fire fighters in your area get a cost-of-living increase? Should the legislature enact a new capital punishment law? Should the police carry loaded guns? Most readers will care about these more specific questions.

Let's go back to that list. It seems pretty obvious that most readers won't care much about your petunias, your cold hot dog, or your problems in American history; and even if they did care, what is there to say beyond pointing out that the flowers are dead, hot dogs should be hot, and your history final frightens you? But before you discard all these beliefs as too narrow and too personal, ask yourself whether your readers might be troubled by similar problems. You're not the only person with a garden: should the city council pass a new leash law or enforce the law that already exists? You're not the only student who eats in the cafeteria: can you start a campaign to get the food service improved? You're not the only person worried about final exams: should the college abolish them? Now that the questions have become slightly broader, you'll have plenty to say, and many of your readers will care about the problems.

As you try to decide which of your beliefs will make the best paper, see whether you can answer yes to all these questions:

1. Do you really care about it yourself?
2. Is it specific enough that your readers will care?
3. Is it narrow enough for you to deal with in a short paper?
4. Is it general enough that your readers will care?
5. Is it broad enough for you to find something to say?

Main Idea Sentences for Persuasion Papers

Asking yourself questions is a good way to find topics for persuasion papers. Should bus fares be reduced? Should husbands share the housework? Is the sales tax fair? The question you ask is not a main idea sentence, but the way you answer it is. Your answer becomes a statement of what you believe and what you are trying to get your readers to believe.

Main ideas for papers of persuasion are easy to recognize because they are always definite statements and because they always contain opinion words. Usually they use words like *should* or *should not, must* or *must not, ought* or *ought not.* Sometimes they use words like *fair* or *unfair, better* or *worse.*

Telephone installation charges *should* be reduced.
Telephone installation charges *should not* be reduced.

Husbands *ought* to help with the housework.
Husbands *ought not* to have to do housework.

A sales tax on food is *unfair* to the poor.
A sales tax is *fairer* than a property tax.

Food and service in the college cafeteria are both *terrible*.
The college cafeteria provides *good* food at *reasonable* prices.

Final exams *should be* abolished.
Final exams *must not be* abolished.

In all these main idea sentences, the opinion words—the words that show the writer's belief—are in italics.

Introductions

The introduction to a paper of persuasion must do double duty. It must make a contract based on the main idea sentence, letting your readers know what your conviction is. This contract is the same kind of promise you began with in your earlier writing. But papers giving directions, papers of explanation, and reports are usually written to satisfy a particular audience that has a definite need. The interest is already there.

In papers of persuasion, however, your readers not only have to be persuaded to agree with you, they often have to be persuaded to read your attempt. Even though you have chosen a topic that many people care about, chances are that most people are perfectly satisfied with what they already believe; they don't much want you to change their minds. So your introduction must do more than make a contract. It must make your readers so curious that they can't help reading the rest of your paper.

If your main idea sentence is "Telephone installation rates should be reduced," the paper might start by saying, "Because of a great injustice, my children went hungry last week." Readers will want to know why the children went hungry and what that injustice was.

> Because of a great injustice, my children went hungry last week. I was robbed. No, not by some shifty-looking thug on the streets; I was robbed right here in my home by someone I had respected and done business with. When I moved across town last month, I had my telephone transferred to my new house— well, actually I didn't *have* it transferred—I unplugged it and carried it to the new house and plugged it in again. And last week, on my phone bill, was a $30 charge for installing my phone. The gall! Since when should I pay the phone company to do work for them? That $30 was enough money to feed my children for a week. Telephone installation charges must be reduced.

That introduction is both melodramatic and exaggerated, and you probably wouldn't want to use it. Nevertheless, it's a great deal better than this beginning:

> Although I know that a lot of people won't agree with me, I think the telephone company ought to reduce its installation charges, at least a little bit, because I think that some people really can't afford to pay so much.

Good introductions find a middle ground between whooping and whining. Just as readers will be quick to see when you're overdoing it, so they'll be quick to stop reading if you underdo it too much, if you sound apologetic and uncertain. Show your readers a believable situation where change is needed. Then they'll be ready to consider your proposals for change:

> Last month I moved across town into a new house. I unplugged my phone in the old house, carried it to the new house, and plugged it in again. After the phone company flipped a switch in their downtown building, my phone began working. Last week I received my phone bill, and on that bill was a $30 charge for installing a phone in my new house (the house is actually five years old—it's just new to me). I promptly called the telephone company customer representative to explain that *I* had, in fact, installed my own phone and should not be charged the entire fee. The reply? The phone company installed my phone because they flipped the switch that started my service. Remember when the man would come

to your house and spend half a day installing your phone? He'd even climb the pole. Since the installation now requires less than a minute of time, and no travel, installation charges should be greatly reduced.

This introduction works by emphasizing how much work the customer does in installing a phone, compared to the amount of work the company does. Readers who have paid high installation fees for something they installed themselves will be reminded of their own anger, and other readers will become aware of a situation they too may consider unfair. Although emotional appeals by themselves are not enough to support a belief, there's nothing wrong with emotion as a way of getting readers involved.

Contrasting one thing with another is also a way to begin. If the main idea sentence is "Final exams should be abolished," you can tease your readers along by comparing the pleasant aspects of college life with one big unpleasantness, the final exam. A satisfactory introduction might go something like this:

> Most students carry away dozens of pleasant memories of their college days. They can look back with fondness on classes, teachers, discussions, and books. They may recall favorite places on the campus—a building, a fountain, a path. Legs broken on ski slopes become souvenirs of wonderful vacations. Bruising, bone-crushing football games become good exercise. Almost everything about college can, with the years, take on a pleasant glow—but not quite everything. No student I've ever talked to has ever said anything like "I'll never forget that wonderful final exam Professor Moriarty gave. Wasn't that *fun?*" The kind of mental bruising and wrenching that goes with final exams is nasty when it happens and stays nasty whenever a student's thoughts carelessly stray to such a gruesome topic. That horror of every college student's life, the final examination, ought to be abolished.

Like the introductions for reducing telephone installation rates and abolishing finals, good introductions often begin by giving specific details and then working up to the main idea at the end of the paragraph. But if you can't think of a lively beginning, there's nothing wrong with a direct approach: "Husbands ought to help with the housework." This start may not be very dramatic, but it is straightforward. It tells your readers without any shilly-shallying what your main idea is, and it's a good deal better than a beginning which tries so hard to be clever that your readers can't figure out what you do believe. The introduction below is unsatisfactory because it fails to make a clear contract:

> Nancy Hanks is always tired, and no wonder. She gets up at six to make the coffee. Then she wakes her husband and kids, rushes back to the kitchen to keep the toast from burning, back to the bedroom to find sonny's shoes, back to the kitchen to pack three lunches, and somewhere between braiding sister's hair and soaking the dishes, she gets her own hair brushed. When she comes home worn out from a day at the office, she doesn't get a drink or a rest with the paper. There's dinner and dishes, diapers and dusting. Weekends are the same old story— mop the kitchen, change the beds, go to the laundromat. It's the same thing over and over. Nancy never catches up.

This introduction gives plenty of specific details, but it never gets to the point and we never discover what the main idea is. What will improve poor Nancy's situation? Better planning? Fewer children? Quitting her job? Hiring some help? If the main idea is "Husbands should help with the housework," beginning with a plain statement would be a great improvement.

Start with your main idea if you want to, but don't stop with a single bare statement. Saying "The food and the service in the college cafeteria are both terrible" isn't enough; you must create a picture that will show your readers just what you mean by "terrible."

> The food and the service in the college cafeteria are both terrible. Yesterday I ordered a sandwich and soup. The lettuce was limp, the bread was moldy, and there wasn't any mustard. The soup was too salty, and it had a hair in it. The day before, the hot dogs were cold. When I complained about the hair, the man at the counter just reached in and fished it out. And when I complained about that, he said, "Eat some place else if you don't like it." I thought a college cafeteria was there to help students instead of make them sick.

Notice that all these introductions use colorful, connotative language—words chosen because of the pleasant or unpleasant associations they have for us. "Pleasant glow" gives us a good feeling about college memories in a way that "bright glare"—a phrase that means almost the same thing—would not give. "Limp," "moldy," "had a hair in it" all take our appetites away; "old," "stale," and "foreign object" are a good deal less repellent. "Bruising," "wrenching," and "gruesome" are all words that invite us to share the writer's disapproval. While colorful words and vivid pictures can't substitute for the reasons you must give in the body of your paper, using them in the introduction will help put your readers in a mood to consider your reasons.

Finding Reasons for Your Belief

Getting your readers in the right mood is a good beginning, but they won't stay in that mood long unless you supply them with reasons. Repeating your opinion over and over won't persuade them, no matter how many exclamation marks you use to emphasize it. In the coffee shop you can pound the table. At home you can shout, maybe loud enough to keep your listeners from asking, "Why? What makes you think that?" Your listeners won't be persuaded, but they may be silenced, and you can think you've convinced them. Writing can't pound or shout, and the readers' "Why?" is always in the background. If the reasons aren't there, the readers won't be there long either.

Before you begin your paper, it's a good idea to make a list of the reasons that will support your main idea sentence. Suppose we take as an example the main idea sentence "Telephone installation rates should be reduced." Our main reason for wanting them reduced, of course, is that we think they're too high; but that isn't really a reason. It's just a way of repeating the main idea in slightly different words. We'll have to do better than that. After a bit of head-scratching, we come up with a list like this:

1. Poor people can't afford phones.
2. High rates make people mad at the phone company.
3. If rates were lower, more people would have phones.
4. The customer actually does the installing.
5. Phone equipment is so sophisticated that it requires less labor.
6. Doesn't require a house visit.
7. Compared to a few years ago, the phone company doesn't have to do much.

Now let's look at our list. Which of these are real reasons and which should we throw away? The first one is probably all right. The phone company is a public utility, with an obligation to serve everybody who needs a phone; when rates get so high that many people can't afford to pay them, the situation needs changing.

What about the second reason? The phone company is certainly concerned about how the customers feel; however, they aren't likely to lower rates just to keep everybody smiling. The reason seems a bit silly. It had better go.

Reason 3 could be all right. If the phone company were convinced that they could get enough additional customers to increase their profits just by lowering installation rates, they might consider doing that.

Reason 4 is probably the most convincing. It should be kept. If the customers are actually doing most of the work, why should they be charged for what they do themselves?

Reason 5 also sounds strong and logical; so do 6 and 7. These reasons, however, are so closely related that it would probably be sensible to group them together; reasons 5 and 6 seem like subdivisions of reason 7.

Now we're left with three reasons, expressed in a slightly different way:

1. Since the telephone company is interested in having customers, they should lower their installation rates so more people could afford to have a phone; thus their overall profits would increase.
2. Customers now do most of the work when installing a phone, so they shouldn't be charged for the work they do.
3. Compared to years past, telephone installation now requires less labor, time, and effort on the part of the phone company.

Notice that the first reason on this list includes the first and third on the original list, and the last reason combines the final three original reasons.

For the main idea that final examinations should be abolished, reasons may be easier to find. Many students know that finals are not a true test of what they have learned in a course because they freeze up in every final they take. And it simply infuriates them to see students in the back row copying from the information written on their white tennis shoes. Besides, these students are sure that if finals were abolished they could focus their attention on the content of the course, where it belongs, rather than concentrating on outguessing the professor about the final. It should not be hard to transform this personal experience into three general reasons for doing away with finals:

1. Finals are not a true test of what the student has learned.
2. Finals lead to cheating.
3. Without finals, students could concentrate on learning instead of on grades.

All three of these seem like strong reasons for abolishing final exams.

Some main idea sentences, however, can be supported by only one really strong reason. For instance, almost the only reason for thinking that husbands should help with the housework is that when both partners work, any other arrangement seems grossly unfair. Instead of looking for more, and weaker, reasons, the writer's job is to find ways of showing the unfairness.

The writer who wants husbands to share the household chores must do more than say "It isn't fair." The paper must first demonstrate the unfairness and then show the improvements that will result from sharing. In the same way, before anybody will believe that everybody will be better off if telephone installation rates are reduced or that cheating will be cut down if final exams are abolished, those reasons must be proved. Beliefs are supported by reasons: reasons, in their turn, must be supported. The four most common ways of supporting reasons are:

1. giving examples
2. citing statistics
3. using authorities
4. predicting consequences

Some of these methods of support work better with some reasons than with others. Use the ones that fit your reason best.

Giving Examples

Most of the reasons that support your belief will be generalizations, and generalizations, as you discovered when you wrote your definition papers, are always clearer when they are illustrated by examples. Examples not only make a generalization clearer, they are likely to make it more convincing, too.

Nearly ten years ago, public reaction to the Vietnam war illustrated how this principle works. We had all been told that war was horrible, that innocent people suffered, that the Vietnamese were not "the enemy" but human beings like ourselves. We knew all those things, but we didn't really believe them until the television news began to show the long lines of starving refugees walking hopelessly down a dusty road and Vietnamese children with their skin burned off. One picture did in sixty seconds what months of explanation couldn't do.

Public understanding of euthanasia, or what is called mercy killing, is another example. Many of us realized that people with no chance of recovery, or even of regaining consciousness, were being kept "alive" indefinitely by elaborate machinery; but unless we actually knew somebody in that situation, we didn't pay much attention, and we cheerfully accepted the notion that "life" was sacred, whatever the circumstances. We were willing to agree that hearts should be kept beating as long as modern science could manage it. It wasn't until we saw the horror and hardship of some actual cases—people so hopelessly injured or ill that for months they had responded to nothing, less alive than the machines to which they were attached, and their families, physically, emotionally, and financially exhausted, pleading with the courts to let the people they loved die decently and naturally—that we understood the reality of such situations and considered whether disconnecting those machines might, in fact, be the humane thing to do.

Most of us remember, when we're talking, that actually seeing something is better than an hour of abstract argument. We say, "Look, I'll show you" or "See for yourself." What's true for talking is true for writing too. We can't produce photographs to make our point, but we can use words to create vivid pictures.

Suppose your main idea is that telephone installation rates should be reduced and your first reason is the generalization that "Since the telephone company is interested in getting customers, they should lower their rates so more people can afford a phone." You *could* begin with that statement and then try to explain yourself by more generalizations:

> Since the telephone company is interested in getting customers, they should lower their installation rates so more people can afford to have a phone; thus their overall business and profits would increase. For people on low incomes, $30 is an awful lot of money. Retired people on small pensions have to watch what they spend. College students don't have much money to spend, either. Rich people might not miss $30 every time they move, but most people would.

You've made a start at explaining who some of the people who can't afford high installation rates are, but you haven't really shown what "afford" means.

Pick one of the general groups you've mentioned—retired people on fixed pensions, perhaps—and then give a real example. Let your readers see old Mr. Clark, who gets a monthly pension check of $300 and spends half of it for rent. Show them his monthly grocery bill—$80—and the bare diet he gets for it, and the prescriptions he has to buy, another $30. Ask them how he's going to afford those installation rates when he has to move into a nursing home that will cost his entire pension, and needs to take his telephone with him.

It doesn't matter much whether Mr. Clark is a "real" old man that you "really" know. Perhaps you made him up. But if there are lots of retired people living on about that amount of money and facing that kind of problem, old Mr. Clark is a perfectly fair example.

As for the reason that expecting working wives to do all the housework is unfair, examples should be easy to find. Glenda Smith works from eight to five, her husband from nine to four, yet he sits in a lounge chair all evening with his feet propped up, watching hockey games on TV. Anita Jones struggles over a stew, with a cookbook in one hand and a baby in the other, while Andy Jones, who boasts about his omelettes, won't go near the stove if Anita is at home. Pete Lang won't change the baby's diaper—that's "woman's work"—but he's all in favor of Pat changing the flat tire—that's "being self-sufficient." All these examples show one partner doing the work, the other partner taking life easy, a situation most readers would find not quite fair. But don't use the McNabs for an example, even though Grant never gets breakfast and seldom changes the baby. He vacuums the rugs and does the laundry, and in spite of Grace's complaining, a lot of readers would find that perfectly fair.

Citing Statistics

Carefully chosen examples can support your reasons by helping your readers to see the problem more vividly and understand it more clearly. But examples cannot include more than one or two cases. If your readers are to believe that the problem is really widespread, you must use some statistics—figures that show *how much, how many, how often.* For instance, the idea that it costs the telephone company less to install a phone today than it did seven years ago seems to invite statistical support. You can find out what it cost the phone company then and what it costs now, and compare the two.

If one of the reasons for wanting final exams abolished is that they encourage cheating, statistical support can be found for that idea too. During one big history final last year, fifteen students caught copying answers were put on probation. Fifteen out of a hundred students is a very high percentage. But there probably were fifteen more who didn't get caught. When this estimate is added, the percentage goes up from fifteen to thirty and the statistical support becomes even stronger.

Sometimes you can provide your own statistics by means of a simple investigation or a little arithmetic. Often, however, you will need to depend on other people's figures. If you want to show the percentage of working wives, consult the most recent census figures. If you want to know how many of them work for fun and how many work because their families need the money they make, look at the Bureau of Labor Statistics or read some magazine articles. You can probably trust the statistics you find in national magazines; but unless you have done the counting and multiplying yourself, you must say where the figures come from. Give credit to your source by mentioning the magazine's name, the date, and the page.

Using Authorities

Just as the library is useful in finding statistical support, so newspapers, magazines, and books will come in handy in finding authorities who will support your reasons. If you want to know how telephone installation rates in your area compare with rates in other areas, you could call the local manager of the phone company and ask. But he may not want to answer that question, and even if you do get an answer the local telephone company is not a very good authority on other cities' prices. Looking in the *Reader's Guide to Periodical Literature* under "utilities" is a better bet.

Sometimes you won't have to search for an authority but will be able to remember something you have already heard or seen. If you are writing on final examinations, you may remember an article you read the other day about Raglan College, where final exams have been abolished. The article quoted Raglan's president as saying he never had been convinced that final examinations were a true test of knowledge. The president went on to say that since finals had been done away with, Raglan had fewer students flunking out and more students enthusiastic about their class work. You can use that comment just as you remember it, mentioning where you saw the article.

Or perhaps you want an authority to back up your belief that reducing installation rates would increase business for the phone company, so you ask two friends who might know. Sarah Graine, who is the finance manager for the Golden Hours Retirement Home, said, "Most of the people who live here wouldn't get a phone anyhow—they can't afford the monthly service charges and long distance rates. Besides, they seem to enjoy the sociability of coming out to the desk, talking to the secretaries, all as a part of using the phone." Well, there goes that lead. A bit discouraged, you next tackle a friend who is a dorm counselor. Would students in the dormitory install phones in their rooms if the installation rates were cheaper? The answer is, "Nope. There are phones on every floor, and the system works fine. People who can afford their own phones have them. For the rest, the charges for installation aren't as important as the monthly bill." With two attempts at authority coming out blank, you wisely decide to leave authorities out.

But even though you have to give up your search for an authority and abandon that reason entirely, your time hasn't been wasted. You've learned something, and it always takes time to learn. Concert pianists practice before they perform, and seamstresses rip out before they produce a professional-looking garment. Writers begin, discard, start over. The difference between a convincing and an unconvincing paper often lies in knowing what to throw away.

Predicting Consequences

Predicting consequences means showing how much better (or worse) things will be if readers do (or don't) follow your advice. Predicting sounds like a simple thing to do. If husbands share the housework, then wives won't be so tired, and rested wives are happier wives. If finals are abolished, there will be less cheating, more real learning, and thus the college will be improved.

But what about the prediction that if installation rates are lowered more people will buy telephone service? Your attempt to find an authority has already shown you the weakness in that prediction. You might, of course, hang on to the reason by just saying, "Anybody can see that reducing installation rates would. . . ." But that's not very persuasive.

Just as a flat statement of belief, or unsupported reasons for the belief, will not convince many readers, a flat prediction is not very convincing either. Wary readers are likely to say, "How do you know?" You must show in some detail why your proposal will inevitably lead to the desirable consequences you predict.

In some kinds of predictions this is fairly easy. You won't have much trouble with the prediction that if the food and service in the cafeteria were improved, more students would eat there. Fresh, crisp salad; hot, appetizing sandwiches; and polite attendants at the counter could make all the difference. Asking a few students who now lunch on an apple from the corner grocer should give you some backing for that prediction. After all, the students who use, or don't use, the college cafeteria are the real authorities on what would happen if conditions were improved.

The prediction that abolishing finals would lead to less cheating is fairly easy, too. Students who are not competing for grades will have less reason to cheat. Once the intense pressure is gone, Rupert will have nothing to gain from copying Tansy's paper, and he might as well write his own.

It will be harder to convice readers that abolishing finals will make for more real learning, instead of more wasted time. Maybe the only successful way to do it is to refer to what happened at a school where finals have been abolished. At Raglan, for instance, the president said that the students got more enthusiastic about their class work. If greater enthusiasm is a sign of more real learning, doing away with finals at Raglan apparently did lead to the predicted result. If it can be shown that students at Raglan are much like students at any other college, readers may be willing to accept the prediction.

Dealing With the Other Side

No matter what logical reasons you have produced or how well you have supported them, there is still something to be said for the other side. Most problems are more complicated than they seem on the surface, and if some of your readers didn't disagree, you wouldn't have to persuade them. Here's where a bit of charm pays off. Instead of assuming that anybody who disagrees with you is an idiot, hardly worth bothering about, you can gracefully admit that your opponents do have reasons, some that seem pretty good. You can, however, show why those reasons are not so good after all.

If you ignore your opponents' reasons, if you leave it to chance, your readers may remember those reasons when you're not around to disprove them. A safer way is to get your licks in first. Anticipate as much of the opposition's argument as you can; then show what's wrong with it.

If you want finals abolished, you can't afford to assume that they continue to exist just because the administration hasn't gotten around to canceling them yet. A standard argument in favor of final exams is that students who have learned anything at all during the course ought to remember it at least until the end of the term. Another argument is that finals are the only way to measure whether students *did* learn anything. The point you are making, however, is not that students didn't learn anything or that they didn't remember it. Your point is that the stress of a two-hour exam, with a whole semester's grade depending on it, is so great that many students can barely remember their own names. When you write the paper, you can say "Some people think. . . ." and then explain why what they think is wrong.

And if you want people to support euthanasia—the "mercy killing" we talked about earlier—you certainly can't ignore the objections to it. Many people believe that euthanasia is a human attempt to play God by deciding when, or whether, people should die. In answer to that argument, you can point out that death is the natural result when hearts can't beat or lungs can't breathe without mechanical help. It's the people who insist on artificially prolonging existence who are "playing God." You could also remind readers that some patients the court ruled should be taken off those artificial aids continued to live without them. The "life support systems" were apparently not the only thing keeping those people alive. If euthanasia means deciding not to maintain life unnaturally, rather than unnaturally causing death, then the "playing God" opposition is not very sound.

Mentioning the arguments for the other side should convince your readers that you have thought carefully about the whole problem and that you are trying hard to be fair. Dealing with the other side can never weaken your position, and often it can strengthen it.

Planning a Persuasion Paper

Once the content of your paper has been worked out, the next step is to arrange your reasons in what you think will be the most effective order. Actually, you have only two choices: you can begin with your strongest reason, or you can save it for the clincher at the end.

Look again at those reasons for reducing installation rates. If you think most readers will be impressed by the unfairness of charging customers for the work they do themselves, put that reason first and support it by your own experience. If you think many readers don't realize how little the phone company does today to install a phone, compared to what they did seven years ago, put that reason next; support it by showing the hours of labor for which the company had to pay seven years ago and the minute or two of labor for which they have to pay now. Then go on to the company's argument and show that it, too, is unfair. Your plan will look something like this:

Reason: customers actually do the installing
Support: (example) your own experience

Reason: compared to seven years ago, the phone company does less work but charges more

Support: (statistics) comparison of company costs then and now; comparison of customer bills then and now

Opposition says: company should recover cost of more sophisticated equipment
Your answer: customer shouldn't have to pay cost of equipment that saves the company money

Try writing it that way. If the reasons don't fit together smoothly, or if you think your response to the opposition argument comes out sounding pretty feeble, don't be afraid to throw the plan away and find a better order, one you think is more likely to convince.

Some writers always like to start with the weakest reason and work up to the one they think is the strongest, convincing their readers little by little. They gradually get stronger and stronger until the knockout in the last paragraph. If you choose this order, you may want to warm up with the opponent's case first, get rid of it, and go on to your own reasons. That's the order used in this plan for a paper on final exams:

Opposition says: ought to remember what's learned; only way to measure what's learned
Answer: not true; stress makes you forget temporarily

Reason: finals not true test of what's learned
Support (example) : freezing up

Reason: finals lead to cheating
Support (statistics) : history exam

Reason: without finals, could concentrate on learning, not grades
Support (authority) : Raglan's president
Support (prediction) : it would happen here, too

This plan assumes that putting the emphasis on real learning is the strongest reason. It may seem to you that getting rid of cheating is stronger. You may be right. Sometimes it is hard to tell which reason will be the most convincing. When you plan your own paper, don't spend too much time worrying over which of two good reasons is really the best. Instead, decide which reason you think you can *write about* most convincingly. In the long run, that's what will convince your readers.

Conclusions

A good conclusion will always emphasize the main idea. If you decide to get this emphasis by repeating or restating the sentence you began with, it's a good idea to change the wording a little:

Introduction: Telephone installation rates should be reduced.
Conclusion: Customers should not have to pay more for less service.

Introduction: Final exams ought to be abolished.
Conclusion: Real education will never take place until we get rid of final exams.

Introduction: Euthanasia should be accepted by society as humane.
Conclusion: Euthanasia is humane; its alternative is not.

A single sentence, clearly and firmly stated, can be a convincing finish for a short paper. Beginning writers, however, are sometimes uneasy with short conclusions, and they are tempted to cloud their sentences with unneeded words:

As I have tried to show in this paper, customers should not have to pay the phone company more for less service; *this is ridiculous and totally unfair and should be against the law.*

As my arguments would seem to show, probably almost all aspects of education *as we know it today* would be improved if grades were abolished, *even though some people might disagree.*

In conclusion, therefore, I think that euthanasia is humane *compared to* its alternative *which* is not *humane.*

You can see for yourself how these namby-pamby phrases weaken rather than strengthen the statements. No matter how brilliantly the reasons are supported, when writers end up apologizing, readers are likely to end up thinking "Well, that writer isn't really sure."

If a single restated main idea sentence seems too abrupt, you may like the summary method better. A summary conclusion gives the reasons, in the same order as in the paper, and then ends with the main idea:

Final exams, then, are no real measure of what students know. Because they are frightened and confused by the exams, the students are tempted to cheat. If they knew all during the term that they wouldn't have to face that ordeal, they'd get a lot more out of every class. Real education will never take place until we get rid of final exams.

Summary conclusions may not seem very exciting, but they are clear and definite. If the reasons have been convincing, the conclusion will be convincing, too.

Sometimes, however, you may want a livelier ending. If you can manage it, a punch line conclusion may work well. In this method, the writing becomes colorful again. You ask a question so pointed that reasonable readers can't possibly disagree. You paint one final word picture so vividly that readers forget their disagreement:

1. While the phone company gets richer, its customers get poorer. While the phone company gets lazier, its customers are overworked. Until downtrodden citizens rise up against their oppressors, the phone company will never care. Don't be a worm forever! Scream! Rebel! Refuse to pay the moneysuckers!

2. The real question is, how much longer are we going to pay the phone company for making us do its work? What will it have us doing next?
3. When you get the next installation bill from the phone company, remember how you unplugged the phone yourself and carried it yourself, and plugged it back in yourself, and how the phone company just flipped a switch. Then call up the phone company's president to see why *he's* charging *you*.

But if you try the punch line method, beware of too much exaggeration, too much sob stuff. Some exaggeration in the introduction, perhaps, can be overlooked—you're trying to arouse interest. The kind of exaggeration the first conclusion employs, however, with its *richer, poorer, lazier, overworked, downtrodden, oppressors, worm,* etc., will strike many readers as hysterical. They won't be convinced; they'll just giggle. The second and third conclusions are a bit better, and many readers will find them effective. Both these conclusions make an emotional appeal, but they do it by making us "see" a real situation, a situation we have to take seriously.

Conclusions are important. Unless they are convincing, nothing in the paper is likely to convince.

Examining a Persuasive Paper

Who Says It's Woman's Work?

[1]   Nancy Hanks is always tired, and no wonder. She gets up at six to make the coffee. Then she wakes her husband and kids, rushes back to the kitchen to keep the toast from burning, back to the bedroom to find sonny's shoes, back to the kitchen to pack three lunches, and somewhere between braiding sister's hair and soaking the dishes, she gets her own hair brushed. She drops the baby at the sitter, edges the car through six lanes of clogged traffic, manages an office for eight hours, collects the baby, plops him in the playpen, gets the dinner. After dinner there are the dishes, and the dusting, and the diapers. She gets the kids to bed, but sonny wants a drink and sister is crying for a story. Weekends are no better—mop the kitchen, change the beds, sew on the buttons, go to the laundromat. Is Nancy widowed or divorced? Of course not. Her husband's in the living room reading the paper. He's sorry she's tired all the time, but cooking and kids and keeping house are "woman's work."

[2]   Is Nancy Hanks's husband especially lazy or especially unsympathetic? No. There are lots more like him. Glenda Smith works from eight to five, her husband from nine to four, yet he sits in a lounge chair all evening with his feet propped up, watching the hockey game on TV. Anita Jones struggles over the stew, with a cookbook in one hand and a baby in the other, while Andy Jones, who boasts about his omelettes, won't go near the stove if Anita is at home. Pete Lang won't change the baby's diaper—that's "woman's

work"—but he's all in favor of Pat changing the flat tire—that's "being self-sufficient."

[3]   If you say to these men that husbands ought to help with the housework, especially if their wives are working, they have a lot of answers. "My mother did *her* housework," they'll say, "and raised six kids besides. She didn't have a dishwasher or a dryer, but she never asked my father to hang out the clothes." Or they'll say, "What would the neighbors think? Wouldn't I look silly in a pink-checked apron?" Sometimes they vary it a little. "I'd like to cook but I don't know how—it's all so complicated." Or "What do you mean, help? I took the kids to the zoo last week, so she could wash the windows." Or even "Nancy *likes* to do those things. She doesn't want me interfering."

[4]   All these answers are pure baloney. His mother may not have complained, but she was an old woman at forty-five, and she didn't manage an office either. The neighbors won't think anything. Grant McNab, a husband worth having, is inside running the vacuum cleaner. And he isn't wearing a pink-checked apron—they're out of style for men this year. The other excuses are even worse. Anybody can cook, if they take the trouble to try. Washing the windows while *she* goes to the zoo might be a pleasant change—for her. And if Nancy says she "likes doing all those things," she's a liar. She'd welcome a little helpful interference.

[5]   The latest census shows that almost half the American women between twenty and thirty are working, but the census doesn't tell us whether their husbands help around the house. The census also tells us that one out of every three American marriages ends in divorce, and the figure is increasing. The census doesn't tell us why people get divorced, but I bet I could guess at some of the reasons. If *he* never lifts a hand to help, if *she* is too tired to have any fun, why stay married?

[6]   I asked Jake Arbur, a marriage counselor at Family Service, what the most frequent problem he heard about was, and he said without any hesitation at all, "Working wives." I indignantly asked him if what he meant was that married women shouldn't work. He laughed and said, "No. If most of them stopped working, then the problem would be starving families. No. The problem is forgetting that marriage is a partnership. If both partners work to earn money, they must share the work of keeping the household going. Sometimes it's the wife's fault—she has old-fashioned notions about woman's work and makes a martyr of herself. But more often it's the husband. He wants his wife to wait on him. He thinks that taking care of the kids is 'woman's work.'"

[7]   That the same problem exists all over the place doesn't make it any better. If Nancy Hanks's husband doesn't change his ways, she'll land in the loony bin, or he'll land in divorce court. If Grace McNab doesn't appreciate her husband, she'll lose him to some other working wife who knows a good thing.

[8]   And when I get married, if I ever do, there'll be a clear understanding of just what "woman's work" is—and I'll get it in writing.

This paper starts with an introduction very much like the one we looked at earlier, but in this version the point is clear. Even though the writer doesn't state her main idea sentence, "Husbands should help with the housework," it would be a pretty dull reader who couldn't figure out what it was. Then she goes on to give more examples, in case the vivid picture of Nancy Hanks's life wasn't enough.

Paragraph 3 gives the opposition's arguments, and paragraph 4 demolishes them. Paragraph 5 uses statistics, paragraph 6 quotes authority, and paragraph 7 predicts some consequences. Paragraph 8 is a kind of punch line conclusion: we find out that the writer isn't married, but that if she does marry, she'll make sure that her husband at least helps with the housework.

Are you convinced by this paper? Are you amused? You can tell that the writer hopes you will laugh—she uses words like "pure baloney," "land in the loony bin," "get it in writing"—but that doesn't mean she isn't serious. She wants you to sympathize with Nancy Hanks; she wants you to believe that husbands *should* help with the housework.

Key Words

Here are some of the important terms used in this chapter. See whether you can answer these questions about them.

1. How is **rational argument** different from instinctive reactions and emotional appeals?
2. What questions should you ask yourself in **deciding on a topic** for a short persuasive paper?
3. How can you recognize **main idea sentences** for persuasion papers?
4. What two things must the **introduction** to a paper of persuasion do? Why can it contain **connotative** words?
5. What question will good readers ask before they accept your belief? How can you **support your main idea?**
6. What are four common ways of **supporting reasons?**
7. Why should you deal with the **opponent's argument?**
8. What is the best **order** for a paper of persuasion?
9. What must the **conclusion** of a paper of persuasion always do? Describe three satisfactory kinds of conclusions.

READINGS
Writing to Persuade

Guaranteed Income

burgher: businessman or citizen (word sounding slightly out-of-date)
circumvent: get around something

Main idea sentence

[1]   The poor don't have enough money. Millions of words and countless hours of agonizing by generations of economists have gone into exquisitely complicated plans to solve this problem. Maybe the time has come to give the poor money. The most practical way to attack poverty in America is to guarantee every family an annual income of $5,000.

First opposition argument: shown to be out-of-date

[2]   The idea of assuring income threatens something dear to Americans—the persistent notion that each man, armed with hoe and axe, is still master of his own livelihood. But the notion resists the harsh reality that a family in the city collapses without a certain level of cash, and so do the chances for fruitful re-employment.

Second opposition argument: proved false by historical example

[3]   The notion also overlooks history. In 1914 Henry Ford shocked respectable burghers when he guaranteed five dollars a day for his workers. Solemn economists and businessmen predicted that workmen would plunge into orgies of drunkenness, crazy spending and a refusal to work a full week. Yet Henry Ford probably did more to insure growing prosperity with that act than he did with his revolution in mass production.

Ben H. Bagdikian, *The Saturday Evening Post*, 1968.

282

Reason 1: we already guarantee some incomes; brief examples

[4]   The country, in fact, already guarantees income, not for the destitute but for the millions of comfortable Americans who quietly accept Social Security, FHA money, agricultural subsidies. Guaranteeing their prosperity has become a complicated game of self-deception. Year by year, in bits and pieces, a crazy quilt of social legislation has been crafted for them, those who have powerful lobbies—big labor, big business, big farmers. But there are few guarantees for the voiceless—the farm laborer, the unorganized worker, the small businessman.

Reason 2: we can afford it; comparison of costs

[5]   Can we afford a $5,000 minimum income? The maximum cost of the program would take a smaller proportion of the American gross national product than is appropriated for family payments in many European countries, including the most free enterprising, West Germany. It would probably not exceed the money cost of the war in Vietnam.

Reason 3: it would be more efficient— prediction; details of how it would work

[6]   Payment could circumvent the cumbersome welfare administration. There would be no means test, no time-consuming detective work. Families would make out income-tax forms, like the quarterly declaration of estimated income. If their income fell under the guaranteed minimum, they would receive the difference in weekly or biweekly checks. Computerized W-2 income forms made out by every employer would permit inexpensive and impersonal random checking to catch cheating and errors.

Third opposition argument: proved false by comparison

[7]   Would America become a nation of sloths? It might, but that is doubtful. Real striving today comes not from those who are so poor that they are out of the system, but from those who are inside the system, beginning to control their income and taste its benefits.

Reason 4: it might revive hand crafts—prediction

[8]   Some believe that such a guaranteed salary would create masses of new jobs in services that society needs but that are not profitable enough to support the worker: homemakers in homes with a sick parent, day-care workers, visitors for invalids. Hand crafts and hand repairs are not profitable in competition with mass-production automated machinery; but people could work at them if their basic living were already provided. The guaranteed income might allow us to abandon the minimum-wage law, so that much work could be done at low rates if the worker preferred to do it.

Reason 5: people wouldn't be afraid to move where jobs were— prediction

[9]   Further, the guaranteed income might help solve one of our economy's worst problems—getting people to go where the jobs are. For when a family is sure of enough to get by on, it will more readily take the chance of moving to a place where there are jobs.

Fourth opposition argument: proved false by examples

[10]   There are fears, of course, that more money for the poor will encourage larger families. In the 60 countries that have family allowances based on family size, all the evidence is that the money has not made families grow—not even in countries where the allowance was started deliberately to encourage child-bearing! Canada has the most generous of family allowances, and its birth rate and ours have risen and fallen together.

Reason 6: would encourage budgeting— prediction

[11]   Experience indicates dependable income actually encourages the poor to budget. Present poor families never can plan. In rent, or food, or medicine, or clothes there is always an emergency. And every purchase must first be passed upon by the welfare worker. A new coat? Ask the welfare worker. Need eyeglasses? Ask the welfare worker. Mosquito netting for the baby? Ask the welfare worker. How much money next month? Next year? Ask the welfare worker. Welfare makes budgeting senseless and impossible.

Extended example, showing effects of increased income:

[12]   Mrs. Louis Robinson is a 39-year-old Negro woman in Issaquena County, Miss. She and her husband had been earning a total cash income of about $15 a week to support their 10 children. As sharecroppers and laborers, they lived for years on credit, plus what they could grow in a garden. Then Mrs. Robinson got a job as a teacher's aide in a Head Start class, at $60 a week. It occurred to me that not many Americans experience a 400 percent increase in income, so not long ago I looked at how they spent their new money.

a. Temporary splurging

[13]   The first week the family splurged: quarts of ice cream, gallons of orange juice, an unending flow of milk and soft drinks. And meat.

b. Paying old debts

[14]   "Then about the third week," Mrs. Robinson said, "we began paying back some old debts, eleven dollars and ninety-five cents on the Deep-Freeze we bought one year when the crops were better, and on stores where we had accounts. My husband and I, we plan now about clothes and what kind of things we can do to the house.

c. Saving money by paying cash

[15]   "Funny thing. We can buy lots cheaper now. We used to have to buy where we had credit, and in those

stores you just had to take what they had at the price they set. When you have cash, you just shop till you get what you want. Why, I get almost twice as much chicken for my money as I used to. And at a white store.

d. Gaining greater community respect

[16]   "And you know? After we leave the white store, the owner says, 'You-all come back.' They never said that before."

Responses

1. This article was written more than ten years ago, but similar arguments are sometimes given today by people worried about unemployment and poverty. Can you find anything in the article that makes it sound dated? If so, what is it?

2. The test of a persuasive paper on a national topic such as guaranteed income is not whether the legislative change it proposes has been adopted—obviously this one has not been—but whether some people who read the article have changed their opinions or become more aware of the problem. Applying this test to the article, do you find it persuasive? Why or why not?

3. How does the writer use the introduction to put readers in a receptive frame of mind? Why do the arguments of the opposition appear immediately after the introduction?

4. Are you convinced by the statistical evidence in paragraph 5 supporting the argument that we can afford a guaranteed income? What kind of statistical evidence might contradict it? Which evidence do you find most convincing? Why?

5. Paragraph 8 suggests, "The guaranteed income might allow us to abandon the minimum-wage law." Which would be easier to enforce, guaranteed income or the minimum-wage law? Which would do more for poor people? Has the writer made clear why the minimum-wage law could be abandoned?

6. Is Mrs. Louis Robinson a fair example? Why or why not? Does Mrs. Robinson earn $5,000 a year? Who takes care of her ten children while she works, for instance? What other reasons can you give showing that Mrs. Robinson is, or isn't, a fair example?

7. This paper ends with a vivid example, rather than a conclusion that restates the main idea. Write a conclusion that summarizes the main points and restates the main idea. Do you think the article is more effective with or without your conclusion? Why?

8. Write a short persuasive paper for or against some government program with which you have had some experience, or some proposed program you know something about: school lunches, Job Corps, aid to dependent chil-

dren, GI benefits, the work study program, etc. Try to use as many forms of support as you can.

Wonderful Weeds

lustre: radiance; desirability (British spelling)
versatility: ability to do different things or be used in different ways

[1]   With spring here, if you are tired of paying high prices for salad making as well as for everything else, maybe you should join the growing number of people who have stopped trying to kill weeds and have started eating them. Many of the common weeds that are met in furious battle all spring and summer long, if looked at from a different perspective, assume lustre and value. Somebody has said that a weed is just a misplaced flower; it is also often a misplaced vegetable—and more.

[2]   Take the dandelion, for instance. Most people know that in spring the young dandelion greens can be used in salad or cooked like spinach. But not everybody knows that the roots can be cooked like carrots. Or that some people roast the roots until they are dark brown throughout, then grind them and brew them as a coffee substitute. Dandelion wine is another of the boons to mankind this much-maligned plant offers. The flavor of the wine, which can be either sweet or dry, has no relationship to that of dandelion greens.

[3]   Another plentiful plant usually regarded as a pest is broadleaf plantain. The young leaves of this lowly perennial can be cooked or used in salad, adding a flavor something like mushroom. Tea can be made from the dried leaves. The green leaves have a reputation in folk medicine for great healing power, accounting for their use as emergency bandages.

[4]   The list of edible plants that are not usually eaten is long, and their versatility is amazing. The green fruit of the common mallow is edible, either raw or cooked. The seeds of lamb's quarters can be ground for flour. The dried young leaves of stinging nettle can be made into a tea rich in vitamins A and C. Purslane, a succulent annual good in salads, also can be used to thicken soups; its large stems can be made into pickles. Cattails, thistles, milkweed, even tumbleweed, are just a few of the other plants that rarely see the candlelight of the dinner table. Yet all of them have edible parts which are usually nutritious and which often have a distinct flavor not available in ordinary vegetables. Salsify, for example, a plant that looks like a skinny dandelion, has a flavor—it is said—which resembles oysters.

[5]   A word of caution is in order. It probably goes without saying that weeds which have been sprayed with herbicides should not be eaten. Some plants, of course, are poisonous. But if you want to try something different, a whole world of new tastes is ready to hand and easy pickin' just outside the back door.

Richard Hawkins, *Columbian,* May 1, 1979.

Responses

1. Why, do you think, was this article included under persuasion rather than in an earlier part of the book? How does it differ from giving directions? From classification or analysis?
2. What two reasons for eating weeds are given in the article? How are the reasons supported?
3. How does Hawkins justify the phrase "and more" at the end of the first paragraph?
4. What cliché is Hawkins playing with in "candlelight of the dinner table" (paragraph 4)? What other meaning does "easy pickin'" have? How does that other meaning help to tie the conclusion to the main idea sentence?
5. If you have a special preference in kinds of food or diet in general, write a short paper persuading your readers to try what you prefer or avoid what you disapprove of. Be sure not to give directions; just try to get readers to change their attitudes.

A Letter from Julian Bond at the Southern Poverty Law Center

blatant: obvious and offensive
repercussions: results, aftereffects

Dear Member,

[1]   In Ft. Myers, Florida, many Black children break out in what the local residents call "sandsores," the result of constant exposure to the grit and dust that blows through their neighborhood from the unpaved roads.

[2]   The all-white Ft. Myers city council persists in using public money to pave roads mostly in white neighborhoods, where residents enjoy well-kept streets lined with beautiful palms.

[3]   A barren field with few facilities serves as a recreation area for Black children in Arcadia, Florida, while an excellent recreation complex, complete with air-conditioned game rooms, is located in the white neighborhood of that town.

[4]   These are just two examples of the blatant discrimination in municipal services practiced against Blacks in south-central Florida, a region that has remained virtually untouched by the civil rights movement.

[5]   Now the Southern Poverty Law Center is assisting the Lawyers' Committee

Julian Bond, Southern Poverty Law Center, Montgomery, Alabama.

for Civil Rights Under Law in class-action lawsuits against three Florida communities—Ft. Myers, Arcadia and Florida City—to win equal municipal services for their Black residents.

[6]   For years, Blacks in these towns have suffered from inadequate street lighting, sewage systems, fire hydrants, street paving and more, while the white sections have been steadily improved with both federal and local funds. . . .

[7]   The health, safety and quality of life for over 12,000 Blacks is at stake in these important suits, and a victory could have repercussions throughout the South, where similar discrimination is widespread.

[8]   In an earlier suit, I asked Center members to help in our effort to gain equal street paving for the Black people of Selmont, Alabama.

[9]   We won that suit, and we can win in Florida, too, with your help.

[10]   Please use the enclosed envelope today to send your tax-deductible contribution of $15, $25, or however much you can spare.

[11]   You have my deepest thanks for your past support of the Center's work, and I know the Black people of these cities will be grateful for your continued generosity.

Most sincerely,

Julian Bond

Julian Bond

Responses

1. This persuasive paper is a fund-raising letter mailed out to a number of Americans not long ago. Is the main idea sentence actually included in the letter? If you think so, what is it? If you think it isn't, write out in your own words what the main idea sentence must have been; then compare your sentence with what other students have written.

2. What reasons are given to support the main idea? How are the reasons supported?

3. Make a list of the connotative words you find in the letter. Then divide the list into those with pleasant associations and those with unpleasant associations. Compare your lists with those other students have made.

4. When this letter was mailed, it enclosed photographs of the two recreation areas in Arcadia. Do you think the pictures would help you see the discrimination more clearly than the words the writer has used? Why or why not? Why do you suppose the pictures were included?

5. The letter contains eleven short paragraphs, each only one sentence long. Try to combine these short-sentence paragraphs into three or four longer paragraphs. Where would you make your divisions? Which version do you prefer? Which is easier to read? What relationship do you see between the readers for whom the letter was written and the way it is paragraphed?

6. Julian Bond is a well-known state senator from Georgia and was once considered as a candidate for Vice President. What does his signature on the letter add to its effectiveness? How might it be considered part of the "support"?
7. Pick some organization or cause you are interested in, and write a letter to members or the general public asking for money to support the cause. Make your appeal as convincing as you can.

The Dollar of the Future

laminate: layer of one substance placed over another
denomination: value of a bill ($1, $5, $10, etc.)
verification: proof
prior to: before

Public Law 95–447, dated October 10, 1978, authorized the issuance of the new Susan B. Anthony dollar coin. It further provided that the minting of the Eisenhower circulating dollar coin be discontinued as of December 31, 1978.

ADVANTAGES OF THE COIN'S COMPOSITION

The Anthony dollar is a copper-nickel clad coin as are all U.S. coins valued at 10¢ or greater. This composition has many advantages, such as superior surface wear and appearance and relatively low cost to produce. Also, because of the unique electrical resistivity and density of the laminate, it is very difficult to counterfeit or slug.

COST ADVANTAGES OF THE ANTHONY DOLLAR

A minimum of $4.5 million will be saved per year, since the old large Eisenhower dollar cost 8¢ to produce and each new Anthony dollar costs only 3¢ to produce.

In addition, any substitution of the dollar coin for the dollar bill will result in savings for private business as well as the Federal budget. The $1 bill costs nearly 2¢ to produce and lasts only 18 months in circulation—frequently in bad shape. The new dollar coin will cost 3¢ to produce and will last 15 years or more in good condition.

The new dollar coin is quick and easy.

QUICK TO IDENTIFY

- Easy to see it is a woman • Susan B. Anthony is the only American woman to be honored on a circulating United States coin

Brochure issued by the Federal Reserve Bank and distributed by banks to their depositors in 1979 and 1980.

- Easy to see the unique eleven-sided inner border on both sides
- Easy to distinguish by size • Larger than the quarter

QUICK TO USE IN VENDING MACHINES

- Easy to insert • Worn and torn bills are often rejected
- Easy to make direct purchase • Reduces the need for bill changers

QUICK TO COUNT AND SORT

- Easy to handle • Unlike bills, coins won't stick together when new and tear when old
- Easy to separate by size • Bills, being all the same size, take time to sort
- Easy to automate counting and sorting operations

QUICK TO SET UP CASH REGISTERS

- Easy to insert and withdraw. Four suggested arrangements to accommodate the $1 coin in cash register drawers are:

Currency				
$1 coin	25¢	10¢	5¢	1¢

Currency				
25¢	10¢	5¢	1¢	$1 coin

Currency					
$1 coin	50¢	25¢	10¢	5¢	1¢

Currency					
50¢	25¢	10¢	5¢	1¢	$1 coin

SOME OF THE BENEFITS OF THE ANTHONY DOLLAR

TO THE RETAIL COMMUNITY—

The new one dollar coins

Save time and reduce errors at the cash register

Are easily withdrawn from and dropped into cash drawers—bills are secured under spring retainer and must be straightened

Save time and reduce errors in counting and handling operations

Are quickly counted and handled (manually or automatically)—bills often stick together and cannot be distinguished by size

Are quick and easy to separate by size—bills must be individually separated by denomination and placed face side up in one direction

TO THE FINANCIAL COMMUNITY—

Substitution of dollar coin for note

Eliminates need for removal of worn and torn bills from circulation

Reduces mistakes resulting from new currency being stuck together or being of mixed denomination

Reduces teller verification time—counterfeit possibility substantially reduced

Speeds up teller transaction time and reduces customer waiting time

Eliminates jamming of currency counting machines

TO THE CONSUMER—

The new dollar coin is

> Easy to carry with other coins—avoids fumbling in both sections of wallet or purse—higher bills remain secure
>
> Easy to find in pocket or change purse, since it is sized between the quarter and half dollar and weighs ⅓ as much as four quarters
>
> Easy for children to use—easy to hear when dropped

The coins are being minted in Philadelphia, Denver, and San Francisco and distributed by the Federal Reserve Banks. The Mint began production in December 1978 in order to accumulate an inventory of 500 million coins prior to their release to local banks in July 1979. Production will continue after release at the rate of 80 million per month.

Responses

1. Who were the readers of this government brochure expected to be? How can you tell? What is the government trying to persuade readers to do?
2. Less than half this brochure is written in regular sentences or complete paragraphs. The rest of it is arranged like an outline, a procedure often followed by businesses in publicizing their products. What are some of the advantages of using this form? What might some disadvantages be?
3. Are all of the reasons given (advantages) equally convincing? How many of the small children you know ordinarily use dollar bills, for instance? What other reasons seem somewhat unconvincing? Why?
4. Does the word "consumer" as it is used in this brochure fit your definition of the word? How does the government's suggestion that these dollars will be "consumed" relate to the statement that the dollars will last 15 years or more in good condition?
5. How useful do you think the diagrams given under "Quick to Set Up Cash Registers" would be? Why do you think they were included?
6. Most of this brochure is a list of reasons, arranged in groups. How many of the reasons are supported? How? Pick three or four of what seem to you unsupported reasons, and suggest the kind of support that might be given.
7. More than a year after it was issued, the Anthony dollar was still not much used. Write a paper with the main idea sentence, "The Anthony dollar is not practical" or "The public doesn't like the Anthony dollar."

The Hazards of Nuclear Power

lethal: poisonous, deadly
toxic: poisonous

WHAT IS A NUCLEAR REACTOR AND WHY IS IT SO DANGEROUS?

[1]   The heart of a nuclear power plant is an array of long, thin rods filled with pellets of uranium fuel. As uranium atoms are split within these fuel elements, energy is produced to heat water circulating through the reactor. This heated water produces steam which is carried to a turbine-generator, which spins to produce electricity.

If a pipe breaks which carries water to the fuel, emergency cooling water needs to reach the fuel *within 60 seconds* to prevent overheating, melting and release of radiation from the massive fuel "core" of the power plant. An emergency core cooling system (ECCS) has been designed to prevent such a catastrophe. If this backup cooling system fails to work effectively, the reactor core would overheat and the stage is set for major radiation release into the environment in which radioactive material in gaseous form could be carried by the wind to nearby cities.

SAFETY SYSTEM IS UNPROVEN

[2]   The public is being asked to accept the word of the nuclear industry that the currently installed emergency core cooling system can function properly to prevent this most dreaded of disasters. The fact remains, however, that there has been only limited testing of the emergency core cooling system—*and some of the tests reveal design defects and indicate that ECCS might fail if actually called upon. Sworn testimony of experts in the field reveals that the effectiveness of this critical reactor safety system has not been properly demonstrated.*

THE PROBLEM OF NUCLEAR WASTES

[3]   Radioactive nuclear wastes are created when nuclear fuel is used up during nuclear power plant operation. These wastes include strontium 90, cesium 137, and plutonium 239—exceedingly toxic substances. By the end of this century, the government estimates there will be hundreds of millions of cubic feet of low and high level nuclear wastes in the United States.

No method for long-term storage or disposal of these radioactive wastes has been proven. All proposed techniques for storing these wastes are in a research or development stage.

Of great concern are the many problems that have already developed in U.S. radioactive waste storage efforts. As an example: In June, 1973, it was discovered that 115,000 gallons of high level radioactive waste had leaked from a tank at the Atomic Energy Commission's waste storage facility in Hanford, Washington. In-

Brochure distributed by the Union of Concerned Scientists, 1980.

vestigation revealed that (1) the tank had been leaking for several weeks; (2) no automatic alarm system alerted anyone to the leak; (3) the management in charge of the storage facility did not review monitoring reports that would have shown the leak; (4) there was no preventive maintenance applied.

WHY IS PLUTONIUM SO DANGEROUS?

[4]   Plutonium is the man-made element used in the atomic bomb that was dropped over Nagasaki, Japan, in 1945. Plutonium's threat to life is more than just the atomic explosions it can be used to produce. A particle of plutonium the size of a large grain of pollen can cause lung cancer if inhaled. A typical nuclear power plant produces several hundred pounds of plutonium each year. *It takes plutonium half a million years to lose its killing power.*

It is feared that if plutonium ever gets into the hands of terrorists, they will gain an immense power to further their ends.

A CALL TO PROCEED WITH CAUTION

[5]   The commercial nuclear power plant program planned for the next 25 years in this country represents a serious threat to your health and safety and to the health and safety of the American people. Yet—despite the hazards, despite the growing danger of sabotage from terrorists, despite the unresolved problem of disposing of lethal nuclear wastes safely—you are asked to accept this program as necessary to solve this nation's energy problems.

[6]   The *Wall Street Journal* labeled these nuclear plants "atomic lemons," pointing out that "their unreliability is becoming one of their most dependable features." Yet, you are asked to accept the program as the mainstay of the nation's future electric power supply.

[7]   The MITRE Corporation, a Virginia think tank, warns that nuclear materials in the hands of a terrorist group "would give it a power of blackmail over the world at large and the U.S. in particular without precedent in history." (Between 1969 and 1975, ninety-nine threats of violence were directed against commercial nuclear facilities.) Yet, you are asked to accept the program as safe.

[8]   Insurance companies have refused to provide the public with full coverage against nuclear accidents because the risk is too great. Yet, you are asked to accept the program as safe.

[9]   Consumer advocate Ralph Nader warns ". . . there is no practical solution for protecting our generation, much less our children's and grandchildren's, from the immense accumulation of lethal wastes that are inevitable in the nuclear power industry." Yet, you are asked to accept the program as safe.

[10]   According to a report by the Atomic Energy Commission's Regulatory Staff, U.S. nuclear plants are "besieged" by serious safety problems arising from faulty design and construction. Yet, you are asked to accept the program as safe.

[11]   The U.S. Geological Survey has found that there aren't enough known uranium reserves in the United States to fuel proposed nuclear power as the answer to the oil crisis. Yet, you are asked to accept nuclear power as the answer to the oil crisis. . . .

[12]   There is an important step you can take to help control the nuclear risks. That step is your becoming a Sponsor of the Union of Concerned Scientists, the organization dedicated to preventing such a disaster.

Responses

1. Like the preceding article, this one was also in the form of a brochure; it was mailed out to a selected group of people across the country. How do you think the readers were selected? This brochure, unlike the one distributed by the government in support of the Anthony dollar, is written in complete sentences and paragraphs. Does that help you to decide who the readers were expected to be? How?

2. How do the apparently factual comments in the first part of the brochure —"not been properly demonstrated," "research or developmental stage," "not proven," etc.—affect the reader's attitude toward nuclear power?

3. The second sentence in paragraph 5 has three parallel phrases (all built according to the same grammatical pattern). Where are these phrases referred to again? In what order?

4. In paragraph 6, the *Wall Street Journal* is quoted as saying "their unreliability is becoming one of their most dependable features." Why didn't the *Journal* just say the plants are unreliable? Is there a contradiction in what they did say? Why or why not?

5. How many sentences in the last half of the article begin with "Yet"? Where do they appear? Are they all alike? Do you think this repetition is effective? Why or why not?

6. This brochure also contained three boxed quotations, all pointing out that at present we have no assurance that nuclear power is safe: one was by Hannes Alfven, Nobel laureate in physics; another was from a *Reader's Digest* article called "The Burning Question of Brown's Ferry" by James Nathan Miller; and the third was a statement by Congressman Morris Udall, chairman of the House Interior and Insular Affairs Committee. Which of these three is most likely to be an authority on the topic? Which the least likely? Why?

7. Although this brochure was distributed early in 1980, it does not mention the Three Mile Island incident. Why do you think it was omitted? Would the article be more effective if it had been included? Why or why not?

8. Write a paper either for or against nuclear power. Find at least one authority supporting the position you take, and quote from that authority. If you are against nuclear power, don't use the authorities quoted in this article; go to the library and find other statements.

Mount St. Helens Proves a Point

epicenter: a point from which the shock waves of an earthquake appear to
 radiate
minion: a slave or follower
abashed: to be ashamed or embarrassed
counter: opposite
utopianism: a belief in an ideal world or society
concomitantly: also, at the same time, correspondingly

[1]   The pilot had just announced that our plane, headed back eastward, would
not turn and go near Mount St. Helens, with its skyfull of ominous dark smoke
and wondrous belches. And there was a disappointed collective sigh. Shucks.
Foiled again. People genuinely were disappointed. And why? Was it just another
"sideshow" of life missed? Why, I had to ask myself, have the sudden volcanic
rumblings, after the giant has slept for some 150 years, so captured everyone's
imagination?
[2]   There is the sheer beauty of this angry outburst from the bowels of the earth,
to be sure. But it is more than that. We had, quite simply, come to such a point
of disassociation from the earth that we thought only dyspeptic old reprobates like
the Ayatollah Khomeini were supposed to rumble and threaten. It has been part of
our arrogance—part of our view of ourselves as the secure little epicenters of the
universe—that we have just taken the earth itself for granted, giving the special
"days" that the powerful grant to their minions but hardly the tribute that the
abashed offer the mystical.
[3]   Oh, floods and earthquakes and ebbtides still happen—we know that. But we
assume they happen in that "other" world. The "Third World." The "Fourth
World." The "developing world." Not to us. We are "developed." Which means,
beyond the touch of an earth we do not control. But the developing world is as removed as we are, just in a different way. Two examples:
[4]   In the haunted beauty of the high, arid Bolivian mountains, the Maryknoll
priests used to pick up the Indians in their trucks to help them along the desolate
highways. But at certain points, the Indians would simply open the door and get
out—while the trucks were in motion. The Indians quite simply had no sense of
motion. Or of gravity. Or of the earth which ostensibly ruled and guided them.
[5]   One day in Cairo recently, I was traveling in a cab down a major boulevard
when a mini-bus full of people suddenly swept down the other side of the street,
turned over on its side and then skidded, still on its side, 50 feet across the entire
intersection. It was horrendous. But what came next was even worse. Egyptians,
always eager to be helpful, emerged running from all directions. They surrounded
the stricken mini-bus on all sides and began swinging it back and forth, back and
forth, to try to right it. How many people died because of that little exercise—a little exercise of "helpful" people who simply did not understand the most elemental
laws of physics—I did not stay around to see.

Georgie Anne Geyer, *Los Angeles Times;* reprinted in the *Spokesman-Review,* April 24, 1980.

[6]   But, while they do not even begin to understand the movements of the earth, we have had the counter arrogance: thinking we understood it all too well. While the Russians found their new religiosity in the secularism of Marxism, many of us have found it in the new environmentalism, in being against nuclear power, in the taming of the earth through an earth day. We have been reveling in our rampant utopianism, really believing that life is perfectible, that truth is knowable, and that, concomitantly, if things are not perfect or true or just or just right, then people are "holding back." Life becomes deliberate, not accidental or naturally imperfect.

[7]   So when you think about it, it all makes sense. It pleases us to take care of earth, the way we do of our bodies, because we own it, too. We accept it on our terms. Until Mount St. Helens' unseemly antics, we had forgotten it had any terms. That is why, I strongly suspect, the hoary old mountain has struck us with its wondrousness. It reminds us, despite our selves, of sticky ancient saps and dark subterranean rivers that we had tried to put aside. It reasserts the mystery.

[8]   But the other mountains beneath me in the plane are behaving nicely. They are glorious, but calm. They lie quietly in their coats of light snow, like good mountains. One can ski on them, gaze at them, mine them, control them. They would never act like Mount St. Helens.

Responses

1. At the end of March 1980, Mt. St. Helens, a 9,677-foot peak in southwest Washington, began to throw ash and steam over itself and the surrounding area. On May 18, 1980 the mountain did erupt. Nearly a hundred people were killed, a third of the mountain was destroyed, and the resulting ash disrupted communities as far away as Montana. How is Geyer using the preliminary rumblings from the mountain to prove her point? Would the point be different if this article had been written in June rather than in April? Why or why not? Is Mt. St. Helens' point, as indicated in the title, the same as Geyer's point? Whether or not you believe the points are the same, write a main idea sentence that you think would fit this article.

2. What does the introduction do? Where does the introduction end? How did you decide?

3. Explain what Geyer means by "developing" and "developed" in paragraph 3. Why does she put these words in quotation marks?

4. What generalization do the examples given in paragraphs 4 and 5 support? How effective are they? Why? What examples are given in paragraph 6? What generalization do they support?

5. Geyer deliberately uses several incomplete sentences—constructions that English teachers often mark as "fragments." Why do you think she uses them? What effect do they create?

6. Would you like this article better if it had ended with paragraph 7? Why or why not? What, if anything, does paragraph 8 add to Geyer's point?

7. Write a paragraph or two defending or attacking the idea that science has conquered nature. Be sure to give at least one extended example to support your position.

Don't Pay the Purists No Mind, Honey

purist: one who insists that rules should be strictly observed
pretentious: full of artificial dignity
intuitively: recognizing a truth immediately without logical proof
eclectic: made up of things from various sources
indomitable: can't be subdued or overcome
orthodox: correct in opinion or doctrine

[1]   The best statement I ever heard on the subject of racial tolerance was uttered some years ago in Anacostia by a Black teenager eating a McDonald's cheeseburger.

[2]   Our family was new to Washington, our children were still infants, and we did not yet fully appreciate the racial geography that defines this city. One evening we went searching for a McDonald's and found one deep in the Southeast, a part of the District where white folks ain't supposed to go.

[3]   In the restaurant, my son stood up on the seat, surveyed the world around him and described it for us with innocent accuracy. One by one, he pointed to each of the customers at other tables—all of whom were Black—and announced their race. He's Black and she's Black and they're Black and so on. Then he observed, with equal clarity and volume, our race. Mommy's white. Daddy's white. I'm white and so on.

[4]   A painful silence. The girl at the next table did not look up from her cheeseburger. She merely remarked: "Don't pay it no mind, honey."

[5]   Don't pay it no mind, honey. Is there a better way to say it? Grammarians may enjoy pointing out the technical flaws in that sentence, but the expression has lived on in our family—an article of enrichment passed on to us by that anonymous girl. We use it on each other. And sometimes, when I hear one of our self-important Washington figures holding forth on his own importance in lifeless but proper English, I get the urge to interrupt: Don't pay it no mind, honey.

[6]   American English is a mongrel language, and it is precisely such small interchanges as ours that keep it vibrant, the most versatile language in the world. One group of Americans borrows or steals from another, modifies a stray idiom, crumples the original meaning and makes it fit their own practical usage. Good talk travels across town, even in segregated Washington, from McDonald's to tables set with china and linen. The well-to-do borrow language from the poor, even from

William Greider, *Manchester Guardian Weekly*, January 6, 1980.

the underworld. Sometimes, the well-to-do repackage and record it and sell it back to the poor. The poor, meanwhile, must clean up their English if they wish to become un-poor.

[7]   The point is that the sterile critics who preach proper English create pretentious arguments that conceal the real importance of these different voices in nonstandard languages. Sure, language is a social and political battle-ground. But our language differences, I believe, also act as lubricants among diverse social groups, even among economic classes. If this weren't true, America would have torn itself apart a long time ago.

[8]   The adaptations of language represent one of America's less obvious strengths, particularly the filtering upward of new words, new idioms, new flavor from whatever caste or class or ethnic group is at the bottom. This doesn't happen in most Western nations, where proper prose is enforced from the top, which is why the government of France worries endlessly about the steady decline of French in the world. The fact is that many in France or Great Britain or West Germany find they can often say more in American English, or express more through the musical language of the Black blues singer. Anything as powerful as the blues must be a powerful language.

[9]   Do we Americans understand this about ourselves? I'm not sure we do. Every other season, a new book hits the best-seller list scolding us for bad English, or someone raises a pious alarm about the threatened status of standard English v Black English v Spanish v whatever else comes along. This is a very old pretention. From the earliest days of the republic, purists have been complaining about the debasement of the King's English. They always lose, as Americans change the language in every generation. But that doesn't seem to deter the scolds.

[10]   My colleague Noel Epstein, who has made a scholarly study of these things, particularly the arguments over bilingual education, suggests to me that Americans are more appreciative today. Epstein believes that, unlike the sixties, when folks were fighting toe-to-toe over standard v minority tongues, they are intuitively realizing now that it doesn't have to be an either-or choice. We can have both; indeed we have always had both, an incredible dimension of our culture.

[11]   Not only are a good number of minority languages and dialects still alive and kicking in this nation, but in a limited way each of us who conducts our life in English is also speaking a little Jewish, a little Italian, a little Spanish, a little Indian, a little black, a little uptown white. The social theorists continue to declaim on the question of whether America is a "melting pot" or a "tossed salad," but Epstein's notion is that we are neither. Maybe American is an Irish stew made with North Carolina barbecue and side orders of potato pancakes, corn bread, chicken soup. An eclectic menu.

[12]   In fact, there is a real social disadvantage for those of us who are limited to one standard language, and others sometimes do a number on us because of it. Black Americans who successfully navigate in the white offices of standard English, for instance, still employ the mother tongue, sometimes to remind the white folks around them that Black is beautiful or proud or indomitable. I have seen Black reporters in the newsroom do the jive routine on white editors, but I admit that it was startling to read in Bob Woodward's and Scott Armstrong's new book "The Brethren" that Justice Thurgood Marshall does it, too.

[13]   "Dat de way it was, sho was." That is not how one expects Thurgood Marshall, the giant of the civil rights era, to talk. Chief Justice Warren Burger may smile, but I feel confident that it also makes him uncomfortable. That, of course, is the point. This is Mr. Justice Marshall reminding Mr. Chief Justice Burger, not very subtly, that one of his "brethren" is Black.

[14]   From deep in the federal labyrinth, a bureaucrat told me about a wonderful variation on the same theme. A Black secretary in this agency speaks a mumbled dialect that her white co-workers and supervisors can barely understand. Sometimes, with embarrassment, they must ask her to repeat for them. But when this same woman telephones another Black secretary to chat, she doesn't speak Black English. She speaks an exaggerated version of standard English—a parody of the way "proper" white folks talk: "Helllooooow, Miss Jones. Would yooou be free for lunch toooday?"

[15]   This is her inside joke, and perhaps she doesn't realize that her white colleagues are on to it. But I suspect she wants them to hear, to know that she can do it their way if she wants to but that she sure isn't about to throw away her own identity in the process. That Black secretary clearly has some moves available to her that most white people don't have.

[16]   White children who grow up exclusively on standard English sometimes discover that they are prisoners of one language, restricted to a single communications channel, no other knobs to turn. For many of them Black English has offered an escape, a way to repudiate their orthodox upbringing. It's impossible to listen to white rock 'n roll without hearing that statement of repudiation. For that matter, listen to groups of white teenagers talking among themselves and you often will hear an awkward mimicry of Black street patter.

[17]   I'm not suggesting that learning other languages of America or the world will make us all love each other; we'll only understand better what the other guy is really after. But it can help us get rid of that feeling of intimidation, that fear of the strange and the alien, and, I suspect, become stronger people in the process. That's why knowing Black English is as important for white children as standard English is for Blacks. Thurgood Marshall couldn't do the Kingfish routine on Warren Burger if Warren Burger were able to respond in kind. Can one imagine the Chief Justice slapping hands with Mr. Justice Marshall and exclaiming: Right on, Thurgood, baby, you my main man?

Responses

1. How does the introduction arouse the reader's interest? Where does the introduction end and the main part of the article begin?
2. What is the technical flaw in the sentence quoted in paragraph 4 and changed slightly to make up the title of the article? What kind of judgment do you make about people who use such sentences? What kind of judgment does Greider think you should make?

3. What reasons does Greider give to support the main point of his article? How are these reasons supported?
4. What three metaphors are suggested in paragraph 11? Which metaphor best fits your idea of what the American language is? Why?
5. How many examples of "a little Jewish, a little Italian, a little Spanish, a little Indian, a little Black, a little uptown white" can you think of? If you are not sure of the origin of some words that occur to you, look them up in a good dictionary.
6. When you were in grade school and high school, were you told that one way of saying something was "wrong" and another way "right"—much as the answer to a math problem is right or wrong—or were these language choices discussed in terms of the effect they have on listeners or readers? Which way would Greider think the choices should be presented? Why?
7. "Pious" (paragraph 9) and "orthodox" (paragraph 16) have religious connotations. How are these connotations related to Greider's point?
8. The argument most frequently presented by people who think everybody should be taught to talk alike is that dialect speakers can't get ahead in the world unless they learn to speak so-called standard English. Write a paper defending this point of view and using examples to support what you say. Or, if you disagree, write a paper maintaining that the schools should not try to change the way American students speak, and give reasons for your belief.

More Suggestions for Writing

The speed limit should (or shouldn't) remain at 55 mph.

Professional athletes should (or shouldn't) be allowed to compete in the Olympics.

Some building in your area should (or shouldn't) be torn down.

Doctors should (or shouldn't) be sued for malpractice.

Teachers or firefighters or police or hospital personnel should (or shouldn't) be allowed to strike.

Women should (shouldn't) be drafted.

Compact cars are (aren't) dangerous.

Spelling is (isn't) important to good writing.

Amateurs should not try to give first aid.

Some traffic intersection you know about is dangerous.

The college needs a new _____.

Putting an ad in the college newspaper is (or isn't) a good way to get a job (or find an apartment or sell a piece of equipment).

Organic foods are (or aren't) better for you.

The sale of mail-order guns should (or shouldn't) be forbidden.

Everybody should know how to swim.

The state should (or shouldn't) require that all automobiles pass an inspection test.

Chapter 10

Fair Persuasion

The world is full of persuasive writing. Some of it is open and aboveboard; some of it hides behind explanations and reports. When you think of persuasive writing, you probably think first of ad writers, for none of us can escape them. Ads are all around us. The radio shrieks at us about newer, bigger, better products. Television issues frank warnings about household germs and offensive body odors. Beautiful people in magazine ads beckon to us from beautiful cars parked on beautifully landscaped driveways in front of beautiful houses. Newspapers squeeze in a dribble or two of world events between the furniture closeouts and the grocery specials. Our mailboxes are jammed with circulars offering everything from life insurance to cemetery plots.

But ad writers are not the only salesmen. Politicians have something to sell, too. Millions a year are spent to persuade you that Senator John S. Goodsell is a plain, earnest farmboy who carries your particular interest engraved upon the gold of his 100 percent American heart. He persuades a group of laborers that he believes unions were made in heaven, and he persuades a group of businessmen that he believes unions were definitely made somewhere else. In the Senate, he persuades his colleagues that the multimillion-dollar project for a grasshopper sanctuary in his state will benefit the national economy, increase our prestige, and preserve a priceless national resource.

Many other people try to persuade us, too. The public-relations woman proclaims the merits of her organization; the president of the United Good Givers Association pleads for the poor; the encyclopedia company suggests you'd *really* be smart if you bought their books. Indeed, so many people are trying to persuade us so much of the time that it is difficult to think of anybody who isn't.

When you try to get other people to agree with you, and try to do it honestly, you give reasons for your opinion and support your reasons. It would seem, then, that when you wanted to act rationally (rather than impulsively) you could expect supported reasons from people who are trying to make you agree with them. But how often do you get any reasons at all? And when you do get reasons, how good are they?

>Buy Lovely Lady Facial Tissue.
>It's used by Hollywood stars.

This advertisement is an attempt to convince you. The main idea sentence is "Buy Lovely Lady Facial Tissue." The reason given to support the main idea is "It's used by Hollywood stars." The name and the claim suggest that if you use it, you will be lovely, too. The notion—an implied prediction—is stupid when stated plainly, but the advertisers don't expect you to state it plainly. They just want you to associate the glamour of Hollywood stars with the use of Lovely Lady Facial Tissue. However, look at what has been left out.

You are not told how many stars use the tissue. The implication is that all stars use it, but it only takes two to make star<u>s</u>. The advertisers are hinting that a survey has been made, but they have concealed the statistics. Nor do you know why the stars use it. Maybe they were paid to endorse it, or maybe Lovely Lady Tissue Company gave them a year's supply of the stuff and hopes they can figure out something to do with it. Certainly you are not told *how* they use it. Maybe it's so rough they sand their furniture with it. Maybe it's so durable they carpet their apartments with it. Or maybe it's so flimsy they tear it to shreds and decorate their Christmas trees with it. If you assume, as the advertisers hope you will, that the stars use it on their faces, thus creating their beautiful complexions, you are being misled by a bad cause-and-effect relationship.

And what is a "Hollywood star" anyway? Boris Karloff and Lassie were Hollywood stars of the first magnitude, but who wants to look like them? *Star* is a word that can be defined several ways. Tansy, who had a thirty-second walk-on part as the maid in the movie *What's Become of Raphael Bogislav?*, is called a star by her press agent. The language the advertisers are using is vague and indefinite.

But even if the stars were Shirley Temple, Katharine Hepburn, and Jane Fonda, would the reason be any stronger? You would ask a banker about a loan, a jockey for a racing tip, Betty Crocker about biscuits. They are experts on these matters. But what makes stars authorities on facial tissue? Do they blow their noses more than ordinary people? True, they wipe thick layers of make-up off their faces. But they do that with towels. In the matter of choosing a facial tissue, you are as much an expert as a Hollywood star. You have a nose, and a harsh tissue will not scratch it less, no matter how many Hollywood stars use the same tissue. Advertisers who imply otherwise are misusing authority.

Slanted Words

Actually, the facial tissue advertisement relies entirely on your willingness to respond emotionally to pleasant words. No advertiser would say, "With this paper you can wipe the grime off your worn-out face in a few hurried swipes. And when you're done fussing with yourself, you can just dump the paper in the garbage can." Ad writers can sell more by saying, "Lovely Lady Facial Tissue restores morning radiance. Its soft caress smoothes away daytime cares. And when you are once again your fresh and lovely self, the tissue is disposable." *Radiance, soft, caress, smooth, fresh,* and *lovely* are all "purr" words that tend to put readers in a good mood, to soften them into buying the tissue. Persuasion that relies on emotion and slanted words is common, and it can be deceptive.

When you wrote objective reports, you had some practice in avoiding slanted words. When you tried persuasive writing, you probably used a few slanted words deliberately, to arouse interest in your introductions. And it may seem to you that advertisers have just as much right to use "purr" words as you had to use colorful language in your examples. Both you and the advertisers are using vivid language for exactly the same purpose: to create a picture in the minds of readers, to remind them of something they have already experienced. But an honest argument does not stop with the picture. It does more than suggest glamour by pleasant associations; it goes on to give sound, supported reasons. Unfair persuasion offers *only* slanted words and colored language; it conceals the reasons.

Using definite, specific language is a good thing, and there's nothing wrong with colorful words. What you need to ask is:

1. Are the vivid words used to make the meaning clearer or just to get readers to purr—or snarl?
2. Is the appeal to your emotions or to your mind?

Glittering Generalities

Much like the use of slanted words is the use of glittering generalities. These are such sweet and general statements that we feel bound to agree—unless we realize they have no specific meaning. Glittering generalities slant by what they don't say. They are used by people who want to avoid definite statements.

Both ad writers and politicians may use glittering generalities. For example, Senator Goodsell may leave more out of his campaign speeches than he puts in. The senator says he is for God, mother, and country; and that he is against atheists and Freudians and communists (those who are anti-God, anti-mother, and anti-country—according to him). In effect he is saying, "I love good and hate evil. Since all of you love good and hate evil, you should support me for the Senate." It is probably true that you do love good and hate evil, but what is "good" and what is "evil"? Does everyone always mean exactly the same thing by "good"? By "evil"? Sometimes people react emotionally without stopping to ask whether the senator's notion of what is good agrees with their own.

To avoid being taken in by such sweet generalities, you must insist on more specific information. In answer to the question "Will you vote for the urban-housing bill?" (a definite question), the senator says:

This bill deserves the serious consideration of all thoughtful people. If we are to win the life-death struggle between the American ideal and the forces that seek to destroy it, we must gird ourselves with moral courage and physical strength. Money for defense is essential to the preservation of our way of life. Yet taxation must not be excessive. We must think this thing out and arrive at a satisfactory solution.

What does this answer tell you? The senator seems to be in favor of America and against the people who are against it, whoever they are. He is in favor of moral courage, and against physical weakness. He believes in defense, and he doesn't want to raise taxes. And it all sounds so good. Unless you are careful you may respond to these soothing comments in the same way people respond to the ad writer's words—with emotion, not reason. You may be so busy agreeing emotionally with the senator's viewpoint that you will forget he was supposed to be talking about improving conditions in the city ghettos. If you see the urban-housing bill as contributing to the American ideal, you are likely to suppose the senator does, too. If you think financial help for poor people is "creeping socialism," it is easy to think that the senator, too, believes the urban-housing bill will destroy the American way of life. The senator hopes that if he avoids a definite statement, all his hearers will go away believing his ideas are the same as theirs.

If you stubbornly insist, as you should, that the senator say something definite about the proposed bill, he is sure to spoon out the sugar coating of slanted language. Even though he plans to vote against it, he will not say, "Let those lazy, good-for-nothing bums fend for themselves." He won't even say, "I intend to vote against the bill." Instead, he will probably say, "The American way is to allow all our citizens the natural dignity that goes with paying their own way."

The ad writer gave you sugared words; Goodsell gives you sugared words and sugared generalities. Both of them are appealing to you emotionally rather than rationally. Don't be persuaded until you get some supported reasons. What *examples* can the senator offer? What *statistical support* has he for the stand he takes? Can he back up his position by appealing to *authorities* on urban conditions? What *predictions* is he making about the effects of the bill? If you don't want to be deceived, you must learn to tell the difference between honest and dishonest support. It's always reasonable to ask:

> *Are the statements clear and definite or are they meaningless pleasantries, meant only to put the reader in a good mood?*

Facts, Inferences, and Judgments

If you do force Senator Goodsell to give a more definite answer, you need to know what kind of statement he's making. Most statements made about the present or the past can be classified as *facts, inferences,* or *judgments.* (Statements made about the future are always predictions of one kind or another.) When you were writing objective reports, you learned to distinguish between *factual statements* (those that can be checked) and *opinion statements* (those that express the speaker's judgment as to good or bad, beautiful, ugly, or ordinary, safe or dangerous, etc.). In between the extremes of fact and opinion are *inferences*—statements about what we think is or isn't so, did or didn't happen, based on some facts we do know. Sometimes inferences are so reliable that we can almost consider them as factual statements; sometimes they are so unreliable that they can lead us wildly astray.

We might begin with the old saying "Where there's smoke, there's fire," to see how these three kinds of statements work. "Hey, the Christmas tree's on fire!" is, of course, a factual statement. You can—and should—check it for accuracy before you call the fire department. Go into the living room and see. But if someone says, "There's smoke in the living room; the Christmas tree must be on fire!" the first half is a factual statement, the second half an inference. If there is a great deal of smoke and nothing else in the living room that will burn very easily, and if we agree that smoke is always a sign of fire, the inference is probably sound. At least, it's dependable enough that you'd better call the fire department without looking to see whether it's the tree or the curtains.

"Abner smokes a pipe—he started the fire," is another inference, but this one is a good deal less reliable. It does relate to some facts: Abner is a pipe smoker; Abner was in the living room for an hour; and the Christmas tree did catch fire. Possibly Abner did leave a smouldering pipe too close to the dried-out fir branches; but it's also possible that the Christmas tree was too close to the fireplace, that little Gracie has been playing with matches, that the Christmas tree lights overheated. If the whole living room is destroyed, any decision as to how the fire started will be an inference—although the fire marshall's inference, that faulty wiring was the culprit, will probably be the most reliable, especially if he discovers that the electric wiring behind the wall has fused. The statement that "Abner has always been careless" would, of course, be a judgment.

When smoke and fire refer to physical things, we're on safer ground than when the old saying is applied to people's behavior. Sometimes you hear people say "Where there's smoke, there's fire" when they're not talking about combustion at all. The neighbors have been gossiping about Rosita. She has a new leather coat; she had steak for dinner three nights in a row; and she came home Saturday in a new sports car. Rosita works in a bank. "She must be taking money out of the till," says Mrs. Grundy. "No other way she could get so much," says Mr. Busybody, whose brother manages the bank. "Where there's smoke, there's fire," says the brother and finds an excuse to fire Rosita because it's a fact that the bank's books were fifty dollars out of balance last Tuesday. The inference, and the judgment based on it, were not investigated.

The kind of judgment (guilty or not guilty) that lawyers call circumstantial evidence is always based on inferences. Just after the drugstore has been robbed, Alfie Brown is seen running down the street as fast as he can go. Later, Alfie is found to have a new transistor radio exactly like the one missing from the drugstore. Furthermore, the druggist, who was in the back room at the time, heard the thief coughing; Alfie has a cold. The running, the radio, and the unidentified cough are the facts. That Alfie robbed the store is the inference based on those facts. Unless Alfie can show a receipt for the radio, the police may consider the inference reliable enough to arrest him.

There's nothing wrong about making inferences; we couldn't live or think without them. Inferences get us into trouble when we forget they aren't facts, and when we forget to question whether they are probable or merely possible. When other people try to persuade us, it's important to know whether we're being given facts, inferences, or judgments, and to ask what's behind the judgments that are being made.

> *Facts* are statements that can be verified; they should be checked for accuracy.
>
> *Inferences* are statements made about what isn't known, based on what is known; they should be checked carefully against the known facts.
>
> *Judgments* are statements about good or bad, desirable or undesirable, guilty or innocent; they should be recognized as opinion and checked against the facts or inferences on which they are based.

Honest Examples

Examples, because they have to be specific, are almost always factual statements. Like any other factual statements, they should be checked for accuracy. But even if they are accurate, they can be misleading in other ways. Senator Goodsell offers his independent old mother, who lives in a fifty-room mansion and owns huge blocks of blue-chip stock, as an example of an elderly person who would be very angry at anyone who offered to subsidize her rent. But old Mrs. Goodsell is hardly a representative example of the people who will be helped by the bill. And the senator is misleading us when he uses such an unfair example. On the other hand, the student who said that final exams are no indication of student learning illustrated the generalization by an actual experience in freezing up and seeing other people cheat. Such cheating and freezing are probably representative enough to be honest examples, especially if there have been lots of cheaters and freezers in most of the finals the writer has taken.

Honest examples can serve two purposes: they can make the meaning of a general statement clear, and they can help readers see a problem more vividly.

As you discovered when you wrote stipulative definitions, some words are so general and so subjective in their meaning that they almost always require examples. The statement "John Smith was *brave*" needs an example to make clear what is meant by bravery. Does it simply mean that John Smith was completely without fear, or does it mean he was so eaten up by fear of spiders that he showed great courage in removing a daddy-long-legs from the baby's crib? When people talk about a great *revival of religion,* do they simply mean that more people are going to church, or are they suggesting that more people are really worried about their souls? Only carefully chosen examples can make the meaning clear.

Sometimes the meaning of the word being used is clear enough, but the full force of what the word represents is not felt by the readers. In such cases, examples help to drive home the point. Even though most people understand what *starve* means, "Five thousand starve to death in India" will not disturb readers nearly as much as the example of one emaciated infant, wailing feebly and hopelessly for the bowl of rice that is not there. Statements such as "Four hundred killed in weekend traffic mishaps" take on more reality with just one headless body, one glimpse of bloody pavement, and one set of grief-shocked relatives. Notice that these examples use definite, specific words that help us see (*emaciated, headless, bloody*), rather than words that stir our emotions vaguely (*life-death struggle, American way, natural dignity*). If we respond to the example with pity or horror, it is because the language is vivid, not sugared.

In dealing with examples, you need to ask:

1. Are the examples honestly representative of the generalizations they illustrate?
2. Do the examples make the meaning clearer or the picture more vivid?

Honest Statistics

Examples are honestly used when they lead to a clearer understanding or a more vivid realization, but they are dishonestly used when they tempt readers to form a generalization based on only one example or one instance. It is unfair to argue that because one baby goes hungry, all the children in town are undernourished; or that because one 1979 car has defective brakes, everyone who drives a 1979 model will be involved in a fatal accident.

Before you can make a sound general statement, you must have enough facts to generalize about. One way of getting enough facts is to take a survey. Suppose you want to know how many students in your school have jobs. It is glaringly obvious that you can't say, "I work; therefore everybody works." It is equally obvious that you don't have time to ask all the students in school whether they are employed, unless you drop all your classes and quit your own job. But you can make a survey.

Your statistics will not be very reliable if you question only the people in the coffee shop and then say, "Four of the forty people in the coffee shop at three o'clock Thursday afternoon said they have jobs. Therefore only 10 percent of the student body work." If your school has a student body of two thousand, a sample of forty students is not enough, anyway. Furthermore, the students in the coffee shop may not be representative of the whole student body. Maybe at three o'clock most of the workers are at work. If you ask fifty people in the library at eight o'clock on Friday morning, 90 percent of them may say they have jobs.

A hundred out of two thousand might be a large enough sample, but if you ask only humanities students, you will not have a representative group. Maybe humanities students are less likely to be working than technical students. Your statistics will not be reliable unless you have used enough examples and unless those examples represent a fair cross section of all the students in school. If you ask a hundred students, if you make sure that they represent every department, and if you ask on more than one day and at different hours during the day, you may come up with a pretty honest estimate of the number of employed students.

Suppose your estimate shows that 33 percent of the student body work. When you present your statistics, be careful not to say "Many students work" or "A large number of students work" or "The average student works" or even "Some students work." All these statements interpret the facts. One person's *many* is another person's *some*. Is thirty-three out of a hundred *many* or *some* or *a few*? And who is the *typical* student? Remember that *typical* and *average,* like *good* and *bad, better* and *worse,* are opinion words. You are not justified in saying anything except "A survey of a hundred students shows that approximately 33 percent of the students on this campus work."

If your survey also deals with how much the students work—whether they work full- or part-time—and if you discover that twenty-three of those thirty-three students work only an hour a day whereas the other ten hold full-time jobs and work eight hours a day, you may be tempted to report that students work for an average of about three hours a day. You have figured it out mathematically:

$$
\begin{array}{ll}
\text{10 students at 8 hours} = & \text{80 hours} \\
\text{23 students at 1 hour} = & \underline{\text{23}} \\
& \text{103 hours}
\end{array}
$$

103 hours divided by 33 students = 3 hours 4 minutes a day

Notice, however, that *no* student actually works three hours a day; and the situation of the majority, who work only an hour a day, is quite different from the situation of those ten who try to combine a full-time job with full-time college attendance. Readers who know that "averages" can be deceptive ought to ask how you arrived at that figure. Did you add all the hours together and divide by the number of people? Did you line up all the responses in order, from most to fewest hours, and use the number that appeared in the middle of the list? Or did you give the number of hours that appeared most frequently? Either of the last two kinds of averages would present a more accurate picture. Unless you're deliberately trying to deceive, you'll have to provide the actual figures: twenty-three students work one hour a day, ten students work eight hours a day.

Perhaps you added a third question to the survey. Perhaps you also asked whether those hundred people thought college students *should* work. Twenty-five said no, twenty-five said yes, and fifty were undecided. It's likely that the twenty-five yeses came from working students; they wouldn't be working unless they had to. And even though you're trying to demonstrate that working doesn't interfere with studying, it's not fair to report that only 25 percent of those you interviewed were opposed to students working. Readers who realize that percentages can deceive are likely to ask, "What did the other 75 percent say?"

If you are trying to use your figures to prove a point, if you have something to gain from the results of the survey, your readers ought to look at your statistics very closely. When Senator Goodsell hires some pollsters to "test" his popularity, the pollsters' statistics may be open to some suspicion; probably his opponent has hired other pollsters to test her popularity, and their results may be quite different. In each case, the survey-taker has a stake in the outcome, and sensible people will be cautious about believing the figures.

What's true for surveys is true for all statistical reports, whether they are experiments, investigations, or simple counting. Science could not progress without using statistics; it was mathematical calculations that put electric dishwashers into kitchens, mathematical calculations that put men on the moon. But good scientists are careful not to let their figures mislead either themselves or other scientists; they're careful to make sure that the statistics are honestly and accurately reported.

Statistics can usually be depended on if:

1. the sample is big enough
2. the sample is representative of the whole group
3. the results are reported in specific, objective language, with nothing left out
4. the person offering the statistics has nothing personal to gain from the outcome

Honest Use of Authorities

Mentioning authorities who agree with you is another acceptable way of supporting reasons; but authorities can be misused, too. Using the name of a famous person who is expert in one field to give evidence for something in another field may be a misuse of authority. If you are looking for an expert on British politics during and just after World War II, you could hardly do better than Winston Churchill, though he was probably not very objective. But if you're looking for an expert on American baseball, French cooking, or what to do with a colicky baby, it would not be fair to use Winston Churchill, even though nearly everybody recognizes his name.

If you're looking for a baseball expert, quote Pete Rose or Reggie Jackson. If you're talking about French cooking, you can refer to Chef Fernande Garvin or Julia Child. If you're writing a treatise on the U.S. Supreme Court, you could hardly improve on Justice William O. Douglas, whose long experience on the Court and carefully written judgments established him as an authority beyond question. If you want an authority on the House of Representatives, you could certainly quote Bella Abzug or Shirley Chisholm. All these people are experts in their fields, and repeating what they say about baseball, cooking, law, and Congress is a perfectly honest use of authority.

It is, of course, possible for a person to be an expert in more than one field. Justice Douglas specialized in law, but that did not keep him from having other interests, too—for example, he was an avid outdoorsman and hiker. And it didn't keep him from making a careful study of America's land preservation policy, especially in national parks, forests, and wilderness areas. He may not have had access to classified information that is available to the secretary of the interior or the director of the Bureau of Parks and Wildlife, but at the same time, because he wasn't a cabinet member or an administrator, his professional career was neither threatened nor advanced by the outcome of political decisions and he therefore was able to make a more independent judgment. Whether or not you agree with the positions he took, Justice Douglas is widely regarded as an authority on the preservation of wilderness areas—certainly much better informed than the person who relies on slogans and hearsay rather than on a thorough study of the situation.

Justice Douglas is much more the exception than the rule. Usually, authorities are quoted out of their fields in an attempt to grab off some of the glory associated with their names and graft it onto whatever is being discussed. We are urged to deposit our money in the Benjamin Franklin High-Interest Savings Bank, buy our cars from the Abraham Lincoln Pre-owned Car Emporium, or purchase our candy from the Martha Washington chain. We are told that Shift City Transmissions are better than Shiftless Transmissions because the world champion heavyweight wrestler says so. In each case, we can be fairly sure that authority is being misused. Mr. Franklin, Mr. Lincoln, and Ms. Washington were dead for decades before these businesses were ever established; the business owners are simply taking advantage of Franklin's reputation for thrift, Lincoln's reputation for honesty, and Martha Washington's prestige as the nation's first first lady. The wrestling champ knows about shoulder joints; he may not know anything about universal joints.

Neither is the imaginary *everybody* very good authority. The case becomes no stronger if we say, "Everybody is doing it, so you should do it, too" or "Everybody knows that; why discuss it?" A careful survey would show that *everybody* is a great exaggeration. But more important, even if the survey showed that 99.4 percent of the population were doing it or believing it, the survey still has not proved that it is worth doing or that it is necessarily so. Large numbers of people have supported actions we now think wrong: the Salem witch burnings, the Nazi book burnings, the Ku Klux Klan cross burnings. Group pressure is group pressure, not rational thinking.

"Everybody says so" is not good authority, and neither is "I heard it on television" or "I read it somewhere." Television programs range from soap operas to *Sesame Street,* from "people" shows to propaganda, and their purpose is often to entertain rather than to inform. Reading is a valuable habit, but not everybody who writes and gets published is a trustworthy authority. The same questions should be asked about what you hear and what you read as are asked about any other authority. If a television or newspaper report begins, "An unidentified source . . ." or "A source close to the mayor . . . ," careful readers will be suspicious. Both the janitor and the errand girl are "close" to the mayor, but their guess as to whether he will approve the next budget is not much better than yours.

What happened in the past is not always good authority, either. "It's always been that way—why change it now?" or "The men who wrote the Constitution wouldn't like it" are not good reasons for being against a proposal made in quite different times, under quite different circumstances. People who say, "We don't need a welfare program. Grandpa always raised enough vegetables to feed the family when he didn't have a job. Why can't those other unemployed people do it, too?" are not using acceptable authority. They are only saying they don't believe in change. The point is not that all changes are either good or bad, but that each change should be judged on its own merits.

To test whether authority is being used honestly, ask:

1. Are the experts speaking in their own fields?
2. If they are out of their fields, are they well informed on the subject?
3. Have they anything to gain by what they say?

Authority is misused if:

1. the argument is just taking advantage of a famous name
2. it uses "everybody knows" or "everybody does"
3. it uses "we have always done it"

Honest Predictions

Predicting the consequences is another much-used method of supporting an argument; but predictions, even more than examples, statistics, and authorities, can be used unfairly. You are always on risky ground when you attempt to foresee the future, but you can be a good deal more certain in some areas than in others. Suppose you say, "If I put a kettle of water on the stove and turn the burner on high, the water will boil." Almost everybody will accept this prediction. Suppose you say, "If I come to class every day and smile sweetly at the teacher, I will pass the course." Almost everybody will want to ask a few questions. Suppose you say, "If we re-elect Senator Goodsell, everybody in the country will get his or her dearest wish, but if we elect Alan James, the roofs of our houses will fall on our heads." At this, everybody should protest loudly.

Predictions that deal with the physical world are usually fairly safe:

Water will boil at 212 degrees Fahrenheit at sea level.

On January 28, 1985, sunrise in Kansas City will be at 7:25 A.M., Central Standard Time.

Low tide in Chesapeake Bay tomorrow will be at 8:33 P.M.

Predictions that deal with the behavior of people are much less safe:

The senator's temper will boil at the mention of the urban-housing bill.

My uncle will rise from bed tomorrow at 7:25 A.M., Central Standard Time.

My automotive teacher will sneeze at 8:33 P.M.

The senator may change his mind about the housing bill, smile blandly, and talk smoothly about our responsibility to the underprivileged. Your uncle may oversleep. Your teacher may have recovered from the hay fever that caused the sneezing.

Even so, if you know the senator well and are well acquainted with your uncle's habits, your first two guesses may be fairly good. If you are predicting something simple about someone you have known for a long time, what you say may often be accurate. But when you move to new situations and attempt to predict the results of something you have never experienced before, then your predictions become less reliable. When you try guessing about complex problems, in situations where a variety of causes might affect the results, your guesses may become wildly unreliable.

A combination of figures and predictions can also be misleading, especially if the figures themselves are accurate. Mark Twain once "proved" that by the year 2600 the lower Mississippi River would be less than two miles long. He did it by beginning with some perfectly reliable figures showing how much shorter the river had become in the last 175 years and then extending those figures into the future. Mark Twain, who was deliberately making a joke, pretended that exactly the same process would continue to happen every year in the future. But people not trying to be funny often make the same kind of inaccurate predictions. Because there was such a great increase in the number of babies born just after World War II, many school districts thought the number of schoolchildren would continue to grow larger forever and so they built a lot of new schools. Now some of those schools are standing empty or being torn down. Using the same combination of statistics and predictions, it would be possible to show that if the number of kindergarten children has decreased by 10 percent in the past ten years, a hundred years from now there will be no five-year-olds at all. This prediction is obvious nonsense if we take it that far, but it can sound pretty convincing if we extend it for only thirty years. Using what happpened in the past to show what might happen in the future can be helpful, but only if we remember that conditions in the future are never likely to be exactly the same as they were in the past.

Before you say, "If we do *this, that* will happen," or "Because it *is* like that, it *will* always be like that," remember that:

1. predictions dealing with the physical world are usually safe
2. predictions dealing with people you know well are fairly safe
3. predictions about new situations and new experiences are often not safe at all

Post Hoc Thinking

Just as fair persuasion avoids simple-minded predictions about future events, so it avoids oversimplified explanations of what happened in the past. When you practiced writing causal analysis, you had some experience in how to tell whether one thing caused another. You discovered that most important human events have more than one simple cause. The old nursery jingle that begins, "Because of a nail, a shoe was lost. Because of a shoe, . . . etc.," makes good children's literature, but not very good reasoning. No reliable historian would say the assassination of Archduke Ferdinand was the *only* cause of World War I. No reliable psychiatrist would say that watching a lot of violence on television was the *only* reason fourteen-year-old Sammy Evans conked his grandfather with a beer bottle. No reliable judge would say that a girl's wearing short skirts and a tight sweater was the *only* reason she was raped. Many events, in fact, have causes so deeply buried so far in the past that we can never be sure what they were.

It's always tempting to think that because two events are related in time—first this happened, then that—the first thing caused the second. This temptation is behind most of the superstitions from which we never quite free ourselves, even though we know better. Once, probably, somebody sprained an ankle just after walking under a ladder, and it was all too easy to think the ladder had something to do with the bad luck. Once, probably, somebody won an unexpected ten dollars just after picking up a pin; it was equally easy to believe that the pin had caused the good luck.

The faulty cause-and-effect relationships that give rise to superstitions are silly but harmless. Probably nobody was ever hurt by knocking on wood or refusing a room on the thirteenth floor. But we can be harmed, or at least misled, if we fall for more serious examples of such bad reasoning. If somebody tells you that in September the teachers got a raise and in November the reading scores went down, so paying teachers more causes them to work less hard, you're justified in saying, "Wait a minute, that's a post hoc fallacy! There's no connection between the salaries and the scores."

Post hoc, ergo propter hoc is a Latin phrase that means "after this, therefore because of this." *Fallacy* simply means "a mistake in reasoning." Remember that:

> *Just because one thing happened before another doesn't mean that one thing caused the other.*

False Analogies

Sometimes, when you are puzzled by complex situations, you may try to simplify them by comparing the unknown to the known. Such comparisons can be dangerous if the differences are more important than the likenesses. A comparison can be fairly made only when the things being compared are alike in significant ways and when the differences have nothing to do with the comparison. It is probably fair to compare conditions at one college with conditions at another college if the two schools have the same kinds of students and if the schools teach the same kinds of courses in about the same way. It is probably fair to compare the results of fluoridation in two different small towns of about the same size in about the same kind of location.

But if the people who are against fluoridation go on to compare the effects of swallowing fluoride with the effects of swallowing arsenic they are using a *false analogy*. An analogy is unfair when it begins with things that are similar and then pretends that they are identical. It is true that both fluoride and arsenic (and table salt and aspirin and a good many other things we regularly put into ourselves) are deadly poisons when taken in large quantities. But it is also generally agreed that flouride in small quantities in drinking water is good for the teeth, while even very small quantities of arsenic do no one much good. The differences are more important than the likenesses.

Let's examine another common kind of comparison. When the Democrats are in power, a Democrat says, "The President is the captain of the ship of state. To criticize him now, when our need for national security is so great, is like starting a mutiny in midocean on a storm-tossed ship." But in what ways is a country's need for national security like a ship working its way across a stormy sea? (And for that matter, what, exactly, is meant by "national security," and how, exactly, is it affected when somebody criticizes the President?) The storm is caused by weather conditions; security is the result of political conditions. Does the president really have as little control over politics as a ship's captain has over the weather? And if the President *is* responsible for "national security"—whatever that means—and if it's now weakened, perhaps he deserves to be criticized. One of the things that makes many U.S. citizens feel secure is their freedom to criticize anyone they want to. Is a ship's captain elected? Is a nation of 200 million people really much like a single ship? In short, since the differences are more important than the similarities, it's unfair to say that the criticism of the administration is the same as mutiny.

Analogies, like examples, are fairly used when they make a situation more vivid or a meaning more clear. A professor who is trying to explain sound waves to a general physics class might compare sound waves to ocean waves. This analogy between something familiar and something unfamiliar is perfectly fair. It helps students form a picture in their minds of something they've never seen. It's also fair because the professor is probably saying the two wave actions are similar but not identical. No sane person would carry the analogy so far as to suppose that a very loud noise might get people salty and wet.

In deciding whether any kind of comparison is fair, you need to ask two questions:

1. Are the things being compared alike in significant ways?
2. Do the differences have anything to do with the comparison?

Inductive and Deductive Reasoning

All the thinking we do can be roughly divided into two kinds: induction and deduction. *Induction* means starting with specific things and making a generalization based on them. *Deduction* means starting with a general statement or belief and applying it to a specific thing or situation.

Usually these two processes of thought are so closely interrelated and occur so fast that we aren't aware of how our thinking works. Tommy is late coming home from school and Tommy's worried mother thinks to herself, "Something terrible has happened." Her thoughts, which she doesn't stop to analyze, go something like this: "Tommy came home on time on Monday, Tuesday, Wednesday, and Thursday"—specific events. "Therefore, Tommy always comes on time unless he's had an accident"—inductive reasoning that produces a generalization. Then Tommy's mother starts with that generalization and applies it to a specific situation—"Tommy is late today"—and arrives at a deductive conclusion—"Something terrible has happened to Tommy." When Tommy does get home an hour late (he's been watching a truck being pulled out of a ditch), his mother goes through another deductive process: "Children who worry their mothers should be punished; Tommy worried me; I won't let Tommy watch television tonight."

Tommy follows the same process. He thinks to himself, "Mothers who love their children don't punish them for silly little things like being late, but my mother is punishing me." So he yells at his mother as he sulks off to bed, "You don't love me any more!" Neither Tommy nor his mother is aware of the thinking processes they have gone through, and neither of them has stopped to question whether their generalizations are reliable.

Both inductive and deductive reasoning are valuable and necessary. We can't do without them in ordinary life, and science uses them both. Almost all the discoveries of modern science have come from inductive reasoning. Let's take an entirely imaginary situation. Suppose a man with a bad skin rash decides to dig the dandelions out of his yard. He works all afternoon, and when the last dandelion is gone, so is the skin rash. He rushes into the house to tell his wife that the dandelions have cured the rash. His wife, however, is a scientist. She is willing to guess that something in the dandelions may have helped the rash go away—scientists call this kind of guess a *hypothesis*—but she also knows that the guess must be tested, over and over again under very careful conditions. If hundreds of cases of the same kind of rash get much better when the same kind of dandelion is rubbed on them, the guess has been proved accurate, and medical science has a useful new generalization to work from: essence of the dandelion venticoma helps certain cases of rash.

Applied science, on the other hand, usually works deductively. A doctor says to herself, "Certain cases of rash are helped by rubbing them with essence of the dandelion venticoma. Eva Baldash has a hand rash. Essence of dandelion venticoma will probably help her." So the doctor writes a prescription for the essence, and if the generalization is accurate—if it has been tested often enough and carefully enough—Eva's hands will get better.

Inductive reasoning *begins with specific things and arrives at a generalization.*

Deductive reasoning *begins with a generalization and applies it to specific things.*

Honest Reasoning

To check whether inductive reasoning is being used fairly, we do the same thing the scientist did in deciding whether dandelions can cure rashes: we ask whether a lot of similar but separate events have always produced the same result. Just as a statistical survey is reliable only if the sample is large enough, so a generalization arrived at inductively is acceptable only when there are enough occurrences to support it. Because cars always stop when they run out of gasoline, you can safely accept the generalization that cars won't run without gas. But if Senator Goodsell tells you that everybody opposes the law that requires cars to be inspected before they're licensed—he's had three angry letters from motorists—you can point out that you know six people who think those inspections reduce accidents and save lives. The senator's attempt at inductive reasoning has led him to a dishonest generalization.

You are always justified in asking what's behind the generalizations other people make, and you can expect that careful readers will question the generalizations that appear in your writing. Don't use such words as *everybody, nobody, always,* and *never,* unless you can demonstrate that your generalization is really accurate. And don't make statements that can be interpreted as including everybody, even though you don't use the word. "A nurse knows what to do in an emergency" means *all* nurses in *all* emergencies. The generalization would be more acceptable if it said "most nurses" or "nearly always." If you say, "Men expect their wives to wait on them hand and foot," any reader who knows just one husband who makes the morning coffee and sews his own buttons on is likely to mistrust your whole argument, no matter how sensible the rest of it may be.

Before you accept a conclusion based on inductive reasoning, ask yourself.

1. Does the generalization claim more than the specific events can support?
2. Are there some cases where the generalization is *not* accurate?

Checking whether deductive reasoning is being used fairly also requires two steps. First, you have to decide whether the generalization is dependable, then you have to make sure that nothing has gone wrong in getting from the generalization to the conclusion. No acceptable conclusion can ever come from a generalization that's too broad. Anybody who starts with such a sweeping generalization as "Today's high-school graduates can't spell" or "Dentists are out for all they can get" might as well stop right there. Any conclusion based on such all-inclusive statements is open to suspicion.

Even if the generalization is more carefully worded, and even if most people will accept it, the conclusion may still be faulty. Reasoning that begins with "Some dentists are out for all they can get" must not end with "Mother didn't need false teeth at all—Dr. Steinmetz just wanted the four hundred bucks." Mother may or may not have needed false teeth; the dentist may or may not have given bad advice for the sake of the money. Deductions that start with "some" or "most" have to end with "maybe," "perhaps," or "probably." The conclusion can never be more definite than the generalization.

In much the same way, you must make certain that whatever you're talking about really fits the generalization. It's accurate to say that all Americans over sixty-five are eligible for Medicare; but if all you're sure about is that Polly Riley looks old and wrinkled, it isn't fair to say that she can have her hospital bills paid by the government. Unless you can show that she's over sixty-five, it's unfair to shift from "looks like" to "is"; honest reasoning requires that the conclusion say "maybe."

Another shift occurs when we try to prove that something *isn't* so because it *doesn't* fit the generalization. When Senator Goodsell says, "All Americans believe in democracy, but Olaf Betubje isn't an American; obviously he doesn't believe in democracy," he hopes you won't see the shift. The senator is pretending that *"All* Americans believe in democracy" is the same as *"Only* Americans believe in democracy."

Other kinds of shifts can lead to faulty reasoning, too. Sometimes the meaning of a word changes half way through an argument. "If this is a free country, and they tell us it is, I shouldn't have to pay to get a driver's license" may sound reasonable until you remember that "free" in "free country" means the right to say what you believe without fear of being arrested; it doesn't have anything to do with paying money.

Deductive reasoning goes on around us all the time. We use it, and so does everybody else. Before we accept the conclusions, however—either our own or those of the people who are trying to persuade us—we need to ask two questions:

1. Is the generalization reliable?
2. Has the meaning shifted between the generalization and the conclusion?

Guilt by Association

Guilt by association is another, and a very common, way that faulty deduction can trick us into unreliable conclusions. The reasoning goes like this:

All pigs have tails.
All cows have tails.
Therefore all cows are pigs.

The conclusion here is such obvious nonsense it's hardly worth discussing; but when this same kind of reasoning is applied to individuals or groups of people, what happens is not so obvious and the results can be damaging and even dangerous.

A neighbor comments casually, "Known criminals eat lunch at the Double X Cafe. The new man across the street ate lunch there today. He's probably a criminal too." Actually, Ralph Upright has only been in town a week; he simply went into the first place that sold hamburgers. But Mr. Upright will have trouble making friends if that neighbor spreads the word that there's something suspicious about his behavior.

In the United States in the fifties, when a congressional committee was looking for communists in every closet, many honest citizens lost their jobs and their reputations by this kind of faulty reasoning. The argument went like this:

> Communists attended the meeting in Anderson Hall.
> Joe Doe was seen at that meeting.
>
> Communists are in favor of public housing.
> Jenny Doe thinks public housing is a good idea.
>
> Communists write articles for *Better World* magazine.
> Jasper Doe wrote an article for *Better World* magazine.
>
> All the Does must be communists.

Guilt by association, which can involve more than one kind of faulty reasoning, is still with us.

Sometimes you hear people say, "I'll never vote for Jones. He's a Republican and they're all crooks!" It's a very clear case of guilt by association. Many aides, advisers, and appointees of Nixon's administration were indeed charged with various crimes; some were convicted and served time. Yet it is not logical to conclude that *all* Republicans are lawbreakers. When we're not emotionally involved, we know better. It is exactly the kind of reasoning that produced "Cows are the same as pigs," but this time the absurdity may be harder to see. We *know* cows are not pigs, but we're not so sure that Jones is not a crook. What we do know is that *some* Republicans were charged, tried, and found guilty—some, not all. To move from the guilt of *some* Republicans (fact) to the condemnation of *all* Republicans (feeling) is perhaps understandable in terms of emotion, but it is certainly unfair reasoning. Maybe Jones is a crook, maybe he isn't, but there are other ways of deciding. Calling him a crook just because he's a Republican is falling for two kinds of bad logic: shifting from *a few* to *all,* and labeling people according to the company they keep. Such methods are smear techniques, not honest ways of supporting opinions or reasons.

Looked at one way, guilt by association is like analogy that has been carried too far. It fastens onto the similarities but completely overlooks the differences, and it destroys, rather than increases, our chance of understanding. Comparing ocean waves to sound waves does help us understand, and we know that the notion of sound waves making anybody wet and salty is absurd. Making judgments about people because they have something in common with other people we disapprove of does not lead to understanding—but it's harder to see the absurdity.

The rule to remember here is:

> *Just because two people (or things) are alike in one way does* not *make them alike in other ways too.*

Either/Or Thinking and Other Bad Logic

It's easy to fall into the trap of supposing that if a thing is not so, its opposite must be; that if a thing is so, its opposite can't be. In many very simple situations, this either/or approach is perfectly logical. Either the basement light is on or it isn't. Either you missed the 8:30 bus or you caught it. Either you can pay the rent this month or you can't. And if you are expecting a baby, it will certainly be either a girl or a boy. But just as the causes of a complicated event are not simple, so more involved situations cannot usually be explained by saying "It must be either this or that."

Senator Goodsell says, "Whose side are you on anyway? Either you're for me or you're against me." Nonsense. Perhaps you agree with the senator that some parts of the income tax law are unfair, but you certainly don't agree that all income taxes should be abolished. "If you don't succeed in life, you're a failure"—but lots of people go happily along, neither making a fortune nor landing on skid road. "The world is divided into good guys and bad guys"—but unlike in television serials, in real life most people are "good" sometimes, "bad" sometimes, and mostly somewhere in between. "Medicine is either helpful or harmful; it can't be both"—but two aspirin tablets will cure a headache and the whole bottle will land you in either the emergency ward or the morgue. In times when war has seemed to threaten, some politicians have argued that "Unless we drop the bomb on them first, they'll drop it on us." So far, however, more reasonable people, aware of other possibilities, have prevented a world disaster.

The old saying that there are two sides to every question would be more accurate if it said *"at least* two sides." We need to be suspicious of people who say there are only two choices; those people may be confused themselves or they may be deliberately trying to trick us.

Another kind of trick, sometimes deliberate and sometimes accidental, is to argue in a circle. Such arguments begin with a belief or reason, but instead of supporting the first statement, they circle around until the original belief is used as proof of itself. "Senator Goodsell says the illegal immigration from Mexico can easily be stopped, and he's an authority on it." "How do you know he's an authority?" "He made two speeches about it." "Why did he make the speeches?" "Because he's an authority—he must know a lot about it." Sensible people will ask for more support than that.

Personal attacks are another way of arguing unfairly. Let's suppose that Senator Goodsell's opponent actually does know a good deal about the Mexicans who come across the border to work in the harvests. She spent a year with Cesar Chavez and she speaks Spanish fluently. When she asks the senator a specific question about the housing conditions of migrant workers, he responds by announcing that she was once almost expelled from college for leading a protest march against the draft. When she asks whether the senator believes farm workers should be allowed to form a union, Senator Goodsell says her husband's income tax was audited last year. Instead of discussing the conditions under which immigrant laborers live, he has made a personal attack on his opponent, hoping voters will forget about the real issue and worry about his opponent's personal life instead. In the same way that arguing in circles makes people forget that nothing was proved, *name-calling* makes people forget what the actual problem is. Both methods of avoiding honest argument are illogical and unfair.

Remember that honest persuasion depends on supported reasons. Watch out for attempts at persuasion that depend on:

1. insisting there are only two choices
2. using a statement as proof of itself
3. calling the other side names instead of sticking to the point

Suspicion, Stampeding, and Sense

In this chapter we've talked about several common errors in reasoning, and although the discussion certainly isn't complete, it does provide some important ways of distinguishing honest from dishonest support. It should help you to be critical of what you read as well as of what you write. But don't suppose that because there are so many ways to cheat, everybody who tries to persuade you is cheating. Lots of examples are lively and useful. Lots of surveys are carefully made and fairly reported. Many authorities are trustworthy. Many predictions, even the gloomiest ones, come true.

Nobody but a fool believes everything, and the person who doubts everything is only a little less foolish. You don't want to be railroaded into believing something, but neither do you want bitter suspicion to keep you from believing anything. Asking for reasons and examining those reasons may not always make you comfortable, but it's a sight better than being either a sucker or a skeptic. Although reason can be misused, it's important to remember that the human ability to reason soundly is the thing that brought us out of the trees and into a rocket ship. Sound reasoning may be the only thing that can keep us from blowing both ourselves and the trees back to the amoeba stage.

Key Words

Here are some of the important terms used in this chapter. See whether you can answer these questions about them.

1. Explain the difference between responding **emotionally** to arguments and reacting **rationally** to them.
2. What do we mean by **slanted words?** How can you tell whether vivid words are being used fairly or unfairly?
3. What are **glittering generalities?** How can you avoid being taken in by them?

4. What are **inferences?** How are they different from **facts** and **judgments?**
5. What two purposes can **honest examples** serve? How can you tell whether examples are honest or dishonest?
6. What four questions should you ask to decide whether or not **statistics** are reliable?
7. What three questions can you ask to decide whether or not **authority** is used honestly? How can you tell when authority is being misused?
8. What kind of **predictions** is likely to be reliable? What kind is unsafe?
9. What does **post hoc thinking** mean? What is a **fallacy?** What can you do to avoid being taken in by post hoc fallacies?
10. What is meant by **false analogy?** What two questions could you ask in deciding whether two things have been fairly **compared?**
11. What is the difference between **inductive** and **deductive thinking?**
12. How can you tell whether the results of **inductive reasoning** are **dependable?** How can you tell whether a conclusion reached by **deductive reasoning** is **acceptable?**
13. What is **guilt by association?** How can it be recognized and avoided?
14. What is an **either/or argument?** How can you recognize a **circular argument?** What's the matter with **name-calling?**

READINGS
Fair Persuasion

Six Advertisements

1. BROWN AND ROOT

Brown&Root may have designed and built the mill where this paper was made, the rail line that brought it to the printer, the highway that carried it across town, the chemical plant that made the ink to print it, the power plant generating the light you are reading it by, and the refineries and pipelines which produced and transported the fuel for all these projects.

We're proud of our work.

And we're even prouder of our people. More than 65,000 of them, serving progress the world over.

The Texas Aggie, December 1979.

2. ALMADÉN

Sunset Magazine, April 1980.

3. DEBEERS

Family Circle, November 1979.

4. DOW CHEMICAL

"Losing a parking lot is a small price to pay– to give these skimmers right-of-way."

Margaret Siemens, Environmental Manager, Oyster Creek Division, Dow Chemical U.S.A.

Every spring since 1968, a flock of black skimmer waterbirds takes over a parking lot inside Dow's giant chemical complex at Freeport, Texas.

"The skimmers lend credibility to our environmental efforts," Margaret says. "When civilization pushed them out of their coastal nesting areas, they sort of 'requisitioned' our oyster-shell parking lot. So we fenced it off and every year now, hundreds of them come back to nest and hatch their young.

"We're always happy to see the skimmers return to Freeport. They remind us that a clean environment is something we owe to people—wherever we operate.

"To me, it's a matter of caring for your products and knowing the people you work with care, too, whether we're monitoring for air quality, taking stream samples for analysis, or working out the environmental impact of a new plant.

"It's a lot of responsibility and the work keeps me busy, but I enjoy it and I enjoy being part of the Dow community in Texas.

"I guess these skimmers do, too. It kind of pleases me they picked us for a neighbor."

DOW
*common/uncommon
sense/chemistry*

NOTICE
BABY SKIMMERS
HAVE
THE
RIGHT OF WAY

*Trademark of The Dow Chemical Company

Texas Monthly, March 1980.

5. PIONEER

PIONEER ANNOUNCES ANOTHER FIRST IN HIGH FIDELITY.

[1]   If you want great high fidelity components, but don't want to pay a high price for them, Pioneer's latest breakthrough will be music to your ears.

[2]   This time it's not a technical breakthrough, but an economical one. It's Pioneer's National Truckload Sale.

[3]   During this sale, Pioneer's reducing prices to their dealers so that they can pass these savings on to you.

[4]   For one month only, Pioneer trucks will arrive at participating dealers, direct from our warehouse, loaded with today's most popular high fidelity equipment, at prices that are guaranteed to be equally as popular.

[5]   Every receiver has been specially priced. Including the industry's most popular receiver, the SX-780. Every turntable. Including Pioneer's new Quartz line.

[6]   Pioneer's National Truckload Sale also covers Pioneer's best selling line of cassette decks. Pioneer speakers. Component ensembles. Headphones. And more.

[7]   Pioneer's National Truckload Sale is being held at every Pioneer dealer that displays the Pioneer Truckload Sale wall poster or banner in their window.

[8]   So if you've been waiting for the chance to buy high fidelity components at just the right price, your truck's come in.

[9]   Come to Pioneer's incredible National Truckload Sale. It's another first from Pioneer that's second to none.

◎ PIONEER®
We bring it back alive.

©1980 U.S. Pioneer
Electronics Corp.,
85 Oxford Drive,
Moonachie, N.J. 07074.

Time, April 14, 1980.

6. MOBIL

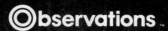

A fable for now. One morning an Elephant strolling to the water hole suddenly found the path blocked by a huge pile of sticks, vines, and brambles. "Hello?" she called out. "What gives?"

Monkey seethes. "Buzz off, snake-snoot," shouted a Monkey from the barricade. "It's an outrage to little folk how much you take in, so the rest of us animals have seized the water hole and food. You're gross, and we're revolting." "What's eating you?" the Elephant asked. "You're the one eating too much," the Monkey declared, "but we're going to change that. No more obscene profiteering at the feed trough. Strict rations for you, fat friend!"

Who can live on peanuts? The Elephant's heart pounded, yet between the ears she was quite unflappable. "Though it may seem that I consume a great deal," she said calmly, "it's no more than my share. Because I am large—not fat—it just takes more to keep me going. How can I work hard if you won't let me have the proper nourishment?" The Monkey sneered. "Knock off that mumbo-jumbo, Dumbo," he said. "You already net more than a million Spiders. You take in more than a thousand Pack Rats. You profit more from the jungle's abundance than a hundred Monkeys."

"Small is beautiful, Raja? Which monkey told you that?"

Swift dam. "But I also can do more," the Elephant said. "I can haul tree trunks too heavy for other creatures. I can clear paths to new food and water. I am full of energy. Why, I even give rides to the little ones. *If* I have enough to keep me going." No one listened, and the Elephant grew hungry and thirsty. But so did the other animals, for their barricade had become a solid dam blocking the stream to the water hole. "Crisis, crisis!" the animals cried.

Ms. Understanding. "Thank goodness I still have some energy left," the Elephant said, pushing earth and pulling plants until the water hole again began to fill. "You see," she said, "you need a big beast for a big job, and a big beast has big needs. Not just to stay healthy, but to put a bit aside for tomorrow. And maybe to have a bit extra for working especially hard, or for sharing with have-not animals." Nobody acknowledged her undamming with even faint praise, yet all resumed drinking thirstily. That tickled her old ivories, for all she really wanted was to go on doing her usual work without any new wrinkles. No need for hurt feelings. After all, who ever heard of a thin-skinned Elephant?

Moral: Meeting America's energy needs is a big job requiring big companies. But if a big company can't earn a profit adequate for its size, it won't be able to meet that need.

Parade Magazine, March 2, 1980.

Responses

1. What do Brown & Root, Inc., do? How do you know? What are they trying to sell in this advertisement? How can you tell? How do you define "progress"? How do Brown & Root expect you to define it?

2. In the Almadén advertisement, what emotions are being appealed to? What is the connection between the question, the picture, and the paragraph at the bottom of the page?

3. Why is the DeBeers diamond called "an eternity ring"? What association are readers expected to make between the name of the ring and the length of a marriage? What is the difference in the way the man looks at life? If you aren't sure what the difference is, why is that comment included? What is the general belief about diamonds that seems to back up what this ad says?

4. Why is it important for Dow Chemical Company to show that it is concerned about the environment? What is the connection between fencing off a bird colony's nesting ground and the production of napalm, manufactured by Dow and used during the Vietnam War?

5. What emotional words are used in Pioneer's advertisement? What other devices are used in this ad? Rewrite the information in paragraphs 5 and 6 in the form of a complete sentence for each paragraph. How does the effect change?

6. What are the similarities between an elephant and the Mobil Oil Corporation? What are the differences? By making one of the speakers in the fable a monkey, what is being said about the people who favor the windfall profits tax on oil companies?

7. What actual information about the product sold by the company does each of these advertisements provide? For each advertisement, write a sentence or a paragraph giving only the factual information presented in the ad. Be sure not to include any emotional appeals or emotional language.

Seven Letters

CURB PROGRAM

To the Editor:

[1]   School District 12 is considering a breakfast program for its schools. The more affluent will freely use the service as they do the lunch program. The poorer families can't always afford the lunches.

[2]   The breakfast program is not necessary for this district. We are not a depressed area.

Printed in the *Sunday Oregonian,* April 27, 1980.

[3]   Some parents now believe education and lunch are entirely the school's business. We have learned that education is more difficult for a child without parental interest and cooperation. More food programs won't aid education.

[4]   We must allow parents to rear and teach their own children the values important to that family and not so often assume we know what is best for each child. The school and teachers continue to assume parental responsibilities and are undermining parental confidence and children's trust in their parents' judgment.

[5]   School District 12 must concentrate on improving basic education. This is a serious undertaking and takes dedication. It must not branch out further into the food business.

Elizabeth Berck
4122 S.E. View Acres Road
Milwaukie

Responses

1. What contradiction is there between the statements made in paragraphs 1 and 2 of this letter? Does the letter contain any circular reasoning? If so, what is it?
2. Which of these general beliefs is behind the argument in paragraphs 3 and 4?
    > A good diet has nothing to do with the ability to learn.
    > Parents whose children eat lunch at school are not interested in their children.
    > Feeding their children at home is the parents' responsibility.
    > Eating lunch is an important part of a value system.
    > Children who eat lunch at school do not trust their parents' judgment.

    Refer to the letter in supporting what you decide.
3. Does "food business" imply that the school is making a profit? Will the teachers themselves provide or prepare the breakfasts or lunches? How does a school that provides a lunch service lose its "dedication" to education? Is this an example of either/or reasoning? Why or why not?
4. Write to the editor, responding to this letter and pointing out the flaws you see in the argument.

SEPARATE CHURCH AND STATE

To the Editor:

[1]   The intention of our forefathers, when they provided for the separation of church and state, has been distorted by the ridiculous regulations now being enforced. They never intended that American schools become godless, atheistic institutions where every reference to the Christian faith that has made our country

great is outlawed and condemned. If they had intended that, they would never have included the words "under God" in the salute to the flag.

[2]   Now they are maintaining that we cannot even sing carols at Christmas or give plays showing the birth of Christ. Next they will be saying that courses in world history cannot mention Martin Luther—after all, he was a good Protestant and that makes any reference to him against the new regulations.

[3]   Either we insist that prayer and Christianity be returned to our classrooms or we will produce a whole generation that knows nothing about the true religion and the morality it teaches. Unless we allow school programs celebrating the Nativity, we will have thousands of young adults believing that sacred holiday was created by a fat man in a red suit with a pack of expensive toys on his back. Refusing to tell children the true meaning of Christmas is like refusing to teach them multiplication tables or telling them that touching toads causes warts.

[4]   To show how bad the situation is: Last year they made the fourth grade teacher at King School stop saying the Lord's Prayer at the beginning of the day. By the end of May there had been five instances of stolen lunch money in that room alone.

[5]   The judge who made that decision for our state has a cousin in the state penitentiary, and the president of the school board has a son who is a Zen Buddhist. What can we expect when we let such irresponsible people make the decisions that will affect our children for the rest of their lives?

Rev. Arnold Breist
Chairman of the Amalgamated Christian
Protestant League

Responses

1. How accurate is the last sentence of paragraph 1? Who wrote the flag salute? When was the phrase "under God" added?
2. Who is "they" in paragraph 1? Who is "they" in paragraph 2?
3. Which kinds of unfair persuasion are used in this letter:
       glittering generalities
       misused statistics
       misused examples
       misuse of authority
       misused predictions
       unfair comparison
       post hoc thinking
       guilt by association
       either/or thinking
       name-calling
   Be ready to show where each kind of unfair persuasion occurs.

4. If you are in favor of prayer in the schools, write a letter to the editor supporting your position but avoiding the unfair persuasion used in this letter. If you are against it, write to the editor giving acceptable reasons for your opposition.

AN APPEAL TO YOUR HEART . . . AND YOUR REASON

Dear Friend:

[1] Tomorrow is election day, and Alderman Ralph Axelrod comes before you with an appeal as timeless and meaningful as those issued by Jewish leaders of the past.

[2] "I need your help," he says.

[3] *He needs your help* . . . an appeal that goes to the heart of Jewish tradition . . . and as a Rabbi I say to you: Do not forsake Ralph Axelrod.

[4] He has served you well for many years with good programs shaped by action, compassion, and kindness.

[5] Do not forsake him now that he calls out to you for help.

[6] Keep competent Jewish leadership in the City Council.

[7] Vote for Ralph Axelrod.

[8] The polls are open Tuesday, March 18, from 6 a.m. to 7 p.m. PULL LEVER 60B FOR RALPH AXELROD.

[9] I appeal to your heart . . . and your reason.

> Rabbi Oscar Lifshutz
> 5029 North Kenmore Avenue
> Chicago

Responses

1. What appeals to emotion are made in this letter? What appeals to reason are made?

2. What factual information is given? What are the examples of compassion and kindness?

3. What words with religious overtones can you find in the letter? Why did the writer use this language?

4. Is your attitude toward this appeal changed by knowing that the opposing candidate was also Jewish? Why or why not?

5. Why, do you think, are the paragraphs in this letter so short? What would be the effect of combining them?

6. Write a letter supporting some candidate for local office (imaginary if you like) in which you give factual information and avoid slanted language.

WINDFALL TAX A RIPOFF

To the Editor:

[1]   I would like to express my opinion on a recent article entitled, "Use windfall tax for elderly, poor, Americans say."

[2]   While I am well aware that our poor and underprivileged are in dire need of financial assistance and rightly deserving, I nonetheless feel that the windfall tax is just another government rip-off.

[3]   I fully realize that these oil companies are reaping huge profits while we sit, frustrated, in long gas lines. But does that give our government the right, under the ruse of a windfall tax, to confiscate funds from private industries?

[4]   I think not. Something must be done, of course, but government intervention is not the answer.

[5]   If the government is suddenly so amicable and willing to give financial aid, then surely, the people of America are more deserving of our funds and sympathy than the hordes of Vietnamese boat people coming into our country at a steady, staggering rate.

[6]   Where, and what, are our priorities? If we want to play the good Samaritan, then why not start at home, with our own? Exactly how much money is being doled out for the search and rescue of these foreigners? Could not the money be put to a needy use here, at home?

[7]   And where will the government stop? Admittedly, the windfall tax appears lucrative and just punishment for the long lines and outrageous prices we are plagued with. But allowing the government free rein to plunder non-government profits is a deadly mistake.

[8]   Take heed America. Unwisely we have condoned this sham. Uncle Sam's appetite has been appeased for now, but, all too soon he will rear his ugly head again. And whose profits willl he devour then?

Kathleen Boehm
Vancouver

Responses

1. Find less slanted substitutes for "reaping," "ruse" and "confiscate" (paragraph 3) "staggering" (paragraph 5); "doled out" (paragraph 6); "plunder" (paragraph 7); "sham" and "devour" (paragraph 8). What is the difference in effect when these words are changed?
2. What is the relationship between a windfall tax on excess oil profits and the refugees from Vietnam?
3. Paragraph 4 says something must be done. About what? By whom? And why does the writer say "of course"?
4. What are non-government profits? The wages of people who work in factories or grocery stores? The earnings of lawyers and doctors? The profits

made by people who operate restaurants or shoe repair shops? What kind of profits does the writer of this letter believe should be taxed?

5. Does an appetite have a head? What is wrong with the metaphor in paragraph 8?
6. How sound is the the prediction the writer makes in the last paragraph?
7. Work out the plan that was apparently followed in writing this letter; begin by writing a main idea sentence.

CONSTITUTIONAL CHANGES

To the Editor:

[1]   When President Reagan swore to uphold the constitution, he meant any constitution, not just the one that has been misused and abused by self-seeking politicians for the last fifty years. All of us need to work for a constitutional convention so we can get control of the country back from the government. Our great Founding Fathers never thought of the way present-day politicians would be serving themselves at the expense of the public.

[2]   And they couldn't have believed that an activist Supreme Court, made up of doddering old men, would care more about making themselves famous than about interpreting the Constitution.

[3]   Why do you suppose Congressmen are so afraid of a constitutional convention that would force the government to balance the budget? It seems clear that a balanced budget would give them less money to buy votes.

[4]   Besides, they know that the public is fed up with inflation, unfair taxes, interfering regulations, a Supreme Court that makes laws instead of interpreting them, a many-tentacled bureaucracy we don't need, a justice system that protects criminals instead of honest citizens.

[5]   The total mess this country finds itself in is caused by all branches of government, and they won't do anything to clean up that mess unless we make them do it.

Ronald Arthur Smith
Marin County

Responses

1. What support is given for the generalization in the last sentence of paragraph 1? For the generalization in paragraph 2? For the series of generalizations in paragraph 4?
2. What is meant by "an activist Supreme Court" (paragraph 2)? What would an inactive court do? Who is supposed to challenge the decisions of the Supreme Court?
3. What is the mess referred to in the last paragraph? Who is "they" in the last half of the last sentence?

4. Rewrite this letter, including only factual information—statements that can be checked. How long is the rewritten letter? Compare your version with those written by other students.

NURSING HOME CARE

The following two letters appeared in the same newspaper on the same day:
To the Editor:

[1]   I was appalled to watch the so-called "exposé" of nursing homes on KSL-TV recently. It is frightening to me that this obviously biased and slanted program was aired for so many people to watch and take as "gospel."

[2]   I previously believed such a "hate" force could only exist under Hitler or Stalin—not in the United States. It's too bad the nursing home industry doesn't have the money to finance an hour-long rebuttal program of prime time TV.

[3]   My grandfather has lived in one of those so-called "pits" for nearly eight years, and in all of those years of my visiting with him, I have only experienced love and concern for him from all involved there. I would just like to encourage people to visit nursing homes and compare, and then decide for themselves the truth and not believe what others decide is the best for us all.

[4]   Thank heavens for people like Mr. McPhie who truly love their fellowmen enough to want to care for them when it is difficult to do so.

Carma Hamilton
Toledo

To the Editors:

[1]   Having read with interest the different articles appearing in the papers and on TV regarding the treatment of patients in nursing homes, it has prompted me to relate my own personal experience.

[2]   My husband was afflicted with severe rheumatoid arthritis. He had entered the hospital on Sept. 11 for a knee replacement. While there, other problems had surfaced which caused him extreme pain and discomfort.

[3]   Because of his long stay in the hospital and the expense involved, it was decided to place him in a rest home where the needed therapy would be available. He was moved to a nursing home on Nov. 10.

[4]   On Tuesday, his third day there, he was tied in a chair and left for 2½ hours. His bottom was burned and raw because of the problems that had developed in the hospital. He begged to be put back into bed and struggled to get out of the chair.

[5]   I was helpless. I had asked for help but was completely ignored and informed that it was for his own good. Finally I was able to find a nurse to help get him into bed. He had been sitting in a mess for some time, which had added to his discomfort.

[6]   After getting him into bed, there weren't any blankets on his bed. The nurse left, promising to get some and be right back. She never came back and I used his

Deseret News, March 12, 1980.

robe, sweater and sheepskin trying to get him warm as he was chilling. Needless to say, I had called his doctor but was unable to reach him at that time. I went home determined to have him removed as soon as possible.

[7]   Wednesday when I arrived I realized there was something very seriously wrong with my husband. Someone had attempted to feed him some breakfast but he had never swallowed it. I tried calling the doctor but was unable to talk to him at that time.

[8]   A nurse came in the room and started to reprimand me for coming before visiting hours. I looked at my watch, it was 11:30 a.m. She left. Immediately two other people entered the room, a husky male and a nurse's aide. They said they had come to give my husband a shower.

[9]   I begged them not to move him but to give him a bed bath. My request was ignored and I was informed that it was state law that every medicine patient had to have a shower every day. He was lifted by the man into the wheelchair, wheeled into the shower dragging his feet on the way. Within seconds he was brought back, placed in bed, and I was told that the doctor was on the phone.

[10]   My husband was unconscious and had been for sometime, even when someone had tried to stuff food in his mouth earlier. He was moved by ambulance to University Hospital, where he died early Thursday morning, never regaining consciousness. At the time of his death, the backs of his legs were black and blue where he had struggled to get out of the chair.

[11]   The memory that I have of the cruel treatment my husband was subjected to has been the hardest thing I have had to cope with since his death.

Alice Hepworth
Salt Lake City

Responses

1. Which of these two letters gives an example creating a clear picture of what happened in the nursing home? Explain your choice by referring to the letters.
2. Which of these seems typical? Why?
3. Which of these letters contains more name-calling? Refer to the letters to back up your answer.
4. Write a persuasive paper either maintaining that most nursing homes for the elderly are well run or arguing that they should be more frequently and carefully inspected. Give reasons for what you say, and make sure that the reasons are fairly supported. (You may have to consult the library for accurate information.)

New Sexual Guidelines*

[1]   We're hearing more about sexual harassment on the job, a detestable practice to be sure, but one that's probably been around since the first Pharaoh hired a shapely secretary to chisel hieroglyphics.

[2]   Every man or woman probably has a pretty good idea of what constitutes sexual harassment in their respective individual cases. The trouble comes in trying to codify all the possible overtures and innuendos that conceivably could be interpreted as a sexual advance.

[3]   But that is what the U.S. Equal Employment Opportunity Commission is up to these days. In a development that bodes nothing but headaches for management, the EEOC has proposed guidelines to spell out just how certain behavior on the job might run afoul of the federal sex-bias laws.

[4]   Obviously, any offer of hiring or advancement conditioned on sexual favors is a no-no that could subject not only the individual but the company to federal punitive action. But what about the hypersensitive soul who reads something sexual into every bit of social interaction with fellow workers?

[5]   With EEOC bureaucrats on the job, any executive had better think twice before uttering some innocent compliment like, "Say, that's a nice looking outfit you have on this morning." Could be sexual harassment, according to the feds.

Responses

1. What argument is implied in paragraph 1? How satisfactory is it? Why?
2. What effect does the writer get by using such phrases as "up to," "a no-no," and "the feds"?
3. Paragraph 2 says the trouble comes in trying to codify; paragraph 3 says the EEOC "has proposed guidelines to spell out . . . ." What, according to this writer, is the "trouble" with the EEOC guidelines? How do you know?
4. Is the example given in paragraph 5 fair? Why or why not?
5. Write your own definition of sexual harassment, giving at least two examples of such harassment and one example showing what it is not.

When You Say Whiskey†

[1]   If when you say whiskey you mean the devil's brew, the poison scourge, the bloody monster, that defiles innocence, dethrones reason, destroys the home, creates misery and poverty, yea, literally takes the bread from the mouths of little

---

*Editorial in the *Sunday Oklahoman,* March 10, 1980.

†Kenneth Vinson, "Prohibition's Last Stand," *New Republic,* October 16, 1965.

children; if you mean the evil drink that topples the Christian man and woman from the pinnacle of righteous, gracious living into the bottomless pit of degradation and despair, and shame, and helplessness, and hopelessness, then certainly I am against it.

[2] But if when you say whiskey you mean the oil of conversation, the philosophic wine, the ale that puts a song in their hearts and laughter on their lips, and the warm glow of contentment in their eyes; if you mean Christmas cheer; if you mean the stimulating drink that puts the spring into the old gentleman's step on a frosty, crispy morning; if you mean the drink which enables a man to magnify his joy, and his happiness, and to forget, if only for a little while, life's great tragedies, and heartaches, and sorrows; if you mean that drink, the sale of which pours into our treasuries untold millions of dollars, which are used to provide tender care for our little crippled children, our blind, our deaf, our dumb, our pitiful aged and infirm; to build highways and hospitals and schools, then certainly I am for it.

[3] This is my stand, I will not retreat from it. I will not compromise.

Responses

1. This brief article makes fun of sweeping generalizations and slanted language; it's amusing to have the writer be "certainly for" and "certainly against" the same thing. Do you find paragraph 1 and paragraph 2 equally convincing? Why or why not?

2. What issues are currently dividing your friends, your campus, or your community into two strongly opposed camps? Write your own two-paragraph "stand" in which you round up exaggerated claims and blames in order to "clarify" the issue.

3. Write three descriptions of the same object. First, describe the object so that it seems desirable; next, describe it so that it seems as unattractive as possible; finally, describe it as objectively as you can, leaving out all opinion words.

In Their Own Best Interests: A Fable for Parents

[1] On April 21, 1978, Steven Jones filed a custody suit in New York County Supreme Court. In his petition, Mr. Jones asked for custody of his two parents, Martin, forty, and Gail, thirty-five. He stated that he wished them to reside with him and his younger sister, Eileen, on a full-time basis at 680 East 51 Street in New York City. The basis of his suit, Jones explained, is that the emotional climate created by "split" parents is an unhealthy one for children. As evidence, he cited his own and his sister's unhappiness, his failing grades in mathematics and French,

Suzanne Ramos, *The Complete Book of Child Custody* (New York: Putnam, 1979).

his sister's temper tantrums, "which she has at least twice a day," and the fact that he bites his fingernails.

[2]   Jones, who is ten years old, is being represented by Marcia Barrett, a well-known attorney in the field of children's rights. "Where did you get the money to retain Ms. Barrett?" Jones was asked by one of the group of reporters who had gathered around him and his lawyer outside the courthouse.

[3]   "Fortunately, I've saved all my birthday, Christmas, Easter and Valentine's gifts from my grandparents," he replied. "Children should always have some money of their own for a legal retainer because lawyers don't like to take on a case and wait to see if the judge will make the parents pay the bill. We, as children, have to become more aware of how we can protect our interests."

[4]   "You have your own attorney. Do you favor your parents having their own legal counsel?" asked a journalist from the *Times*.

[5]   "I don't think that will be necessary," he answered. "We have their best interests at heart."

[6]   "If you do win this case, Mr. Jones," another reporter asked, "will you permit visiting privileges for your mother's boyfriend and your father's second wife?"

[7]   "I'll give that careful thought," he said, "but, according to the psychiatric consultation I had, that would be giving them a double message and would probably be very confusing to them."

[8]   "Have you consulted your parents as to their wishes on this?" he was asked.

[9]   "My sister and I have talked to them, but we feel we can't put too much stock in any living arrangement they request. Last year they wanted to live together. Then they wanted to live by themselves. Now they want to live with other people. Who knows what they'll want next year? In this case, we'll have to decide what's best for them."

[10]   "Suppose your parents aren't happy together? Suppose they have problems adjusting?"

[11]   "We'll get professional help. Eileen and I feel that it's important for them to work through their feelings and to talk about any anger they are experiencing. And we'll give them a lot of love. After that," Jones continued, "I feel that if my sister and I set clear limits from the start, they will learn to cope with each other."

[12]   "After all," he went on, "we feel that's part of being a parent."

Responses

1. Are readers expected to believe that Steven Jones hired a lawyer and filed a suit in the New York County Supreme Court? If not, why did Ramos write this article?

2. Make a list of what Ramos thinks is wrong with the way child custody cases are normally handled. Compare your list with the lists other students have written.

3. Is this method of persuasion more or less effective than a straightforward argument? Why?

4. Using the list you made for the second response, write a straightforward persuasion paper urging that changes be made in the way child custody cases are dealt with.

5. Try writing a fable that indirectly presents your attitude toward some problem or situation. Use either Ramos' article or the Mobil advertisement (page 77) as a model for what you might do.

More Suggestions for Writing

Conduct a survey among students in your class on any subject that most people are currently interested in. Prepare four or five questions, and make sure you always ask them in the same order. Compile the results of the survey and report them in a short paper.

Write three or four detailed examples that illustrate some condition you think should be changed. Read only the examples to the other students in the class, and see whether they can tell what condition you are describing and what your attitude toward it is.

Pick out some law or local regulation that makes you angry; find, in the library, some qualified authority that supports your point of view; then write a short paper using that authority as support for your position.

Find an editorial or letter in your local paper that you think uses slanted language, name-calling, or guilt by association; write a paper quoting these flaws in reasoning, and explain what is wrong with them.

Write two accounts of the same event, slanting one account so that readers will be sympathetic and slanting the other so that readers will be unsympathetic. Don't change any of the actual details of what happened in either version.

Write an advertisement for a perfume, a soft drink, or a fast food store; then write an objective description of whatever the ad has been trying to promote.

Write to the editor of your local paper, protesting something that is going on in the community.

Chapter 11

Summarizing and Reviewing

Imagine how little we'd know about the world if people couldn't summarize. Before you went in to vote, for instance, you'd have to listen to every politician's speech in full, or read every word of it. If you were conscientious, you could spend hours going through the same old declarations about the nation's best interests, the same protestations of integrity and efficiency, the same background information you're already familiar with. Because summaries exist, however, you can just switch on the television or scan the headlines to discover that Representative Angela Murphy has made a long speech in favor of a new mass transit system. It may have taken her an hour or more to give all her reasons, but it takes the announcer only ten seconds, or the headline writer only five words, to tell you what the main point was. Both the television announcer and headline writer have given a summary. News programs and newspaper reports, too, are composed mainly of summaries. Even if you read beyond the headlines, the news article on Murphy's talk will probably not include more than a fraction of what she said; instead, the writer will merely summarize the most important points.

Not only news reporters make summaries. Much of our conversation with family and friends is summarizing. A mother asks, "What did you do in school today?" and the child answers, "Dissected a frog," leaving all the gory details to the mother's imagination. A friend asks you about Saturday night's show, and you answer: "Two people from outer space tried to take over a radio station, but they were killed in the end."

Such summaries are much like condensed reports; they give just the main facts. If the child who dissected the frog goes on to say, "It was icky. I hated it," the mother is being given more than a summary. She's being told what the child thought about the lesson. And if you go on to say, "The movie was terrible—the acting was clumsy, the plot was unconvincing, and the ending too abrupt," you're giving more than a quick *summary;* you're offering a quick *review* of the film. In casual conversations, we don't worry much about separating our summaries from our reviews. The mother may be more interested in the child's reaction to dissecting a frog (review) than in the science lesson itself (summary). Your friend may be trying to decide whether a particular movie is worth the admission price. The question, "Was it any good?" may sometimes be more important than the question, "What was it about?"

Throughout your life you have been making this kind of simple summary, and often you have commented on your summary as you went along. You have listened to other people talk, and, if you got the point of what they were saying, you could, without too much strain, tell somebody else what had been said. As you were telling them, you shortened the original a lot or a little, repeating what seemed to you to be the highlights of the discussion. Sometimes you added your own comments, sometimes you didn't. Such summarizing is simple and easy, and adding your own opinions is natural. For ordinary situations this system works very well, but you're bound to encounter other situations in college or on the job where your summaries must be more precise and more complete. Furthermore, your summary—a condensed version of the original—must be carefully separated from your review—what you think about it. Because summaries and reviews each serve a different purpose, it's important to understand the differences between them and to practice each skill separately.

> *A summary shortens what somebody else has said or written.*
> *A review includes comments about the original.*

Taking Notes for a Summary

One use for making a summary is to acquire new information; another is to make sure that you understand the new material. Summarizing can help you in studying, and summarizing well can make the difference between a satisfactory answer to a test question and a rambling, unsuccessful response. Good summaries, in other words, can also convince other people that you understand the material you are summarizing.

Suppose the subject of boll weevils has come up in your ecology class, and nobody seems to know much about them. You're asked to find out about them and then to share your information with the class the next day. Nobody will be much helped if all you can say is, "Boll weevils are bugs that are bad for cotton." The first step is to visit the library, find the information, and prepare a summary. Here is what one encyclopedia says:

> **Boll Weevil** is a small beetle that feeds inside the *bolls* (seed pods) of cotton plants. Native to Mexico, it crossed into Texas about 1890. Since then, it has spread into most cotton-growing areas of the United States. This insect causes damage to U.S. cotton crops of $200 million or more each year.
>
> Brownish to black in color, the boll weevil is about ¼ inch (6 millimeters) long. It is one of a group called *snout beetles,* because of the long beaks or snouts

with which they feed. The boll weevil's snout is about half as long as the rest of its body.

In winter, adult boll weevils hide in trash in or near cotton fields. When buds appear on the cotton plants in spring, female boll weevils open them with their snouts. They lay eggs inside the buds, and the eggs soon hatch into wormlike grubs. The grubs feed inside the buds, usually causing them to fall off the plant. Continuing to feed, the grubs become adult boll weevils in about 2½ or 3 weeks. They then eat their way out of the buds and attack other buds. Later in the season, they attack the bolls, where the females deposit more eggs. Several generations of boll weevils may be produced in a single season. Many insecticides are used to control boll weevils. Large fields are often sprayed with insecticides from airplanes.

The coming of the boll weevil to the United States caused great damage to cotton crops, yet it produced some good results, too. It forced many farmers to plant other crops, and to use some of their lands for raising cattle, hogs, and chickens. Many are now more prosperous than when they raised only cotton.[1]

Although this explanation of boll weevils is clear and simple enough, you probably will not be able to remember the details unless you take some brief notes.

If your notes are complete, they should begin with the *purpose* of the article: "explanation of boll weevil." They should include the main idea: "boll weevil is a beetle that does great damage to cotton crops." They should include the main subdivisions: where the boll weevil comes from, what it looks like, how it destroys cotton, how it is controlled, and how it has changed farming. Since the most important thing is how it destroys cotton, the notes on this part should be the most detailed. They might look something like this:

Purpose: explanation of boll weevil

Main idea: a beetle that does great damage to cotton crops

Subdivisions:
Came from Mexico around 1890
$200 million damage annually in U.S.
Brownish or black, ¼ inch long—beak or snout ½ length of body
Female lays eggs first in buds, then in bolls later in season
Eggs hatch into grubs which feed on plants
Grubs mature in 2½–3 weeks, several generations per season
Controlled by insecticides sprayed from airplanes
Good result: forced farmers to vary crops

Notice that these notes follow the order and keep about the same proportion as the original material. Following the same order makes for clarity, and keeping the same proportion helps you give the same emphasis to each point as the original does. The notes, as given above, leave out only one thing that should be included, information telling where the material came from. Here, too, it is necessary to be

[1] "Boll Weevil," *The World Book Encyclopedia* (Chicago, 1976), p. 358. From *The World Book Encyclopedia.* © 1976 Field Enterprises Educational Corporation.

complete and accurate. Copy the author's name, the book title, the place of publication, the publisher, the date, and the pages you read (*The World Book Encyclopedia,* 1976, page 358). Since the piece on boll weevils came from an encyclopedia article, no author and no separate publisher is given but, when your material does give an author's name or a publisher different from the name of the book, you must give it, too.

Good notes for a summary should always include:

1. the purpose of the original writing
2. the main idea
3. the main subdivisions
4. the source of the material

Putting Notes into a Paragraph

If you have taken your notes carefully, you will be ready to share your information with the class. If you want to use your notes as you talk, fine; if you don't, just having written them down will help you remember the important points in the right order. Perhaps you will be asked to write out the information. Here is a written summary based on the notes shown earlier.

> The boll weevil is a type of beetle that does great damage to cotton. It came to the United States from Mexico around 1890 and now destroys $200 million worth of cotton annually. It is brownish or black in color, about one-quarter inch long, with a long snout or beak that the female boll weevil uses to open the cotton buds. She lays her eggs first in the buds and then, later in the season, in the bolls (or seed pods) of the plants. The eggs hatch into grubs, which feed on the plant and within two or three weeks grow into adult boll weevils. Thus, several generations are produced each season. The boll weevil can be controlled by insecticides sprayed from airplanes. Its one advantage is that it has forced farmers to raise a greater variety of crops. (This information was taken from *The World Book Encyclopedia,* 1976, p. 358.)

This summary differs from the encyclopedia article in two important ways. It's less than half as long, and it uses the writer's own words, not those of the *World Book.* The summary is shorter because it leaves out some of the information. It omits the kind of livestock the farmers raised after the boll weevils had damaged the cotton, and it shortens the explanation of how the grubs eat. These details are interesting, but they are not really necessary for the summary. Notice, too, that although the last sentence ("Its one advantage . . .") looks like the writer's own comment, it is actually based on the judgment expressed in the final paragraph of the original article. Even though the person who wrote this summary is violently opposed to insecticide spraying, that personal disapproval doesn't appear in the written summary. Instead, it's saved for the class discussion, where the writer is encouraged to express an opinion about the indiscriminate use of poisonous chemicals.

The process used to write this summary will work for any summary, although it may need to be changed a little depending on the purpose of the material you are summarizing.

When you turn your notes into essay form:

1. Keep the same order as the original.
2. Keep the same proportions as the original.
3. Use your own words.

Summarizing a Summary

The *World Book* gave five paragraphs on boll weevils, which were shortened very neatly into one paragraph. Some writing, however, seems so packed with information and so hard to understand that a single paragraph may deserve a summary by itself. And after you have summarized the paragraph, you may want to shorten it still more—to summarize your own summary. For example, look at this explanation of the kind of people who will enjoy being sociologists:

> People who like to avoid shocking discoveries, who prefer to believe that society is just what they were taught in Sunday School, who like the safety of the rules and maxims of what Alfred Schuetz has called the "World-taken-for-granted," should stay away from sociology. People who feel no temptation before closed doors, who have no curiosity about human beings, who are content to admire scenery without wondering about the people who live in those houses on the other side of that river, should probably also stay away from sociology. They will find it unpleasant or, at any rate, unrewarding. People who are interested in human beings only if they can change, convert or reform them should also be warned, for they will find sociology much less useful than they hoped. And people whose interest is mainly in their own conceptual constructions will do just as well to turn to the study of little white mice. Sociology will be satisfying, in the long run, only to those who can think of nothing more entrancing than to watch men and to understand things human.[2]

Before you begin to summarize, read the paragraph again all the way through. You may find some words you will need to look up. What is a "maxim"? What are "conceptual constructions"? What does "entrancing" mean?

Even after you have all the words under control, you may still not be sure what the main idea sentence is. If you aren't, jot down, point by point, what the author is saying. This paragraph provides some easy clues as to what the separate

[2] Peter L. Berger, *Invitation to Sociology: A Human Perspective* (New York: Doubleday & Company, 1963). Published in 1973 by Overlook Press. Copyright © 1973 by Peter L. Berger. Reprinted by permission of Doubleday & Company, Inc.

points are. Each time Berger begins a sentence with "people," he is beginning another point. Glancing through the paragraph again, you can see that there are four
such sentences and that each one explains a different kind of person who should
stay away from sociology. Your notes, then, will look something like this:

> Stay away if—
>   take world for granted, easily shocked;
>   not curious about people;
>   want to reform people;
>   see things in terms of own theories.
> *Will* like if—
>   find people fascinating and want to understand them.

Once the notes are down on paper, it is fairly easy to see Berger's purpose, to
explain, and to see the main idea in the last sentence—that people who find other
human beings fascinating and want to understand them are the only ones who will
like sociology. Quite often, summarizing not only shortens the material and thus
makes it easier to remember, but it also leads to a clearer understanding of the
material itself.

Now that you have found the purpose and have stated the main idea clearly
in your own words, writing the summary should be easy. Since the author kept his
main idea for the end of the paragraph, you should, too. Work from your notes
rather than from the paragraph itself, so you won't be tempted to use the author's
words. Your summary should look something like this:

> Peter Berger says there are four kinds of people who should stay away from
> sociology: those who take the world for granted and are easily shocked by what
> other people do; those who aren't curious about other human beings; those who
> want to reform other people; and those who like to see the world in terms of their
> own theories. People who find other human beings fascinating and want to under-
> stand them are the only ones who will really like sociology.

Although this paragraph does summarize the original, it is still fairly long—nearly
half the length of Berger's paragraph. It could be shortened even more:

> Peter Berger says people who are easily shocked, incurious, given to reform,
> or sure of what they think will not like sociology. Only people who find other
> people fascinating and want to understand them will like being sociologists.

This shortened summary keeps Berger's method of development—contrasting the
people who won't like sociology with those who will—but it gives much less detail.
Part of the point would be lost by taking out this contrast, since by first showing
the kind of people who will dislike sociology, Berger suggests quite a bit about the
people who will like it. Nevertheless, if you need to shorten the summary still more,
perhaps down to a single sentence, that sentence must contain the main idea.

> Sociology is satisfying only to people who are fascinated by other human beings
> and want to understand them.

Remember, no matter what length your summary is:

All summaries must contain the main idea.

Summarizing by Paragraphs

Some writers make it easy for you to take notes by separating each of their points into paragraphs, much as you did when you were trying to make it easy for your readers. Notice how the first four paragraphs in this essay each deal with a different kind of example:

A Note on Verbal Taboo

[1]   In every language there seem to be certain "unmentionables"—words of such strong affective connotations that they cannot be used in polite discourse. In English, the first of these to come to mind are, of course, words dealing with excretion and sex. We ask movie ushers and filling-station attendants where the "lounge" or "rest room" is, although we usually have no intention of lounging or resting. "Powder room" is another euphemism for the same facility, also known as "toilet," which itself is an earlier euphemism. Indeed, it is impossible in polite society to state, without having to resort to baby talk or a medical vocabulary, what a "rest room" is for. (It is "where you wash your hands.") Another term is "John." There is now a book on the best "Johns" in New York.

[2]   Money is another subject about which communication is in some ways inhibited. It is all right to mention *sums* of money, such as $10,000 or $2.50. But it is considered in bad taste to inquire directly into other people's financial affairs, unless such an inquiry is really necessary in the course of business. When creditors send bills, they almost never mention money, although that is what they are writing about. There are many circumlocutions: "We beg to call your attention to what might be an oversight on your part." "We would appreciate your early attention to this matter." "May we look forward to an early remittance?"

[3]   The fear of death carries over, quite understandably in view of the widespread confusion of symbols with things symbolized, into fear of the *words* having to do with death. Many people, therefore, instead of saying "died," substitute such expressions as "passed away," "went to his reward," "departed," and "went west." In Japanese, the word for death, *shi,* happens to have the same pronunciation as the word for the number four. This coincidence results in many linguistically awkward situations, since people avoid *"shi"* in the discussion of numbers and prices, and use *"yon,"* a word of different origin, instead.

[4]   Words having to do with anatomy and sex—and words even vaguely suggesting anatomical or sexual matters—have, especially in American cul-

ture, remarkable affective connotations. Ladies of the nineteenth century could not bring themselves to say "breast" or "leg"—not even of chicken—so that the terms "white meat" and "dark meat" were substituted. It was thought inelegant to speak of "going to bed," and "to retire" was used instead. In rural America there are many euphemisms for the word "bull"; among them are "he-cow," "cow-critter," "male cow," "gentleman cow." But Americans are not alone in their delicacy about such matters. When D. H. Lawrence's first novel, *The White Peacock* (1911), was published, the author was widely and vigorously criticized for having used (in innocuous context) the word "stallion." "Our hearts are warm, our bellies are full" was changed to "Our hearts are warm, and we are full" in a 1962 presentation of the Rodgers and Hammerstein musical *Carousel* before the British royal family.

[5]   These verbal taboos, although sometimes amusing, also produce serious problems, since they prevent frank discussion of sexual matters. Social workers, with whom I have discussed this question, report that young people of junior high school and high school age who contract venereal disease, become pregnant out of wedlock, and get into other serious trouble of this kind are almost always profoundly ignorant of the most elementary facts about sex and procreation. Their ignorance is apparently due to the fact that neither they nor their parents have a vocabulary with which to discuss such matters: the nontechnical vocabulary of sex is to them too coarse and shocking to be used, while the technical, medical vocabulary is unknown to them. The social workers find, therefore, that the first step in helping these young people is usually a linguistic one: the students have to be taught a vocabulary in which they can talk about their problems before they can be helped further.

[6]   The stronger verbal taboos have, however, a genuine social value. When we are extremely angry and we feel the need of expressing our anger in violence, uttering these forbidden words provides us with a relatively harmless verbal substitute for going berserk and smashing furniture: that is, the words act as a kind of safety valve in our moments of crisis.[3]

The first paragraph says that certain "verbal taboos" exist in every language and gives some examples from English of ways we say "rest room." The second, third, and fourth paragraphs give further examples. Paragraph 5 explains some of the problems created by verbal taboos, and paragraph 6 explains how they can be valuable. Good notes, paragraph by paragraph, would look something like this:

Paragraph 1: Some words, mainly those dealing with excretion and sex, aren't normally used in "polite conversation"; this taboo gives rise to such words as *rest room.*

Paragraph 2: Society also has taboos on talking about money.

[3] S. I. Hayakawa, *Language in Thought and Action,* 3rd ed. (New York: Harcourt Brace Jovanovich, 1972), pp. 65–67. From *Language in Thought and Action,* Third Edition, by S. I. Hayakawa, Copyright © 1972 by Harcourt Brace Jovanovich, Inc. Reprinted by permission of the publisher.

Paragraph 3: Many people avoid using the word *death* because of the fear of dying.

Paragraph 4: Words dealing with human anatomy and sex are another group that people avoid.

Paragraph 5: Such taboos cause numerous problems; young people often shy away from getting help with their problems because they don't know the language to use in public to discuss them.

Paragraph 6: But verbal taboos are not completely unhealthy; using the taboo words provides us with a means to get rid of frustration and anger without being physically destructive.

Actually, what this paragraph-by-paragraph note-taking does is to pick up the main idea of each paragraph. Then it is easy to combine the notes into a paragraph of your own:

> Certain words are considered so offensive that we avoid using them; words dealing with excretion, money, death, the anatomy, and sex are "verbal taboos" in today's society. Such taboos can cause communication problems; because people don't know the words to explain a problem, they avoid talking about the problem and it goes unsolved. But the taboos have one advantage: using the words helps us vent anger and frustration without physically harming ourselves or others.

Fine so far, but you also need to let your readers know that these ideas belong to S. I. Hayakawa, not to you, and you need to say where you found them so that readers who want to know more will be able to find the original essay. The easiest way is to give Hayakawa credit right at the beginning:

> S. I. Hayakawa, in his book *Language in Thought and Action,* says that. . . .

Then you go on with your summary.

> *In summarizing an article of several paragraphs, include the main idea of each paragraph.*

Analyzing Mixed Purposes

The purpose of all three of the articles already summarized is explanation. The first explains what a boll weevil is; the second explains who will like sociology; the last explains the inhibitions people have about using certain words. These are all fairly straightforward purposes, and they are all developed in a fairly straightforward way. Sometimes what you read, however, will be mixed in its purpose, and a mixed purpose is harder to be sure about. For instance, what is the writer doing in this selection?

The Intellectual Taxicab Company

[1]   My friend Danny hung his Boston University diploma below the hack license in his cab. After seventeen years of education in the finest schools in America, Danny, at 22, couldn't fix his stopped sink, repair a burnt connection in his fuse box, replace a pane of glass in his kitchen or locate the carburetor in his car.

[2]   Danny is an educated man. He is a master of writing research papers, taking tests, talking and filling out forms. He can rattle off his social-security number as easily as he can his name because it was also his student identification number. He can analyze Freud from a Marxian viewpoint and he can analyze Marx from a Freudian viewpoint. In short, Danny is an unskilled worker and he has a sociology degree to prove it. He is of very little use to American industry.

[3]   This is nothing new. Colleges have been turning out unskilled workers for decades. Until five years ago, most of these unskilled workers took their degrees in sociology, philosophy, political science or history and marched right into the American middle class. Some filled executive positions in business and government but many, if not most, went into education, which is the only thing they knew anything about. Once there, they taught another generation the skills necessary to take tests and write papers. But that cycle broke down. Teachers are overabundant these days, college applications are down, plumbers are making $12 an hour and liberal-arts graduates are faced with a choice—graduate school or the taxicab.

[4]   Danny chose the taxicab because driving was about the only marketable skill he possessed. Danny refers to his job as "Real World 101." He has been shot at, punched, sideswiped and propositioned. But he has also acquired some practical skills—he can get his tickets fixed; he knows how to cheat the company out of a few extra dollars a week; he found his carburetor and he can fix it.

[5]   Soon, I will be in the same position. I'll graduate from Boston University with a B.S. in journalism. Whatever skills that degree symbolizes are not currently in demand. I suppose I could go to graduate school, but, . . . I've been doing the same thing for seventeen years and I'm getting a little tired of it. Besides, there are a lot of grad-school graduates who are driving cabs, too.

[6]   And that brings me to the Intellectual Taxicab Company. Danny and I were discussing the hack business recently and we came up with the idea. It is the simple answer to a simple question: why should all that college education go to waste reading road signs when masses of people are looking for knowledge and riding in cabs?

[7]   What America needs is a system to bring together all the knowledgeable cabbies and the undereducated rest of the country. The system we propose is the Intellectual Taxicab Company. The Intellectual Taxicab Company would consist of a dispatcher and a fleet of cabs driven by recent college graduates. When you need a ride, you call the company and say some-

thing like: "I'd like to go from Wall Street over to East 83rd and I'd like to discuss the world monetary situation."

[8]   "All right, sir, we'll have an NYU economics graduate over in five minutes."

[9]   Or: "Hello, I'm in Central Square and I'd like to go to Brookline and discuss whether or not there is a God."

[10]   "You're in luck, madam, we have a Harvard philosophy graduate who minored in Comparative Religions right in the neighborhood."

[11]   The educational possibilities of this plan are staggering. English and Drama graduates could take the after-theater run, explaining the literary ramifications of the shows. Political Science graduates could hack around Capitol Hill or City Hall. Regular bus runs could be set up to conduct seminars on popular topics. The Intellectual Taxicab Company would bring adult education to the streets. It would also give all those alienated college graduates a feeling that they didn't waste four years and all that tuition money. And it would elevate the snotty cabdriver to an art form: cabbies would quote Voltaire while they rant about how bad the mayor is.

[12]   Surely there must be some foundation money or unimpounded Federal funds available to begin such a noble experiment in education. If there is, Danny and I are ready to start immediately. In fact, Danny is licking his lips in anticipation. "Just think how much my tips will go up," he said.[4]

The first step is to look up any words you don't know or that you guess may have been used with specialized meanings—*hack? ramifications?* Then try to figure out what Carlson is doing in this article. Certainly he's inviting readers to laugh, but is entertainment his main purpose? The first part of the article introduces us to Danny. Danny's situation lets us see what the problem is: students are graduating from college every semester, failing to find jobs in their own field, and having no useful skills to fall back on. Then the writer makes clear that Danny isn't the only one; Carlson will soon share the problem. Finally, he proposes a solution: since some graduates are forced to take jobs driving taxis, society could take advantage of their education by organizing an "Intellectual Taxicab Company." The last part of the article tells how the company would work and outlines its advantages.

Once we realize that Carlson has stated a real problem and proposed an absurd solution, we understand that he wants us to recognize his solution as ridiculous and start thinking more deeply about how the problem might be solved. His essay is a criticism of an education that produces people with no practical, marketable skills—except training other people in the same impractical, unmarketable skills—and college teaching jobs are very scarce. It's also a criticism of society for permitting such waste.

The main purpose is to *persuade,* but Carlson uses *telling what happened* to Danny to back up that persuasion. The method of development is irony—saying something readers are not expected to believe, but actually meaning quite the opposite—and satire—showing human foolishness through exaggeration. We can

[4] Peter Carlson, "The Intellectual Taxicab Company." Copyright 1974, by Newsweek, Inc. All rights reserved. Reprinted by permission.

see the irony in paragraph 4: Carlson doesn't really expect us to agree that getting tickets fixed and cheating the company are "practical skills." "Simple answer to a simple question," in paragraph 6, is ironical too: the question isn't simple, and neither are the answers. Common sense tells us that the Intellectual Taxicab Company couldn't possibly exist, but Carlson ends by solemnly asking for foundation money. He also pokes fun at some other American characteristics: people's tendency to talk to cab drivers; and drivers' "snottiness" and habit of offering political comment, as well as their eagerness to collect tips.

The underlying main idea is never clearly stated; we have to figure it out for ourselves. It seems to be more than "Many college graduates can't get jobs," but Carlson offers no actual solution. Probably he's saying, "A liberal arts education that leaves graduates unable to get a job is wasteful and unfair." You need to know what the point of the essay is, but when you write your summary, your job is only to shorten what Carlson actually said:

> In "The Intellectual Taxicab Company," Peter Carlson illustrates through Danny, a friend, the problems college graduates face when trying to enter the job market. Danny couldn't find a job in his field so he hung his diploma in his cab. Since many college graduates are being forced to take jobs similar to taxicab driving (after ruling out the only other possibility—graduate school), Carlson ironically proposes an Intellectual Taxicab Company: clients could call for an expert to discuss economics or religion while being chauffeured about town, and English and Drama graduates could "take the after-theater run."

In an article that has mixed purposes, be careful to distinguish between the main purpose and the method of development.

Using Your Own Words

In writing that is mostly explanation or persuasion, it is fairly easy to condense the idea without repeating exactly what the original has said. But someimes the idea of an article seems less important than the way the writer says it. Look at this selection, for instance:

> There are roughly three New Yorks. There is, first, the New York of the man or woman who was born here, who takes the city for granted and accepts its size and its turbulence as natural and inevitable. Second, there is the New York of the commuter—the city that is devoured by locusts each day and spat out each night. Third, there is the New York of the person who was born somewhere else and came to New York in quest of something. Of these three trembling cities the greatest is the last—the city of final destination, the city that is a goal. It is this third city that accounts for New York's high-strung disposition, its poetical deportment, its dedication to the arts, and its incomparable achievements. Commuters give the city its tidal restlessness; natives give it solidity and continuity; but the settlers give it passion. And whether it is a farmer arriving from Italy to set up a

small grocery store in a slum, or a young girl arriving from a small town in Mississippi to escape the indignity of being observed by her neighbors, or a boy arriving from the Corn Belt with a manuscript in his suitcase and a pain in his heart, it makes no difference: each embraces New York with the intense excitement of first love, each absorbs New York with the fresh eyes of an adventurer, each generates heat and light to dwarf the Consolidated Edison Company.[5]

This paragraph uses several words you may not know: *turbulence, inevitable, deportment, incomparable, continuity, indignity, generates.* But in spite of using more hard words than the other paragraphs, this one presents more vivid pictures. White makes us see some of the people who come to the city, the grocer from Italy, the girl from Mississippi, the boy from Iowa. He uses some unusual comparisons that make us think of familiar things in a fresh, new way. Everybody knows that commuters come and go, but when White says that they are like locusts who eat up the city in the morning and spit it out at night, we get a fresh vision of the crowds of people who pour in and out of the railroad stations and along the highways. We are not used to thinking of a city as having a "high-strung disposition" or a "poetical deportment," but when White makes these comparisons, we think of the noise and movement of the streets, and we wonder whether tall buildings and long avenues may be a little like a poem. White makes us think of New York as though it were a person. His purpose is to describe New York, not its physical appearance, but its atmosphere. He wants his readers to feel about it the way he feels.

Because so much of the meaning of this paragraph depends on the words White uses, it is tempting to use his words instead of your own. Undoubtedly White can say it better, but the student who writes a summary by lifting a sentence here and there will come up with something like this:

> There are roughly three New Yorks. Of these three trembling cities the greatest is the last—the city that is a goal. Each embraces New York with the intense excitement of first love.

This "summary" not only cheats by copying White's words, it also confuses and misleads the reader. It breaks one of the main rules of writing: never use more than three consecutive words belonging to another writer without putting quotation marks around them. Properly punctuated, this attemped summary would be nothing but a long quotation; it would not be a summary at all. Further, it destroys the proportions of the original, and it leaves the reader wondering what on earth the three New Yorks are. Why are they trembling? What is meant by calling a city a goal, not a place? And who are the "each" who embrace New York so excitedly? This attempted summary does not keep the flavor of White's writing, as it tries to do; it does spoil his meaning.

Let's look again at what White is doing in his original paragraph. Actually, he is classifying the people who live or work in New York into three groups. When he

---

[5] E. B. White, *Here Is New York* (New York: Harper & Row, 1949), pp. 17–18. Copyright 1949 by The Curtis Publishing Company. Reprinted by permission of Harper & Row, Publishers.

begins with what is probably the main idea sentence of the paragraph ("There are roughly three New Yorks"), he doesn't mean that there are three cities, or three geographical divisions within the city; he means that there are three different ways of thinking about New York, and that these ways depend on who is doing the thinking. The people who were born there see one city; the commuters see another; and the people who come from far away, looking for something or hoping for something, see the city in still a third way. We san say, then, that White describes the atmosphere of New York by giving examples and classifying.

Here is a much better summary, which includes all three of White's divisions:

> In an essay on New York, E. B. White says that there are three different ways of thinking about the city. The people who were born there take it for granted. Commuters come and go every day and give the city its restless feeling. But the people who come to New York from far away come because the city represents something wonderful to them, and they are the ones who find it exciting and love it most passionately.

Certainly this summary is not as good as White's original. In trying to be both accurate and honest, it leaves out White's carefully chosen words; and in shortening the paragraph, it leaves out the examples. It keeps the *idea* of the original, but it loses much of the *effect*. Nevertheless, it is an acceptable summary because it neither misleads nor cheats.

> *Always use quotation marks if you repeat more than three consecutive words of the original.*

Keeping the Same Tone

In material like White's where much of the effect depends on the flavor of the writing, losing some of that flavor in a summary is probably unavoidable. There's not much that can be done about it. However, in most summarizing it is possible to do something about keeping the *tone* of the original. Although you always use your own words when you summarize, you must try as hard as you can to use the same *kind* of words the original writer used. If there is a lot of slang, you may use slang, too. If the writer was trying to be funny, you may try to capture the humor. But if the writer was being serious, your summary must be serious, too, even though you simplify the language so it will be easier to understand.

For example, it would be misleading to begin a summary of Carlson's article like this:

> In "The Intellectual Taxicab Company," Peter Carlson exposes the current injustice toward college graduates entering the job market and expounds upon the complexities of such a dilemma.

Although Carlson's problem is not simple, his language and tone are, and it's unfair to suggest that his paper is dull and dry by writing a summary that is dull and dry. You must avoid slanting in summaries just as carefully as you avoided it in reports.

Honest summaries reflect the spirit, as well as the ideas, of the original.

Summarizing What Happened

Most of the material you summarize will be explanations and arguments. However, you may sometimes have to summarize a third kind of writing purpose, telling what happened. For a class in contemporary problems you may need to report on some world event. For a literature class you may have to summarize the plot of a short story or a novel. When you do summarize what happened, here are a few pointers that will help. First, say where it happened and when it happened. Second, don't just dump in a name you haven't mentioned before and assume that your readers can guess who it is. Third, repeating conversations or long descriptions will waste so much time you may have to skimp on events that are important to the story. And finally, whether you are summarizing an actual event or an imaginary one—the battle of Bunker Hill or the fire at the shoe factory, Ulysses' long journey home or Holden Caulfield's weekend in New York—it would be a mistake to spend a lot of space on one incident you found especially interesting at the expense of another that is just as long in the original and probably just as important. In other words, when you summarize what happened, it is as necessary as ever to keep the proportions right.

In summarizing reports or stories:

1. Say where it happened and when.
2. Identify all the people you mention.
3. Don't repeat conversations or long descriptions.
4. Don't overemphasize one event or part of an event at the expense of another.

Summarizing Fiction

In keeping the proportions of fiction right, you will not have the same clues that helped guide you through explanations and arguments. Certainly there won't be main topic subdivisions in heavy type. Such useful separators as *further, second, next, another reason* will be missing. There will only be the story itself.

Neither will fiction openly state the main point. When you wrote about your own experiences, sometimes you didn't put the main point into your paper, although you had to keep very clear in your own mind what it was. In the same way, when you read an account of what happened to other people, either real or imaginary, you will have to figure out what the main point is. You will not state it openly if you are writing a straight summary. But keeping the main point in mind as you write will help you decide what to put in the summary and what to leave out just as it helped you decide what to include when you were writing about what happened to you.

For instance, if you were summarizing the story "Little Red Riding Hood," it might help you to remember that the point of the story is that little girls who don't mind their mothers will get into trouble. Another point, perhaps, is that little girls ought not to talk to strangers, no matter how much sweet talking the strangers do. If you think minding mother is the main point of the story, you will not want to leave out the mother's warning as she ties the strings on the little red cape and sends her daughter out into the big woods. If you think the main point is not talking to strangers, you will want to emphasize the way the wolf flattered the innocent little girl. What is true for summarizing a nursery story is true for summarizing a longer tale, although the point may not be quite so easy to find.

If you have read George Orwell's *Animal Farm,* you know that the main point, or one of them, is that people who seize power often forget their promises and become even worse tyrants than the people they overthrew. If you are summarizing *Animal Farm,* you will want to keep that idea in mind. Remembering it will remind you to include what the pigs were like before they got rid of the farmers, and what they were like afterward. But you will not include the idea in the actual summary, any more than you will include the comment that the pigs remind you of fascists or communists. If you are asked to summarize *and comment* on what you have read, then certainly you will put in what you thought the point was, and what the pigs reminded you of.

> *In summarizing fiction, use the main point to help you decide what to include, but don't state the point unless the original states it.*

Summarizing Longer Material

All the articles summarized in this chapter have been very short, sometimes a paragraph, sometimes a page or two. We don't have enough space here to reproduce a twelve-page article or a full-length book and the summaries that should go with them. Although the general principles are much the same, the way you go about summarizing longer material is a bit different. If what you are summarizing is fairly short, you can read it all the way through and then go back to take notes on it. If what you are summarizing is long, you may want to take notes as you go. Material divided into sections will be easier if you treat each section separately, deciding what the purpose is, finding the main point, and noting the important subdivisions. In textbooks the subtopics will often be printed in heavy type to help you further. This heavy type gives a strong hint of what the author intends the point to be.

The longer the material you are summarizing, the more you will have to condense. If you are summarizing an entire book, it is especially important to keep the proportions right. Work on one chapter at a time, but be sure to work on all the chapters. If you are getting tired when you reach Chapter 6, you may be tempted to do a thorough job on the first five and then skimp on the rest. But if you have taken it section by section, making brief notes on each section as you finished reading it, you may be able to resist the temptation. Remember that the most important ideas ofen come at the end.

This system is useful both for summarizing long material and as preparation for writing a review. When you write the review, you may not use all of your summary, but you will know what parts you're leaving out, and why you're doing it.

In summarizing long material:

1. Treat each section separately.
2. Take notes as you go.
3. Keep the proportions right.

Writing a Review

Some time while you are in college—or out of it, for that matter—you will probably need to write a review. You may be asked to summarize and comment on a book, an article, a film, a play, or even a concert. The review may be a class assignment or your contribution to the program of a community group. Or it may even be a part of your job: perhaps the company you work for will ask you to review the newest book on advertising techniques or an article on imported bicycles. You may be given a specific assignment: if your company is especially interested in *Word of Mouth Advertising: How to Make It Work,* you may be asked to read it, or your sociology instructor may ask everybody to read Lincoln Steffens' *Shame of the Cities.*

Often, however, if you are asked to prepare a review, the choice of the book or article will be up to you, and you will be restricted only by your own tastes and the interests of the people who will read your review. Don't decide too hastily; first make a trial run through the material. If you are considering a book, look at the table of contents, or glance through the introduction. Flip through for illustrations or diagrams. Read the first page, and read here and there in the middle. You can tell fairly quickly whether the book is a good risk for you and whether your audience will care about it. The Friday Night Consumers Association is not likely to care much about *The Home Life of the Etruscans,* no matter how fascinating you find it; they would prefer Ralph Nader's latest publication. On the other hand, if the book review is for a course in the modern American novel, the teacher probably won't consider what Nader writes as "literature" and certainly not as a novel.

You'd do better to try Ralph Ellison's *Invisible Man* or Margaret Walker's *Jubilee*. But the world is full of books, and on most topics, for most purposes, you have a wide choice. If you don't like the first book you examine, keep trying until you find one you do like. Then read it well before the time you must write the review so you'll have time to think about what you have read. Make a summary of what the book actually says. Then when you begin to write the review, you'll have all the facts right in front of you.

The following advice relates mainly to book reviews, which are the most common and sometimes the most troublesome assignment for inexperienced writers. However, the advice can be adapted, with only slight changes, to any kind of review.

Good reviews always:

1. Identify what's being reviewed.
2. Include some summary.
3. Include some evaluation.

Identifying Your Subject

The first part of your review should state clearly what you are reviewing. If it's a book, give the full name of the author; the exact title of the book; the publisher and city of publication; and the date the book was first published. (In printed material, the title of a book will be set in italic. Since you can't use italics in handwriting or typing, underline the title.)

> *The Daughter of Time* was written in 1947 by Elizabeth Mackintosh, under the better-known pen name of Josephine Tey; the copy I read was a Berkley Medallion paperback reprint, published in New York in 1970.

If you are reviewing an article, give much the same information—author, title of the article (in quotation marks), name of the magazine (underlined), and date of the magazine:

> David S. Rubsamen, in an article called "Medical Malpractice," published in the August 1976 issue of *Scientific American,* says that patients expect so much of modern medicine they are quicker to sue when it is unsatisfactory.

For a review of a concert, film, or play, say who directed it and who the leading performers were; for a review of a speech, say who gave it. And in all cases tell your readers *when* ("last Saturday night," for instance, or "playing from September 22 through 29") and *where* ("at the Coliseum in Tacoma" or "to an audience of more than one hundred X-ray technicians at St. Mary's Hospital").

Somewhere in the review, either near the beginning or near the end, you should give your readers some background information about the person who wrote the book or article—or gave the speech or directed the play. If you are reviewing a novel, what is the author's reputation among people qualified to judge fiction? If you are reviewing nonfiction, what makes the writer an authority on the subject? If you are reviewing a speech or a production, what is important in the background of the speaker or the producer? If you don't know the answer, and often you won't, there are places to find this information. Sometimes the blurb on the cover of a book, or a brief note at the beginning or end, will tell a little about the author's life and list other books the author has written. Often near the front or the back of a magazine, you can find a paragraph about each of the writers who are featured in that issue. The program for a concert or a play will usually tell you something about the main performers.

But if these sources fail, try the library. If you can't find anything on your own, ask the librarian for help. And if neither of you can produce any information, be honest about it. It does no harm to say, "I couldn't find any material about this writer—or this producer or this speaker."

If you do find a lot of biographical material, however, don't use details that have no bearing on what you are reviewing. It doesn't really matter that the author's mother's maiden name was Smith, or that the speaker's father kept pet snakes—unless, of course, the subject of the lecture was a discussion of poisonous reptiles. Make sure that the biographical details you include are clearly related to the topic of the book, article, or play.

An identification must include who, what, where, and when.

Using Your Summary

The summary you have written can be included in your review in two ways. You may decide to plunge in and give your readers the whole thing at once—tell the story if you're reviewing a novel, movie or play; outline all the main points if you're reviewing nonfiction or a speech; list all the numbers performed if you're reviewing a concert. You can then devote the rest of the review to your opinions. But this method, even though it is sometimes acceptable, is usually pretty dull. A better way is to give a brief indication of what the material covers—a one- or two-sentence summary of your summary—and then to use the rest of the information in your summary to support the comments you want to make. This second mehod will make your review easier to read. It will not be broken into two parts, first all summary, then all comments, and readers won't have to jump back and forth, wondering which comments refer to which part of the summary.

The only danger in evaluating as you go lies in separating what you say from what the original writer or speaker said. That won't be a problem if you remember to use such phrases as "according to the author" or "it seems to me" whenever you shift from summary to evaluation. Here are some samples of how to show the separation:

The author says that because most divorced women blame their husbands for the failure of their marriages, they are unlikely to be happy if they marry again. Although she gives two or three examples to support her belief, *I don't think* the examples are typical. The divorced women *I know* blame themselves as much as their former husbands, and five out of six of *my* acquaintances have had successful second marriages.

In Barzone's new twenty-minute work, "Salute to a New Dawn," with which the concert ended (*summary*), the drums seemed too loud. They overpowered the string section, which was carrying the melody, and drowned out the vocalist. The audience seemed to share my opinion. They were restless all during the final number, and many of them left before it was over (*evaluation*).

In the following review of the children's story, "Little Red Riding Hood," the summary has been interwoven with the evaluation. The summary sections have been underlined so you can easily see the distinction:

Little Red Hiding Hood, that old nursery story grownups keep on telling children, seems to me so silly that bright children would laugh themselves sick when they heard it. What child would believe stuff like that? As everybody knows, Little Red Riding Hood is the story of a little girl in a red cape who walks through the woods to take a basket of food to her bedridden old grandmother. In spite of her mother's warning to go straight there and not talk to anybody on the way, the little girl gets into conversation with a wolf who hurries ahead, gobbles up the grandmother, and disguises himself enough to fool the little girl.

In the first place, what was the mother doing, letting the child out alone? If the woods were so dangerous, why didn't she go herself or drive her in the car? Even the child's name shows she wasn't used to walking—Little Red Riding Hood. And the mother must have known the child was a little retarded. Some children I know can't tell dogs from wolves, but they can sure tell wolves from human beings. Some versions of the story say the wolf just shut the grandmother in the closet instead of eating her. But if that's what happened, what was the matter with the old woman? Why didn't she pound and scream to warn the child? In the original version, after the wolf had eaten the grandmother, he dressed up in her cap and got into bed. Here's where it really gets silly. At the very first question "Why are your ears so big, grandma?" you'd think the child would have noticed that the old woman could hear all right last week, when her ears were not only smaller but also a different shape. But no. The stupid child just stands there asking questions until the wolf, who is almost as stupid as she is, gets out of bed and tries to eat her up. Why didn't he just eat her in the woods when it would have been easy and safe? What's all this foolishness about dressing up in a lace cap?

Whichever way you handle your summary—giving it all at once or weaving it in—the summary shouldn't outweigh the comments. It's never acceptable to spend a long time retelling a story, condensing a report, repeating an argument, or listing a chain of events, and then end abruptly by saying "I liked it" or "I was bored."

Give just enough summary that your readers will understand what you liked, or just enough that they can tell why you were bored.

When you write your own reviews, naturally you won't mark which part is summary and which part comment, as we have done here. But unless you keep the distinction straight in your own mind, your readers will be confused or maybe even deceived.

> *In writing reviews, always make a clear distinction between what is in the original and what you think about it.*

Giving Your Evaluation

If you are reviewing nonfiction—a book, an article, or even a speech—and if your summary has been carefully done, you already know what the author's purpose and main idea are. Now you can ask the same questions you asked in revising your own papers. Are the explanations clear? Do the examples that are used make the meaning easier to understand or the situation more vivid? Are they fair examples? Are all the important terms carefully defined? If the subject is a report, does it seem accurate and objective? If it's an attempt to persuade, are the methods it uses fair?

Don't be afraid to make judgments. After all, you are writing a review, and it is your responsibility to evaluate. Remember, though, that an unsupported evaluation will not be very convincing to your readers. If you think the examples in the original are especially well chosen, then include one of them in your review. If you think the method of persuasion is unfair, explain what it is and say what's the matter with it. Be specific, rather than general, in all your comments.

If you are reviewing fiction—a novel, a short story, a play, or a movie—finding the purpose and the main idea is not quite as easy. When you wrote your summary, you knew that the obvious purpose was telling what happened, and although it wasn't included in the summary, you tried to figure out the main point to use as a guide in deciding exactly what events to include or omit in your summary. That main point—often called "the theme" in discussions of fiction—has also guided the author in creating imaginary people in an imaginary world. The theme has determined how those imaginary people will react to the events of their lives, and your discovery of the theme will help you understand the book, or the play, or the movie. Once you understand what the main idea is, you can write a more sensible evaluation.

Writers of good fiction always keep their main ideas clearly in mind. When Sinclair Lewis wanted to dramatize the cloddishness of a middle-class businessman, he made Babbitt convincingly human and even somewhat likable, but Lewis never let us lose sight of his message: that Babbitt's life is futile and meaningless. In writing a review of *Babbitt,* don't just say, "Mr. Lewis wrote this book to show what it was like to live in Zenith in the 1920s." That won't help your audience much. You must make clear what Lewis' convictions were, and then you must refer to parts of the book in order to back up your interpretation.

You can use your previous knowledge and experience to support your evaluation. Although the characters and events in fiction are imaginary, fiction succeeds only when authors can make us believe in the people they have created and in the things that happen to those people. One way of judging fiction is to test its reality. Are the characters like people you have read about or have known? Does the author describe places well enough that you can see them? Are the events believable?

Naturally, some characters, places, and incidents will be unfamiliar to you. Some may even seem revolting. But you probably do not want to condemn a book or a movie just because its characters and events disgust you or because they are outside your own experience. Instead, try to discover the reasons for using such characters and events. Not all fiction attempts to be true to life. *Animal Farm* and *Watership Down* use animals for characters, but George Orwell and Richard Adams knew that pigs and rabbits don't talk. *Lord of the Flies* takes place on a tropical island after an atomic war, but William Golding knew that there had been no such war. *A Connecticut Yankee in King Arthur's Court* tells about a man traveling through time and space, but Mark Twain, although he knew about science and history, deliberately ignored scientific and historical facts. Ursula LeGuin was aware that no human beings have ever landed on the planet Winter, but she created a history of that planet and its odd inhabitants in *The Left Hand of Darkness*. In evaluating fantasies, like any fiction, you must always do three things:

1. Discover the author's aim.
2. Decide whether the aim is accomplished.
3. Judge whether it is an aim worth accomplishing.

Your review can discuss more than just the author's main point or the aim in writing; you may want to comment on how the material was presented. The "how" is sometimes called *style*—something unusual about the way a book is written, or a speech given, or a play performed. Perhaps the entire book is written in the form of questions and answers. Or, perhaps, the author tries too hard to be funny. Perhaps the speaker talked so softly you had trouble hearing the words or made so many odd gestures that you were distracted from what was being said. Perhaps the play was performed without any scenery at all or with costumes that didn't seem to fit with the backdrop. Perhaps the photography in an otherwise satisfying film was too often deliberately out of focus or used too many unnecessary closeups.

If you do comment on style, be sure to support your comments with specific examples. Here, as always, your opinion is worth reading only if your readers can understand why you hold that opinion.

Don't give unsupported opinions.
Always refer to definite examples taken from whatever you are reviewing.

Examining a Book Review

How to Lie with Statistics

[1]   *How to Lie with Statistics* is an old book. It was written in 1954 by Darrell Huff and published by W. W. Norton & Company, New York. It's been nearly thirty years since its first publication, but the information it gives and the advice it offers are just as useful today as ever. Advertisers still use statistics to con people into buying their products. Government agencies still try to make conditions look better than they actually are by presenting their figures in the most favorable light. "Cost of living declines" may make you think the cost of groceries is going down, until you discover that even though meat prices have gone down one-tenth of one percent between August and September, they are still 15 percent higher than they were a year ago.

[2]   The title of the book may seem a little misleading. It is not really written for advertisers or statisticians who want to mislead us; it's a book for consumers who want not to be misled. As Huff says in the introduction, "It may seem altogether too much like a manual for swindlers. Perhaps I can justify it. . . . The crooks already know these tricks; honest men must learn them in self-defense."

[3]   I wasn't able to find out much about Darrell Huff's background, but I did discover that he relied on a number of standard books on statistics and had help with his examples from members of the American Statistical Association. It really doesn't make a great difference who he is, as long as his book keeps us from accepting all the statistics that bombard us without asking some questions about where the statistics come from and what they mean.

[4]   Huff begins by explaining the many ways in which statistical samples can be biased and offers a question we can ask to decide whether a sample is really random: "Does every name or thing in the whole group have an equal chance to be in the sample?" The other chapters cover such topics as what "average" and "actual test" mean and what they often do not mean; why we should mistrust the scores on intelligence tests; how graphs can be distorted to create almost any impression; the way the old *post hoc* fallacy can be used to make people believe in relationships that don't exist at all; and "How to Talk Back to Statistics."

[5]   The section on averages was especially interesting. Like a lot of other people, I supposed that an "average" was what you got when you added up several things and then divided the total by the number of things you had included. Now I know that there are three kinds of averages: mean, median, and modal. I can see how unscrupulous people can choose whichever kind fits the point they want to make, without actually lying. Huff uses as an example the "average income" of a given neighborhood. If you want to make it look big, you can use the *mean* average—add up all the incomes and divide. In Huff's example, that comes to $15,000 a year. If you want to make it look

smaller, you can use the *median* average—the middle figure in the whole list of incomes. That was $3,500. Still another way would be to use the *modal* average—the figure that appears most often on the list. That was $5,000. I was surprised at the different "averages" you could get, all based on the same figures. This is also a good illustration of what I mean by the book's not being out-of-date. Although the inflation of the last twenty years would make today's income figures be more like $50,000, $8,000, and $10,000, the principle is exactly the same.

[6]   Aside from the useful information this book contains, Huff's style is lively and very easy to read. He never just makes abstract statements; he always gives examples. In talking about IQ tests, for instance, he talks about Peter and Linda, and shows us why their parents might mistakenly think that Linda was brighter because her score was five points higher and that Peter was below average. Then he goes on to show why "such conclusions as these are sheer nonsense."

[7]   The names of the chapters are also a good indication of Huff's style. He calls them things like "How to Statisticulate" and "The Gee-Whiz Graph." Illustrations throughout the book, drawn by Irving Geis, fit well with the informal style. Some of the cartoons are just there to be funny, to keep you amused and interested, like the drawing of the baby in the high chair, smoking a cigar and reading the Kinsey report. This one comes during the discussion of what a "normal" baby is. Other illustrations, not drawn by Geis, are adaptations of actual charts and graphs, with an explanation of how pictures can deceive us.

[8]   I not only think everybody should read this book but everybody should own a copy, too. It is short, only 142 pages long, and even with inflation, it cannot cost very much more than it did last year.

Does the writer begin by identifying what is being reviewed? Yes. In the first paragraph, we are told *what* (a book called *How to Lie with Statistics*); *who* (the author is Darrell Huff, and the publisher is W. W. Norton); *where* (the book was published in New York); and *when* (1954). In paragraph 3, the writer admits frankly that it wasn't possible to find out much about Huff's background and compensates for that omission by telling us where some of the examples came from. It might be an improvement, however, to mention that the information in this paragraph came from the introduction to the book. Unless we are told that, we are left wondering how the writer knew that members of the American Statistical Association helped by providing examples. The mention of that reputable association does help convince us that what Huff says is reliable.

Paragraph 1 tells us indirectly what the purpose of the book is—giving information on how statistics are used to deceive and advice on avoiding deception. The same paragraph makes clear why we, the readers, might want that information and advice.

Paragraph 4 is straight summary. It tells what the first chapter is about and gives samples of the topics covered in other chapters.

Paragraph 5 begins by saying which chapter the writer found especially interesting and then goes on to explain why. The definitions of averages given in this paragraph are part summary—the writer's own words tell us what Huff said in the book—and part evaluation—the writer uses the examples to show that the book is not out-of-date.

Paragraphs 6 and 7 make comments about style—the specific, easy-to-understand examples Huff uses and the amusing chapter titles.

The final paragraph recommends the book—a recommendation that is supported by what the writer has said in the earlier paragraphs.

There is a clear separation between what Huff says and what the writer thinks. In paragraph 2, for instance, we know that the first two sentences are the reviewer's opinion. Then the phrase "As Huff says. . . ." lets us know that the rest of the paragraph comes from the book. And the writer has been careful not to give unsupported opinions. In the comments on style, we're not just told that the style is "lively and very easy to read"—we're shown the liveliness.

Altogether, this is a good book review.

Key Words

Here are some of the important terms used in this chapter. See whether you can answer these questions about them.

1. What is the difference between a **summary** and a **review?**
2. What should good **notes for a summary** include?
3. In turning notes into a **paragraph of summary,** what three things must you do?
4. No matter how long or short your summary is, what is the one thing it must always include?
5. If you are **summarizing an article of several paragraphs,** what is the easiest way to go about it?
6. When is it especially necessary to distinguish between **main purpose** and **method of development?** Why?
7. When must you use **quotation marks** in a summary?
8. What is meant by **keeping the same tone** as the original?
9. In **summarizing what happened,** what four things must you watch out for?
10. How do you use the main idea in a **summary of fiction?**
11. What is the best method of **summarizing long material?**
12. What three things should be included in a **good review?**
13. What information must the **identification of a review provide?**
14. What should you remember in **using your summary in your review?**
15. What should you do in your **evaluation?**

READINGS

Summarizing and Reviewing

The End and Means of Meaning

Here is a short article taken from Charlton Laird's book, *The Miracle of Language:*

[1] How is it possible that two people who may never have seen each other before, or who may not even live on the same continent, or be alive in the same century, have immediate, similar, and complicated ideas in the presence of a sound? Especially is this event amazing when we consider that there are hundreds of thousands of these sounds with millions of meanings and still more millions of implications so delicate that they cannot be defined. Some millions of people have agreed, at least roughly, as to the meaning of the word *wrist* and the other countless words in the language, and this in spite of the fact that the human animal is so varied and contentious that seldom will two human beings agree about anything, whether the subject be religion, politics, or what will "go" with that hat.

[2] Of course when the word *wrist* is spoken by one person and heard by another, little communication has as yet taken place. The single word raises almost as many questions as it answers. Is the speaker thinking that his wrist is arthritic, or that certain brush strokes can best be made with the wrist? These questions can be partially answered by adding a few more words, but in spite of anything he can do the speaker is likely to remain to a degree ambiguous. He cannot be precise because the syllable he is uttering has no precise meaning.

[3] Thus "the miracle of the desert" is far enough from the divine to exhibit a human flaw. Exact communication is impossible among men. Gertrude Stein may have felt that "a rose is a rose is a rose," but our speaker, if he considers the matter carefully, must know that a wrist is not necessarily a wrist. It may be some bones hung together by ligaments. It may be the skin outside these bones. It may be the

Charlton Laird, *The Miracle of Language* (New York: World Publishing, 1953).

point which marks the end of the sleeve. If the speaker is a tailor, *wrist* may be a command to hem a glove. But even granted that both speaker and hearer agree that *wrist* is here associated with the bones, flesh, and skin at the juncture of the human hand and arm, they may associate highly varied feelings with this part of the body. The speaker may have big, bony wrists, and have hated them all her life. The hearer may have been forced out of an Olympic skiing contest when he fell and broke a wrist. There is no one thing which *wrist* calls up in exactly the same form to everyone; there are not even areas of meaning which are the same for everybody. Meanings exist only in minds, and minds result from beings and experiences; no two of them are alike, nor are the meanings they contain. Still, granted that meaning is not and never can be exact, there remains a body of agreement as to the association to be connected with certain sounds which is staggering to contemplate.

[4]   But we have only begun, for we started with the simplest sort of example of spoken language. A word like *no* can mean *no, damn it,* or *yes,* or dozens of things between and among these meanings, depending upon the way in which the word is pronounced and the sounds modulated. The uttering and grasping of words, furthermore, become immeasurably complicated as soon as a speaker starts running them together into sentences. But for the moment let us complicate the situation only slightly by making the speaker also a writer, and let him make a few marks on any sort of an object. These marks can now take the place of sound and can call up the concepts associated with *wrist* wherever they go. They can continue calling up these concepts long after the man who made them is dead; they can do so for hundreds, even thousands, of years. Clay cones and slabs of stone, scratched with marks which were long undecipherable, could still produce something like their original meaning when their language was rediscovered, although no living man had known how to speak or write or think the language for thousands of years.

[5]   Man, then, can be defined, if one wishes, as a languagized mammal. A cow can communicate in a cowlike way by bawling and dogs can express themselves to a degree by looking soulfully from one end while wagging the other, but man is probably more significantly distinguished from his fellow creatures by his complicated means of communication than by any other difference. In short, man as we know him could not exist without language and until there was language. Civilization could not exist until there was written language, because without written language no generation could bequeath to succeeding generations anything but its simpler findings. Culture could not be widespread until there was printed language.

[6]   In the beginning was the word. Or, if in the beginning was the arboreal ape, with the word and an opposable thumb he scrambled down from the trees and found his way out of the woods.

Here is a review of Laird's essay:

[1]   Laird says that it is amazing that millions of people who don't even know each other can get "immediate, similar, and complicated ideas" when they hear the same sound. He illustrates what he means by using the word "wrist," and he goes on to say that if "wrist" is said by itself, not everybody will get exactly the same idea as everyone else when they hear the sound, although they will all get the same

general idea. Some people will think of a part of the body, but a tailor might think of a glove. And part of what people will think will be influenced by what has happened to their own wrists.

[2]   What Laird says is interesting because it makes you stop and think about words. It is easy to think of words as being things instead of just sounds. After I read Laird, I sat and said some words very slowly, listening to myself make the sounds. I said "rist" and "wist" and "rit" and "ris." After awhile I couldn't remember which sounds were words and which weren't. But when my brother came in, he said. "What are you mumbling about? The only thing I can make any sense out of is *wrist*. Did you sprain it or something?" I could see what Laird meant. It was amazing that my brother could sort the word out of all the sounds I was making.

[3]   Laird says it is just as amazing that people can make marks on stone or paper and other people can get the same ideas from them thousands of years afterward. I wasn't so surprised by what he said about writing, although I can see how much information would be lost if nobody could read or write. Once or twice I've wanted to leave somebody a note when I didn't have pencil and paper. I should think the cavemen would have been awfully frustrated.

[4]   Laird ends by defining people as "languagized mammals." He thinks the main difference between people and animals is that people have a complicated means of communication.

[5]   I found the essay very interesting because I had never thought much about language before. I can't remember not being able to talk, and so I just took talking for granted. But now I can see what Laird means by calling it a miracle.

Responses

1. Has the writer of this review sufficiently identified what is being reviewed? If you think the identification is adequate, list what it includes and where it can be found. If you think it is inadequate, write a paragraph that does give enough identification.

2. Which parts of this review are summary? How has the writer distinguished between what Laird said and what the reviewer is saying?

3. How has the reviewer supported the evaluation? Where is this support given?

4. Write a paragraph-by-paragraph summary of Laird's essay. If you were reviewing the essay, what would you include that has been omitted here? Why?

What Is Obscenity?

[1]   To date there exist, I think, no thorough-going studies by competent persons which justify the conclusion that normal adults' reading or seeing of the "obscene" probably induces anti-social conduct. Such competent studies as have been made do conclude that so complex and numerous are the causes of sexual vice that it is impossible to assert with any assurance that "obscenity" represents a ponderable causal factor in sexually deviant adult behavior. "Although the whole subject of obscenity censorship hinges upon the unproved assumption that 'obscene' literature is a significant factor in causing sexual deviation from the community standard, no report can be found of a single effort at genuine research to test this assumption by singling out as a factor for study the effect of sex literature upon sexual behavior." [social psychologist Leo Alport] . . . Macaulay, replying to advocates of the suppression of obscene books, said: "We find it difficult to believe that in a world so full of temptations as this, any gentleman, whose life would have been virtuous if he had not read Aristophanes and Juvenal, will be made vicious by reading them." Echoing Macaulay, "Jimmy" Walker remarked that he had never heard of a woman seduced by a book. . . .

[2]   Most federal courts . . . now hold that the test of obscenity is the effect on the "mind" of the average normal adult, that effect being determined by the "average conscience of the time," the current "sense of what is right"; and that the statute does not intend "to reduce our treatment of sex to the standard of the child's library in the supposed interest of a salacious few. . . ."

[3]   However, there is much pressure for legislation, designed to prevent juvenile delinquency, which will single out children, i.e., will prohibit the sale to young persons of "obscenity" or other designated matter. . . .

Responses

1. Find the main idea sentence of this article, and make brief notes in your own words on what Frank said.

2. Use your notes for a brief oral summary, probably given to the small group of students you are working with. Compare your report with the report given by other people in the group. Have all of you included the same things? If you haven't, discuss what ought to be included, what ought to be left out.

3. Using either your original notes or your notes as you have changed them after the group discussion, write a summary of Judge Frank's opinion, making it about half as long as the original.

Judge Jerome Frank, from the U.S. Court of Appeals opinion in *United States v. Roth,* 237 F. 2nd Series (2nd Circuit 1956).

Remarriage of Women

[1]   Remarriage rates for divorced women depend on a number of factors, a new study shows. Race, age at divorce, and schooling are important in determining, or predicting, how soon a woman may remarry after divorce, according to data compiled by the National Center for Health Statistics in its National Survey of Family Growth. The center is part of the U.S. Department of Health, Education and Welfare Office of Health Research, Public Health Service.

[2]   In the United States in 1976, there were about 6 million women 15–44 years of age whose first marriage had ended in divorce. About 92 percent remarried within 5 years after divorce—21 percent during the first year. The data showed that the likelihood of remarriage was greater for white women than for black women, greater for those who were divorced before age 25, and greater for those with less than a high school education than for those with one or more years of college.

[3]   The study interviewed more than 3,000 Black women and 5,600 women of other races. White women had a higher probability than Black women of remarrying within one year after divorce, and the racial differential increased so that by the third year the difference was nearly twice that of the first year. For Hispanic women, the rate of remarriage was about the same in the first year, but increased rapidly over the next two years.

[4]   Women whose divorce occurred prior to age 25 had higher probabilities of remarriage (women divorced before 1970 were more likely to have divorced prior to age 25 than those divorced after 1970). The duration of a woman's first marriage had little or no effect on the likelihood of her remarrying, and the number of children a woman had did not influence her probability of remarrying during the first 5 years after divorce.

[5]   Another finding: the more education, the lower the probability of having remarried. A woman with less than 12 years of education would remarry within two years, compared with college-educated women who would remarry within four years. The religion of a woman appeared to have little relationship to whether or not she will remarry, the survey showed, nor did geographic area affect remarriage rates.

[6]   For the full report in *Advance Data,* Number 58, write HEW, National Center for Health Statistics, 3700 East-West Highway, Hyattsville, MD 20782.

Responses

1. Where and how does the writer give credit to the original source?
2. Find all the words and phrases by which the writer reminds readers that this material is a condensation of what someone else has written.
3. Are the statistics given in paragraph 2 necessary? Why or why not?
4. Is this article a summary or a review? How can you tell?

Women Today, March 7, 1980, p. 38.

The Evolution of a Monster

[1]   Frankenstein's creation has fascinated audiences for more than 150 years. In *Mary Shelley's Monster,* Martin Tropp explores the history and psychology of the story and its themes. He believes that most of the characters in *Frankenstein* represent aspects of author Mary Shelley: her fears, the conscious and unconscious levels of her mind, her wariness of what new science promised.

[2]   Shelley's work questioned the value of technology devoid of ethics and emotion. Frankenstein disregards all natural feelings to stitch an assortment of dead parts into a living whole. And it is isolation from any affection that turns his Monster to brutal murder.

[3]   The Frankenstein myth has been interpreted in dozens of films—each influenced, says Tropp, by the events and attitudes of the society in which it was made. In the 1931 *Frankenstein,* with James Whale directing Boris Karloff, the Monster does not learn to speak, nor does it harbor malice and revenge. Instead, it remains both ignorant and innocent, an outcast misunderstood and tortured by society.

[4]   In Whale's 1935 film, *The Bride of Frankenstein,* we find that the Monster has survived the villagers' attempts to immolate it in the first movie, but its innocence is gone. It no longer kills merely to save itself; it now kills out of hatred and revenge.

[5]   During the '40s, Tropp says, the film image of the Monster was altered from isolated outcast to controlled weapon, reflecting the wartime environment. In 1942, *The Ghost of Frankenstein* introduced the idea of the brain transplant. The film became popular because it also expressed a fear of the times—the ability of science to control and change personality, to change people to automatons.

[6]   In the late '50s, a new series of films resurrected the Monster, but Tropp notes that its creation is no longer the core of the film. "It is accepted that such things can be done with little trouble. More important is the attitude of the creator, and the motivation that keeps him at it . . ."

[7]   The later Baron Frankensteins are often insane, sadistic and violent. Tropp explains that these films ". . . place the blame for a sterile future squarely on consciously repressive, sadistic, scientific attitudes rather than on noble motives distorted by ignorance and arrogance." These interpretations have recently been reinforced by two TV versions of the novel.

[8]   The newest films have turned satiric. Andy Warhol's *Frankenstein,* a gory 1974 film, is an "effective if stomach-turning parody," says Tropp. Mel Brooks's comic *Young Frankenstein* is respectful satire. These films are diametrically opposed in viewpoint, the first showing man as a machine, the second illustrating a comfortable cohabitation with technology. In one form or another, the Frankenstein myth is still very much with us.

[9]   *Mary Shelley's Monster* is published by Houghton Mifflin Co., $7.95.

Sherida Bush, *Psychology Today,* August 1976.

Responses

1. Is this article a summary or a review? Support what you say by referring to the article.
2. List all the words and phrases by which Bush lets you know when the ideas expressed belong to Tropp rather than to Bush. Are there any places where you are in doubt? If so, where are they?
3. In which paragraphs does Bush use the exact words from Tropp's book? Why do you think these parts were quoted? Which of the quotations could be most easily summarized without losing the tone or the intention of the original?
4. Have you read Shelley's novel *Frankenstein* or seen any of the films based on it? Do you need to have read the original book or seen any of the films to understand this article? Why or why not?
5. Find a magazine article of at least six to ten pages on a subject that interests you, and write a short paper based on it. Your paper may be either a summary or a review, whichever you prefer. Then exchange papers with another student to see whether the other person can tell whether you intended to write a review or a summary.

The Carson Factor by William Ashworth

In the spring of 1947, the farmers of Klamath County, Oregon, began a widely publicized "war of extermination" against the coyote. The campaign, which was designed to eliminate predators from the area and thereby make it "safe for mankind," was well organized, heavily financed, and extremely successful. The farmers of Oregon were pleased; they had eliminated a source of danger from their county. What they did not realize was that they also had eliminated nature's greatest check on the rodent population. All the mice needed now was a mild winter (excellent for breeding) combined with a few more fateful errors on the part of mankind, and they could literally take over.

Then in 1957 it happened: Suddenly the mice were everywhere. Mice-breeding burrows appeared throughout the county, leaving thousands of acres looking as though they had been dive-bombed. Potato farmers dug up their crops and found the mice—now as many as 10,000 inhabiting a single acre—nesting inside. Haystacks weighing up to 150 tons disappeared overnight as terror gripped the residents of Klamath County. A massive poisoning program was initiated. It had little effect on the mice, but five thousand snow geese died.

And so it went, all through that long, disastrous winter.

According to William Ashworth, one of the most compelling and dramatic environmentalist writers today, it was not really the absence of the coyote that led

Hawthorn Books, Inc., 1979.

to the mouse war but ignorance of what he terms the Carson Factor—Rachel Carson's plea, in *Silent Spring,* for universal "awareness that we are dealing with life."

"When we ignore it," Ashworth writes, "when we base our actions and our attitudes toward living things on the biological equivalent of the flat-earth theory, then our progress will be false, and the unforeseen results of it will continue to come back and haunt us."

The Carson Factor is more than the true-to-life story of the Klamath County mouse wars. It is a gripping tale of the consequences of humankind's tampering with the balance of nature. It is, in effect, the most effective plea for man-beast coexistence to date.

William Ashworth, active in environmentalist causes, is a free-lance writer living in Ashland, Oregon. His works have appeared in a number of publications, including *American Heritage* and *True;* for a number of years he served as the editor of the *Northwest Conifer,* a quarterly publication of the Pacific Northwest Chapter of the Sierra Club. Ashworth is the author of *Hells Canyon* and *The Wallowas,* both of which were published to critics' acclaim. His next book, which will expose the ways in which private interest groups manipulate Congress, will be published by Hawthorn in 1980.

Responses

1. This discussion of a book written by William Ashworth appeared on the front and back flaps of the book's dust cover. Such a discussion is usually called a "blurb." Its purpose, of course, was to encourage people to buy the book. Does it give enough information (summary) to arouse your interest? Why or why not? How does knowing that the evaluation was written by the publisher affect your reaction to it?

2. Which parts of the article are summary, which parts review? Would you like the article better if the summary and comments were more closely combined? Why or why not?

3. Is all the information given about Ashworth necessary to establish his qualifications for writing this book? If you think some of the information is unnecessary, which parts would you leave out? Why?

4. Are you given complete enough information about *The Carson Factor?* If not, what else would you like to know before deciding to read (or not read) the book?

5. Pretend that you are the publisher of some book you have liked. Then write a cover blurb that could be used on a new paperback edition of the book.

Kramer vs. Kramer

[1]   Normally I am a person who is willing, even eager, to suspend all rational judgment at a sad movie. I cry, therefore, I enjoy. *Kramer vs. Kramer* was this sort of movie, a three-hankie flick, if I ever saw one. So, I indulged in it like a chocoholic at the Godiva counter. However, in the cold light of the morning after the binge, the plot weighs a bit more heavily on my mind, if not on my hips. It occurs to me that the scales of Justice were tipped by the heavy hand of Hollywood.

[2]   The movie, for those of you who have been busy Star-Trekking, is about the transformation of a fairweather father into a full-time father. Mommy takes off for California and daddy takes over. Eventually mommy returns, and the stage is set for the ultimate custody battle. By the time Kramer and Kramer hits the courtroom, we are all on the side of the father. But, in a tribute to the acting powers of both Dustin Hoffman and Meryl Streep, by the end of the pivotal trial scene, both come across as perfectly decent, nonvillainous, equally loving parents genuinely concerned for their child.

[3]   Which is more than you can say for the legal system. *Kramer vs. Kramer* makes good drama out of lousy law. The judge awards the boy to the mother, because she is a "Mother"—and he does so without even chatting in chambers with this delightfully articulate 7-year-old boy.

[4]   Now, I grant you that there are, Lord knows, any number of arbitrary judges. But the fact is that in 1980, and especially in a major metropolitan area, the court is less likely to give instant primacy to Motherhood (especially deserting Motherhood) and extremely unlikely to make any custody decision without some evaluation of the kid. In real life, the Kramer boy would probably have had his own court-appointed attorney, or psychiatrist.

[5]   It also struck during my morning-after hangover that in the real world of divorce Mr. and Mrs. Kramer would have been more likely to share than to fight these days. They were perfect candidates for joint custody. The fact is that while millions of Americans sat in dark movie theaters across the land, sniffling over Kramer's farewell pep talk to his boy, we are seeing a strong trend toward shared divorced parenting. "Joint custody is not exactly sweeping the country, but the concept and actual practice is spreading," says Dr. Doris Jonas Freed, chair of the committees on child custody and on research of the family law section of the American Bar Association.

[6]   On Jan. 1, for example, a brand-new law went into effect in California which makes joint custody the first choice of the state courts. The California law was passed to assure that kids have the maximum contact with both parents and to encourage parents to share the rights and responsibilities of child rearing. Sole custody remains an option, as it should, but if a court in California does NOT grant joint custody, it has to have a reason.

[7]   This isn't just a piece of California-ism. Five other states provide for joint custody, and courts across the country are accepting it or even ruling on it. In

Ellen Goodman, *Boston Globe,* reprinted in the *San Antonio Light,* January 13, 1980.

New York recently, in Adler vs. Adler, each parent asked for sole custody of an 11-year-old, but the court opted for joint custody.

[8]   This doesn't mean splitting weeks or years down the middle, shuffling children back and forth from one school or town to another. It doesn't necessarily mean a 50–50 deal. It establishes a legal principle of the sharing of decision-making and of physical time, according to any sensible plan the parents can devise. It seems that if two parents can fashion an agreement together (and it does require cooperation) they are more likely to avoid the pitfalls of divorce—from child snatching to defaulting payments to disappearing acts.

[9]   Even the father's rights advocates have turned their interest from sole male custody to shared. As Dr. Freed said, "It's more important for children to have access to both parents, the love and affection of both. You know the old cliché, 'You don't divorce your children?' This will make it a reality." Neither parent need "lose" their child.

[10]   I grant you that a scene of the Kramers sitting down and bargaining would have meant fewer handkerchiefs. But what's bad for the movies may well prove better for many of the one million kids who go through divorce each year. After all, a tearjerker isn't much fun in real life.

Responses

1. What is the main point of this article? Can you find it stated in a single sentence? If not, write a main idea sentence for the article in your own words and then compare your sentence with those other students have written.

2. Where does Goodman summarize the plot of the film? Does the summary give enough information? If you have seen the movie, what would you add to her summary?

3. Which paragraphs of this article seem not to be discussing the film at all? Why has Goodman included them?

4. How does the conclusion of the article tie in with the introduction?

5. Compare what Goodman is saying in this article with what Ramos says in the article on page 377. What are the points of agreement? What are the differences? Write a short letter pretending you are Goodman responding to Ramos or Ramos responding to Goodman—or one of the Kramers responding to either of them.

6. Write a review of a movie you have seen recently. You may either confine your comments to what you thought of the movie, or you may use the theme of the film as a taking-off place for further discussion.

There's a Thumb in My Soup

Finger's
53 NW 1st Ave.
Phone: 223-0743
Lunch: 11:30 am to 2:30 pm
Dinner: 6 pm to 11:30 pm
Closed Sunday and Monday
Visa accepted

[1]   Great cuisines have always included an abundance of fine ingredients, a variety of cultural influences, and a leisured class that could afford creative chefs in great kitchens. Considering these requirements, we were intrigued to learn that Finger's, Portland's newest bid for dining elegance, had conceived the "New American Cuisine." After all, culinary models do not spring from heads as did Athena from Zeus'.

[2]   Owner-chef Fred Finger laid the visionary egg for this endeavor in the form of a mangled omelet at age 9—inauspicious beginnings for the founder of a new culinary movement. Nevertheless, Finger eventually developed a local following and gained respect for his cooking skills, first at Father's, a dining house in Manzanita, and, more recently, as head chef at The Gazebo, in Lake Oswego. With financial backing, he recently opened his own restaurant in Old Town's newly renovated Norton House.

[3]   The interior of this "fine arts restaurant" aims at seducing the tweed-and-silk set. Brick walls are hung with contemporary pieces, woolen lampshades hover over boxy white tables, and armless chairs, upholstered in dark cotton, project a clean and proper upper-middle-class image. Oak floors and cedar ceilings provide a sleek finishing touch to this perfect rendering of a cool, chic eating space. Taste is the object, but gallery-like sterility prevails.

[4]   At first perusal, the menu is riveting, punctuated by French and Italian preparations, complete with enticing descriptions. The thirteen-page wine list easily qualifies for a Library of Congress number. You assume that whoever arranged this selection of food and drink must be driven by passion, a good sign in the restaurant business. But after sampling various offerings on three recent visits, we must conclude that this passion is nothing more than skillful marketing.

[5]   Our first clue that Finger's' execution does not match its ambitions came with the hors d'oeuvres. A scoop of pinkish chicken-liver *pâté* ($2.50), meagerly garnished with four cucumber slices and a lone radish rose, will please only those who love pure liver, as this spread contains no other flavors. (We are not members of this minority group.) It also would take a strange breed to enjoy *crudités* ($1.95), crisp vegetable sticks attended by two blue-cheese balls of dry peanut-butter texture and soapy flavor. How crude indeed!

[6]   Our next warning came with the onion soup *gratinée* ($2.50). Onion strands

Karen Brooks and Gideon Bosker, *Willamette Week,* November 8–14, 1979.

swim in an aggressive beef-flavored stock while the oven-toasted bread, floating like a life preserver, is as indestructible as rubber food from a magic shop. Cream of broccoli soup ($1.95) is of the skimmed-milk variety, but we enjoyed cream of celery ($1.95), a hot and fatty chicken broth coarse with puréed vegetables.

[7]   Being great lovers of pasta, we sampled two of three available. *Linguini* with clams and *pesto* ($4.95 à la carte) deserves high marks. Warm, freshly cooked noodles are tossed with *pesto,* a Genoese sauce of fresh basil, Parmesan, and olive oil, all macerated in a mortar with a pestle from which this dish takes its name. The entire production is artfully rimmed with shells of briny baby clams. Less inspired is spaghetti *carbonara* ($4.95 à la carte), which is almost as good as buttered spaghetti, but not quite. Bits of rosy ham and peppery *prosciutto* (see if you can find them) contribute minimal flavor, while the thimbleful of Parmesan cheese provides none.

[8]   Don't look to the entrées for excellence—they are of little distinction and hardly warrant their princely price tags ($8.95 to $14.95), despite the addition of soup, salad and vegetables. Two veal dishes are offered, and they offer little. *Scaloppine* of veal *piccata* with rosemary potatoes ($10) is poorly treated: browned thin slices of high-quality meat are cooked to a dry and crusty state of sorrow. Although the menu claims the veal is sautéed with lemon, capers, and oregano, it would take a chemical analyst to detect any trace of these. And while we appreciate vegetables on the crispy side, a serving of half-cooked potatoes is stretching the concept. Veal *marsala* ($10) is little more than the *piccata* with a mask of sautéed mushrooms, although on one occasion the shavings of veal were moist and tender. The accompanying shoestring potatoes are hash browns raised to a low art, while crowns of naked broccoli cry out for their lemon garnish. We cannot comment on the salad because it never arrived.

[9]   Supreme of chicken with crab sauce ($10.95) consists of juicy, boned and skinned fowl, but the sauce does a terrific imitation of melted processed cheese. The best thing we can say about the saffron rice is that it never appeared.

[10]   If there is any gratification to be experienced at Finger's, it is of the delayed variety. After enduring several disappointing courses, our spirits were boosted by the most impressive selection of desserts in town. Coffee-tinged mocha-walnut torte ($1.95) is so deliciously rich with butter cream it should carry a warning from the surgeon general. *Sacher torte* ($1.95) is a wonderful layering of dense, deeply flavored chocolate cake, apricot jam, and gooey black icing. Our *bombe glacée* ($1.50), which varies nightly, was a mousse-like ice cream imbued with rum and capped with crushed walnut pralines. Pass on *grand marnier* soufflé ($3.50), a cup-cake-size meringue that reeks more of exploitation than of orange liqueur.

[11]   There may be a Finger in the kitchen, but the service is all thumbs. Waiters lack the confidence to assume any identity—not even a pompous one—and appear stressed by the unpredictability of the kitchen, both with respect to preparation time and availability of ingredients. No backroom escapades, however outrageous, could possibly explain their disorientation on two of our visits. On one, our waiter went underground for forty-five minutes, finally resurfacing to inform us that our chocolate soufflé had burned. On another, bread refills were so slow in coming that we were sure a rationing order was in effect.

[12]   Finger's suffers from an image problem. What it appears to offer, at first glance, diverges considerably from what it delivers. Menu misrepresentations abound on every level. The eloquent preamble primes you for a unique blend of European and Oriental cooking, yet the influence of the latter is nonexistent and the former makes an average showing at best.

[13]   The only thing revolutionary about the "New American Cuisine" is its inflationary pricing. Although integrity is evident in the use of fresh herbs, quality meat, and homemade bread, this alone cannot compensate for a succession of flawed, expensive dishes. Except for a dessert stop, our advice is: Let your fingers do the walking . . . past this place and into one more deserving of your patronage.

Responses

1. In this review of a restaurant, why is all the specific information given in a list at the beginning of the article? Would the article have read more smoothly if the name, location, times, etc. had been worked into the first paragraph? Why or why not?
2. Underline all the factual information—free of any opinion—given in the body of the article. Then compare what you have underlined with what other students have done.
3. What is the writers' attitude toward this restaurant? Make a list of the vivid words that show how they reacted to both the place and the food.
4. What comparisons do the writers use? How effective do you find the comparisons? How fair do they seem to be?
5. Write a review of some eating establishment at which you have eaten recently—any place, from a hamburger stand to a fancy French dining salon complete with wine and candles; write about the college dining room if you like. But be sure your review includes both factual information and your attitude toward the restaurant.

More Suggestions for Writing

Summaries—

    any chapter in any textbook you're using—a very good way to study and remember the material

    any material assigned for outside reading

    your lecture notes, before they get cold

    any article you've read, or speech you've heard, that seems important or interesting

Reviews—
    a record or tape or album of music
    a concert
    a play
    a television program—soap opera, talk show, special feature, whatever
    a school program
    a story
    a poem
    a book
    a street fair

Appendix One/ Writing Business Letters

Some time or another, whether or not the job you hold requires it, you're likely to have to write some business letters. You may conduct most of your business by phone, but that doesn't mean you will not also need letters. If you've called to let a company know you're not pleased with their services and want things changed, your message will go further if you follow the call with a letter to the right people. If you have a job where you need to place or take orders for supplies, offer or receive estimates, report to the boss or communicate with other employees, you'll want some kind of written record. And if you want to switch jobs, you may use the phone as a first step, but you'll certainly want to write a letter of application as well, both as a way of getting clear in your own mind what your qualifications are and as a way of presenting those qualifications in the most attractive, orderly, and efficient form. Clearly, letters have an advantage over phone calls: letters can be kept, referred to, verified, reread. Phone calls can't. Letters last, phone calls don't.

For all these reasons, knowing how to write a good business letter is important. Business writing is generally the same as other kinds of successful writing. Business letters should be clear, make a point (have a main idea), be carefully organized, and be easy to understand. Where business writing differs from the writing you have been doing, the difference lies in a slightly greater formality and a slightly more crisp tone than you may have been accustomed to using.

Being formal, however, does not mean using jargon. No good modern business writer uses such out-of-date phrases as "Yours of the 4th inst. duly received" or "Hoping to hear from you soon, I remain, your obedient servant." Good business writing comes to the point and sticks to it. Good business writers seldom include personal chit-chat, but neither do they avoid using "I" and "you" if they mean *I* and *you*. The tone is straightforward and natural.

Application Letters

Perhaps the most important type of business letter you'll ever write is a job application—the letter itself and the personal information sheet (resumé) that goes with it. Being straightforward and natural is essential in an application. Even though you've been remembering your readers' needs in other writing, here you should go one step further and actually put yourself in the reader's place. For *you,* your letter means, "I want a job with this company." For the *employer,* the letter means, "The writer of this letter is (or is not) able to do a good job for my company." Since the success of your letter depends on pleasing the person who reads it, you must try to imagine what you would want to hear if you were doing the hiring. Your letter must do more than just say, "I want the job."

One way of pleasing the reader is to keep the letter short, usually not more than four or five paragraphs. If at all possible, keep it to one page. The letter should include:

1. how you heard about the vacancy (from an advertisement, a friend, a placement service)
2. your most important reasons for thinking you're suited for the position
3. a word or two about your reasons for thinking the job would suit you
4. a brief statement about your present circumstances (status in school, reasons for wanting to change jobs or location)
5. the best way to get in touch with you and, if the job is within traveling range or if you can expect a visit from a representative, a request for an interview.

If you are answering an advertisement, you might begin by saying, "I saw your advertisement for an administrative assistant in the *Northfield News* of April 3, and I would like to apply for the position." Or if you heard about the vacancy from a friend who is employed by the same company, you might start with, "Thelma Gervitz, who works in your department, told me that you are looking for an administrative assistant. I am writing to apply for the job."

In explaining why you are qualified for the position, follow any clues you have about the requirements of the job. If it's construction work (or any other work that may be physically demanding), be sure to say you're in good health—if you are—and add anything else that will make you sound healthy: the jogging you do, the volleyball you play, your experience as a logger or a camp counselor or a furniture mover. If the job is in sales, think of qualities that relate to selling: your pleasing personality (as demonstrated by the college offices you have been elected to, perhaps); your aggressiveness (as demonstrated by your sales record on your present job or the promotions you've been given); your active imagination (as demonstrated by the sales campaign you suggested or the successful advertisement you wrote); your leadership ability (as demonstrated by your volunteer work with the Girl Scouts or the East Side Improvement Association).

If you have had actual experience in the kind of job you're applying for, certainly that experience is your best recommendation. Be sure to mention it, saying exactly when, where, and how long you worked: "From June through September 1975, I worked as research assistant to Mr. Oscar Salmon, at Dynamic Services in Wichita."

But even if you have never had any direct experience in the special kind of job you're trying for, there's no reason to give up if the job sounds interesting and you believe you could do it well. Most people have *something* in their backgrounds that relates to nearly any job. A little thought will help you see how to make the most of your experiences and relate them to the job you want.

Take your clues from the advertisements. Look carefully at the "Help Wanted" section of the Sunday newspaper. For instance, what kinds of words appear over and over in the ads for accountants? "Budget analyst, performance evaluation, capital investment, managerial experience, growth potential, billing expert, operational audits, long-range planning." If you want to be an accountant, and if you've had the training for it, use some of those words when you write your letter. Whatever job you're looking for—in administration, sales, education, programming, health services, or anything else—you will sound like a more attractive candidate if you take a hint from the ad writers.

If you are applying for a job as an administrative assistant, for example, talk about some of your old experiences in some of the new, fashionable words. If you have been a camp counselor, you can justifiably say that part of your job was as "assistant administrator," in charge of thirty-five girls; that you arbitrated grievances, made time-flow charts, helped develop goals and objectives, were involved in short- and long-range planning, and helped with the final evaluations. Don't say any of that if it wasn't so, of course, but even if you just made out the summer schedules, deciding who got the canoes and who got the tetherball, you did some short- and long-range planning. And even if you just wrote to the parents at the end of the camp session telling them how well their daughters adjusted, you've done some evaluations and handled some correspondence.

Does the job you're applying for require you to work with the general public? Selling tickets to the sophomore play, or collecting for the United Fund, is "working with the public." Does it ask for planning and management ability? If you've had a successful delivery route, or handled the budget for the annual awards banquet, you've done some "productive planning" and can demonstrate some "efficient management."

Once you have explained why you think you are suited for the job, mention why the job would suit you. Unless you are contented in your work, you won't be a very good employee and employers realize this. Don't say selling automotive parts will be your life work unless you really have no other ambitions, but do emphasize the parts of the job you'd like. Say, for example, "I like working with the general public, and I enjoy methodical attention to detail."

Be sure to say what you are doing now. If you are going to school, say when you expect to finish. If you are working part-time, say where. If you are unemployed, you can just say, "I will be available to begin work at any time that is convenient for you." And of course, if you are answering an advertisement, you will have to include any other information the ad asks for. A request to "state salary expected" sometimes appears in job advertisements. Expected salary is awkward to discuss in a letter. You may ruin your chance at the job if you ask for too much, but if you ask for too little, you risk getting hired for less than the company might have been willing to pay. You can't ignore the specific request, but you might sidestep it by saying, "I would expect to be paid at the usual rates for beginning administrative assistants," or "The salary is negotiable."

As for how the employer can get in touch with you, be sure to give both an address and a phone number. If you are away at school from eight to five every day, say, "I can be reached at 968-6092 any evening after five o'clock." An offer to come in for an interview whenever it's convenient for the employer makes a good closing line. Your last paragraph should also mention that you are enclosing a personal information sheet, giving specific details about your education, experience, and references, unless you have referred to this fact sheet earlier in the letter.

It's particularly important to edit and proofread your letter before you mail it. The care with which you prepare your letter may be the employer's best indication of the care with which you will do your job. Some ads even ask you to reply in your own handwriting, rather than typing the letter, since handwriting is another possible index of care and character. Whether you write or type, however, a sloppy, misspelled letter may prejudice the employer against you, even though the job you are applying for may never require you to do any spelling at all.

Other simple things that may determine whether or not you get a response from the company are the neatness of your typing, the form of your letter, and your ability to balance between boastfulness on the one hand and an apologetic overmodesty on the other. Don't worry about beginning your sentences with "I." After all, you are telling about yourself, and saying so straight out is better than awkward attempts at avoiding what would be the normal wording.

Don't hesitate to get help on the wording, spelling, or typing. Once you've gathered the information, decided what you want to say, and written a draft of the letter, get somebody else to read what you have written and make suggestions about improving it. Ask somebody else to read it even though you're pretty confident you're done a good job. Full professors writing for foundation grants get help on their applications, and unless they have secretaries they often ask friends to do the typing for them.

Remember, the point is not how much you can do without help but how attractive you can make your letter. If your application letter and personal information sheet are neat, well organized, complete, and courteous, employers who value competence and efficiency will give your application serious attention.

Sample Application Letter

4039 State Street, Apt. 6
Bethel, New Jersey 18404
April 17, 1981

Mabel Parsons, Personnel Director
Bosell Optical Supply Company
353 Main Street
Baxter, New Jersey 18600

Dear Ms. Parsons:

Please consider this letter my application for the position of administrative assistant, as advertised in last week's Sunday Gazette.

My experience as an assistant administrator comes from two sources, my position as business manager for the Bethel Bugle (the college newspaper) and my job as counselor at Camp Nokomis. As business manager for the paper, I was responsible for selling advertisements, handling the billing and collecting, helping with the layout of the paper, and supervising student assistants. As camp counselor, I was in direct charge of thirty-five adolescent girls. I arbitrated grievances, made time-flow charts, helped develop goals and objectives, worked on long-range planning, and wrote evaluations.

At present I am a business major at Bethel Community College, where I expect to graduate in May. I have been on the Dean's Honor Roll each semester. My courses have included "Business Management," "Management Theory and Practice," and "Advanced Accounting."

I am especially interested in the position with your company since photography is one of my hobbies and I know a little about lenses and lens-grinding.

I am enclosing a personal information sheet with this letter, and I will be glad to come to Baxter for an interview. I can be reached at the above address or by phone (688 037-6620) any day after 4:30 p.m.

Sincerely,

Roselle Peters

Roselle Peters

enclosure

Personal Information Sheet

Your personal information sheet, sometimes called a resumé, should give a complete and accurate account of:

1. all the personal details employers are curious about
2. your education
3. your work experience
4. at least three references

All this information could be included in the letter, of course, and some of it probably has been, but it looks stronger and clearer in outline form. Besides, if you keep a copy for your own records, all the information will be at hand when you need to apply for another job. Each application letter you write will be slightly different, but most of your personal information sheet will stay the same.

You may wish to give personal information about age; health; citizenship; whether you are single, married, or divorced; number of children, if you have any; and hobbies or special interests. However, regulations against discrimination prohibit employers from demanding this information.

The order of the rest of the information sheet will depend on whether you think education or experience is more likely to get you the job. If you've had experience in the field, then that is probably more important than your education. But if your work experience is not directly related to the job you are applying for, you'll probably want to list your education first, especially if your degree or training does relate to the job.

Your educational record should begin with the school you last attended and work backward to grade school. Give the name of the school, the city and state where it is, the years you attended, and, for high school and college, the date of your graduation. Be sure to list any specific courses that you think the employer would be interested in.

Job experience, too, should begin with the present and go backward. Give the dates of your employment; the name of the person or company you worked for; the address; the name of your immediate supervisor, if it is different from the name of your employer; and a description of the kind of work you did, unless it's obvious from the job title. Ordinarily, your educational record and your job record taken together should account for your time after you got out of high school. If there are any large gaps, they may lead a prospective employer to wild speculation about what you were doing in that unexplained year or two. Better satisfy that curiosity; you can say, "September 1975–March 1976, unemployed" or "August 1972–August 1973, stayed home with small baby." Unless your record of full-time employment is fairly long, it is better to include all the jobs you have ever had—paper routes, baby-sitting, lawn-mowing. Though these jobs may seem unimportant and quite different from the job you are applying for, the habits of responsibility and self-control demanded by any regular work may be just what will sway the employer in your favor. If the list is long, you may want to group part-time jobs or those that you held for a short time under a section "Miscellaneous Jobs."

If you're participated in any activities or joined any clubs, be sure to mention it. Be creative in your thinking. Maybe you sang in the church choir or helped out at Boys' Club or played some sport (even city league or church league). Think of how you spent your time outside of class or after work. You may be surprised to discover that much of that time was spent helping others or organizing events.

You should give at least three references, including at least one person you have worked for and at least one of your college teachers. It's all right to include a couple of character references, but they should not be relatives, and they ought not to be such close friends that they would obviously be prejudiced in your favor. Except for previous employers, it's a good idea to ask for permission before you list anyone as a reference. For one thing, asking permission is an ordinary act of politeness; for another, you shouldn't take the chance of naming someone who might be unwilling to write a letter recommending you.

Like your application letter, your personal information sheet must be neat, carefully organized, and complete.

Sample Personal Information Sheet

Roselle Peters   Age: 29
4039 State St., Apt. 6   Health: excellent
Bethel, New Jersey 18404   Citizenship: U.S.
Phone: 688 037-6620   Divorced, one child, 6
                                  Hobbies: photography
                                            hiking

Education
1979-1981:   Bethel Community College, Bethel, New Jersey
                A.A., May, 1981, in Business Administration,with
                    special course work in photography, journalism,
                    and communications

1970-1972:   evening courses in secretarial science at
                    Richardson Community College, Richardson,
                    California, including typing, business
                    machines, and shorthand

1966-1970:   Northland High School, Richardson, California
                Graduated in June 1970, in the top 10% of the
                    class

Experience
1980-1981:   Business manager of Bethel Bugle, published
                    weekly at Bethel Community College
                Responsibilities: selling advertisements,
                    billing, collecting, layout, supervision
                    of student assistants
                Immediate supervisor: Professor Arnold Getz,
                    journalism instructor

1979-1981:   Waitress, part-time, The Salad Bar
                Immediate supervisor: Mary Bettesford,
                    owner, 7831 Elm St., Bethel, New Jersey
                    18406

1977-1979:   Counselor for three months each summer at Camp
                    Nokomis, Forest Heights, New Jersey 18333
                  Responsibilities: leading adolescent girls,
                    arbitrating grievances, making time-flow
                    charts, developing goals and objectives,
                    working on long-range planning, and
                    writing evaluations
                  Immediate supervisor: Antoinette Smith, Camp
                    Nokomis

1975-1977:   Stayed at home caring for baby daughter

1973-1975:   Stenographer, Rutherford Lumber Company,
                    Rutherford, Oregon 97330
                  Immediate supervisor: Nelson Lundgren,
                    same address

1971-1972:   Clerk-typist, Ingalls Insurance Company,
                    Richardson, California 93266
                  Immediate supervisor, Allan P. Jones, same
                    address

Fall 1970:   Waitress, Blondie's Cafe, Richardson,
                    California
                  Immediate supervisor: Blondie Welch, 36
                    Highway 99, Richardson, California 93267

References

Professor Arnold Getz   Professor J.S. Rutherford
Journalism Department   Business Administration
Bethel Community College   Division
Bethel, New Jersey 18406   Bethel Community College
                                    Bethel, New Jersey 18406

Antoinette Smith, Director
Camp Nokomis   Mary Bettesford
Forest Heights, New Jersey 18333   The Salad Bar
                                    7831 Elm Street
                                    Bethel, New Jersey 18406

Letters of Request

Even though application letters are actually requests that you be considered for a job, we have dealt with them separately here because they are likely to be more important to you than more casual requests and because they call for very specialized kinds of information. But application letters are not the only kind of request letters you will need to write. You may need to ask, in writing, about a variety of other things:

What courses are scheduled at the college you plan to attend?
Would one of your professors, or the family you used to baby-sit for, be willing to write a recommendation letter for you?
Where can you order parts for an old sewing machine?
Can the local historical society provide information about the earliest church in your community?

That sort of thing.

Whenever you write a letter of request, the letter should include three things:

1. an explanation of exactly what you want
2. an explanation of why you want it
3. an expression of appreciation for the help you hope to get.

In very short requests these three things can sometimes be combined. For instance, if you are writing to Oakton Community College asking for information about the fall schedule, your letter might just say:

I'm planning to take some courses in data processing at Oakton Community College this fall. Since I will probably have to attend classes after work, could you please send me a copy of your evening class schedule? Thank you very much.

Most of the letters you write, however, will need to be slightly more detailed than that request and will probably require three or four paragraphs.

Letters of request, like most other business correspondence, are set up on the page in the same way as the application letter shown on page [385]. All business letters contain at least six parts:

1)	**Heading**	The complete address of the writer, with the date beneath it. If the letter is written on paper with the company or organization's name printed at the top—called the "letterhead"—only the date is typed in.
2)	**Inside Address**	The name and address of the company, person, or organization you're writing to.
3)	**Salutation**	A conventional greeting to the person you're writing to, usually beginning with "Dear." If you're writing just to a company or organization, the usual salutation is "Gentlemen." However,

		if you are a supporter of the women's movement, you may want to omit the salutation and just say "Attention Personnel Manager" or "Attention Credit Department," whatever seems appropriate.
4)	**Body**	Whatever you need to say in the actual letter. Especially in typed letters, you need to leave a double space between paragraphs.
5)	**Complimentary Closing**	Some conventional expression at the end, such as "Yours truly," "Sincerely," or even, if you know the person well, "With best regards."
6)	**Signature**	Your typewritten or hand-printed name, with your written signature above it.

These six parts can be arranged on the page in more than one acceptable way. The application letter on page [385] is set up in *block form;* that is, the inside address, the salutation, and the body are all lined up even with the left-hand margin, and the heading, the complimentary closing, and the signature are lined up in the middle of the page. Block form is the most usual in typewritten letters, but *modified block form*—just the same except that the first line of each paragraph in the body is indented about half an inch—is probably better for hand-written letters.

Once the letter is written, addressing the envelope is simple. Your name and address go in the upper left-hand corner. The name and address of the person or organization you're writing to go in the center of the envelope, with both pieces of information written in block form. Until recently it was good practice to copy these names and addresses just as they appeared in the letter. Now, however, the post office is requesting that the official two-letter state abbreviations be used. Instead of "Maine," write ME; instead of "Minnesota," write MN. Using these abbreviations not only makes it easier for the computers to sort the mail, it also makes it more likely that your letter will be delivered promptly. If you want to be consistent, you can, of course, use these new abbreviations in the heading and the inside address of the letter.

Sample Letter of Request

Heading

2215 56th Street
Riverview, Arizona 73811
April 8, 1981

Inside Address

Professor Elizabeth Stevens
Mt. Hope Community College
El Capitan, California 53409

Salutation

Dear Professor Stevens:

Body in Modified Block Form

    I hope you will remember me. I took your course in child care at Mt. Hope Community College in the fall semester, 1979, and received an A. You told me during our last conference that you would be glad to give me a reference whenever I needed one.

    I am applying for a position as assistant director of Mayfield Day Care Center and have been asked to give a reference who can speak to my experience with children. Can you write a letter for me? Please send the letter to

Mr. Roger Anderson
Mayfield Day Care Center
1506 River Street
Riverview, Arizona 73824

The letter should reach him before May 15, when applications for the job will be closed.

    Thank you very much for whatever help you can give me.

Complimentary Close

Cordially,

Barbara Jenkins

Signature

Barbara Jenkins

Sample Envelope

```
Barbara Jenkins
2215 56th Street
Riverview, AZ 73811




                        Professor Elizabeth Stevens
                        Mt. Hope Community College
                        El Capitan, CA 53409
```

Letters of Complaint

Letters of complaint are often much harder to write than other request letters. Probably you are already furious. You have been threatened with a collection agency for a bill you have already paid, or the merchandise you sent a check for six months ago has not yet arrived and nobody has bothered to answer the letter you've already sent.

Before you begin the next letter, decide what your aim is: Do you want to blow off steam or do you want to get a bad situation improved? If blowing off steam is what you're after, use your own creativity—you don't need a model. But if you are really trying one more time to get the problem straightened out, keep your temper and sound reasonable. Say exactly what happened, exactly what you're complaining about, exactly what you want done. Set a deadline if you like ("by return mail"), but don't threaten suit unless you actually mean to hire a lawyer.

In other words, a letter of complaint has a lot in common with any other business letter. It needs to be clear, complete, and reasonably polite, although there's certainly no need to say thank you for the mistake that has been made. Succesful letters of complaint will always include:

1. a detailed explanation of what the problem is
2. a suggested solution to the problem
3. a request for some response to your letter

Sometimes such letters need more support or explanation than can be given in the body of the letter. You may want to send a copy of an earlier letter or a canceled check. If you do send something more than the letter itself, type the word "Enclosure" at the left-hand margin, below your typed signature. If you are sending more than one extra thing, you can say "Enclosures 2" or "Enclosures 3."

Sometimes, too, you may want to send a copy of your letter to somebody else, either because you think they can help or because you think they should know what the situation is. Whenever that happens, type "cc" (for "carbon copy") followed by the name of the person or organization that is getting the copy. The abbreviation "cc" is used even if what you are sending is a photocopy rather than a carbon. This information, like the information that something is being enclosed, is typed at the left-hand margin, below the signature line.

Finally, if you want to make extra sure your letter is received, you can send it by certified or registered mail, and pay the postal service for sending you a card saying the letter was actually delivered. The letter should also contain this information, typed as the last item, against the left-hand margin.

Sample Letter of Complaint

```
                                  9876 Towne Ave., Apt. M-5
                                  Hampstead, NB 77015
                                  February 22, 1981


Happy Seed Company
P. O. Box 35
Flackmore, IN 34567

Attention:  Order Department

On April 5, 1980, I sent you a check for $35.19 to cover
my order for your Special Blooms Catalog ($2.00) and your
special offer of 25 miscellaneous seedlings ($31.00). The
check included $2.19 for postage, the amount asked for in
your advertisement.

When the order did not arrive, I wrote to you in June and
again in July. I have not received either my order or any
answer to my letters. With this letter I am enclosing photo-
copies of my canceled check, endorsed by your company on
April 8, 1980, and the two earlier letters I sent you.

By return mail I would like to have either my money back or
the goods I have paid for.

I am sending a copy of this letter to the Flackmore Better
Business Bureau. Both letters are going by registered mail.

                                  Yours truly,

                                  Edgar Steel
                                  Edgar Steel

Enclosures 3
cc: Flackmore Better Business Bureau
Registered Mail
```

Business Writing on the Job

So far, we have been talking about the kind of business letters you may need to write for yourself. Many jobs, however, will require you to write letters for your organization—placing orders, answering inquiries or complaints, promoting special events, or just providing information. Such letters follow the same rules that have already been given, with a few minor differences:

1. When you're writing for an organization, you'll probably use letterhead stationery. In that case, the part of the heading you add will be only the date.
2. Because you're only part of the organization, you will need to show what your position is. Under your typed signature, put "Order Department" or "Assistant Membership Chair" or whatever your accurate title is.
3. If your organization has a typist who prepares the letter for you, the letter should show that help. Your initials are typed in capitals at the left-hand margin, followed by a slash mark and the initials of the typist, usually in small letters: JFK/mw. Remember, however, that you're responsible for any letter you sign, so read it carefully to be sure there are no omissions or mistakes.
4. If you have letterhead stationery, you will probably also have envelopes with the organization's name and address printed on them. You can either let the printed return address stand as it is or, if the organization is large, type your name and position just below the printed material.
5. Your organization may have a special style or special models for you to follow. If that is so, follow them.

Sample On-the-Job Letter

NORTHWEST PRESERVATION ASSOCIATION
813 Overland Road
South Little Fork, Idaho 63334
Telephone: 866 731-8698

October 30, 1981

Ms. Agatha Trent
84 N.E. Graham St.
Lasser, Kansas 41444

Dear Ms. Trent:

I'm glad to tell you that membership in the Northwest
Preservation Association is not limited to people who live
in the northwest. We welcome anyone interested in pre-
serving our mountains, streams, and forests.

Dues in the association are $10.00 a year. For that you
will receive a subscription to our quarterly, God's Country,
with professional photographs and articles on the animals,
wild flowers, and shrubs of the forest. You will also
receive, every other month, a detailed map of a different
wilderness area, showing trails, campsites, etc.

I am enclosing a membership application form, and I hope I
will hear from you soon. Without the support of people like
you, we have little hope of keeping this remarkable area
unspoiled.

Sincerely,

Harry J. Roth

Harry J. Roth
Membership Department

HJR/ECK
Enclosure

If you need to write to someone in your own organization, perhaps so there will be an official record of some action, explanation, or request, the general rules are the same, but the form is a bit different. In places where there are no printed sheets for interoffice memos, you can create your own. The heading will contain four items:

To:
From:
Subject:
Date:

Then the body of the memo proceeds in much the same way as any other piece of business writing. Like anything else you write, a memo needs to be signed, either by your written name after the last paragraph or by your written initials at the end of the "from" line.

Sample Interoffice Memo

```
TO:  Catherine Larson, Assistant Vice-President

FROM:  Oscar Brown, Mailing Room Supervisor

SUBJECT:  Fire in the mailing room

DATE:  September 6, 1981

Yesterday, September 7, 1981, waste material in the back
hall of the mailing room, just south of where the packing
is done, caught on fire.  Marcia Means, who was the only
employee working at the time, smelled smoke and investigated.
Her prompt action in using the fire extinguisher on the wall
just outside the shipping room door prevented the fire from
doing much damage.  She noticed the smoke at 3:15 p.m. and by
3:20 the flames were completely out.

The paint on the south wall is somewhat dirty from the
smoke, but otherwise no property was damaged, since the
waste material was all contained in the large metal barrel
provided for it.

Marcia did not set off the fire alarm, since she had already
put out the fire, but she does tell me that the smoke detector
in the mailing room did not go off.  That detector should
probably be inspected and replaced.

I cannot determine what caused the fire.  Marcia, who was
working alone, does not smoke, and there appeared to be
nothing but the usual scraps, stuffing material, and paper
in the barrel.
```

Appendix Two/
Writing
Longer Papers

Even though you have written ten or twenty successful short papers, and been rather proud of your efforts, there's something about the announcement "term paper" that may make you forget everything you know about writing. It's true that you will have to spend more time on a long paper than on a short one, and it's true that a bigger proportion of your semester grade may depend on how successfully you write it. But there is no need to fall into a state of hysterical alarm just because some teacher says, "Term papers will be due the last week of the semester," and casually adds, "Make it about two thousand words long." There's no need to count up on your fingers (two thousand words is about eight typed pages) and decide you can't possibly do it.

Actually, the main difference between a term paper (or a reference or a research paper, whatever it's called) and any other college paper is just that—length. You'll be all right if you remember that you are almost never expected to produce eight pages out of your own unassisted head. Long assignments usually take it for granted that you will get some of your material from magazine articles and books. There are some exceptions, of course, but those exceptions often make the paper even easier to write. Suppose you are taking a course in child development: your term paper may consist of the observations you have made all semester in the day care center, together with the conclusions you have drawn from what you have observed. In that case, you will have known about the assignment from the beginning of the semester, and the careful day-by-day notes you have taken will form the bulk of your paper. Or suppose you are taking diesel mechanics: your term paper may be a careful report of the repair job your group did on one truck. These two papers are not much different from the kinds of reports you may have to write when you are actually out on a job.

Whatever form your term paper takes, be sure to find out exactly what you are expected to do. If the assignment isn't completely clear, ask the teacher to repeat it or stay after class and get a fuller explanation. If the assignment is a reference paper—that is, one in which you are expected to use books or magazines to collect your information—be sure to ask what style manual you need to follow. Then get a copy and follow it exactly when you put your paper in final form.

Be sure, also, that you leave yourself plenty of time to do the necessary research. A term paper, even though it isn't much different from any other writing you have been doing, cannot be completed between midnight Friday and 9 A.M. Monday. Take it seriously, but don't worry yourself sick over it.

The Reason for Research Papers

No teacher, in an English class or any other course, asks you to do a research paper just to make life hard for you. Good research papers are more than an exercise in following what may seem tiresome steps, one by one, and then submitting the results in conventional form. Good research papers, like any other kind of looking-and-finding, can be an exciting experience in discovery.

They also provide good practice in making discoveries. People in hundreds of different kinds of jobs are required to find information—from the law clerk who hunts for old legal decisions to help prevent your neighbor from damming up your creek, to the lab assistants who helped Salk isolate the polio vaccine. The people who hold such jobs not only have to find information, they have to evaluate it and decide how it relates to the question with which they began. They have to locate, examine, sometimes discard, and always summarize accurately.

Good research always begins with a question. Unlike some other papers you have written, you don't start with a main idea and look for things that will support it. Instead, you start with a topic, ask yourself something about it, and set out to find an answer.

You'll do a better job, and stand a better chance of enjoying the process, if you begin with a question you really care about. In some classes, a general topic will be assigned, in much the same way that the investigations you do on a job will be determined by the needs of the job. If you are given a topic, narrow your question to the part you find most interesting. If that's impossible, ask your teacher whether you can change to some other topic related to the course, something you *can* get involved in. Most teachers don't really want you to waste your time on a topic that bores you.

If a topic has not been assigned, the possibilities are wide open. Are you curious about whether windmills are a real alternative to nuclear energy? Do you want to know whether there are too few, or too many, hospital beds in your area? What's involved in starting a small weekly newspaper? One student, whose aunt refused to buy a tuna sandwich, began to wonder whether boycotting tuna would really help porpoises. Once she got started, she read a lot of material not actually connected with her question. She explored whether dolphins can talk, and she grew indignant about what has happened to whales. She might have switched to either of those topics, but she decided to stay with the porpoise controversy because it seemed more timely.

In working out your question, don't worry about making a world-shaking discovery. College students are not expected to do the kind of research that results in a cure for cancer or an idea nobody has ever had before. One writer commented not long ago that most of our so-called intelligence is not in our heads but in the libraries of the world. A research paper is a chance for you to find some of it in your own library, evaluate it, and use it.

Finding Material

Suppose you are interested in American Indian treaties. Before you decide that your main idea will be that most of the treaties were unfair to the Indians, or that almost all of them have been broken, you'll need to spend a good deal of time in the library, finding out all you can about the treaties. Almost any college library can give you three sources of help: the card catalog, the magazine index, and the reference librarian. You may want to try the card catalog first. In it you will find listed all the books the library owns, cross referenced under author, title, and subject. At this point in your search, the "subject" cards (or, in some libraries a big book called "subject index") will give you the most help. Look both under "Indians" and under "treaties." You will probably find that most of the books you're interested in are shelved very close together, under the same general classification number. Jot down a number or two and, if your library has "open shelves"—that is, if you are allowed to go where the books are shelved and look through them—find the right section and begin browsing through the books you find. If the library has "closed shelves"—that is, if you must take a call slip to the desk and have them bring the books to you—you can still browse through several to see which will be most useful, but the process will be slower.

If your subject is Indians, you will probably want to deal with some events more recent than can be found in most books, the troubles at Wounded Knee, perhaps, or the attempt some west coast Indians made a few years ago to capture and hold Alcatraz. For this information, you will need to go to the magazine index, the *Readers' Guide to Periodical Literature,* a series of bound volumes which lists all the articles that have been published in most magazines of general circulation. It comes out by the month; then the last few monthly editions are combined into slightly bigger paper editions; and finally the paper editions are combined into big volumes, each of which covers two years. If you are looking for recent material, the best way to start is by beginning at the present and working back toward the past. The front of each volume carries a list of the abbreviations used. *Sat R,* for instance, means the *Saturday Review,* and the numbers following it show the page numbers of the article and the date of the magazine. You can easily find out what magazines your library stores back issues of, either bound or on microfilm. When you have copied down the notations for the articles that interest you, take your list to a librarian who will get them for you. And finally, of course, if you have not found enough material, ask the reference librarian whose job it is to help you find the things you need.

Don't try to read all of everything you have found. Instead, glance rapidly through each book or magazine, trying to find material that relates to your specific topic. Then you can read the ones that will be most useful.

As you read, take notes on all the information you think you will want. Most people find that 3 × 5 notecards are the simplest way to record information—that's why they're called "notecards," of course. But whether you use notecards or a notebook, there are a few standard procedures you ought to follow:

1. Keep your notes brief, but accurate; if you copy too much, it will be hard to sort out when you begin to plan your paper.
2. Put the information you find into your own words or, if you can't always do that, use quotation marks when you copy more than three consecutive words from somebody else.
3. Be sure to record the exact source of every note you take; nothing is more exasperating than having to go back through every book you have read, looking for where you found an important piece of information.

If there's someone in your area who's an expert on your subject, you might try for an interview, either in person or on the telephone. Perhaps there's a lawyer who defended some Indians arrested for spearing salmon, or perhaps you know the Indians who did the spearing. If the student writing about porpoises had lived in San Diego or Astoria, Oregon, she might have been able to talk to some of the men who go out on the tuna boats. If you do ask for an interview, be sure to have one or two specific questions ready, and be sure to take careful notes of what you hear, just as you would on material from a book or magazine.

Planning the Paper

Once you have made yourself something of an expert on your topic, or at least have found out a good deal about it, you can decide what the main idea of your paper will be. You have already found the support for it, so your main idea can rest firmly on the material you have collected.

Now the job is much like the job in writing any other paper. You will make a plan, showing the order in which you will use your material. Your introduction will make the limits of your topic clear and give readers an indication of what your purpose is. If your paper—the report of what you have discovered—is to be successful, it should have only one general purpose, but you will probably need to use many of the other writing purposes, too. (The exceptions, in most reference papers, are giving directions and personal experience.) But you will need to *define* the most important terms you use; you may find *comparisons* or *classifications* helpful; you'll want to *analyze* how something works or what caused it. Even though you take a position for or against something—those Indian treaties were unfair, or we do need stricter rules about killing porpoises—you will need to *tell what happened,* and you will need to keep your writing as objective as possible. You'll need to support what you say by examples, statistics, authorities, and probably predictions. You'll want your conclusion, whatever it is, to be logical. And without some careful *summary* of what you have read, you can't write the paper at all.

Perhaps you'll be asked to turn in a formal sentence outline as part of the paper. Here's an outline of the porpoise paper. It's not quite the one that the student made before she started to write; instead, it shows the changes she made as she was writing. Notice that she put each main division into a complete sentence, and that she never subdivided unless she had at least two subtopics.

The Plight of the Porpoises

   I. Attempts to save porpoises have caused much argument.
  II. Considerable information about porpoises (dolphins) exists.
     A. Tales are told about their friendliness to people.
       1. The Greeks told about a man saved by a dolphin.
       2. The Romans told of a dolphin playing with a boy.
       3. In New Zealand a dolphin played with children.
     B. Modern science has studied dolphins.
       1. Bottle-nosed dolphins live well in captivity.
       2. Dolphins are mammals, belonging to the whale family.
       3. Dolphins are intelligent.
         a. They probably have a language.
         b. Their responses fit the definition of intelligence.
         c. They can be trained to fight for the navy.
 III. The tuna industry "fishes on dolphins."
     A. Superseiners throw nets around both dolphin and tuna.
     B. Attempts to free the dolphin often don't succeed.
 IV. Laws and litigation began in the early 1970s.
     A. In 1972 Congress passed the Marine Mammal Protection Act.
     B. In 1974 environmentalists filed suit against the government permits.
     C. In 1976 the suit was decided in favor of the dolphins and the court asked for more information.
       1. An international commission defined "optimum sustainable population."
       2. The report was published in late 1976.
     D. In 1977 environmentalists filed another lawsuit, which they lost.
     E. The tuna industry began to lobby for more lenient legislation.
  V. Scientists found better ways to get dolphin out of the nets.
     A. In 1975 *The Bold Contender* tested five improvements.
     B. In 1976 *Elizabeth C. J.* tested refinements of those improvements.
       1. These ships had good dolphin records.
       2. *Elizabeth C. J.* operated under special conditions.
 VI. The tuna industry responded to the 1977 regulations.
     A. They threatened to sell ships to foreign countries.
     B. They warned that business and jobs would suffer.
VII. We're not doing enough to save the dolphins.
     A. No international agency protects them.

B. Tuna could be caught by other methods and the tuna industry could still survive.

C. Even if present regulations were enforced, too many dolphins would still continue being killed.

Giving Credit

Because many of the things you will be saying in this long paper really belong to somebody else—that is, you are depending on facts other people have gathered or statements they have made—you will need to let your readers know where your material came from. There are two standard ways of giving credit to the original author.

The first method—footnoting—is used for specific borrowing. You must give the original writer the credit whenever you use

1. statistics collected by someone else
2. a piece of information or an example that is not common knowledge
3. more than three consecutive words taken from someone else
4. even your own very slightly changed version of someone else's words.

The test for common knowledge is not whether *you* already knew it, but whether someone fairly familiar with your subject would have known it. That Abraham Lincoln was born in a log cabin, was president of the United States during the Civil War, and when he was young may have walked many miles to return a penny is common knowledge. What Carl Sandburg (a Lincoln expert) says about Lincoln's personal sorrows during the war years is not common knowledge, and if you use Sandburg's information, you must give Sandburg credit.

There are three good reasons for doing your footnoting carefully. One, of course, is to avoid being accused of plagiarism. The second reason is so that readers who are genuinely interested in what you're saying can go to your sources and read more about it if they want to. The third reason is self-protection: if some of the information you find turns out to be inaccurate, it's the original writer's fault, not yours.

The second method of giving credit is a bibliography. A bibliography is simply a list of everything you read in getting ready to write your paper. It should contain not only the sources you footnoted from, but the sources you got your general ideas from, too.

Using a Style Manual

When the assignment is made, your teacher will probably tell you how your footnotes should be arranged, and what form your bibliography should follow. Be sure to follow these directions exactly. It may seem to you a little silly to fuss about whether footnotes come at the bottom of each page or all together at the end of the paper; whether the name of the book you're referring to is followed by a period or a comma. Many teachers, however, care a lot about these minor details, and it shouldn't be much extra trouble for you to follow the directions.

Or your teacher may just refer you to a style manual where advice on a standard form for term papers is clearly explained. The style manual will also tell you how wide the margins should be, how the title should be spaced, whether or not to use a table of contents—things like that. And even if your teacher does not specifically require that your term paper be typed, it's a good idea to type it, or have it typed, if you possibly can. Typing will make it look better, and every little bit helps. If you do have someone else type it, however, be sure to read the finished copy just as carefully as you read the paper before you gave it to the typist. Your teacher is likely to hold you responsible for the typist's mistakes.

And don't hesitate, naturally, to have someone else read it over before you hand it in. We don't know anybody who presented a master's thesis without having a friend or two read it first.

Examining a Sample Research Paper

The Plight of the Porpoises

Evelyn Umgartner
English 101
December 1, 1978

The Plight of the Porpoises

Introduction begins with general problem of extinct species, then makes clear this paper is concerned with porpoises killed by tuna fishing.

For centuries human beings have been acting as though the earth belonged to them and they had no responsibility for the other creatures that lived on it with them. We have almost exterminated species after species because money could be made from them. When our advanced technology had so nearly wiped them out that killing them was no longer profitable, we have passed laws to "protect" them. It's only recently that environmentalists have been trying to protect some living things before it is too late. One of these attempts--to save the porpoises that tuna fishermen have been killing by the hundreds of thousands--has caused much controversy in the last ten years. Perhaps the slaughter of porpoises has gained more attention than most efforts to save an endangered species because the porpoises (more accurately classified as dolphins) are so friendly, harmless, and endearing.

Comment about friendliness of dolphins serves as transition to next paragraph.

Telling what happened, in Greece, in Rome, and in New Zealand.

Human beings have known and loved dolphins for a long time. An old Greek story tells about a man who was saved by a dolphin. When he jumped into the sea to keep from being killed by sailors, a dolphin carried him to shore on its back.[1] A Roman story tells about a dolphin who made friends with a boy, would come when the boy called it, and would eat out of the boy's hand.[2] Much more recently, in 1946 in New Zealand, a porpoise named Opo came regularly to play beach ball with children swimming near the shore until she was stranded on the beach one day when the tide went out.[3] There have been many other stories of dolphins befriending people or keeping them from drowning. And almost everybody who has lived near the ocean or been out to sea in a boat has seen porpoises leaping in and out of the water.

Singles out bottle-nosed dolphins, the kind we know most about.

Probably most of the stories are about bottle-nosed dolphins (<u>Tursiops truncatus</u>), which are the most sociable of all the dolphins. They live well in captivity and are the ones that do tricks in circus acts and aquariums; a bottle-nosed dolphin starred in a television series not long ago. Much research has been

---

[1]Winthrop N. Kellogg, <u>Porpoises and Sonar</u> (Chicago: Phoenix Books, 1961), p. 12.

[2]<u>Ibid</u>., p. 13.

[3]<u>Ibid</u>., pp. 18-19, quoting from <u>Life</u>, April 23, 1956, pp. 105-110.

done on these dolphins in ocean laboratories, where scientists have been able to watch them taking care of other, injured dolphins, helping them get to the surface to breathe and staying close to protect them. Dolphin mothers have been seen to carry sick or dead babies on their backs for several days, and other dolphin females behave like "aunties," helping take care of the young dolphins.[4]

Some classification; a scientific definition of dolphins.

Although they live in the water, dolphins are not fish at all. They are classified as Cetacea, a group that includes toothed whales, dolphins, and actual porpoises. Cetacea were once land animals, but millions of years ago they went back to the water, for reasons nobody knows. All of them are warm-blooded animals that give birth to their young alive and feed them on milk, just as human beings do. They have to breathe air to live, although they can stay under water without breathing longer than humans can. Cetacea vary in size from sperm whales (what Moby Dick in Melville's famous novel was) that can be sixty feet long and

This information is not footnoted, since it is general knowledge to anyone who has studied marine mammals.

---

[4] D. J. Coffey, _Dolphins, Whales, and Porpoises, an Encyclopedia of Sea Mammals_ (New York: Macmillan, 1977), p. 23.

weigh sixty tons, to the smaller dolphins, which are about eight feet long and weigh about three hundred pounds.

Possibility of dolphin language is also general knowledge.

Most people know about the studies indicating that dolphins, as well as whales, have a structured language, even though nobody so far has been able to translate it. Underwater recordings of clicks and whistles of varying length and intensity seem to show that these noises are used for sophisticated communication and are more than the mere "signals" of danger or pleasure that other animals use.

The probable possession of a language is not the only proof that dolphins are extremely intelligent. Their brains are larger and apparently more complex than ours are. A human brain weighs 1,400 grams; a dolphin's weighs 1,700 grams, and the cerebral cortex is larger and more convoluted than a human's. One book,

Definition of intelligence is quoted because exact wording is important.

called <u>Smarter Than Man?</u>, points out that animals with a physical structure different from creatures that live on land cannot have their intelligence measured by the usual way. It suggests that a fair definition might be

> the ability to differentiate, to combine
> and generalize, to analyze and associate,
> to perceive continuity and arrive at the

concept of cause and effect, to imagine
the results of contemplated actions, to
deliberate and find the means of reaching a desired goal.[5]

Evidence is cited to show that dolphins can do
all of these things. They are easily trained,
can invent new tricks by themselves, and
cooperate with people to such an extent that
during the Vietnam war the United States Navy
used them to retrieve practice torpedoes, fast-
en bombs to the hulls of enemy ships, and place
and retrieve chemical "bugs" in enemy harbors.[6]

Even though this is a transition paragraph, the statistics need a footnote.

The Greeks had so much respect and admiration for dolphins that they considered them
sacred. We Americans, however, not only send
them on suicide missions to fight our wars for
us but allowed tuna fishermen to kill between
three and five million of them in the years
from 1960 to 1970,[7] not because the fishermen
had anything against the dolphins or wanted to
use them for anything, but just because killing
dolphins made it easier to catch tuna.

---

[5] Karl-Erik Fichtelius and Sverre Sjolander,
Smarter Than Man?, tr. by Thomas Teal (New
York: Random House, 1972), p. 29.

[6] Coffey, op. cit., p. 73.

[7] Stanley M. Minasian, "Dolphins and/or Tuna,"
Oceans, 10 (November 1977), pp. 60-63.

Explanation of how fishing on dolphins works.

For reasons nobody understands, dolphins and yellowfin, a variety of tuna that is sold as "light tuna," are almost always found together. The dolphins swim in herds near the surface of the water, and the tuna are farther down under them where the fishermen can't see them. Until about 1960, when fishermen saw a herd of dolphin they put out hooks, lines, and live bait. The dolphins were too intelligent to take the bait, so the fishing boats caught the tuna without harming the dolphins. About twenty years ago, however, the industry began using fast speedboats and huge purse-seine nets instead of bait. When the fishermen saw a herd of dolphin, the speedboats would chase them close together, throw a net a mile long and three hundred feet deep around both the dolphins and the tuna, and pull the net together at the bottom like the drawstring of a purse. Many of the dolphins were tangled in the net or trapped under water, and since they have to breathe air, more than 300,000 of them died every year.[8]

---

[8] Vic Cox, "Murder of the Porpoise: Closing In on a Solution," Science Digest, 82 (July 1977), pp. 46-47.

Definition of backdown procedure.

Some effort was made to let the dolphins out of the net. Sometimes the captain of the fishing boat could pull up most of the net, put the boat into reverse, and slide the net down under the dolphins without letting the tuna out. But this "backdown procedure" was hard to do, and unless weather and water conditions were just right, the procedure didn't work.

Second use of the word "slaughter" hints at the position the writer is taking.

In an attempt to cut down on this slaughter before the dolphins were wiped out, the U.S. Congress, in October 1972, passed the Marine Mammal Protection Act. This act set limits on the number of dolphins the tuna fishing fleet could kill but gave the industry two years before it had to observe the limits, provided all available ways of protecting the dolphins were used in the interval. During these two years the National Marine Fisheries Service, a division of the Commerce Department, was to work with the tuna industry to find ways of reducing the dolphin killings to almost nothing.

Telling what happened again: chronological account of laws and lawsuits.

The number of dead dolphins did go down somewhat. According to Dr. William W. Fox, Jr., chief scientist for the National Marine Fisheries Service's research program, an average of

Statistics are footnoted, but other straightforward account of events is general knowledge (or could be).

137,000 dolphins a year were killed in 1973 and 1974.[9] At the end of 1974, the Commerce Department gave the tuna industry a blanket permit to continue fishing on dolphins if they all used the backdown procedure and a new fine-meshed netting at the end of the net where the dolphins were. In October 1974 a group of environmentalists filed a federal lawsuit asking that the permit be withdrawn. Late in 1975 the department issued another permit for the 1976 season, and the environmentalists filed another suit. The two suits were combined, and in May 1976 Federal Judge Charles Richey ruled that all fishing on dolphins was to be stopped by June 1, 1976. The tuna industry appealed the decision and was allowed to continue fishing until the appeal was decided. Even though the appeal was denied, the tuna industry was allowed to fish on dolphins for

Because "Said it would create a hardship" might be a controversial interpretation, a source is given here.

the rest of the year because they said that stopping immediately would create a hardship for them.[10]

---

[9] William W. Fox, Jr., "Tuna/Dolphin Program," Oceans, 11 (May 1978), pp. 57-59.

[10] Minasian, op. cit.

Judge Richey had said in his decision that the Commerce Department had no authority to issue the permits, and that the intention of the 1972 act was "to protect marine mammals and not necessarily to protect an industry to the exclusion of the dolphins."[11] The decision was based on the fact that the Commerce Department didn't know what the dolphin population was, what effect the killing had on it, or how many animals were actually involved. To get more accurate information, Dr. Fox of the National Marine Fisheries Service called a conference of twelve international scientists to work out a definition of "optimum sustainable population" (the number of dolphin necessary to keep the species from dying out) and to make an assessment of all twenty-one kinds of dolphin. The National Marine Fisheries Service adopted this definition and published the report in September 1976.[12]

The 1977 permit issued by the department was based on this report. The permit set a preliminary quota and said the eastern spinner

Original wording is quoted to avoid distortion.

"Optimum sustainable population" is briefly defined.

---

[11]Minasian, op. cit.

[12]Fox, op. cit.

dolphin was below the optimum sustainable population and could not be killed. After these 1977 regulations were announced, the Committee for Humane Legislation filed suit again, but in June 1977 Judge Richey ruled that there was now enough information to justify the quotas. After hearings were held in San Diego and Washington, D.C., a quota of 59,050 dolphins was set for the year. The tuna industry immediately began an intensified lobbying effort for more lenient legislation. The <u>New York Times</u>, in commenting about the protests of the tuna industry, said:

> The Federal Government has shown elaborate concern for the tuna industry in carrying out a Congressional mandate to reduce the porpoise kill "to insignificant levels approaching a zero mortality."
>
> A two-year grace period, followed by three years of indulgence, has cost the lives of 800,000 porpoises. . . . It is against this background that the country must judge the government's attempt to reduce this year's slaughter from 100,000 to 50,000.[13]

The industry's efforts resulted in a compromise bill, which was put before Congress in September 1977. The bill would have somewhat increased the quotas for 1977, but it would have required a 50 percent reduction by 1980

---

[13]Quoted in Cox, <u>op</u>. <u>cit</u>.

Quoting the *New York Times* comment, with its "elaborate concern," "three years of indulgence," is another indication of the position the writer is taking.

The proposed bill seems worth including, even though it apparently didn't pass in 1977; see the explanatory footnote.

and an additional 50 percent reduction each year after that. It also called for a complete observer program on the tuna ships; two million dollars from the tuna industry for further research; rewards for the captain and crew of a ship with a below-average tuna kill; and observers on foreign ships selling tuna to the United States.[14]

Meantime, experiments in ways of protecting dolphins had developed better gear and procedures. In 1975 the National Marine Fisheries Service chartered a tuna ship, The Bold Contender, which made twenty-five sets--that is, threw the purse-seine net around herds of dolphin and tuna twenty-five times--and killed only 1.44 dolphin per set, compared to the 12.8 dolphin per set killed by other tuna boats that year.[15] The Bold Contender used a new type of net, with a lip on it; one-and-a-quarter-inch webbing in the backdown part of the net; a man wearing a snorkel on a rubber raft; "porpoise grabbers" to pull the dolphins out;

A "set" is defined.

Short explanatory footnote is used for information that would seem to interrupt the paper.

---

[14]Minasian, op. cit. (This bill apparently did not pass the Senate; I could find no later reference to it.)

[15]Fox, op. cit.

and speedboats to hold the net open and help the dolphins over it. In 1976 this system was tested by comparing the results of ten ships using it with ten other ships, and although one report said that "the results persuaded the fleet owners to order $2.5 million worth of new webbing," Dr. Fox of the National Marine Fisheries Service merely said that "several problems were noted."[16] He went on to point out, however, that Judge Richey's ruling had interrupted the test and made interpreting the data very difficult. It was ironic, he said, that "the suit brought by the environmental groups . . . delayed implementation of the most effective dolphin rescue gear by about one year."[17]

In another test cruise, by the Elizabeth C. J. from October to December 1976, a scientist found that he could hear the clicks and whistles of the porpoises when he was under water, and a man on a raft could signal the captain when the dolphins were all out. In forty-five sets the Elizabeth C. J. made, only

---

[16]Cox, op. cit.; Fox, op. cit.

[17]Fox, op. cit.

The writer notes differences in two different interpretations of the results; exact wording is quoted and the sources are given in a single footnote.

420

sixteen dolphins were killed.[18] This gear was not required in 1977 but it is required under the 1978 regulations.

The figures given by the president of the Save the Dolphins Association are slightly different; he says over five hundred tons of tuna were caught and less than half a dozen dolphins were killed. But he also points out that what the Elizabeth C. J. did does not represent actual fishing conditions. The ship was the best and most sophisticated in the fleet, it had a very conscientious captain and crew, and it fished under the best weather conditions and without any mechanical breakdowns or competition from other fishing boats.[19] (The test voyage was made by special permission during the closed season.)

Meantime the tuna industry's response to the milder regulations proposed in 1977 was a threat to sell their ships to foreign countries not bound by United States regulations. According to an article in Business Week, by January, 9 of the ships in the 140-vessel United States

---

[18]Cox, op. cit.

[19]Minasian, op. cit.

Another difference in interpretation; the point of view of one author is given; the other is apparently neutral.

Cause and effect; analysis of why this record was not representative.

The writer may be interpreting by saying "response . . . was a threat"; the article, slanted in favor of the tuna industry, said they were being forced to sell by the regulations.

tuna fleet had applied for transfer to foreign registry, where there are no porpoise limits. One San Diego owner of two boats said he wanted to sell them to Mexico, continue to fish for tuna, and sell the catch to United States canneries duty-free.[20]

Tuna is a big industry. The wholesale value of tuna canned in the United States in 1976 was $800 million. The president of H. J. Heinz Co. said that more than 40 percent of its $83-million earnings comes from Star-Kist tuna, and Ralston Purina gets about 15 percent of its even larger profits from Chicken of the Sea. The article in Forbes magazine giving these figures used a headline saying, "In their zeal to protect the lovable porpoise, environmentalists may inadvertently sink the U.S. tuna fleet --and do the porpoise no good at all."[21] The article ended by saying that if the tuna industry buys more foreign-caught tuna, even more porpoises will be killed.

Exact quotation here shows the slant of the *Forbes* article; *Forbes* is read mainly by business people.

---

[20] "The U.S. Tuna Fleet Fishes for Foreigners," Business Week, January 24, 1977, p. 25.

[21] "Troubled Waters," Forbes, 119 (April 1, 1977), p. 56.

Comparison of whale situation to dolphin situation.

There is no international agency that controls the killing of dolphins. In 1946, when it became apparent that many kinds of whales were becoming extinct, an International Whaling Commission was set up. It is a voluntary organization of fifteen member countries, with no powers of enforcement and subject to political pressures from the whaling industry even in the recommendations it makes.[22] There

A prediction.

seems no likelihood that an international commission for dolphins could do any better, even if one could be organized in time.

Alternate way of catching tuna, and explanation of why it isn't used.

The tuna industry does not have to fish on dolphins. Tuna can be caught in other ways. Albacore (canned as "white tuna") are not found near dolphin herds; they are caught by setting out miles of line with baited hooks every few yards. Even the yellowfin can be caught by "school fishing"--setting nets around tuna feeding near the surface. But the tuna industry, with money invested in superseiners costing over five million dollars apiece, does not find these methods "efficient."

Dealing with the argument of the other side.

The industry argues that if it is forced to abide by the government regulations, and

---

[22]Coffey, op. cit., pp. 35-37.

especially if it is not allowed to kill any of
the endangered eastern spinner dolphin, it
can't operate at a profit, jobs will be lost,
and the whole economy will suffer. This is

**Analogy—what businesses
said in the past and what
the tuna industry says now.** the same argument that was used by businesses
when child labor laws and the eight-hour day
were first proposed, but businesses kept operating. It seems likely that the tuna industry
could keep operating, too.

What will happen to the porpoises seems
less certain. One small hopeful sign is that
in 1977 some of the tuna vessels came back
sooner than they expected, saying that the dolphins were not guiding them to the tuna.[23]
These intelligent animals may be taking some
steps to save themselves, but they may be unable to prevent the yellowfin tuna from following them.

**Conclusion: the writer
comes out in support of
killing fewer dolphins than
the government allows.** At present, the government regulations are
saving some dolphins that would otherwise be
killed. But even the United States, which has
tried to do something about it, still allows
the killing of many thousands every year. We
are not doing enough to help these intelligent

---

[23]Minasian, op. cit.

animals about which Plutarch wrote nearly two thousand years ago:

> To the dolphin alone, beyond all others, nature has granted what the best philosophers seek: friendship for no advantage. Though it has no need at all of any man, yet it is a general friend to all and has helped many.[24]

Nobody killed dolphins with technology in Plutarch's day. Today the dolphins do need humane human beings to help them survive.

---

[24]Quoted in Kellogg, op. cit., p. 23.

Quotation contrasts friendliness of dolphins with callousness of human beings.

Bibliography

Coffey, D. J. Dolphins, Whales, and Porpoises, an Encyclopedia of Sea Mammals. New York: Macmillan, 1977.

Cox, Vic. "Murder of the Porpoise: Closing In on a Solution." Science Digest, 82 (July 1977), pp. 46-47.

Fichtelius, Karl-Erik, and Sjolander, Sverre. Smarter Than Man? Tr. by Thomas Teal. New York: Random House, 1972.

Fox, William W., Jr. "Tuna/Dolphin Program." Oceans, 11 (May 1978), pp. 57-59.

Kellogg, Winthrop N. Porpoises and Sonar. Chicago: Phoenix Books, 1961.

Minasian, Stanley M. "Dolphins and/or Tuna." Oceans, 10 (November 1977), pp. 60-63.

"Troubled Waters." Forbes, 119 (April 1, 1977), p. 56.

"The U.S. Tuna Fleet Fishes for Foreigners." Business Week, January 24, 1977, p. 25.

Wursig, Bernd, and Wursig, Melany. "The Photographic Determination of Group Size, Composition, and Stability of Coastal Porpoises." Science, 198 (November 18, 1977), pp. 755-756.

Bibliographies are always listed alphabetically by the author's last name; if there is no author, the title of the article is used.

This bibliography lists one article not included in the footnotes; it provided general information on how dolphins can be counted.

Appendix Three/ Editing

Whatever you're writing, the first—and most important—step is to get your ideas down on paper as clearly, forcefully, and gracefully as you can. Make sure your paper says what you want it to say. Make sure you're pleased with what you have written. Then, and only then, can you go on to the final step: editing what you've written.

"Editing" means going back over your paper, checking for such things as spelling and punctuation. These represent the "etiquette" of writing—a set of conventions that have developed during the five hundred years since the printing press was invented. Like any other kind of good manners, their main purpose is to make other people comfortable, to make reading smooth and easy.

As a writer, these conventions are important to you because many readers will form judgments about you and the value of what you say based on how carefully you observe their notions of writing etiquette. It's not much use arguing that these are surface matters, quite separate from the worth of your report or your argument. It's not much use offering such clichés as "Clothes don't make the man (or woman)," or "You can't judge a package by its wrapping." We do make superficial judgments about strangers in terms of their appearance, although first impressions usually tell us nothing of real value. We do reach for the pretty package before the one in the battered box. Most of us do enjoy a dinner more when the tablecloth is clean and the goblets glitter, even though we know these niceties can't compensate for soggy potatoes and a limp salad. A careful cook will first time the potatoes and chill the salad, then turn to serving the dinner as attractively as possible. Careful writers will organize their ideas and put them into words, then go back over what they have written to "make it look good."

For some writers, however, that plan is easier to make than to follow. How do you know what to look for? How can you tell what to change? Where can you get help?

Beginning writers certainly can't look for everything all at once. The best solution, probably, is to break the problem into parts. What is sometimes called "mechanics" can be divided into five parts: spelling, punctuating, paragraphing, capitalizing, and smoothing out the wording. Go through your paper once, just concentrating on spelling. Go through it again, this time looking at punctuation, paragraphs, and capital letters. Finally, read it again, this time watching for words you may have left out or minor things you may want to change. As you grow more skillful in proofreading and more sure of yourself, you will be able to combine these operations; but some very experienced writers still read their papers more than once, catching changes on a second reading that they missed the first time through.

As for where you can get help, there are lots of sources: your teachers, your friends, the other students in your class. The best and most permanent source, however, is a good college dictionary. Modern dictionaries are more than just lists of words and their meanings. Most of them have supplements on usage and punctuation, sometimes listed under the heading "Manual of Style." Make sure your dictionary is up-to-date—the conventions of writing change, just as other conventions do—and then get thoroughly familiar with all the kinds of information it can give you. Don't try to edit your papers without your dictionary handy, and don't try to edit without using it.

Spelling

There's nothing magic or sacred about spelling. It's just a method of using symbols—letters of the alphabet—to represent the sounds we make when we talk. In an ideal system, we'd have a separate letter to represent every meaningful sound, and each letter would always represent the same sound, and only that sound. When you saw the letter *s,* for instance, you would know that it stood for the sound you hear in *sit* and never for anything else. Unfortunately, the system isn't that reliable. The letter *s,* as everybody knows, can represent several different sounds: *s*it, *s*ugar, *s*hould, bee*s*, grea*s*y (the way some Americans say it), or no sound at all, as in i*s*land. What's true for *s* is true for most of the rest of the alphabet. Letters do double duty or pop up in places where they don't seem to do anything at all. We have at least one letter we could dispense with entirely: *C* could be replaced by *s* in such words as *century* and *civic,* or by *k* in such words as *cat* and *come.*

Naturally, this bad fit between sounds and letters is not deliberate. Five centuries ago, before Caxton brought the printing press to England, people spelled words however they thought they sounded, and nobody made any fuss about it. The early printers, however, decided their lives would be easier if everyone spelled words the same way, so gradually they "standardized" the system, using the spellings they saw most frequently. Sometimes they were printing very old manuscripts, written when the sounds of the language were quite different. Englishmen used to say *night* so you could hear the sound represented by *gh;* they said *knight* so you could hear the *k* sound at the beginning of the word. The printers tried to make letters represent sounds, and they did a fairly good job of it for that time and that place. But the sounds of a language keep changing, and what seemed a logical spelling in 1470, in London, can seem pretty illogical in 1970, in Omaha, Nebraska, or Melbourne, Australia. And though the sounds of speech are always slowly changing, the writing system doesn't change much for either time or geography. That it doesn't change makes reading easier and spelling harder.

As for making the system fit the language better, there isn't much hope there either. George Bernard Shaw, the famous British playwright, left a million pounds to "reform" the spelling system, but the English courts threw that provision out of his will. One objection to change is that all the books in all the libraries would immediately become out-of-date and very hard to read. Another objection is that English has so many dialects, with so many differences in the way English speakers pronounce words, that it would be difficult to decide whose pronunciation to use. And a final objection, perhaps the most important, is that people who have learned the system just don't want things any different.

Nevertheless, if you think of yourself as a poor speller, here are a few facts that may comfort you:

1. *The ability to spell well is not a measure of intelligence, nor is it a measure of the ability to write well.* Apparently, good spellers are people with good visual memories: their minds "photograph" the appearance of words on a page, and they can produce that photograph when they need to write a word. These are the people who, when you ask them how to spell something, say, "Wait a minute. Let me write it down." They judge spelling by the way it looks. Other people, whose memories depend more on sound than on sight, have more trouble with spelling and have to work harder at it.

2. *Nobody can spell everything; all of us have some words we always have to look up.* The trick, of course, is to learn what those words are. If you can't keep the *i/e, e/i* problem straight, in words like *believe* and *receive,* just accept the situation and plan to use your dictionary every time these words occur. It's only when your list of uncertainties gets too long, when it contains too many of the words you use regularly, that you have a real spelling problem. The best—probably the only —solution here is to take a few words at a time and just learn them. Some people have had good luck by developing their muscular memories. Using a child's crayon, they write the word very large, over and over, until it is imprinted in their minds. Other people use a rote system, saying *"w, h, i, c, h* spells *which"* until the spelling becomes automatic. If you have a genuine spelling problem, try to really look at the letters in each word every time you edit.

3. *Most spelling difficulty comes in the ordinary words of daily life; more than 80 percent of the words in the language are "regular"—that is, they follow a logical system.* More people have trouble with a word like *writing,* for instance, than with a word like *insoluble.* If you can learn the common words, the "hard," unusual words will take care of themselves. Even if they don't, you can use the dictionary for obscure words without slowing yourself down much.

4. *The spelling of "sound-alike" words always depends on meaning. Peace* and *piece,* for example, are not the same word at all. We just happen to say them the same way. With homophones—words that sound alike but mean something different—learning the difference takes two steps. First you become aware that the pairs exist (or quadruples, as in *since, sense, scents,* and *cents*). Then you deter-

mine which is which. For some pairs, memory clues will work. Some people use "piece of pie" to remind themselves that a part of something is always spelled *piece*. They tell themselves that their high school principal (the "main" person in the school) was (or was not) "a pal," to distinguish *principal*—meaning main or important—from *principle*—meaning a rule or basic law. You don't have to be told these tricks; you can invent your own. But if you can't find or invent dependable memory clues, you're back to the usual solution; when in doubt, use your dictionary.

5. *Finally, in spite of the apparent confusion, there are some spelling guides that almost always work.* One of them deals with *i/e, e/i*. If you use the whole jingle, instead of just half of it, you can spell more than a dozen common English words. It's a good idea to reverse the order of the jingle:

**I/E,
E/I**

**W
O
R
D
S**

> When said like *me*,
>
> It's *i* before *e*,
>
> Except after *c*.

Changing the order will help you remember that the guide doesn't work for words like *friend* and *neighbor,* because they don't have the same sound as *me*. Then you can use the jingle where it will work: *receive, relieve, chief, niece, belief, grief, conceive,* and so on. This guide will mislead you in two words, *seize* and *protein*. And depending on where you live and what your pronunciation is, it could steer you wrong in three other words: *leisure,* if you say the first syllable to rhyme with *me* rather than with *met;* and *either* and *neither,* unless you live on the East Coast. Learn these exceptions, remember the pronunciation part of the old saying, and you will save yourself a good deal of dictionary checking.

Most of the other useful guides have to do with suffixes—adding endings to words you can already spell.

> If a short word has one vowel,
>
> followed by one consonant,
>
> double the consonant when you add
>
> *-ed, -er, -est, -ing*

It works like this:

trim + *ed*   becomes   *trimmed*

win + *er*   becomes   *winner*

hot + *est*   becomes   *hottest*

stop + *ing*   becomes   *stopping*

If the word has more than one vowel,

or more than one consonant,

don't make any change when you add

-ed, -er, -est, -ing

---

nail + *ed*	becomes	*nailed*	*suck* + *ed*	becomes	*sucked*
deal + *er*	becomes	*dealer*	*kiss* + *ed*	becomes	*kissed*
sweet + *est*	becomes	*sweetest*	*long* + *est*	becomes	*longest*
fool + *ing*	becomes	*fooling*	*match* + *ing*	becomes	*matching*

This same guide works for longer words *where we emphasize the last syllable:*

corral + *ed*   becomes   *corralled*

begin + *ing*   becomes   *beginning*

Kidnap and *cancel* usually don't double the consonant, *because we emphasize the first syllable* rather than the last one: *kidnaped, canceling.*

If a word ends in *e*,

drop the *e* before adding

-ed, -er, -est, -ing

---

hopҿ + *ed*	becomes	*hoped*	*savҿ* + *ed*	becomes	*saved*
safҿ + *er*	becomes	*safer*	*balancҿ* + *ed*	becomes	*balanced*
nicҿ + *est*	becomes	*nicest*	*balancҿ* + *ing*	becomes	*balancing*
writҿ + *ing*	becomes	*writing*	*believҿ* + *ing*	becomes	*believing*

This guide will keep you from writing, "Jackie hopped for a bike for Christmas" (when you mean wanted it), or "Jackie hoped all the way home" (when you mean bounced up and down).

hop + ed	becomes	*hopped*	hop + ing	becomes	*hopping*
hope + ed	becomes	*hoped*	hope + ing	becomes	*hoping*

W
O
R
D
S

E
N
D
I
N
G

I
N

-Y

> If a word ends in *y*
>
> 1. change *y* to *i* before
>   all endings except *-ing*
>
> 2. add *-es* instead of just *-s*
>   after the *i*

It works like this:

copy	becomes	*copy + i + es*	(*copies*)	but *copying*
marry	becomes	*marry + i + ed*	(*married*)	but *marrying*
carry	becomes	*carry + i + er*	(*carrier*)	but *carrying*
snappy	becomes	*snappy + i + est*	(*snappiest*)	
happy	becomes	*happy + i + ness*	(*happiness*)	
mercy	becomes	*mercy + i + ful*	(*merciful*)	
cozy	becomes	*cozy + i + ly*	(*cozily*)	
merry	becomes	*merry + i + ment*	(*merriment*)	

The only place this guide does not work is where the *y* comes after another vowel instead of after a consonant, as it does in words like *day, honey, boy,* or *buy.* These words follow the guide given on page 431—if a word has more than one vowel, don't make any change when you add the suffix.

A
D
D
I
N
G

-LY

> When you add *-ly,*
> don't change anything else
>
> **EXCEPT**
>
> 1. when the original word ends in *y*
>
> 2. when you'd get three *l*'s together
>
> 3. when you'd get *le* and *ly* together

cold + ly	becomes	*coldly*	but *angry + ly*	becomes	*angrily*
live + ly	becomes	*lively*	but *full + ly*	becomes	*fully*
hopeful + ly	becomes	*hopefully*	but *terrible + ly*	becomes	*terribly*

Apostrophes are another part of English spelling that worry many people. Actually, we use apostrophes in only two main ways:

> Apostrophes are used
>
> 1. to spell contractions
>
> 2. to show possession after nouns and a few pronouns (*anybody's*)

A contraction occurs when we shorten a word (*o'er* for *over*) or push two words together to form a single word (*don't* for *do not*). The guide for contractions goes like this:

> To spell a *contraction*
>
> 1. Write the combined words as a single word.
>
> 2. Use an apostrophe to replace the letter or letters left out.
>
> 3. Make no other spelling change.

can n̸o̸t becomes *can't*		*would n̸o̸t* becomes *wouldn't*
it i̸s becomes *it's*		*they a̸re* becomes *they're*
I w̸i̸ll becomes *I'll*		*I w̸o̸u̸ld* becomes *I'd*
Bertha i̸s becomes *Bertha's*		*that i̸s* becomes *that's*
we h̸a̸ve becomes *we've*		*who i̸s* becomes *who's*

The only contractions in which we do change the spelling—*will not* becomes *won't* and *shall not* becomes *shan't*—seldom give anybody much trouble.*

We get into trouble when we make oversimplified, incomplete statements about the other function of apostrophes: "Use an apostrophe to show possession." That's accurate enough, as far as it goes, but it doesn't go far enough. We need to add something:

Never use apostrophes to show possession in eight common English pronouns: *I, you, he, she, it, we, they,* and *who.*

All these pronouns have special possessive forms—*my* or *mine; your* or *yours; his; her* or *hers; its; our* or *ours; their* or *theirs; whose*—and these pronouns are never spelled with an apostrophe. That guide, too, is simple and reliable. The confusion comes because we run into homophones again. Several of these pronouns sound exactly like contractions. It's hard to see much difference between these pairs:

You're (contraction of *you are*) leaving *your* hat (belongs to you).

The typewriter came with *its* (belongs to typewriter) own cover, but *it's* (contraction of *it has*) been lost for a long time.

They're (contraction of *they are*) planning to sell *their* car (belongs to them).

There's (contraction of *there is*) some question about whether *it's* (contraction of *it is*) really *theirs* (belongs to them).

Who's (contraction of *who is*) going to decide *whose* (belongs to somebody) car it is?

Probably the only sure way to decide between *its* and *it's, your* and *you're, they're* and *their, who's* and *whose,* is to apply the kind of test illustrated in the sentences just given. If reading it as a contraction makes sense—that is, if you can substitute *it is, you are, they are, who is,* for instance—use an apostrophe. If that substitution doesn't make sense, leave the apostrophe out.

Here is a simple guide for using apostrophes to show possession in everything except those eight pronouns:

---

* We also change the spelling in *ain't,* the contraction for *am not,* but most writers have been taught to avoid that one, except in quoted conversation.

A
P
O
S
T
R
O
P
H
E
S
/
P
O
S
S
E
S
S
I
O
N

> Use an apostrophe for any relationship that can be put into an *of* phrase.
>
> Put the apostrophe after the end of the word as it stands in the *of* phrase.
>
> If the word in the *of* phrase doesn't end in *s,* put *s* after the apostrophe.
>
> If the word in the *of* phrase does end in *s,* add an apostrophe and nothing else.

mother *of Helen*   becomes   *Helen's* mother

problems *of everybody*   becomes   *everybody's* problem

friend *of the children*   becomes   the *children's* friend

den *of the lion*   becomes   the *lion's* den

den *of the lions*   becomes   the *lions'* den

novel *of Dickens*   becomes   *Dickens'* novel

job *of Charles*   becomes   *Charles'* job

On the last two, some people write *Dickens's* novel and *Charles's* job, as you would probably hear it in speech, but either way is all right, and if apostrophes seem to you mysterious and important, you'll be safer with the *of* guide.

Using these spelling guides may seem like a slow process at first. And it is. But since you should never bother with them when you're actually writing—that would interfere with your thinking—the slowness isn't serious. And it's true that there are many spelling difficulties these guides don't cover. Maybe you can find other guides to help with words that bother you: in all words where -*phon*- means "sound," for instance, the *f* sound is spelled *ph.* But if you can't find the guides, or if the guides don't work, use your dictionary.

Punctuation

Punctuation marks are a set of symbols that try to reproduce in writing the pauses, the inflections, and the intonations used naturally in speech. Granted, the few symbols we have are clumsy and inadequate; still, they're better than nothing. Remember, using commas and periods and question marks in the conventional ways is not a matter of being "correct" or "incorrect"; it's a matter of helping your readers "hear" what you've written. If you don't believe that, try reading the following unpunctuated paragraph:

> just by learning to talk even if you hadn't learned to read and write you have become a master of a subtle and complex system the proof of your mastery is that you can understand what other people who speak your language say to you at least most of the time and they can understand what you say to them it is exactly this mastery of language that distinguishes the dullest humans from the brightest and most accomplished animals an animal may grunt howl whine scratch or even point to express what it feels at the moment but only a human being has words for feelings and only humans can talk about what they felt yesterday and what they may feel tomorrow only humans can talk about what happened the day before yesterday the past can make guesses about what may happen next month the future and can discuss things that have never happened and perhaps never will happen by language by using words humans have learned to get outside the present

It's obvious that using commas, periods, and capital letters in the usual places makes reading easier. What is a good deal less obvious is where "the right places" are. A lifetime of listening to people talk provides very little direct help. People don't go around saying, "That's what I mean period don't you agree with me question mark" unless they're sending an old-fashioned telegram or dictating to a stenographer they don't trust much.

That nobody ever goes around saying "period . . . comma . . . question mark" is only one reason people have trouble with punctuation. The other reason is that the usual directions are hard to follow. The "rules" are almost always written in terms that involve a good deal of specialized knowledge. The rules for using commas, for instance, are given to saying such things as "Use a comma after a subordinate clause at the beginning of a sentence" or "Set off nonrestrictive clauses with commas." That's fine—if you know for sure what subordinate and nonrestrictive clauses are.

Another reason the conventional directions are not much help is that the sentences offered as examples tend to look quite different from the ones we write ourselves. If you have a sample pattern to follow, it's fairly easy to insert commas into sentences like these:

Hoping for rain tomorrow_____we did not water the lawn.

My mother-in-law_____who once lived in Boston_____makes baked beans.

These practice sentences lie quiet and unresisting while you stick commas in them. The sentences you write yourself, however, may be wriggling and full of life, and they seldom follow a neat textbook pattern. If your sentences don't look much like the patterns in the book, that doesn't necessarily mean your sentences are bad. On the contrary, it may be a sign you are an effective and vigorous writer. There's no reason to limit yourself to a few simple patterns, even though the livelier sentences may seem harder to punctuate. If you don't understand the terminology the handbooks use, don't just give up. Remember that the basic purpose of all punctuation marks is to help you express what you mean, to guide your readers so they can read what you have written with intelligence and understanding. Your job is to decide where commas and periods will help, where they will hinder.

If the problem is a comma, for instance, one good way is to ask yourself whether, if you were reading it instead of writing it, a comma would guide you in seeing what parts of the sentence belong together. The short pauses we make in talking sometimes mean we need commas, but sometimes they mean we've just stopped to think. The pauses we make at the ends of sentences are a more reliable guide. Periods are symbols of longer pauses. When people talk, they pause briefly between one sentence and the next. When they have finished a "complete declaratory sentence," to use the handbook's phrase, they lower the pitch of their voices. When they have asked a question, whether or not they expect an answer, they raise the pitch slightly at the end of it.

Just as you know a great deal of English grammar even though you cannot use all the terminology, so you know almost perfectly how this system of emphasizing, pausing, and pitching your voice works, even though you may not be able to define such terms as "pitch" and "stress." To remind yourself of what you already know, try reading these sentences twice each, first as though you were making an announcement, and then as though the news were more than you could believe and you were asking if it was *really* so:

> John was elected president of his class.
> *John* was elected president of his class?
>
> Mary is going to marry George.
> Mary is going to marry *George?*
> Mary is going to *marry* George?

You, like everybody else, can hear a big difference. You are hearing punctuation, or at least, you are hearing what punctuation stands for.

That's why it will help to read what you have written aloud to yourself, listening carefully to your own pauses and your own intonation. When you lower the pitch of your voice and come to a full stop, put in a period. When you raise the pitch of your voice and come to a full stop, put in a question mark. When you pause a little, but not much, and change the pitch just a little, you *may* need a comma. That's when you should examine how the parts of the sentence are put together.

If you can find a friend to listen to you read, that's even better. When someone else is listening, you are likely to read a little more carefully in an effort to help the other person understand your meaning. No matter how carefully you put in the periods and question marks, however, you won't be able to catch all the variations of your voice. Punctuation marks can only hint at the shocked disbelief your voice showed when you turned "Mary is going to marry *George"* into a question.

It's important that you figure out some reliable way of identifying sentences, since knowing where one sentence stops and another begins is your readers' most pressing need. You can't do it by length. Some sentences are short, some very long:

> The doctor came immediately.

**P
E
R
I
O
D
S**

Although there was no apparent reason for her discomfort, whenever Marcia tried to stand up, and especially if she stood up suddenly, her face would twist with pain, tears would streak her face, and she would fall back to the chair, whispering, "It hurts, mommy, it hurts me."

Some things that are not sentences are also fairly long:

When it is time for little boys to go to bed, even though they have eaten a big dinner and everybody knows that they can't possibly be hungry. . .

People do say such things in conversation, either in answer to a question ("When do kids ask for snacks?") or as an invitation for someone else to ask, "Well, what does happen at bedtime?" Even though we might *say* something like "When it is time . . . ," if we write just that much, followed by a period, we'll confuse or annoy our readers. Before you use a period to punctuate a group of words beginning with "when," make sure you have said what happens after that *when.* Before you use a period to punctuate a group of words beginning with *because* or *although,* make sure you have included what occurred as a result of that, or in spite of that, whatever that was. As you edit, look at the words you have punctuated with a period to make sure your readers won't be left saying "So what?" or "What about it?"

PERIODS

1. are used at the end of all sentences,
   unless the sentence asks questions
   or makes an exclamation

2. show a falling inflection and a full pause

Periods are also used for most abbreviations:

P.M.   Colo.   c.o.d.   Ms.   Feb.   U.S.S.R.   B.C.

If you're not sure what the abbreviations are, your dictionary can tell you. But ordinarily, except for time designations such as P.M. or B.C., or titles such as *Ms. Chisholm* or *Dr. Boneset,* we don't use abbreviations in the middle of an ordinary paragraph.

The other end mark you will need is a question mark. We hear lowered pitch at the end of statements, raised pitch at the end of most questions. Again, the first step is to read and listen. Even though the question you have written does not require an answer, even though it cannot be answered, you should still use a question mark:

When will people learn to live together in peace?

If listening to yourself read doesn't help enough, paying a little attention to English word order may be useful. When we shift from making statements to asking questions, we shift the order of our words:

Cuthbert *was* eating *cauliflower.*
    becomes
Was Cuthbert eating cauliflower?
Why *was* Cuthbert eating cauliflower?
What *cauliflower was* Cuthbert eating?

Whenever a group of words begins with such words as *is, was, are, will,* or *do,* or such words as *when, where, why,* or *what,* immediately followed by *is, was, are, will, do,* and so forth, it should be punctuated with a question mark. That guide works for quotations, too. Notice the difference in word order between these two statements:

Hazel asked, "Why is the tax so high?"

Hazel asked why the tax was so high.

The first one needs a question mark, the second a period.

QUESTION MARKS

are used for

1. full pause and rising inflection

2. changed word order that signals a question

Commas are separators, too, but they represent smaller divisions within sentences. We use them when we offer lists:

A frightened, trembling, tear-stained child stumbled down the steps of the bus.

Mushrooms, oysters, snails, rattlesnakes, and chocolate-covered grasshoppers are all considered delicacies by some people somewhere.

We use them when we give dates or addresses:

January 4, 1823

1403 Newberry Street, Joplin, Missouri

We use them when the main part of what we're saying is interrupted by something else. Interruptions can occur at the beginning, before the main part of the sentence:

Nevertheless, I won't answer that advertisement.

Slipping and skidding on the icy pavement, my grandfather finally made it across the street.

Whenever I have a bad nightmare, I feel jittery all the next day.

Interruptions can occur in the middle, separating one main part of the sentence from the rest. Whatever the purpose of these interruptions, they need commas at both ends:

My uncle, a nice old man with a long white beard, is coming to town next week. (interruption to explain)

My uncle, however, will not stay with us. (interruption to show contrast)

I wouldn't do that, Mr. Peters, if I were you. (interruption to be polite)

Interruptions can come at the end:

Radial tires certainly give better traction, although they are more expensive than the ones we've been using.

Quoting the exact words someone else said is considered an interruption, even though we often don't pause when we're talking:

Patrick Henry said, "Give me liberty or give me death," and his words encouraged the southern states to join the revolution.

COMMAS

are used

1. to separate the parts of a list

2. to separate parts of a date or
   an address

3. to show interruptions
   at the beginning
   in the middle
   at the end
   of the main part of the sentence

Finally, another useful guide to commas is, "When in doubt, leave it out." Unnecessary commas sprinkled through your writing may bother your readers more than a needed comma or two will help. If you don't hear any interruption, it's better not to use commas:

The old doctor who delivered me is taking care of my baby now.

DO NOT USE COMMAS

Too many unnecessary commas will drive some readers frantic.

When commas are used between two sentences that should be separated by a period or a connecting word, the resulting punctuation is known as a "comma splice" or "comma error." Committing a comma splice is not a capital crime; but teachers who are particular about punctuation often think it means you don't know what a sentence is, and they are so upset by this failure to use conventional punctuation that they may fail the paper. This is where examining how the parts fit together will pay off. Look at the following collection of words; the two parts need to be separated by more than a comma:

A COMMA IS NOT ENOUGH HERE: Many people believe solar energy is better than nuclear energy, the sun can heat our houses without hurting the atmosphere.

There are several ways to show how the parts do (or don't) fit together:

USE A PERIOD: Many people believe solar energy is better than nuclear energy. The sun can heat our houses without hurting the atmosphere.

ADD A CONNECTING WORD: Many people believe solar energy is better than nuclear energy because the sun can heat our houses without hurting the atmosphere.

REARRANGE THE WORDS: The sun can heat our houses without hurting the atmosphere, so many people believe it is better than nuclear energy.

COMMAS

are

not used

1. between the main parts of two sentences
2. unless the main part of a sentence is interrupted by extra information

or

3. unless the two sentences are joined by a connecting word (and, but, or, so, etc.)

Periods, commas, and question marks are the most essential kinds of punctuation, and the only ones we can really hear. All the others are visual conventions: symbols that give sophisticated readers a little more information than they would otherwise have.

Q
U
O
T
A
T
I
O
N

M
A
R
K
S

The most important visual symbol is the quotation mark. We use quotation marks whenever we write down *exactly what someone else has said or written.* We use these marks whether what was said is one word, three words, a sentence, a paragraph, or a whole page of someone else's writing. We do *not* use quotation marks when we repeat just the sense of what was said but change the wording slightly. It works like this:

Grandpa Squeers was always using strange oaths.
Grandpa Squeers was always saying "dadniggled" and "jumping jeepers."

The camp counselor warned the girls not to throw gasoline into a lighted bonfire.
The camp counselor repeated, "Never throw gasoline into a lighted bonfire."

Nathan Hale commented that he was sorry he had only one life to give to his country.
Nathan Hale said, "My only regret is that I have but one life to give for my country."
Nathan Hale said his only regret was that he had "but one life" to give for his country.

We use quotation marks to show the beginning of someone else's exact words and again to show the end. If the quoted words run to more than a paragraph, we use quotation marks at the beginning of each new paragraph, to remind readers that we are still quoting. We do not use quotation marks at the end of paragraphs, however, unless we have stopped quoting.

If what we're quoting already contains a quotation, we use apostrophes to show the inside quotation, so readers won't be confused by thinking too soon that the main quotation has ended. It works like this:

Grandma Squeers said, "I wish Pa would stop using those funny words. I sure get tired of hearing 'dadniggled' and 'jumping jeepers.' "

Use a comma before you begin a direct quotation (there's a pause there) and whatever mark is appropriate at the end, usually a period. Periods and commas always go inside the quotation marks. Sometimes a question is involved, though, and you must decide whether the question mark goes before or after the quotation mark. Then you have to decide which part is the question, the whole sentence or just the quoted part. The whole sentence is a question when we write:

Did Dr. Holmes say "aggravated eye infection"?

Here the quotation mark comes before the question mark. But the main sentence is a statement, and only the quoted part a question, when we write:

Dr. Holmes asked, "What on earth did you do to that eye?"

Here the question mark goes inside the quotation mark, and we skip the period that would ordinarily belong at the end of a statement. It's a safe guide never to use two pieces of end punctuation at the close of a single sentence.

> ## QUOTATION MARKS
>
> are used
>
> 1. at the beginning and the end of someone else's exact words
>
> 2. at the beginning of each paragraph in a long quotation, but not at the end until the quotation is finished

Other punctuation marks such as colons, semicolons, parentheses, and dashes have specialized uses. They are fairly easily learned, but for most ordinary writing, commas and periods will usually do just as well.

Colons are always a signal that something else will follow. We use them at the beginning of business letters, showing that the rest of the letter will follow:

C
O
L
O
N
S

> Dear Senator Underwood:
>
> Dear Bob:

We use them to make clear that an example is coming, exactly as we have been doing all through this section. We also use them to introduce long quotations, especially when the quotation will be separated from the words that introduce it by an indented margin (see the unpunctuated paragraph on page 450). And we use a colon, occasionally, in an ordinary sentence to show that the rest of the sentence is just an explanation of what we have already said:

> The plumber's excuse was not very satisfactory: merely that he'd been "awfully busy."

In all these places, even at the beginning of a business letter, you could use a comma without confusing your readers.

> ## COLONS
>
> 1. show that something will follow
>
> 2. are often used
>   at the beginning of business letters
>   at the beginning of examples, long lists, explanations, and long quotations
>
> 3. can usually be replaced by commas

S
E
M
I
C
O
L
O
N
S Semicolons are sometimes used in place of commas in long sentences:

> Jason Slumber has had a legal office in a corner of the Mercantile Building, at Fourth and Commerce Streets, since November 1960; but the office isn't well-known, since Mr. Slumber only comes in once a week and seldom has a client oftener than once a month.

Using a comma between "1960" and "but" would certainly not be either "wrong" or very confusing. All the semicolon does is warn the reader that the separation here is a little more important than the separations shown by the other three commas in the sentence.

Semicolons are also sometimes used in place of periods when two sentences are very short and seem to belong together:

> Jason Slumber is a wealthy man; he inherited a million dollars.

If you read that sentence aloud, you will hear something close to a period; you might as well put it in, just as you could put a period instead of a semicolon in the sentence you are now reading.

Probably the place semicolons are most useful is in separating the parts in a long, complicated list:

> Besides the bride and groom, the wedding party consisted of Roger Simpson, the bride's father; Eleanor Chamberlain, the bride's mother; Angus McDoom, the groom's brother; and Agnes Smith.

Here semicolons help readers to understand that the wedding party was made up of four people, in addition to the two that got married, rather than seven, as commas might lead readers to suppose.

SEMICOLONS

1. separate the parts of a complicated list

2. can otherwise usually be replaced by
   periods for big pauses
   commas for smaller pauses

D
A
S
H
E
S In other words, you can do a lot of successful writing without worrying too much about semicolons.

Dashes and parentheses are used for interruptions that really break into the main idea of the sentence:

> Clay is an extremely plastic material—far more plastic than most so-called plastics—and is easily shaped into pots.

If you are doubtful about using dashes, you have two choices in sentences like this. You can substitute commas, or you can rewrite the sentence:

> Clay is an extremely plastic material, far more plastic than most so-called plastics, and is easily shaped into pots.

> Clay is much more plastic than many so-called plastics. Because it is so moldable, it is easily shaped into pots.

Parentheses are not quite as easy to eliminate as dashes, since they usually give additional information, but they too can be replaced by commas or rewriting:

> Some kinds of clay (the common varieties are explained in the introduction) can be found within twenty-five miles of any city in this country.

> A kind of clay, one of the common varieties explained in the introduction, can be found within twenty-five miles of any city in the country.

> The eclipse is predicted for 10:34 A.M., Eastern Standard Time (7:34 A.M. in San Francisco).

> The eclipse is predicted for 10:34 A.M., Eastern Standard Time, 7:34 A.M., Pacific Standard Time.

P A R E N T H E S E S

The main thing to remember about parentheses is: always use two. The first without the second will leave your readers wondering when you are going to get back to the main part of the sentence, or whether they're the ones that missed something somewhere. Parentheses are sometimes used around whole sentences, or even several sentences. In that case, it's especially important that both of them be there.

DASHES and PARENTHESES

1. are used for interruptions

2. can usually be replaced by commas,
    except when the parentheses enclose
    a complete sentence

As you edit your papers, remember that the guides given here are just that—guides. Probably no two copy editors (people hired to make corrections in professional writing before it is printed) would ever punctuate a book in exactly the same way. All the copy editors try for is consistency and clarity. They want to use the same kind of punctuation for the same kind of thing, rather than jump from parentheses to dashes and then to commas. They want to make reading clear and comfortable. That's all you need to try for, too.

Paragraphs

If you have organized your paper carefully and followed the advice on pages 64–65 to move from one paragraph to another as you move from one section of your paper to the next, you probably won't have much trouble with paragraphs.

You might want to remember, however, that paragraphing helps readers in two ways:

PARAGRAPHING

1. provides a convenient separation of the parts of a paper

2. rests the eyes and makes reading easier

Because that's one of the purposes—to make your writing "look good"—try to avoid a series of very short paragraphs or any extremely long ones. If you find you have written a lot of two- or three-sentence paragraphs, try combining them into one. If they won't combine smoothly, you may need better transitions. And if you have a very long paragraph, filling a whole page or more, find a place to break it up. If you look carefully, you can probably see a natural division.

When you write in longhand, or type double space, the usual way to show paragraph divisions is by starting the first word of each new paragraph at least an inch in from the margin. When you type single space, as you do in business letters and some reports, skip a space between paragraphs and begin the first sentence at the usual margin, like this:

We regret that 42 cartons of size C batteries in our last shipment to you were improperly labeled.

The defective batteries are being replaced at once, by air mail special delivery, and we will appreciate your keeping the 42 cartons now in your possession until one of our salesmen can call for them.

Capitalization

Deciding where to use capital letters in modern English is not as much of a problem as it would have been a century or so ago, when many writers capitalized the first letter of every important word, as we still do in writing titles. Nowadays capitals appear in only three places:

1. We use a capital to begin a sentence—that is, after you have used a period or a question mark, begin the next word with a capital letter.

2. We use a capital to name specific, individual people or things:

   Jennie Jones   Fourth Street   the Singer Building

   Chief Justice Warren   the United States

   Words that are not used as part of the name are usually not capitalized:

   A street near the river is being torn up.

   The building Singer built has forty stories.

   Earl Warren was chief justice of the United States from 1953 to 1969.

   The first thirteen states were united in 1787.

3. We use a capital to begin the first word inside quotation marks whenever we are quoting a whole sentence of what someone else said:

   At the end of the conference, the governor commented,
   "Seems like I'm damned if I do and damned if I don't."

   We don't use capitals when we quote indirectly—change the words a little and omit the quotation marks:

   At the end of the conference, the governor commented that he seemed to be damned if he did and damned if he didn't.

CAPITAL LETTERS

are used

1. to begin sentences

2. to name specific people or things

3. to begin direct quotations

Smoothing Out the Wording

As you read your paper aloud the final time before you copy it, watch for words you may have left out by accident. (Read the final copy for left-out words, too; it's even easier to omit things when you are copying.) Watch for places that *sound* clumsy; often the ear can hear awkwardnesses that the eye won't see. You want to make your writing smooth and natural.

Making it natural, however, doesn't mean making it sound just the way you talk. Many American dialects leave out both words and word endings that edited American English usually includes. Even though you normally say "Josh step right in front of the bus last night," the conventions of editing will require "Josh stepped."

All writers have to make this kind of adjustment, and the more formal the kind of writing, the more the adjustments they must make. It's lucky for most of us, both writers and readers, that American writing has become much less formal in the last few years. People used to be told never to use "I" when they wrote a paper; now almost everybody would agree that we should. And we used to be warned about contractions, also. " 'Don't' is acceptable in speech, but in writing always use 'do not.' " Now most people think the difference in tone between the rather threatening "do not" and the more comfortable "don't" is more important than formality.

One thing you will probably want to watch for, and avoid, is sexist language. The old handbooks used to be very insistent about our using "he" or "his" if we began with "everybody." We were urged to write such things as:

When the speech was finished, everybody clapped *his* hands.

A careful writer will avoid using words that will offend some of *his* readers.

The women's movement has reminded us, however, that most audiences contain both men and women, and that it's insulting to assume that all careful writers are men. If you want to stop assuming that women don't matter, you'll try to avoid using "he" and "his" unless you mean men only. One easy way is to talk about people, rather than "a person," when people is what you mean, anyway:

Careful writers will avoid using words that will offend some of their readers.

If "everybody" seems inevitable, forget the niceties and write "their," just as you would say it. Surely all those people didn't clap the same pair of hands, anyway. Or you can fall back on "his or her," if you're really nervous about it. But just as careful writers avoid using such derogatory words as *Polack, nigger,* or *honky,* unless they deliberately want to be offensive, so careful writers will avoid sexist language.

Editing isn't an impossible job, although all the advice we've given here may make it seem to be. All it takes is care and practice. If you are uneasy about possible differences between the dialect you speak and the dialect you want to write, get a friend, or friends, to go over your paper and pay special attention to the suggestions they make. There's nothing wrong with that kind of help—remember the copy editors who go over those professional manuscripts.

Editing In-class Writing

So far we have been talking about the writing you do at home, when you have plenty of time to edit carefully and make a clean copy after all the changes have been made. But even when you're writing under pressure, for an essay test or an in-class paper, you're still responsible for some quick editing.

It's a good idea to get an inexpensive paperback dictionary and carry it with you. Most teachers, unless they're giving a vocabulary quiz, will be glad to let you use your dictionary to edit any kind of writing. (But maybe, unless it's an English class, you'd better ask.)

Usually you won't have time to make a second copy of what you have written, but you can make changes neatly by crossing out and writing above the line. Before you begin to edit, try to separate yourself from what you have written, even only slightly. Stop a minute; look out the window, or think of something else. Then read what your paper says, pretending that it's not yours at all. The more you separate yourself, the more likely you are to catch left-out words or silly mistakes, such as writing "life" when you mean "like." At best, a quick rereading will catch all those unnecessary confusions; at worst, the changes you do make will convince whoever reads your paper that you've tried to be careful.

Glossary

abstract word—a word that refers to an idea, attitude, or kind of behavior; something that can't be seen or heard or touched: *mischief, imagination, democracy.*

accuracy—getting facts right and presenting them honestly.

active voice—a sentence that follows normal English word order; the first noun (or noun substitute) does whatever is being done: "The child beat the dog." (The child is doing the beating.)

adjective—traditionally, a word that modifies a noun. Adjectives can fit the pattern: "It was a _____ thing" or "It seemed _____." And they can show comparisons: "a *quicker* route"; a *more graceful* action."

adverb—traditionally, a word that modifies a verb, an adjective, or another adverb. Adverbs can fit the patterns: "He worked _____." Adverbs tell *how, when, where, how much.* Adverbs that tell *how* are usually formed by adding *-ly* to adjectives; adverbs that tell *when, where, how much,* usually don't end in *-ly: today, there, very.* Adverbs that tell *how* can fit the pattern: "He worked very _____."

agreement, in sentences—(1) making the subject fit with the verb: "A fire burn*s*. Fire*s* burn." (2) making pronouns fit the nouns they refer to: "One *girl* ate *her* dinner. Both *girls* ate *their* dinners."

analogy—a comparison of two things that have at least one similarity.

analysis—a method of explanation that examines the parts of a process or event.

apologies, in writing—overuse of such phrases as "in my opinion," "it seems to me," or other wording that makes the writer seem unsure of what's being said.

apostrophe—a mark used (1) in place of an omitted letter or letters in contractions: *can*'t; *aren*'t (2) to show possession in nouns and some pronouns: *man's* hat; *anybody's* guess.

audience—the person or people who will read what's been written.

authority—someone expert in the subject being discussed, whose comments or judgment will carry some weight with readers.

auxiliary verb (sometimes called helper verbs)—verbs that combine with the main verb to show differences in time, intention, or possibility:

He *is* eating the pie.

He *had* eaten the pie.

He *might* eat the pie.

Did he eat it?

bibliography—an alphabetical list of the sources used in preparing a paper; appears at the end of the paper.

brainstorming—writing down everything you can think of related to a topic or idea, in random order, without regard to importance; a way of getting ideas flowing.

capital letters—used to begin sentences, to name things or people, to begin actual quotations:

*T*he man hollered at us.

We went to the *W*hite *H*ouse."

He asked, "*W*hy do you do that to me?"

causal analysis—an explanation of why something happens or happened.

cause and effect—an examination of whether one thing (or things) actually caused another thing.

circular argument—the mistake of beginning with a belief and, instead of supporting it, circling around until the original belief is used as proof of itself.

circular definition—an unsatisfactory attempt to explain meaning, in which one word is defined by another version of the same word: "A plagiarist is a person who plagiarizes."

clarity, in writing—the relationship between words, sentences, and paragraphs shown so plainly that there is no room for confusion and no question about what the writer means.

class definition—a method of explaining a word by putting it in a big group and showing how it differs from other members of the big group: "A chair / is a piece of furniture / with four legs and a back, used for one person to sit in."

classification—a method of explanation that (1) groups similar things together, and then subdivides the group, becoming more specific at each step or (2) starts with a specific thing and places it in a larger group of similar things.

classification chart—a diagram showing divisions and subdivisions in a classification system.

clause—a group of words that have both a subject and a predicate. (1) *Independent clauses* are complete by themselves: "The bridge over the Columbia has been recently painted." (2) *Dependent clauses* are not complete when standing alone; they must be attached to an independent clause by a subordinator: "[When the bridge was being painted,] my car got spattered." Or by a relative pronoun: "The man [who was painting the bridge] just laughed."

comma error—same as *comma splice*.

comma splice—a punctuation problem that occurs when two sentences are separated by a comma instead of a period.

Example: Comma splices are not as serious as confused thinking, many readers get upset by them, however.

Solution: Use a period or a semi-colon, or rearrange the sentence:

Comma splices are not as serious as confused thinking. Many readers get upset by them, however.

Comma splices are not as serious as confused thinking; many readers get upset by them, however.

Even though comma splices are not as serious as confused thinking, many readers get upset by them.

comparison—a method of explanation that points out similarities and differences.

conclusion, in writing—the last sentence or last paragraph of a paper; makes the paper sound finished.

conclusion, in logic—the result of a reasoning process. If you know that Alfred was born in Kansas, and that people born in Kansas are U.S. citizens, your *conclusion* would be that Alfred is a U.S. citizen.

conjunctions—connecting words. (1) Coordinating conjunctions (*and, but, or, nor*) can connect words, phrases, or sentences. (2) Subordinating conjunctions (*when, although, because,* etc.) connect dependent clauses to the rest of the sentence.

connotation—the emotional overtones that collect around some words: *home* has a pleasanter connotation than *house; mother* than *stepmother;* etc.

consonant—the sounds we make when we partly stop the air with our tongues, teeth, or lips. English has about twenty-four consonant sounds and twenty-two consonant letters: *b, c, d, f, g*—all the letters of the alphabet except *a, e, i, o,* and *u.*

contraction—word that results when two words are pushed together: "She *isn't* coming." "*Mary's* coming tomorrow." Contractions are used in speech and in informal writing.

dangling modifier—see *misplaced modifier.*

data sheet—see *personal information sheet.*

deduction—the kind of reasoning that begins with a generalization and applies it to a specific thing.

definition—explanation of what a word or phrase means.

denotation—the meaning of a word, separate from any emotional overtones; all words have denotation whether or not they have connotation.

dependent clause—see *clause.*

details—the specific information that helps readers "see" the person or event being written about.

developing a paper—providing specific details, examples, and support for the main idea.

dialect—a set of variations within a language, great enough to be noticed but not great enough to keep the speakers of one dialect from understanding the speakers of a different dialect. Dialect differences can occur in pronunciation, vocabulary, and usage, and dialects can be regional, social, or economic. Everybody speaks a dialect, sometimes more than one.

directions—telling other people how to make or do something.

draft—the first or second version of a piece of writing, before the last revision has been made.

echo transition—showing the relationship between one paragraph and the next by repeating a word, phrase, or idea from the end of one paragraph at the beginning of the next.

editing—going over the final version of a paper to check for spelling, punctuation, pronoun confusion, etc.

either/or thinking—the fallacy of believing there are only two sides to any question or only two solutions to any problem: "If it's not this, it's got to be that."

example—a specific illustration of a general statement.

explaining—writing that tells what something is or how it works by defining, comparing, classifying, or analyzing.

fact—a statement that can be checked and has been found to be accurate.

factual statement—a statement that can or could have been checked, whether or not it's accurate.

fallacy—a mistake in logic or reasoning.

false analogy—a comparison that has been carried so far that it's misleading; pretending that two things which have some similarity are identical or will have identical effects.

fiction—writing that is about imaginary people and imaginary events: novels, short stories, etc.

footnotes—a method of giving credit to other people's work. Footnotes can appear at the bottom of the page or at the end of an essay. Since several forms are acceptable, consult the recommended style manual.

fragment—a part of a sentence that depends on something else to be understandable: "Of course." "Whenever you're ready." Also, the punctuation problem that occurs when part of a sentence is punctuated with a period.
Solution: Attach the fragment to the sentence it belongs with.

general words—words that refer to a group of things: *furniture* or *animals.* The more things a word refers to, the more general it is. *Furniture* is more general than *chair; chair* is more general than *recliner.*

generalization—a statement made about a group of people, or things, or covering more than one situation. Generalizations can be acceptable or unacceptable, depending on what kind of support there is for the statement.

gerund—the *-ing* form of a verb used in a noun position: "I like *skating.*" "*Being criticized* discourages some people."

glittering generality—statements so sweet and vague that they have little meaning: "I believe in giving all people the natural dignity they deserve."

grammar—(1) the way a language conveys meaning: in English, grammar enables us to understand the difference between "Man bites dog" and "Dog bites man," for instance; (2) the analysis of that system: learning to define verbs, prepositions, etc., and examining how they work; (3) certain choices, more accurately called usage or *dialect variations:* the difference between saying "he doesn't" and "he don't," for instance.

guilt by association—a fallacy which results from thinking that because two people or groups like the same thing, know the same people, or do the same thing, they are alike in other ways too:

Football players wear helmets.

Mary wears a helmet.

Mary is a football player.

independent clause—see *clause.*

induction—the kind of reasoning that starts with specific things and arrives at a generalization.

inference—a statement about what isn't known, based on what is known.

infinitive—a phrase made up of *to* + a verb: *to understand, to want,* etc. Infinitives are most often used in noun positions, but they can serve as adjectives:

To cry is childish. (noun position)
He wanted *to see* me. (noun position)
The man *to see* is my uncle. (adjective position)

interruptions—words, phrases, or clauses that could be left out of a sentence without destroying the basic meaning. In writing, interruptions need commas to separate them from the rest of the sentence:

My aunt, *an old battleaxe,* threw a lamp at the cat.
The lamp, *by great good luck,* missed the cat.
The cat, *when it saw my aunt,* howled and ran away.

introduction—usually the first paragraph of a short paper; makes clear what the paper will cover and serves as a contract between writer and reader; usually contains the main idea sentence.

italics—in print, shown by slanted letters; in handwriting or typing, shown by under-lining.

judgment—a statement expressing opinion: a *bad* idea; a *brave* action.

language—the oral symbolic system by which human beings communicate; written lan-guage uses an additional set of symbols (the alphabet) to represent the sounds of speech.

link transitions—words such as *first, next, after, however,* etc., that show relationships of time, space, or contrast.

linking verbs (sometimes called helper verbs)—verbs that connect the first noun to the second, or the first noun to an adjective; they operate much like an equal sign. The most common linking verb in English is *be* (*is, are, was, were, been*):

The girl *is* my sister. (Both nouns have the same referent)

The girl *is* pretty. (pretty girl)

Other linking verbs are *seem, become, look,* etc.

logic—the process of thinking straight; careful reasoning.

main idea sentence—a statement showing what the writer means to say in the paper; usually includes the narrowed topic and indicates both the purpose of the writing and the writer's attitude toward it.

metaphor—an implied comparison: "A temper tantrum can be a safety valve."

misplaced modifier—a phrase in the wrong position, so readers can't easily tell what it belongs with:

Apartment wanted by single man with bay window.
Coming in on Highway 99, the lake looks enormous.

Solution: Rearrange the order of the sentence:

Apartment with bay window wanted by single man.
Coming in on Highway 99, we thought the lake looked enormous.

mixed metaphor—two different implied comparisons used in the same sentence: "My aunt was *blinded* by her *thirst* for revenge."

name-calling—making a personal attack on the other side in an argument, instead of sticking to the subject being argued about; a side-stepping technique, always unfair.

narrowing a topic—moving from a very general subject to some smaller part of it.

natural-sounding language, in writing—using words that avoid sounding stilted or over-formal, but that also avoid the fragments and repetitions that occur in speech.

nonfiction—writing based on facts or actual events: textbooks, biographies, histories, news reports, etc.

noun—traditionally, the name of something. Nouns are words that

1. can fit the patterns: "The _____ seems interesting" or "I like _____."
2. can follow such words as *a, the, some, any,* etc.: an *apple,* some *difficulties*
3. can be made plural by adding *-s* or by a pronunciation change: two *girls;* three *peaches;* four *women*
4. can form possessives: Matilda's *shoes,* a dollar's *worth.*

objective writing—writing that keeps the writer's attitudes and opinions out.

operational analysis—explanation of how something works by examining it piece by piece.

opinion statement—a statement that expresses the writer's attitude or judgment; *good, bad, beautiful, large,* etc., are opinion words.

opposition—an opinion or point of view different from the writer's; in persuasion, it's a good idea to discuss the opposition's argument and show what's wrong with it.

order, in writing—the logical arrangement of ideas and paragraphs. The most common are (1) *chronological order* (arranged by time); (2) *order of importance* (saving the most important point for the end or mentioning it first); (3) *spatial order* (moving from one part or area to the next).

outline—a formal plan showing what a paper will cover or has covered, usually divided and subdivided by the use of numerals and letters.

paragraph—a related group of sentences all dealing with the same general idea. Paragraphs break up the writing and give readers a short rest. Typical paragraphs contain three to eight sentences, although they can sometimes be shorter or longer. The first word of each paragraph is started about an inch in from the left-hand margin.

participle—a form of a verb used in an adjective position:

The *crying* child is hurt. (present participle)

The dog, *beaten* and *battered,* put its tail between its legs. (past participle)

passive voice—a rearrangement of normal English sentence order so that the noun or noun substitute that usually follows the verb comes in front of it:

The child smashed the vase. (active voice)

The vase was smashed. (passive voice)

The vase was smashed by the child. (passive voice)

Good writing does not use the passive voice much, except when whoever did whatever it was is unknown or unimportant: "A fire was set in the old building," or, "The vase was knocked down by the cat, not by the child."

pedantic language—stiff, overly formal writing.

periodical—a magazine.

personal experience—a piece of writing about yourself and your own experiences, written in such a way that readers can see the significance.

personal information sheet—a personal record included with an application letter, listing education, experience, references, etc.

persuasion—writing that tries to get readers to change their attitudes, beliefs, or behavior; argument.

phrase—a group of words that belong together but do not have both a subject and predicate:

I went *to the store.* (prepositional phrase)
I want *to see that man.* (infinitive phrase)
The man *traveling on the train* is my neighbor. (participial phrase)
I hate *washing dishes.* (gerund phrase)
I *will be leaving* tomorrow. (verb phrase)

plagiarism—copying what someone else has written without giving credit to the original writer.

plan for a paper—a list of the ideas that will be in the paper, arranged in the order in which they will appear.

post hoc—from a Latin phrase (*post hoc, ergo propter hoc*) meaning "After this, therefore because of this." Post hoc fallacy is the mistake of assuming that because one thing happened after another, the first caused the second.

précis—same as *summary.*

precision—being exact; finding the right words to express a definite meaning.

predicate—the part of a sentence that contains the verb and what follows it: "The train *went through the tunnel.*" "Riding horseback *can be very tiring.*"

prediction—statement about what will or could happen in the future, based on what has happened in the past.

preposition—a connector that shows the relationship between a noun, or words filling a noun position, and the rest of the sentence: *to* the store; *behind* the desk; *by* asking questions; *about* the question you asked.

private writing—writing not intended for many readers or for unknown readers: love letters, diaries, etc.

pronoun—a word that can substitute for a noun. Common pronouns are divided into five groups: personal, interrogative, demonstrative, indefinite, and relative.

Personal pronouns:
   I, me (my, mine)
   you (your, yours)
   he, him (his)
   it (its)
   she, her (her, hers)
   we, us (our, ours)
   they, them (their, theirs)

The words in parentheses are **possessive** pronouns, which **substitute** for possessive nouns:
   That book is *Elizabeth's.*
   That book is *hers.*
Possessive personal pronouns are not written with apostrophes.

Interrogative pronouns:
   who, whom (whose)
   whoever, whomever
   which
   whichever
   what

Interrogative pronouns indicate questions. The possessive **form** (whose) is not written with an apostrophe.

Demonstrative pronouns:
   this, these
   that, those
   such

Demonstrative pronouns refer to things that have been mentioned earlier. They do not have possessive forms.

Indefinite pronouns:	Indefinite pronouns refer to a
words such as	group of things or people, even
all	though conventional usage treats
any	them as though they were always
anybody (anybody's)	just one: Everybody *is* angry.
everybody (everybody's)	Nobody (none of a group) *is*
few	coming.
nobody (nobody's)	When these words have possessive
none	forms, they *are* written with apos-
	trophes.
Relative pronouns:	Relative pronouns connect clauses
that	to the rest of the sentence:
which	The police told the man/*whose*
who, whom (whose)	truck was blocking the fire hy-
	drant/to get the truck out of
	there in a hurry.

pronoun antecedent—the noun for which a pronoun is substituting. In the sentence "I voted for the candidate who seemed the most honest," *candidate* is the antecedent of *who.*

pronoun confusion—(1) changing from one personal pronoun to another in the same sentence or same paragraph: shifting from *one* to *you* to *anybody; Example:* "One doesn't always know what they want, do you?" *Solution:* "You don't always know what you want, do you?" or, "People don't always know what they want, do they?" (2) failing to make clear who or what a pronoun refers to: In the sentence "Jack told Jim that he won the prize," who is "he," Jack or Jim?

public writing—writing that is intended to be read by other people: college assignments, business letters, job reports, articles for publication in magazines, etc.

purpose—what the writer hopes the writing will accomplish: giving directions, explaining, telling what happened, persuading, summarizing, etc.

"purr" words—words that express the writer's approval and not much else; words meant to put readers in a good mood (term invented by S. I. Hayakawa).

quotation marks—punctuation that shows someone else's words are being quoted exactly:

He said, "I'm not coming."

Quotation marks are not used when the wording has been changed:

He said he wasn't coming.

rational argument—an attempt to persuade that depends on reasons rather than emotional appeals.

referent—the thing, idea, person, object, that is symbolized by a word: "The round red fruit you can actually eat" is the referent of *apple;* "a collection of behaviors" is the referent of *fright.*

relative clause—a kind of dependent clause that is connected to the rest of the sentence by a relative pronoun: "The hamburger *that I like best* is made at Yummy's Drive-in," or "That's the man *who was elected yesterday."*

report—writing that tells what happened, without the writer's interpretation or judgment about the events.

résumé—see *personal information sheet.*

review—writing that evaluates a book, movie, etc. Whereas a report merely summarizes, a review includes the writer's opinion.

revising—going back over what you have written, rewording sentences, rearranging the order, cutting some things and adding others; revising is best done a day or so after the first draft has been finished.

run-on sentence—a punctuation problem that occurs when two separate sentences have no punctuation between them: "Blow-outs can be serious they cause an inexperienced driver to lose control of the car." *Solution:* use a period or rewrite the sentence: "Blow-outs can be serious. They cause an inexperienced driver to lose control of the car," or, "Because blow-outs can make an inexperienced driver lose control of the car, they can be serious."

sentence outline—a formal plan for a paper, in which all the ideas to be covered in the paper are written in complete sentences.

sexist language—using only masculine pronouns when both men and women are meant: "A writer must polish *his* writing." Solution: change to the plural: "Writers must polish *their* writing"; or use "his or her" (but that's a bit awkward); or write, "Everybody must polish *their* writing" (defying the foolish rule that says *everybody* is singular).

slang—street language or faddish use of new meanings for old words: *bad* to mean *good,* etc. Slang usually gets quickly out of date and disappears; but sometimes it becomes accepted into the language as a "regular" word. *Mob,* for instance, was once slang. In writing, slang should be used only for special effect; it should always be avoided in formal writing.

slant—selecting words that influence the readers' judgment, in writing that pretends to be factual: *old hag* is a slanted term for *elderly woman; staggered* is a slanted word for *walked.* Slant can also occur when a writer who wants to create a favorable impression leaves out facts that might create a different impression.

"snarl" words—words that express the writer's disapproval and not much else; words meant to create an unfavorable impression on readers (term invented by S. I. Hayakawa).

source—the book, article, etc., in which the writer found the information being used.

specific statement—a statement made about a particular thing that happened at a particular time.

specific words—the fewer things a word refers to, the more specific it is.

statistics—numbers that show how much, how many, how often.

stereotyping—putting a label on a person or group of people that disregards their own characteristics:

Everybody from Edinburgh is stingy.

Nobody on welfare wants to work.

New Yorkers think nothing important happens west of Philadelphia.

stipulative definition—explanation, often through the use of examples, of how a word is being used in a certain situation by a certain person.

style manual—a booklet giving directions for margins, spacing, footnotes, bibliography, etc., in a formal reference paper.

subject, in writing—the topic being written about.

subject, in grammar—the part of the sentence that comes before the verb: "*Davenports* are comfortable." "*Dinner* was eaten hurriedly."

subjective writing—writing that includes the writer's attitudes and opinions.

subordinate clause—same as *dependent clause.*

summary—in writing, a shortened version of what someone else has said or written, using the second writer's own words.

syllogism—the formal pattern of deductive reasoning that includes a generalization (major premise), a statement relating a specific thing to the generalization (minor premise), and a conclusion. The relationship between the three terms determines whether the reasoning process is logically valid or invalid. The most famous example of a valid syllogism is:

All men are mortal. (major premise)

Socrates is a man. (minor premise)

Therefore, Socrates is mortal. (conclusion)

synonym—a word that means the same, or almost the same, as another word: *obese* is a synonym for *fat.*

tense—a grammatical term applied to verbs, that shows time; indicates when an action took place. Tenses in English are

present: She works. She is working today:

past: She worked. She was working yesterday.

future: She will work tomorrow. She will be working all week.

Other different time relationships are shown by other tense changes:

She has been working all day.

She had been working nights before she got this job.

By next month, she will have been working there a year.

thesis statement—see *main idea sentence.*

title—the name given to a piece of writing. The title is centered at the top of the first page and important words in it are begun with capital letters.

tone—a reflection of the writer's attitude toward the subject and toward the audience, the people who will read what has been written; the tone of a piece of writing can be light or serious, humorous or straightforward, etc.

topic—the general subject the writing is about; the topic can be expressed in a word or a phrase.

topic outline—a formal plan in which all the ideas covered in the paper are expressed in a series of single words or phrases.

topic sentence—similar to *main idea sentence,* except that topic sentences show what the main idea of a paragraph is.

transitions—wording that guides readers from one idea to the next and shows the relationship between the parts of a paper.

usage—the choices available within the grammar of a language. The difference between saying to a dog "Lie down" or "Lay down" is a usage difference; but the first has more prestige than the second.

verb—traditionally, a word (or words) that show action or state of being. Verbs are words that can fit the pattern: "They ＿＿＿ well," or "They ＿＿＿ it." Verbs can have *-ing* added to the base form.

vowel—the sounds we make by letting our breath come out of our mouths in a clear stream. English has thirty or more vowel sounds but only five or six vowel letters: *a, e, i, o, u,* and sometimes *y.* Every syllable must have one vowel sound in it.

Index